GENERALIZED METHOD OF MOMENTS ESTIMATION

Editor:

LÁSZLÓ MÁTYÁS
Budapest University of Economics

CAMBRIDGE
UNIVERSITY PRESS

PUBLISHED BY THE PRESS SYNDICATE OF THE UNIVERSITY OF CAMBRIDGE
The Pitt Building, Trumpington Street, Cambridge, United Kingdom

CAMBRIDGE UNIVERSITY PRESS
The Edinburgh Building, Cambridge CB2 2RU, UK   http://www.cup.cam.ac.uk
40 West 20th Street, New York, NY 10011-4211, USA   http://www.cup.org
10 Stamford Road, Oakleigh, Melbourne 3166, Australia

© Cambridge University Press 1999

First published 1999

Printed in the United States of America

Typeset in Century Schoolbook 11/13 pt. and Courier in LaTeX 2_ε [TB]

*A catalog record for this book is available from
the British Library*

Library of Congress Cataloging-in-Publication Data
Generalized methods of moments estimation / editor, László Mátyás.

    p.   cm.
    Includes bibliographical references and index.
    ISBN 0-521-66013-0 (hardbound)
    1. Econometric models.   2. Moments method (Statistics)
3. Estimation theory.   I. Mátyás, László.
HB141.G463   1998
330'.01'5195 – dc21   98-51529
                                                        CIP
ISBN 0 521 66013 0 hardback
ISBN 0 521 66967 7 paperback

Contents

Contributors

SEUNG C. AHN, Arizona State University

JOERG BREITUNG, Humboldt University, Berlin

J.S. BUTLER, Vanderbilt University

MATTHEW J. CUSHING, University of Nebraska–Lincoln

ALASTAIR HALL, North Carolina State University and
University of Birmingham

DAVID HARRIS, University of Melbourne

FRANK KLEIBERGEN, Erasmus University

MICHAEL LECHNER, Mannheim University

ROMAN LIESENFELD, University of Tübingen

LÁSZLÓ MÁTYÁS, Budapest University of Economics and
Erudite, Université de Paris XII

MARY McGARVEY, University of Nebraska–Lincoln

MASAO OGAKI, Ohio State University

GABRIEL PICONE, University of South Florida

JAN M. PODIVINSKY, University of Southampton

PETER SCHMIDT, Michigan State University

PREFACE

The standard econometric modelling practice for quite a long time was founded on strong assumptions concerning the underlying data generating process. Based on these assumptions, estimation and hypothesis testing techniques were derived with known desirable, and in many cases optimal, properties. Frequently, these assumptions were highly unrealistic and unlikely to be true. These shortcomings were attributed to the simplification involved in any modelling process and therefore inevitable and acceptable. The crisis of econometric modelling in the seventies led to many well known new, sometimes revolutionary, developments in the way econometrics was undertaken. Unrealistically strong assumptions were no longer acceptable. Techniques and procedures able to deal with data and models within a more realistic framework were badly required. Just at the right time, *i.e.*, the early eighties when all this became obvious, Lars Peter Hansen's seminal paper on the asymtotic properties of the generalized method of moments (GMM) estimator was published in *Econometrica*. Although the basic idea of the GMM can be traced back to the work of Denis Sargan in the late fifties, Hansen's paper provided a ready to use, very flexible tool applicable to a large number of models, which relied on mild and plausible assumptions. The die was cast. Applications of the GMM approach have mushroomed since in the literature, which has been, as so many things, further boosted recently by the increased availability of computing power.

Nowadays there are so many different theoretical and practical applications of the GMM principle that it is almost impossible to keep track of them. What started as a simple estimation method has grown to be a complete methodology for estimation and hypothesis testing. As most of the best known "traditional" estimation methods can be regarded as special cases of the GMM estimator, it can also serve as a nice unified framework for teaching estimation theory in econometrics.

The main objective of this volume is to provide a complete and up–to–date presentation of the theory of GMM estimation, as well as insights into the use of these methods in empirical studies.

The editor has tried to standardize the notation, language, exposition, and depth of the chapters in order to present a coherent book. We hope, however, that each chapter is able to stand on its own as a reference work.

***

We would like to thank all those who helped with the creation of this volume: the contributors, who did not mind being harassed by the editor and produced several quality versions of their chapters ensuring the high standard of this volume; the Erudite, Université de Paris XII in France and the Hungarian Research Fund (OTKA) in Hungary for providing financial support; and the editors' colleagues and students for their valuable comments and feedback.

The camera–ready copy of this volume was prepared by the editor with the help of Erika Mihalik using TeX and the Initbook (Gábor Kőrösi and László Mátyás) macro package.

László Mátyás

Budapest, Melbourne and Paris, August 1998

Chapter 1

INTRODUCTION TO THE

GENERALIZED METHOD OF

MOMENTS ESTIMATION

David Harris and László Mátyás

One of the most important tasks in econometrics and statistics is to find techniques enabling us to estimate, for a given data set, the unknown parameters of a specific model. Estimation procedures based on the minimization (or maximization) of some kind of criterion function (M–estimators) have successfully been used for many different types of models. The main difference between these estimators lies in what must be specified of the model. The most widely applied such estimation technique, the maximum likelihood, requires the complete specification of the model and its probability distribution. The Generalized Method of Moments (GMM) does not require this sort of full knowledge. It only demands the specification of a set of moment conditions which the model should satisfy.

In this chapter, first, we introduce the Method of Moments (MM) estimation, then generalize it and derive the GMM estimation procedure, and finally, analyze its properties.

1.1 The Method of Moments

The Method of Moments is an estimation technique which suggests that the unknown parameters should be estimated by matching population (or theoretical) moments (which are functions of the unknown parameters) with the appropriate sample moments. The first step is to define properly the moment conditions.

1.1.1 Moment Conditions

DEFINITION 1.1 **Moment Conditions**

Suppose that we have an observed sample $\{x_t : t = 1, \ldots, T\}$ from which we want to estimate an unknown $p \times 1$ parameter vector θ with true value θ_0. Let $f(x_t, \theta)$ be a continuous $q \times 1$ vector function of θ, and let $E(f(x_t, \theta))$ exist and be finite for all t and θ. Then the moment conditions are that $E(f(x_t, \theta_0)) = 0$.

∎

Before discussing the estimation of θ_0, we give some examples of moment conditions.

EXAMPLE 1.1

Consider a sample $\{x_t : t = 1, \ldots, T\}$ from a gamma $\gamma(p^*, q^*)$ distribution with true values $p^* = p_0^*$ and $q^* = q_0^*$. The relationships between the first two moments of this distribution and its parameters are:

$$E(x_t) = \frac{p_0^*}{q_0^*}, \qquad E\left(x_t - E(x_t)\right)^2 = \frac{p_0^*}{q_0^{*2}}.$$

In the notation of Definition 1.1, we have $\theta = (p^*, q^*)'$ and a vector of $q^* = 2$ functions:

$$f(x_t, \theta) = \left(x_t - \frac{p^*}{q^*}, \left(x_t - \frac{p^*}{q^*}\right)^2 - \frac{p^*}{q^{*2}}\right)'.$$

Then the moment conditions are $E(f(x_t, \theta_0)) = 0$.

∎

EXAMPLE 1.2

Another simple example can be given for a sample $\{x_t : t = 1, \ldots, T\}$ from a beta $\beta(p^*, q^*)$ distribution, again with true values $p^* = p_0^*$ and $q^* = q_0^*$. The relationships between the first two moments and the parameters of this distribution are:

$$E(x_t) = \frac{p_0^*}{p_0^* + q_0^*}$$

$$E(x_t^2) = \frac{p_0^*(p_0^* + 1)}{(p_0^* + q_0^*)(p_0^* + q_0^* + 1)}.$$

With $\theta = (p^*, q^*)'$ we have

$$f(x_t, \theta) = \left(x_t - \frac{p^*}{p^* + q^*}, x_t^2 - \frac{p^*(p^* + 1)}{(p^* + q^*)(p^* + q^* + 1)} \right)'.$$

∎

EXAMPLE 1.3

Consider the linear regression model

$$y_t = x_t'\beta_0 + u_t,$$

where x_t is a $p \times 1$ vector of stochastic regressors, β_0 is the true value of a $p \times 1$ vector of unknown parameters β, and u_t is an error term. In the presence of stochastic regressors, we often specify

$$E(u_t|x_t) = 0,$$

so that

$$E(y_t|x_t) = x_t'\beta_0.$$

Using the Law of Iterated Expectations we find

$$E(x_t u_t) = E\Big(E(x_t u_t|x_t)\Big)$$
$$= E\Big(x_t E(u_t|x_t)\Big) \cdot$$
$$= 0$$

The equations

$$E(x_t u_t) = E\Big(x_t(y_t - x_t'\beta_0)\Big) = 0,$$

are moment conditions for this model. That is, in terms of Definition 1.1, $\theta = \beta$ and $f((x_t, y_t), \theta) = x_t(y_t - x_t'\beta)$.

∎

Notice that in this example $E(x_t u_t) = 0$ consists of p equations since x_t is a $p \times 1$ vector. Since β is a $p \times 1$ parameter, these moment conditions exactly identify β. If we had fewer than p moment conditions, then we could not identify β, and if we had more than p moment conditions, then β would be over–identified. Estimation can proceed if the parameter vector is exactly or over–identified. Notice that, compared to the maximum likelihood approach (ML), we have specified relatively little information about u_t. Using ML, we would be required to give the distribution of u_t, as well as parameterising any autocorrelation and heteroskedasticity, while this information is not required in formulating the moment conditions. However, some restrictions on such aspects of the model are still required for the derivation of the asymptotic properties of the GMM estimator.

It is common to obtain moment conditions by requiring that the error term of the model has zero expectation conditional on certain observed variables. Alternatively, we can specify the moment conditions directly by requiring the error term to be uncorrelated with certain observed instrumental variables. We illustrate with another example.

EXAMPLE 1.4

As in the previous example, we consider the linear regression model
$$y_t = x_t'\beta_0 + u_t,$$
but we do not assume $E(u_t | x_t) = 0$. It follows that u_t and x_t may be correlated. Suppose we have a set of instruments in the $q \times 1$ vector z_t. These may be defined to be valid instruments if $E(z_t u_t) = 0$. Thus the requirement that z_t be a set of valid instruments immediately provides the appropriate moment conditions
$$E(z_t u_t) = E\Big(z_t(y_t - x_t'\beta_0)\Big) = 0.$$
That is,
$$f((x_t, y_t, z_t), \theta) = z_t(y_t - x_t'\beta).$$

There are q equations here since there are q instruments, so we require $q \geq p$ for identification.

■

1.1.2 Method of Moments Estimation

We now consider how to estimate a parameter vector θ using moment conditions as given in Definition 1.1. Consider first the case where $q = p$, that is, where θ is exactly identified by the moment conditions. Then the moment conditions $E(f(x_t, \theta)) = 0$ represent a set of p equations for p unknowns. Solving these equations would give the value of θ which satisfies the moment conditions, and this would be the true value θ_0. However, we cannot observe $E(f(.,.))$, only $f(x_t, \theta)$. The obvious way to proceed is to define the sample moments of $f(x_t, \theta)$

$$f_T(\theta) = T^{-1} \sum_{t=1}^{T} f(x_t, \theta),$$

which is the Method of Moments (MM) estimator of $E(f(x_t, \theta))$. If the sample moments provide good estimates of the population moments, then we might expect that the estimator $\widehat{\theta}_T$ that solves the sample moment conditions $f_T(\theta) = 0$ would provide a good estimate of the true value θ_0 that solves the population moment conditions $E(f(x_t, \theta)) = 0$.

In each of Examples 1.1–1.3, the parameters are exactly identified by the moment conditions. We consider each in turn.

EXAMPLE 1.5

For the gamma distribution in Example 1.1, $f_T(\widehat{\theta}) = 0$ implies

$$T^{-1} \sum_{t=1}^{T} x_t - \frac{\widehat{p}^*}{\widehat{q}^*} = 0,$$

and

$$T^{-1} \sum_{t=1}^{T} \left(x_t - \frac{\widehat{p}^*}{\widehat{q}^*} \right)^2 - \frac{\widehat{p}^*}{\widehat{q}^{*2}} = 0.$$

Defining the sample mean $\bar{x}_T = T^{-1}\sum_{t=1}^{T} x_t$ and sample variance $s_T^2 = T^{-1}\sum_{t=1}^{T}\left(x_t - \bar{x}_T\right)^2$, we find

$$\widehat{q}^* = \frac{\bar{x}_T}{s_T^2},$$

and

$$\widehat{p}^* = \frac{\bar{x}_T^2}{s_T^2}.$$

∎

EXAMPLE 1.6

For the beta distribution in Example 1.2, $f_T(\widehat{\theta}) = 0$ implies

$$T^{-1}\sum_{t=1}^{T} x_t - \frac{\widehat{p}^*}{\widehat{p}^* + \widehat{q}^*} = 0,$$

and

$$T^{-1}\sum_{t=1}^{T} x_t^2 - \frac{\widehat{p}^*(\widehat{p}^* + 1)}{(\widehat{p}^* + \widehat{q}^*)(\widehat{p}^* + \widehat{q}^* + 1)} = 0.$$

With the sample mean and variance defined as in Example 1.5, we solve these equations to obtain

$$\widehat{p}^* = -\bar{x}_T\left(1 - \frac{\bar{x}_T(1 - \bar{x}_T)}{s_T^2}\right)$$

and

$$\widehat{q}^* = (\bar{x}_T - 1)\left(1 - \frac{\bar{x}_T(1 - \bar{x}_T)}{s_T^2}\right).$$

∎

EXAMPLE 1.7

For the linear regression model, the sample moment conditions are

$$T^{-1}\sum_{t=1}^{T} x_t\widehat{u}_t = T^{-1}\sum_{t=1}^{T} x_t(y_t - x_t'\widehat{\beta}_T) = 0,$$

and solving for $\widehat{\beta}_T$ gives

$$\widehat{\beta}_T = \left(\sum_{t=1}^{T} x_t x_t'\right)^{-1}\sum_{t=1}^{T} x_t y_t = (X'X)^{-1}X'y.$$

That is, OLS is an MM estimator.

∎

EXAMPLE 1.8

The linear regression with $q = p$ instrumental variables is also exactly identified. The sample moment conditions are

$$T^{-1} \sum_{t=1}^{T} z_t u_t = T^{-1} \sum_{t=1}^{T} z_t (y_t - x_t' \widehat{\beta}_T) = 0,$$

and solving for $\widehat{\beta}_T$ gives

$$\widehat{\beta}_T = \left(\sum_{t=1}^{T} z_t x_t' \right)^{-1} \sum_{t=1}^{T} z_t y_t = (Z'X)^{-1} Z'y,$$

which is the standard IV estimator.

∎

EXAMPLE 1.9

The Maximum Likelihood estimator can be given an MM interpretation. If the log–likelihood for a single observation is denoted $l(\theta|x_t)$, then the sample log–likelihood is $T^{-1} \sum_{t=1}^{T} l(\theta|x_t)$. The first order conditions for the maximization of the log–likelihood function are then

$$T^{-1} \sum_{t=1}^{T} \frac{\partial l(\theta|x_t)}{\partial \theta} \Big|_{\theta=\widehat{\theta}_T} = 0.$$

These first order conditions can be regarded as a set of sample moment conditions.

∎

1.2 Generalized Method of Moments (GMM) Estimation

The GMM estimator is used when the θ parameters are over–identified by the moment conditions. In this case, the equations $E(f(x_t, \theta_0)) = 0$ represent q equations for p unknowns which are solved exactly by θ_0. If we now proceed as in the exactly identified case to obtain an estimator, we would have

$$f_T(\widehat{\theta}_T) = 0,$$

which is also q equations for p unknowns. Since there are more equations than unknowns, we can not find a vector $\widehat{\theta}_T$ that satisfies $f_T(\theta) = 0$. Instead, we will find the vector $\widehat{\theta}_T$ that makes $f_T(\theta)$ as close to zero as possible. This can be done by defining

$$\widehat{\theta}_T = \mathrm{argmin}_\theta Q_T(\theta)$$

where

$$Q_T(\theta) = f_T(\theta)' A_T f_T(\theta),$$

and A_T is a stochastic positive definite $O_p(1)$ weighting matrix whose role will be discussed later. Note that $Q_T(\theta) \geq 0$ and $Q_T(\theta) = 0$ only if $f_T(\theta) = 0$. Thus, $Q_T(\theta)$ can be made exactly zero in the just identified case, but is strictly positive in the over–identified case. We summarize this in the following definition.

DEFINITION 1.2 **GMM Estimator**

Suppose we have an observed sample $\{x_t : t = 1, \ldots, T\}$ from which we want to estimate an unknown $p \times 1$ parameter vector θ with true value θ_0. Let $E(f(x_t, \theta_0)) = 0$ be a set of q moment conditions, and $f_T(\theta)$ the corresponding sample moments. Define the criterion function

$$Q_T(\theta) = f_T(\theta)' A_T f_T(\theta),$$

where A_T is a stochastic $O_p(1)$ positive definite matrix. Then the GMM estimator of θ is

$$\widehat{\theta}_T = \mathrm{argmin}_\theta Q_T(\theta).$$

■

EXAMPLE 1.10

For the linear regression model with $q > p$ valid instruments, the moment conditions are

$$E(z_t u_t) = E\Big(z_t(y_t - x_t'\beta_0) \Big) = 0,$$

and the sample moments are

$$f_T(\beta) = T^{-1} \sum_{t=1}^{T} z_t(y_t - x'_t\beta) = T^{-1}(Z'y - Z'X\beta).$$

Suppose we choose

$$A_T = \left(T^{-1} \sum_{t=1}^{T} z_t z'_t\right)^{-1} = T(Z'Z)^{-1},$$

and assume we have a weak law of large numbers for $z_t z'_t$ so that $T^{-1}Z'Z$ converges in probability to a constant matrix A. Then the criterion function is

$$Q_T(\beta) = T^{-1}(Z'y - Z'X\beta)'(Z'Z)^{-1}(Z'y - Z'X\beta).$$

Differentiating with respect to β gives the first order conditions

$$\frac{\partial Q_T(\beta)}{\partial \beta}\Big|_{\beta=\widehat{\beta}_T} = T^{-1}2X'Z(Z'Z)^{-1}(Z'y - Z'X\widehat{\beta}_T) = 0,$$

and solving for $\widehat{\beta}_T$ gives

$$\widehat{\beta}_T = \left(X'Z(Z'Z)^{-1}Z'X\right)^{-1} X'Z(Z'Z)^{-1}Z'y.$$

This is the standard IV estimator for the case where there are more instruments than regressors.

$\blacksquare$

1.3 Asymptotic Properties of the GMM Estimator

We present here some sufficient conditions for the consistency and asymptotic normality of the GMM estimator, along with outlines of the proofs. We also consider the asymptotic efficiency of the GMM estimator for a given set of moment conditions.

1.3.1 Consistency

For consistency, we require some assumptions about the structure of $f(x_t, \theta)$, x_t and the parameter space. First, we need an assumption to ensure that the true value of θ is identified.

ASSUMPTION 1.1

(i) $E(f(x_t, \theta))$ exists and is finite for all $\theta \in \Theta$ and for all t.

(ii) If $g_t(\theta) = E(f(x_t, \theta))$, then there exists a $\theta_0 \in \Theta$ such that $g_t(\theta) = 0$ for all t if and only if $\theta = \theta_0$.

∎

Part (i) of Assumption 1.1 states that the population moments exist, which implies some more primitive assumptions about x_t and $f(.,.)$. Part (ii) assumes that θ_0 can be identified by the population moments $g_t(\theta)$. That is, the population moments take the value 0 at θ_0 and at no other value of θ. If there were more than one value of θ such that $g_t(\theta) = 0$, then even full knowledge of the population moment conditions would not allow a true value of θ to be identified.

We consider the property of weak consistency of $\hat{\theta}_T$, that is $\hat{\theta}_T \xrightarrow{p} \theta_0$. Consistency is derived from a consideration of the asymptotic behavior of $Q_T(\theta)$. In particular, we require an assumption about the convergence of the sample moments $f_T(\theta)$ to the population moments $g_T(\theta) = T^{-1} \sum_{t=1}^{T} g_t(\theta)$. Note that $f_T(\theta)$ and $g_T(\theta)$ are q-vectors, and we refer to their individual elements as $f_{Tj}(\theta)$ and $g_{Tj}(\theta)$ respectively, for $j = 1, \ldots, q$.

ASSUMPTION 1.2

$(f_{Tj}(\theta) - g_{Tj}(\theta)) \xrightarrow{p} 0$ uniformly for all $\theta \in \Theta$ and for all $j = 1, \ldots, q$.

∎

This assumption requires that $f(x_t, \theta)$ satisfies a uniform weak law of large numbers, so that the difference between the average sample and population moments converges in probability to zero. The uniformity of the convergence means that

$$\sup_{\theta \in \Theta} |f_{Tj}(\theta) - g_{Tj}(\theta)| \xrightarrow{p} 0, \text{ for } j = 1, \ldots, q.$$

Note that this is a stronger requirement than pointwise convergence in probability on Θ, which simply requires that $(f_{Tj}(\theta) - g_{Tj}(\theta)) \xrightarrow{p} 0$ for all $\theta \in \Theta$. The importance of the uniformity of the convergence for the proof of consistency is that it implies that $(f_{Tj}(\theta_T^*) - g_{Tj}(\theta_T^*)) \xrightarrow{p} 0$, where θ_T^* is some sequence. If we only have pointwise convergence in probability then $(f_{Tj}(\theta_T^*) - g_{Tj}(\theta_T^*))$ may not converge to zero. *Amemiya* [1985, p. 109] provides two such examples.

We also make an assumption about the convergence of the weighting matrix A_T.

ASSUMPTION 1.3

There exists a non–random sequence of positive definite matrices $\bar{A}_T$ such that

$$A_T - \bar{A}_T \xrightarrow{p} 0.$$

■

With these assumptions, the weak consistency of $\hat{\theta}_T$ can be shown.

THEOREM 1.1 **Weak Consistency**

Under Assumptions 1.1 to 1.3, the GMM estimator $\hat{\theta}_T$ defined in 1.2 is weakly consistent.

■

PROOF OF THE THEOREM

The basic steps to prove the consistency of $\hat{\theta}_T$ are as follows.
(i) Deduce from Assumptions 1.2 and 1.3 that there exists a non–random sequence

$$\bar{Q}_T(\theta) = g_T(\theta)' \bar{A}_T g_T(\theta)$$

such that

$$Q_T(\theta) - \bar{Q}_T(\theta) \xrightarrow{p} 0 \text{ uniformly for } \theta \in \Theta. \qquad (1\text{--}1)$$

(ii) Deduce from Assumption 1.1 that $\bar{Q}_T(\theta) = 0$ if and only if $\theta = \theta_0$, $\bar{Q}_T(\theta) > 0$ otherwise, and hence

$$\theta_0 = \mathrm{argmin}_{\theta \in \Theta} \bar{Q}_T(\theta). \qquad (1\text{--}2)$$

(iii) Show that (1–2) and (1–1) imply that $\hat{\theta}_T \xrightarrow{p} \theta_0$. That is, $\hat{\theta}_T$ minimizes $Q_T(\theta)$, θ_0 minimizes $\bar{Q}_T(\theta)$ and $(Q_T(\theta) - \bar{Q}_T(\theta)) \xrightarrow{p} 0$, and hence $\hat{\theta}_T \xrightarrow{p} \theta_0$.

∎

Given our assumptions, the intuition of the proof is clear. A textbook presentation of the formal details of the proof can be found in *Amemiya* [1985, p. 107].

Assumptions 1.1 to 1.3 provide sufficient conditions for the weak consistency of $\hat{\theta}_T$. However, Assumptions 1.2 and 1.3 are quite high level and not easily related to a given sample x_t and function $f(.,.)$. We consider more primitive assumptions that are sufficient for Assumptions 1.2 and 1.3 to hold.

There is a considerable literature devoted to the question of sufficient primitive conditions for Assumption 1.2. A thorough discussion of the technicalities of proving uniform laws of large numbers is beyond our scope, so we just give an outline of some of the important issues. One approach is to make use of the fact that the uniform convergence in probability in Assumption 1.2 can be shown to be a consequence of the following three more basic assumptions.

ASSUMPTION 1.4

Θ is compact.

∎

ASSUMPTION 1.5

$$(f_{Tj}(\theta) - g_{Tj}(\theta)) \xrightarrow{p} 0 \text{ pointwise on } \Theta \text{ for } j = 1, \ldots, p.$$

∎

ASSUMPTION 1.6

$f_{Tj}(\theta)$ is stochastically equicontinuous and $g_{Tj}(\theta)$ is equicontinuous for $j = 1, \ldots, p$.

∎

Assumption 1.4 requires that the parameter space be closed and bounded. From a practical point of view, this assumption is not always desirable. For example, the parameter space for a variance parameter (say σ^2) may consist of the positive real line $\mathbb{R}^+$. That is, $\{\sigma^2 \in \mathbb{R} : \sigma^2 > 0\}$, which is neither closed nor bounded. Even with some upper bound B for σ^2, the set $\{\sigma^2 \in \mathbb{R} : 0 < \sigma^2 \leq B\}$ is only semi–closed. Alternative assumptions and situations in which Assumption 1.1 can be relaxed are considered in *Hansen* [1982], *Andrews* [1992] and *Potscher and Prucha* [1994]. *Hansen* [1982] discusses a particular structure for the moment conditions for which compactness is not required. This structure includes linear models such as in Examples 1.3 and 1.4. For our general results, we maintain Assumption 1.1 for simplicity and consistency with much of the existing literature.

Assumption 1.5 requires that $f_{Tj}(\theta)$ converges in probability to $g_{Tj}(\theta)$ for all $\theta \in \Theta$. That is, a weak law of large numbers must hold for $f_j(x_t, \theta)$ for each θ, which requires further assumptions on x_t and $f(.,.)$. For example, if x_t is i.i.d. and $E|f_j(x_t, \theta)| < \infty$ for all θ and j, then $g_{Tj}(\theta) = Ef_j(x_t, \theta)$ is not a function of T and Assumption 1.5 is the result of a standard i.i.d. weak law of large numbers for each $\theta \in \Theta$. If the assumption that x_t is i.i.d. is relaxed, then other weak laws can be applied. If x_t is allowed to be heterogeneously distributed then additional moment conditions must be imposed. As a simple example, if x_t is independently and heterogeneously distributed such that $\sup_t E\left(f_j(x_t, \theta)^2\right) < \infty$ for all j and θ (*i.e.*, $f(x_t, \theta)$ has bounded variance for all t) then Assumption 1.5 follows. Note that this is not the weakest assumption available, but is easy to interpret. If x_t is also be allowed to be dependent, then there are various sets of conditions that are sufficient for Assumption 1.5. In general, it is necessary to control the degree of dependence in x_t, and hence $f_j(x_t, \theta)$, so that as two elements x_t and x_{t+k} become further apart (*i.e.*, as k increases) their dependence decreases towards zero. For example, we may assume that x_t is stationary and ergodic, or we may assume that

x_t is mixing. Both ergodicity and mixing are concepts of asymptotic independence. The use of a mixing assumption is common because it allows x_t to be both dependent and heterogeneous, and also makes explicit the trade–off in the amount of dependence and heterogeneity allowed for a weak law of large numbers to hold. If x_t is mixing and $f_j(x_t, \theta)$ is a function that contains at most a finite number of lags of x_t, then $f_j(x_t, \theta)$ is also mixing and satisfies a weak law of large numbers for mixing processes. If $f_j(x_t, \theta)$ contains an infinite number of lags of x_t (*e.g.*, an autoregression), then it need not be mixing. In this case, we can impose the additional assumption that $f_j(x_t, \theta)$ is near–epoch dependent on x_t. This is an assumption which implies that $f_j(x_t, \theta)$ is almost completely dependent on the most recent lags of x_t (or the near–epoch of x_t). For the example of an autoregression, near–epoch dependence requires that the zeros of the autoregressive polynomial lie outside the unit circle. If $f_j(x_t, \theta)$ is near–epoch dependent on x_t, then it can be shown that $f_j(x_t, \theta)$ is a mixingale for which weak laws of large numbers can be derived. In all cases, the emphasis is on controlling the degree of dependence of $f_j(x_t, \theta)$, so that it is only weakly dependent on its distant past. Processes with strong dependence such as unit root and many long memory processes are excluded by such assumptions. Processes with deterministic trends are also generally excluded, although *Andrews and McDermott* [1995] provide asymptotic theory for this case.

The many technical details underlying these concepts are beyond the scope of this introductory chapter. *White* [1984] provides a textbook treatment of limit theorems under various regularity conditions, as well as specific concepts such as stationarity (p. 40), ergodicity (p. 41) and mixing (p. 45). *Davidson* [1994] also discusses these concepts, along with mixingales (Chapter 16) and near–epoch dependence (Chapter 17). *Gallant and White* [1988] and *Potscher and Prucha* [1991a, b] both provide unified and rigorous expositions of the use of these ideas in the derivation of properties of estimators computed from the optimisation of some criterion function (of which GMM is an example).

Assumption 1.6 (along with 1.4) provides sufficient regularity to convert the pointwise convergence of Assumption 1.5 into the uniform convergence of Assumption 1.2. The idea is that some form of smoothness condition on $f_{Tj}(\theta)$ is required for uniform convergence. Stochastic equicontinuity can be obtained by making a stochastic Lipschitz–type assumption on $f_j(x_t, \theta)$. That is, if there exists a uniformly bounded random sequence b_t (*i.e.*, $\sup_t E(b_t) < \infty$) and a non–negative deterministic function $h(.)$ such that $h(x) \to 0$ as $x \to 0$ such that

$$|f_j(x_t, \theta_1) - f_j(x_t, \theta_2)| < b_t h(\|\theta_1 - \theta_2\|) \text{ for all } \theta_1, \theta_2 \in \Theta, \quad (1\text{--}3)$$

then $f_{Tj}(\theta)$ can be shown to be stochastically equicontinuous and $g_{Tj}(\theta)$ can be shown to be equicontinuous (see Corollary 3.1 of *Newey* [1991]). In Equation (1–3), $\|x\|$ denotes the vector norm $\left(\sum_{j=1}^p x_j^2\right)^{1/2}$. Intuitively, this condition requires that if θ_1 and θ_2 are arbitrarily close together, the difference between $f_j(x_t, \theta_1)$ and $f_j(x_t, \theta_2)$ should also be arbitrarily small. In this sense, it is a smoothness condition related to, but generally stronger than, the continuity of $f_j(.,.)$ with respect to θ. Stochastic equicontinuity is a property of both $f(.,.)$ and x_t. There is a considerable literature devoted to deriving sufficient conditions for stochastic equicontinuity, including *Andrews* [1987, 1992], *Potscher and Prucha* [1989a, 1994], *Newey* [1991] and *Hansen* [1996]. *Davidson* [1994] (Chapter 21) provides a textbook treatment of uniform convergence. The Lipschitz condition given here is only one example of a sufficient condition.

Note that in order to show strong consistency of the GMM estimator (as does *Hansen* [1982], for example), it is necessary to strengthen Assumptions 1.3 and 1.4 by replacing convergence in probability with convergence almost surely. This in turn requires stronger primitive assumptions about x_t and $f(.,.)$ than those required for convergence in probability. For example, *Davidson* [1994, p. 339] points out that the extra regularity required to obtain strong stochastic equicontinuity can be considerable.

1.3.2 Asymptotic Normality

Assumptions in addition to those required for consistency are needed to derive an asymptotic normality result for the GMM estimator.

ASSUMPTION 1.7

$f(x_t, \theta)$ is continuously differentiable with respect to θ on Θ.

∎

That $f(x_t, \theta)$ is differentiable is required for the maximization of $Q_T(\theta)$ to proceed via the solution of the first order conditions $\partial Q_T\left(\hat{\theta}_T\right)/\partial\theta = 0$. It follows from this assumption that $f_T(\theta)$ is continuously differentiable, and we denote its first derivative as

$$F_T(\theta) = \frac{\partial f_T(\theta)}{\partial\theta'}.$$

Note that

$$\frac{\partial f_T(\theta)}{\partial\theta'} = T^{-1}\sum_{t=1}^{T}\frac{\partial f(x_t, \theta)}{\partial\theta'},$$

so the following assumption requires that a weak law of large numbers applies to the first derivative of $f(x_t, \theta)$ in a neighbourhood of θ_0.

ASSUMPTION 1.8

For any sequence θ_T^* such that $\theta_T^* \xrightarrow{p} \theta_0$,

$$F_T(\theta_T^*) - \bar{F}_T \xrightarrow{p} 0,$$

where $\bar{F}_T$ is a sequence of $q \times p$ matrices that do not depend on θ.

∎

ASSUMPTION 1.9

$f(x_t, \theta_0)$ satisfies a central limit theorem, so that

$$\bar{V}_T^{-1/2}\sqrt{T}f_T(\theta_0) \xrightarrow{d} N(0, I_q),$$

where $\bar{V}_T$ is a sequence of $q \times q$ non–random positive definite matrices defined as

$$\bar{V}_T = T\mathrm{var}f_T(\theta_0).$$

∎

Sufficient primitive conditions on $f(., .)$ and x_t can be found for Assumptions 1.8 and 1.9. For example, Assumption 1.9 may follow from a central limit theorem for independent and heterogeneously distributed processes (*e.g., White* [1984, p. 112]), stationary and ergodic processes (*e.g., White* [1984, p. 118]), mixing processes (*e.g., White* [1984, p. 124]) or near–epoch dependent functions of mixing processes (*e.g., Davidson* [1994, p. 386]). In general, the weakest available conditions for such central limit theorems are stronger than those for the corresponding weak laws of large numbers referred to in relation to Assumption 1.5. Thus, given the way in which such assumptions are presented, we make relatively weak assumptions about $f(x_t, \theta)$ for all $\theta \in \Theta$ to obtain uniform convergence in probability, and relatively strong assumptions about $f(x_t, \theta_0)$ to obtain the central limit theorem. It is not necessarily the case that a central limit theorem need apply to $f(x_t, \theta)$ for $\theta \neq \theta_0$.

We now give an asymptotic normality result for the GMM estimator. The method of proof involves an expansion of the moment conditions about the true value of θ_0, which is a standard technique in showing asymptotic normality. Our steps follow those of *Hansen* [1982].

THEOREM 1.2 **Asymptotic Normality**

Under Assumptions 1.1 to 1.3, and 1.7 to 1.9 the GMM estimator $\widehat{\theta}_T$ has the asymptotic distribution

$$\left(F_T \left(\widehat{\theta}_T \right)' A_T \bar{V}_T A_T F_T \left(\widehat{\theta}_T \right) \right)^{-1/2} \left(F_T \left(\widehat{\theta}_T \right)' A_T F_T \left(\widehat{\theta}_T \right) \right) \times$$
$$\times \sqrt{T} \left(\widehat{\theta}_T - \theta_0 \right) \xrightarrow{d} N \left(0, I_p \right).$$

∎

PROOF OF THE THEOREM

Consider a mean–value expansion of the vector of moment conditions around θ_0 :

$$f_T \left(\widehat{\theta}_T \right) = f_T \left(\theta_0 \right) + F_T \left(\theta_T^* \right) \left(\widehat{\theta}_T - \theta_0 \right),$$

where θ_T^* lies between $\widehat{\theta}_T$ and θ_0. Note that $\theta_T^* \xrightarrow{p} \theta_0$ because $\widehat{\theta}_T$ is consistent. If we pre–multiply this equation by

$$F_T\left(\widehat{\theta}_T\right)' A_T$$

we get

$$F_T\left(\widehat{\theta}_T\right)' A_T f_T\left(\widehat{\theta}_T\right) =$$

$$F_T\left(\widehat{\theta}_T\right)' A_T f_T\left(\theta_0\right) + F_T\left(\widehat{\theta}_T\right)' A_T F_T\left(\theta_T^*\right)\left(\widehat{\theta}_T - \theta_0\right) = 0,$$

since the left hand side represents the first order conditions for the minimization of $Q_T\left(\theta\right)$. Re–arranging and multiplying by $\sqrt{T}$ gives

$$\left(F_T\left(\widehat{\theta}_T\right)' A_T \bar{V}_T A_T F_T\left(\widehat{\theta}_T\right)\right)^{-1/2} \left(F_T\left(\widehat{\theta}_T\right)' A_T F_T\left(\theta_T^*\right)\right)$$

$$\times \sqrt{T}\left(\widehat{\theta}_T - \theta_0\right)$$

$$= -\left(F_T\left(\widehat{\theta}_T\right)' A_T \bar{V}_T A_T F_T\left(\widehat{\theta}_T\right)\right)^{-1/2} F_T\left(\widehat{\theta}_T\right)' A_T \bar{V}_T^{1/2} \bar{V}_T^{-1/2}$$

$$\times \sqrt{T} f_T\left(\theta_0\right).$$

In view of Assumption 1.9, the right hand side of this expression is asymptotically distributed as $N\left(0, I_q\right)$. On the left hand side, we can use Assumption 1.8 to replace $F_T\left(\theta_T^*\right)$ with $F_T\left(\widehat{\theta}_T\right)$ with no change to the asymptotics.

∎

The asymptotic distribution result in Theorem 1.2 is not operational for the derivation of test statistics because $\bar{V}_T$ is unknown and must be estimated. There is a considerable literature on the consistent estimation of $\bar{V}_T$, see *Andrews* [1991], *Newey and West* [1994] and *den Haan and Levin* [1996] for a survey. See also Chapter 3, or further reference, we simply assume that such a consistent estimator can be obtained.

ASSUMPTION 1.10

We can calculate $\widehat{V}_T$ such that $\widehat{V}_T - \bar{V}_T \overset{p}{\longrightarrow} 0$.

∎

Since $\bar{V}_T = T\mathrm{var} f_T(\theta_0)$ and θ_0 is unknown, the consistent estimator $\widehat{V}_T$ is calculated using $f_T\left(\widehat{\theta}_T\right)$.

1.3.3 Asymptotic Efficiency

We consider the asymptotic efficiency of the GMM estimator the perspective of choosing the appropriate weighting matrix A_T. Following Definition 4.20 of *White* [1984], Theorem 1.2 implies that the asymptotic covariance matrix of the GMM estimator for a given set of moment conditions is

$$\left(\bar{F}'_T \bar{A}_T \bar{F}_T\right)^{-1} \bar{F}'_T \bar{A}_T \bar{V}_T \bar{A}_T \bar{F}_T \left(\bar{F}'_T \bar{A}_T \bar{F}_T\right)^{-1}.$$

The weighting matrix A_T can be seen to have an effect only on the variance of the asymptotic distribution of the GMM estimator, and not on the consistency. We therefore choose A_T to minimize the asymptotic covariance matrix. The appropriate choice of A_T is suggested by the following lemma.

LEMMA 1.1

$$\left(\bar{F}'_T \bar{A}_T \bar{F}_T\right)^{-1} \bar{F}'_T \bar{A}_T \bar{V}_T \bar{A}_T \bar{F}_T \left(\bar{F}'_T \bar{A}_T \bar{F}_T\right)^{-1} - \left(\bar{F}'_T \bar{V}_T^{-1} \bar{F}_T\right)^{-1}$$
is positive semi–definite for all $\bar{A}_T$.

∎

This suggests that we should choose $A_T = \widehat{V}_T^{-1}$. Then we can deduce from Theorem 1.2 that the asymptotic covariance matrix of this GMM estimator is $\left(\bar{F}'_T \bar{V}_T^{-1} \bar{F}_T\right)^{-1}$, which is the smallest possible for the given moment conditions. This choice of A_T requires a two step estimation procedure because consistent estimation of $\bar{V}_T$ requires a consistent estimator of θ_0. An initial consistent estimator of θ_0 can be calculated for some arbitrary choice of A_T (say $A_T = I_q$), which can then be used to calculate $\widehat{V}_T$ and the asymptotically efficient GMM estimator.

A disadvantage of this two step approach is that the resulting asymptotically efficient GMM estimator is not unique depending on which arbitrary weighting matrix was used to calculate the initial estimator. That is, different estimators are obtained depending on the initial choice of A_T. Although there is no difference asymptotically, this is still an undesirable feature. There are some alternative estimators that have been proposed to avoid this problem. *Hansen, Heaton and Yaron* [1996] suggested two approaches. The first is to iterate the estimation procedure until the parameter estimates and the weighting matrix converge. The second is to acknowledge the dependence of the optimal weighting matrix on the parameter vector and minimize

$$Q_T(\theta) = f_T(\theta)' A_T(\theta) f_T(\theta)$$

with respect to θ. For the i.i.d. case

$$A_T(\theta) = T^{-1} \sum_{t=1}^{T} f(x_t, \theta) f(x_t, \theta)',$$

while if dependence and heterogeneity is allowed in x_t then more complicated forms of $A_T(\theta)$ are necessary, see Chapter 3. Also, *Imbens* [1997] and *Smith* [1997] provide developments of GMM estimation based on non–parametric approximations to the likelihood function. Each provides asymptotically efficient estimation without being dependent on an initial choice of weighting matrix.

Note, that this discussion applies only to the over–identified case where there are more moment conditions than parameters ($q > p$). If $p = q$ (*i.e.*, θ is exactly identified) then no choice of A_T is required since $\widehat{\theta}_T$ can be calculated by solving the sample moment conditions $f_T\left(\widehat{\theta}_T\right) = 0$ exactly. If estimation were to proceed by the minimization of $Q_T(\theta)$, the above expression for the asymptotic covariance matrix reduces to $\bar{F}_T^{-1} \bar{V}_T \bar{F}_T^{-1\prime}$ for any choice of A_T.

1.3.4 Illustrations

In order to illustrate the concepts of the previous sections, we consider two examples. The first shows how things simplify when i.i.d. observations are assumed, and the second considers again the instrumental variables estimation of a linear regression.

1.3.4.1 GMM With i.i.d. Observations

If x_t is assumed to be i.i.d., $f(x_t, \theta)$ is also i.i.d. and $E(f(x_t, \theta)) = g_t(\theta) = g(\theta)$ for all t. In this case, Assumption 1.1 requires that the expectation exists and $g(\theta_0) = 0$ if and only if $\theta = \theta_0$. Then $g_T(\theta)$ also simplifies to $g(\theta)$, so that Assumption 1.2 requires that $f_{Tj}(\theta) \xrightarrow{p} g_j(\theta)$ uniformly on Θ for all j. We can also replace Assumption 1.3 with the simplified statement $A_T \xrightarrow{p} A$, where A is a non–stochastic positive definite matrix. Then the proof of consistency given in Theorem 1.1 involves us showing that $Q_T(\theta) \xrightarrow{p} Q(\theta)$ uniformly on Θ, where $Q(\theta) = g(\theta)' Ag(\theta)$. It follows that $\theta_0 = \mathrm{argmin}_{\theta \in \Theta} Q(\theta)$, from which consistency can be shown.

With respect to asymptotic normality, Assumption 1.8 requires that the first derivative of the moments satisfies

$$\left. \frac{\partial f_T(\theta)}{\partial \theta'} \right|_{\theta = \theta_T^*} = F_T(\theta_T^*) \xrightarrow{p} F$$

for any sequence θ_T^* such that $\theta_T^* \xrightarrow{p} \theta_0$, where F is a non–stochastic $q \times p$ matrix of full column rank. Since $f(x_t, \theta)$ is i.i.d., the central limit theorem of Assumption 1.9 can be expressed as

$$\sqrt{T} f_T(\theta_0) \xrightarrow{d} N(0, V),$$

where $V = \mathrm{var}(f(x_t, \theta_0))$. If, as in the proof of Theorem 1.2, we perform a mean–value expansion of $f_T\left(\widehat{\theta}_T\right)$ about θ_0, pre–multiply by $F_T\left(\widehat{\theta}_T\right)' A_T$ and re–arrange, we obtain

$$\sqrt{T}\left(\widehat{\theta}_T - \theta_0\right) =$$

$$-\left(F_T\left(\widehat{\theta}_T\right)' A_T F_T(\theta_T^*)\right)^{-1} F_T\left(\widehat{\theta}_T\right)' A_T \sqrt{T} f_T(\theta_0)$$

$$\xrightarrow{d} N\left(0, (F'AF)^{-1} F'AVAF (F'AF)^{-1}\right).$$

The asymptotic covariance matrix of $\widehat{\theta}_T$ is therefore

$$(F'AF)^{-1} F'AVAF (F'AF)^{-1},$$

which in view of Lemma 1.1 is minimized if we can choose A_T such that $A = V^{-1}$. Then the asymptotic covariance matrix would reduce to $(F'V^{-1}F)^{-1}$. We therefore require a consistent estimator of V. Since $f(x_t, \theta)$ is i.i.d., a consistent estimator, if we knew θ_0, would be

$$\widehat{V}_T = T^{-1} \sum_{t=1}^{T} f(x_t, \theta_0) f(x_t, \theta_0)'.$$

Since θ_0 is unknown, we can calculate an initial consistent (but asymptotically inefficient) estimator $\widehat{\theta}_T^{(1)}$ using $A_T = I_q$ (or some other known matrix), and calculate the estimator $\widehat{\theta}_T$ using $A_T = \widehat{V}_T^{-1}$, where

$$\widehat{V}_T = T^{-1} \sum_{t=1}^{T} f\left(x_t, \widehat{\theta}_T^{(1)}\right) f\left(x_t, \widehat{\theta}_T^{(1)}\right)'.$$

For a given set of moment conditions, $\widehat{\theta}_T$ is asymptotically the most efficient GMM estimator.

1.3.4.2 Regression With Instrumental Variables

We can use the example of a regression estimated using instrumental variables to illustrate the preceding ideas. In particular, we can show how the properties of the estimator can be derived working only with the moment conditions and criterion function given in Example 1.10, without explicitly writing down the estimator. For the linear regression model with $q > p$ instruments considered in Example 1.10, we have the sample moments

$$f((x_t, y_t, z_t), \beta) = z_t (y_t - x_t'\beta)$$
$$= z_t (u_t - x_t'(\beta - \beta_0)).$$

Assuming that (x_t, z_t, u_t) is i.i.d., we have

$$f_T(\beta) = T^{-1} \sum_{t=1}^{T} z_t u_t - T^{-1} \sum_{t=1}^{T} z_t x_t'(\beta - \beta_0)$$
$$\xrightarrow{p} \Sigma_{zx}(\beta - \beta_0)$$
$$= g(\beta),$$

where the admissability of the instruments guarantees that

$$T^{-1} \sum_{t=1}^{T} z_t u_t \xrightarrow{p} E(z_t u_t) = 0,$$

and

$$T^{-1} \sum_{t=1}^{T} z_t x_t' \xrightarrow{p} E(z_t x_t') = \Sigma_{zx},$$

where Σ_{zx} has full column rank. Note, that the admissability of the instruments also guarantees that $g(\beta) = 0$ if and only if $\beta = \beta_0$, thus identifying β_0. Furthermore,

$$
\begin{aligned}
Q_T(\beta) &= f_T(\beta)' A_T f_T(\beta) \\
&\xrightarrow{p} g(\beta)' A g(\beta) \\
&= Q(\beta)
\end{aligned}
$$

for a suitable choice of A_T such that $A_T \xrightarrow{p} A$, and hence $\beta_0 = \operatorname{argmin}_\beta Q(\beta)$. Therefore the consistency of the IV estimator can be shown without writing down the closed form of the estimator.

With respect to asymptotic normality, we have

$$
\frac{\partial f_T(\beta)}{\partial \beta'} = -T^{-1} \sum_{t=1}^{T} z_t x_t' \xrightarrow{p} -\Sigma_{zx} = F,
$$

and

$$
\operatorname{var} f\left((x_t, y_t, z_t), \beta_0\right) = \operatorname{var}(z_t u_t) = \sigma_u^2 \Sigma_{zz} = V,
$$

where $\sigma_u^2 = E\left(u_t^2 \mid z_t\right)$ and $\Sigma_{zz} = E(z_t z_t')$. Thus for any A_T we have

$$
\sqrt{T}\left(\hat{\beta}_T - \beta_0\right) \xrightarrow{d}
$$

$$
N\left(0, \sigma_u^2 \left(\Sigma_{xz} A \Sigma_{zx}\right)^{-1} \Sigma_{xz} A \Sigma_{zz} A \Sigma_{zx} \left(\Sigma_{xz} A \Sigma_{zx}\right)^{-1}\right).
$$

If, as suggested in Example 1.10, we choose

$$
A_T = \left(T^{-1} \sum_{t=1}^{T} z_t z_t'\right)^{-1}
$$

so that $A_T \xrightarrow{p} A = \Sigma_{zz}^{-1}$, the asymptotic distribution of $\hat{\beta}_T$ becomes

$$
\sqrt{T}\left(\hat{\beta}_T - \beta_0\right) \xrightarrow{d} N\left(0, \left(\Sigma_{xz} \Sigma_{zz}^{-1} \Sigma_{zx}\right)^{-1}\right).
$$

In view of Lemma 1.1, this is the asymptotically most efficient instrumental variables estimator using z_t.

1.3.5 Choice of Moment Conditions

It is also important to consider unconditional asymptotic efficiency, that is, which moment conditions provide the most asymptotically efficient GMM estimator. One can argue that the more orthogonality conditions are used (the larger the information set) the more asymptotically efficient the GMM estimator is. It is true in general that including extra moment conditions will not reduce asymptotic efficiency. However, we now give two examples that caution against the indiscriminate use of large numbers of moment conditions.

EXAMPLE 1.11

Consider again the example of regression with instrumental variables given in Section 1.3.4.2. Suppose for simplicity that x_t is a single stochastic regressor and z_t is a single instrumental variables such that (x_t, z_t, u_t) is zero mean and i.i.d. and $E(u_t|z_t) = 0$. From this conditional expectation we can derive an infinite number of moment conditions $E(u_t h(z_t)) = 0$ where $h(.)$ is any function of z_t. For example, $E(u_t z_t) = 0$ and $E(u_t z_t^2) = 0$ may be admissable instruments for x_t. Following the notation of 1.3.4.2, the IV estimator using these instruments and the efficient weighting matrix has asymptotic variance $(\Sigma_{xz}\Sigma_{zz}^{-1}\Sigma_{zx})^{-1}$, where

$$\Sigma_{zx} = \begin{pmatrix} E(x_t z_t) \\ E(x_t z_t^2) \end{pmatrix},$$

and

$$\Sigma_{zz} = \begin{pmatrix} E(z_t^2) & E(z_t^3) \\ E(z_t^3) & E(z_t^4) \end{pmatrix}.$$

However, it is important that in addition to $E(u_t z_t^2) = 0$ we know that $E(x_t z_t^2) \neq 0$. That x_t and z_t are highly correlated does not imply that x_t and z_t^2 are correlated. If $E(x_t z_t^2) = 0$ then

$$(\Sigma_{xz}\Sigma_{zz}^{-1}\Sigma_{zx})^{-1} = \frac{E(z_t^2) - E(z_t^3)^2/E(z_t^4)}{E(x_t z_t)^2}.$$

Thus, if $E(x_t z_t^2) = 0$ and z_t is symmetrically distributed then there is no improvement in asymptotic efficiency by including z_t^2 as an additional instrument.

■

The previous example illustrates that additional moment conditions will only improve asymptotic efficiency if they contribute extra information to that contained in the existing moment conditions. The following example further illustrates this point using a panel data model.

EXAMPLE 1.12

For the dynamic error components panel data model (*Sevestre and Trognon* [1995])

$$y_{it} = \delta y_{it-1} + x'_{it}\beta + u_{it} \quad u_{it} = \mu_i + v_{it}$$
$$i = 1, \ldots, N \ \ t = 1, \ldots, T$$

$$E(\mu_i) = E(v_{it}) = 0, \quad E(\mu_i^2) = \sigma_\mu^2,$$
$$E(v_{it}^2) = \sigma_v^2, \quad E(\mu_i v_{it}) = 0$$

the "usual" OLS, (F)GLS, Within, Between, etc. estimators are inconsistent when $N \to \infty$ (but T fixed). The GMM technique now consists of estimating this model by using the

$$E(y_{i0} - x'_{i0}\beta) = 0$$
$$E[(y_{i0} - x'_{i0}\beta)^2] = \sigma_\mu^2$$
$$E[(y_{i0} - x'_{i0}\beta)(y_{it} - \delta y_{it-1} - x'_{it}\beta)] = 0 \quad \forall \quad t = 1, \ldots, T$$
$$E(y_{it} - \delta y_{it-1} - x'_{it}\beta) = 0 \quad \forall \quad t = 1, \ldots, T$$
$$E[(y_{it} - \delta y_{it-1} - x'_{it}\beta)(y_{is} - \delta y_{is-1} - x'_{is}\beta)] = 0$$
$$t, s = 1, \ldots, T \quad t \neq s$$
$$E[(y_{it} - \delta y_{it-1} - x'_{it}\beta)(y_{it} - \delta y_{it-1} - x'_{it}\beta)] = \sigma_\mu^2 + \sigma_v^2$$
$$\forall \ t = 1, \ldots, T$$
$$E[y_{i0}(y_{it} - \delta y_{it-1} - x'_{it}\beta)] = c \quad \forall \quad t = 1, \ldots, T$$
$$E[(y_{i0} - x'_{i0}\beta)x_{it}^k] = 0 \quad \forall \quad t = 1, \ldots, T \quad k = 1, \ldots, r$$
$$E[(y_{it} - x'_{it}\beta)x_{i0}^k] = 0 \quad \forall \quad t = 1, \ldots, T \quad k = 1, \ldots, r$$
$$E[(y_{it} - \delta y_{it-1} - x'_{it}\beta)x_{is}^k] = 0$$
$$\forall \ t, s = 1, \ldots, T \quad s \neq t \quad k = 1, \ldots, r$$
$$E[(y_{it} - \delta y_{it-1} - x'_{it}\beta)x_{it}^k] = 0 \quad \forall \quad t = 1, \ldots, T$$
$$k = 1, \ldots, r$$

orthogonality conditions. In this case the GMM estimator has no closed analytical form. Also, the number of moment conditions is proportional to the time dimension T. As $N \to \infty$ these moment conditions become perfectly collinear so that some are redundant in the sense they provide no extra information.

∎

EXAMPLE 1.13

Hansen and Singleton [1982] considered the estimation of a consumption based capital asset pricing model. This is a non–linear rational expectations model where agents maximize

$$\sum_{t=1}^{\infty} E_t \left(\beta^t U \left(C_t \right) \right),$$

subject to the budget constraint

$$C_t + P_t Q_t \leq V_t Q_{t-1} + W_t.$$

In this model, C_t is real consumption in period t, W_t is real labor income, β is the discount factor and $U \left(C_t \right)$ is a strictly concave utility function. In this simplified version of the model, there are bonds of one period maturity available at price P_t and with payoff V_{t+1}. Agents hold a quantity Q_t of these bonds at each time period. If $U \left(C_t \right) = \left(C_t^\alpha - 1 \right) / \alpha$ then the first order condition for utility maximization is

$$E_t \left(\beta \left(\frac{C_{t+1}}{C_t} \right)^{\alpha - 1} R_{t+1} - 1 \right) = 0,$$

where $R_{t+1} = V_{t+1} / P_t$ is the return on a bond held from time t to $t+1$. This first order condition then gives moment conditions of the form

$$E \left[\left(\eta \left(\frac{C_{t+1}}{C_t} \right)^{\alpha - 1} R_{t+1} - 1 \right) z_t \right] = 0,$$

where z_t is any vector of variables drawn from the information set available at time t. This may include lags of C_{t+1} / C_t and R_{t+1}. This type of application was important in the development of GMM in econometrics. It allowed the estimation of the parameters of economic models that do not have explicit solutions to their first order conditions. Furthermore, it did so without the imposition of specific statistical restrictions such as distributional assumptions for the generation of the data.

■

1.4 Conclusion

In this chapter we introduced the basic ideas behind the Generalized Method of Moments estimator and, also, derived its main properties. With the help of several examples, we showed how this approach relates to other estimation techniques used in econometrics and statistics.

Most of the methods and procedures presented in Chapter 1 are studied in more depth in the following chapters of the volume. The next chapter analyzes in detail the GMM estimation of various econometric models using several different assumptions about the data generating process. Chapter 3 deals with issues related to the estimation of the optimal weighting matrix, while Chapter 4 shows how hypothesis testing is performed in the GMM framework. Chapter 5 collects the main results available in the literature about the finite sample behavior of the GMM estimator for the most frequently used econometric models. Chapters 6 and 7 show how the GMM techniques can be applied to different time series models. Chapters 8 and 9, through the examples of panel data models, show how to derive different types of GMM estimators and also analyze many important practical problems like the choice of moment conditions (instruments) or the trade off between asymptotic efficiency and small sample performance. Chapter 10 takes the reader to the frontiers of this methodology, and finally, Chapter 11 illustrates the usefulness of the GMM approach through a theoretical application.

References

Amemiya, T. [**1985**]: *Advanced Econometrics;* Basil Blackwell, Oxford.

Andrews, D.W.K. [**1987**]: Consistency in Nonlinear Econometric Models: A Generic Uniform Law of Large Numbers; *Econometrica,* 55, 1465–1471.

Andrews, D.W.K. [**1991**]: Heteroskedasticity and Autocorrelation Consistent Covariance Matrix Estimation; *Econometrica,* 59, 817–858.

Andrews, D.W.K. [**1992**]: Generic Uniform Convergence; *Econometric Theory;* 8, 241–257.

Andrews, D.W.K. and C.J. McDermott [**1995**]: Nonlinear Econometric Models with Deterministically Trending Variables; *Review of Economic Studies,* 62, 343-360.

Davidson, J. [1994]: *Stochastic Limit Theory;* Oxford University Press, Oxford.

den Haan, W.J. and A. Levin [1996]: *A Practioner's Guide to Robust Covariance Matrix Estimation;* Manuscript.

Gallant, A.R. and H. White [1988]: *A Unified Theory of Estimation and Inference for Nonlinear Dynamic Models;* Basil Blackwell, New York.

Hansen, B.E. [1996]: Stochastic Equicontinuity for Unbounded Dependent Heterogeneous Arrays; *Econometric Theory,* 12, 347–360.

Hansen, L.P. [1982]: Large Sample Properties of Generalized Method of Moments Estimators; *Econometrica,* 50, 1029–1054.

Hansen, L.P., Heaton, J. and A. Yaron [1996]: Finite Sample Properties of Some Alternative GMM Estimators; *Journal of Business and Economic Statistics,* 14, 262–280.

Hansen L.P. and K.J. Singleton [1982]: Generalized Instrumental Variables Estimation of Nonlinear Rational Expectations Models; *Econometrica,* 50, 1269–1286.

Imbens, G.W. [1997]: One–Step Estimators for Over–Identified Generalized Method of Moments Models; *Review of Economic Studies,* 64, 359–383.

Newey, W.K. [1991]: Uniform Convergence in Probability and Stochastic Equicontinuity; *Econometrica,* 59, 1161–1167.

Newey, W.K. and K.D. West [1994]: Automatic Lag Selection in Covariance Matrix Estimation; *Review of Economic Studies,* 61, 631–653.

Potscher, B.M and I.R. Prucha [1989]: A Uniform Law of Large Numbers for Dependent and Heterogeneous Data Processes; *Econometrica,* 57, 675–683.

Potscher, B.M. and I.R. Prucha [1991a]: Basic Structure of the Asymptotic Theory in Dynamic Nonlinear Econometric Models, Part I: Consistency and Approximation Concepts; *Econometric Reviews,* 10, 125–216.

Potscher, B.M. and I.R. Prucha [1991b]: Basic Structure of the Asymptotic Theory in Dynamic Nonlinear Econometric Models, Part II: Asymptotic Normality; *Econometric Reviews,* 10, 253–325.

Potscher, B.M. and I.R. Prucha [1994]: Generic Uniform Convergence and Equicontinuity Concepts for Random Functions; *Journal of Econometrics,* 60, 23–63.

Sevestre, P. and A. Trognon [1995]: *Dynamic Models;* in Matyas and Sevetre (eds.) "The Econometrics of Panel Data", Kluwer Academic Publishers, Dordrecht.

Smith, R.J. [1997]: Alternative Semi–Parametric Likelihood Approaches To Generalised Method of Moments Estimation; *The Economic Journal,* 107, 503–519.

White, H. [1984]: *Asymptotic Theory for Econometricians;* Academic Press, Orlando.

Chapter 2

GMM ESTIMATION TECHNIQUES

Masao Ogaki

In this chapter, GMM estimation techniques are discussed in the context of empirical applications. The first section presents GMM applications for stationary variables. The second section discusses applications in the presence of nonstationary variables. In the third section, general issues for GMM estimation techniques are discussed.[1]

2.1 GMM Estimation

This section defines a GMM estimator in a framework which is applicable to the applications covered in this chapter. This framework is simpler than the general framework presented in Chapter 1.

2.1.1 GMM Estimator

As in Chapter 1, GMM is based on moment conditions,

$$E(f(x_t, \theta_0)) = 0, \tag{2-1}$$

for a $q \times 1$ vector function $f(x_t, \theta_0)$, where θ_0 is a p–dimensional vector of the parameters to be estimated. We refer to $u_t = f(x_t, \theta_0)$ as the GMM disturbance. In this chapter, it is assumed that $\{x_t :$

---

[1] See *Ogaki* [1993a] for an nontechnical introduction to GMM. *Ogaki* [1993b] describes the use of the Hansen/Heaton/Ogaki GAUSS GMM package.

$t = 1, 2 \ldots\}$ is a stationary and ergodic vector stochastic process unless otherwise noted. Let A_T be a sequence of positive semidefinite matrices which converge to a non–stochastic positive definite matrix A, $f_T(x_t, \theta) = T^{-1}\Sigma_{t=1}^T f(x_t, \theta)$, and $Q_T(\theta) = f_T(\theta)' A_T f_T(x_t, \theta)$. The matrices A_T and A are refereed to as distance (or weighting) matrices. The basic idea of GMM estimation is to mimic the moment conditions (2–1) by minimizing a quadratic form of the sample means $Q_T(\theta)$, so that the GMM estimator is

$$\widehat{\theta}_T = \mathrm{argmin}_\theta Q_T(\theta).$$

As shown in Chapter 1, the GMM estimator is weakly consistent, and is asymptotically normally distributed. It should be noted that strong distributional assumptions such as $f(x_t, \theta_0)$ is normally distributed are not necessary.

When the number of the moment conditions (q) is equal to the number of parameters to be estimated (p), the system is just identified. In the case of a just identified system, the GMM estimator does not depend on the choice of distance matrix. When $q > p$, there exist overidentifying restrictions and different GMM estimators are obtained for different distance matrices. In this case, one may choose the distance matrix that results in an asymptotically efficient GMM estimator. As shown in Chapter 1, an asymptotically efficient estimator is obtained by choosing $A = V^{-1}$, where

$$V = \lim_{j \to \infty} \sum_{-j}^{j} E(u_t u'_{t-j}) \qquad (2\text{--}2)$$

is called the long–run covariance matrix of the GMM disturbance u_t. With this choice of the distance matrix, $\sqrt{T}(\theta_T - \theta_0)$ has an asymptotic normal distribution with mean zero and the covariance matrix $\{F' A^{-1} F\}^{-1}$.

Let V_T be a consistent estimator of V. Then $A_T = V_T^{-1}$ is used to obtain θ_T. The resulting estimator is called the optimal or efficient GMM estimator (see, also, Chapter 3). It should be noted, however, that it is optimal given $f(x_t, \theta)$. In the context of instrumental variable estimation, this means that instrumental variables are given. The selection of instrumental variables will be discussed in Section 4. Let F_T be a consistent estimator of F. Then the standard errors of the optimal GMM estimator θ_T are calculated as square roots of the diagonal elements of $T^{-1}\{F_T' V_T^{-1} F_T\}^{-1}$. The appropriate method for estimating V depends on the model. This problem will be discussed for each application in this chapter. It is usually easier to estimate F by $F_T = (1/T) \sum_{t=1}^{T} (\partial f(x_t, \theta_T)/\partial \theta')$ than to estimate Ψ. In linear models or in some simple nonlinear models, analytical derivatives are readily available. In nonlinear models, numerical derivatives are often used.

Depending on how the distance matrix is estimated, there exist alternative GMM estimators. The two stage GMM estimator uses an identity matrix as the distance matrix in the first stage, then the first stage estimator is used to estimate V, which will be used for the second stage GMM estimator. The iterative GMM estimator repeats this procedure until θ_T converges or until the number of iterations attains some large value. In some nonlinear models, the iterations may be costly in terms of time. In such cases, it is recommended that the third, fourth, or fifth stage GMM to be used because the gains from further iterations may be small. Monte Carlo experiments of *Kocherlakota* [1990] suggest that the iterative GMM estimator performs better than the two stage estimator in small samples.

For some applications, small sample properties of these conventional GMM estimators are reasonable as *Tauchen* [1986] shows. In other cases, small sample biases of GMM estimators are large as shown by *Kocherlakota* [1990]. More recently, many authors have shown that the conventional GMM estimators have serious small sample problems in certain applications (see, *e.g.*, *Altonji and Segal* [1996], *Burnside and Eichenbaum* [1996], *Christiano and den Haan* [1996], and *Ni* [1997]).

Partly in response to these studies, alternatives to the conventional GMM estimators have been proposed. *Hansen, Heaton, and Yaron* [1996] propose the continuous-updating estimator. The idea is to minimize $f_T(\theta)' V_T(\theta)^{-1} f_T(x_t, \theta)$ by choice of θ by allowing V_T to vary with θ. Their Monte Carlo experiments suggest that the continuous-updating estimator typically has less median bias than the two stage and iterative estimator, but its distribution has fatter tails. *Imbens* [1997], *Kitamura and Stutzer* [1997], and *Imbens, Johnson, and Spady* [1998] use information theoretic approaches to propose alternatives to the conventional GMM estimators. These new estimators seem to perform better than the conventional GMM in many cases. As is the case with any new estimators, however, much work remains in order to understand exactly when and which of these new alternative estimators should be used.

2.1.2 Important Assumptions

This section discusses two assumptions under which large sample properties of GMM estimators are derived. These two assumptions are important in the sense that applied researchers have encountered cases where these assumptions are obviously violated unless special care is taken.

In *Hansen* [1982], X_t is assumed to be (strictly) stationary. A time series $\{X_t : \infty < t < \infty\}$ is stationary if the joint distribution of $\{X_t, \ldots, X_{t+\tau}\}$ is identical to those of $X_{t+s}, \ldots, X_{t+s+\tau}\}$ for any τ and s. Among other things, this implies that when they exist, the unconditional moments $E(X_t)$ and $E(X_t X'_{t+\tau})$ cannot depend on t for any τ. Thus this assumption rules out deterministic trends, autoregressive unit roots, and unconditional heteroskedasticity. On the other hand, conditional moments $E(X_{t+\tau} \mid I_t)$ and $E(X_{t+\tau} X'_{t+\tau+s} \mid I_t)$ can depend on I_t. Thus the stationarity assumption does *not* rule out the possibility that X_t has conditional heteroskedasticity. It should be noted that it is not enough for $u_t = f(X_t, \beta_0)$ to be stationary. It is required that X_t is stationary, so that $f(X_t, \beta)$ is stationary for all admissible β, not just for $\beta = \beta_0$ (see Section 8.1.4 for an example in which $f(X_t, \beta_0)$ is stationary but $f(X_t, \beta)$ is not for other values of β).

Gallant [1987] and *Gallant and White* [1988] show that the GMM strict stationarity assumption can be relaxed to allow for unconditional heteroskedasticity. This does *not* mean that X_t can exhibit nonstationarity by having deterministic trends, autoregressive unit roots, or an integrated GARCH representation. Some of their regularity conditions are violated by these popular forms of nonstationarity. Recent papers by *Andrews and McDermott* [1995] and *Dwyer* [1995] show that the stationarity assumption can be further relaxed for some forms of nonstationarity. However, the long–run covariance matrix estimation procedure often needs to be modified to apply their asymptotic theory. For this reason, the strict stationarity assumption is emphasized in the context of time series applications rather than the fact that this assumption can be relaxed.

Another important assumption is Assumption 1.1 in Chapter 1 for identification. This assumption is obviously violated if $f(x_t, \theta) \equiv 0$ for some θ which did not have any economic meaning.

2.2 Nonlinear Instrumental Variable Estimation

GMM is often used in the context of nonlinear instrumental variable (NLIV) estimation. This section describes NLIV estimation as a special case of GMM estimation, and explains how the long–run covariance matrix of the GMM disturbance, V, depends on the information structure of the model.

Let $h(y_t, \theta)$ be a k–dimensional vector of functions and $e_t = h(y_t, \theta_0)$. Suppose that there exist conditional moment restrictions, $E[e_t \mid I_t] = 0$. Here it is assumed that $I_t \subset I_{t+1}$ for any t. Let z_t be a $q \times k$ matrix of random variables that are in the information set I_t.[2] Then by the law of iterative expectations, we obtain unconditional moment conditions:

$$E[z_t h(w_t, \theta_0)] = 0.$$

Thus we let $x_t = (w_t', z_t')'$ and $f(x_t, \theta) = z_t h(w_t, \theta)$ in this case. *Hansen* [1982] points out that the NLIV estimators discussed by *Amemiya* [1974], *Jorgenson and Laffont* [1974], and *Gallant* [1977] can be interpreted as optimal GMM estimators when e_t is serially uncorrelated and conditionally homoskedastic.

The form of the long–run covariance matrix of the GMM disturbance depends on the information structure of the economic model as in the following three cases. An example of each of these cases will be given in the next section.

The simplest case is when e_t is in I_{t+1}. Then u_t is serially uncorrelated because $E(u_t u_{t+j}') = E(E(u_t u_{t+j}' \mid I_{t+1})) = E(u_t E(u_{t+j}' \mid I_{t+1})) = 0$ for $j \geq 1$. Therefore, $V = E(u_t u_t')$, which can be estimated by $(1/(T-p)) \sum_{t=1}^{T} f(x_t, \theta_T) f(x_t, \theta_T)'$.

The second case is when e_t is in the information set I_{t+s+1}, where $s > 0$. Then $E(u_t u_{t+\tau}') = E(E(u_t u_{t+\tau}' \mid I_{t+s+1})) = E(u_t E(u_{t+\tau}' \mid I_{t+s+1})) = 0$ for $\tau \geq s+1$. Thus the order of serial correlation of u_t is s, and u_t is a moving average of order s. In this case, $V = \sum_{j=-s}^{s} E(u_t u_{t-j}')$, whose natural estimator is a truncated kernel estimator (see, *e.g.*, *Ogaki* [1993a]). If the

---

[2] In some applications, z_t is a function of θ. This does not cause any problem as long as the resulting $f(x_t, \theta)$ can be written as a function of b and a stationary random vector x_t.

truncated kernel estimator results in a non–positive semidefinite matrix, another method must be used.

The third case is when e_t is not in the information set I_{t+s+1} for any $s > 0$. Unless some other restrictions are imposed, the serial correlation structure of u_t is not known. The long–run covariance matrix of the GMM disturbance is given by (2–2) in this case, and an estimator of V should allow an unknown order of serial correlation.

2.3 GMM Applications with Stationary Variables

This section illustrates GMM estimation techniques for models with stationary variables by discussing examples of empirical applications. Problems that researchers have encountered in applying GMM and procedures they have used to address these problems are discussed.

2.3.1 Euler Equation Approach

Hansen and Singleton [1982] show how to apply GMM to a Consumption-Based Capital Asset Pricing Model C-CAPM. Consider an economy in which a representative agent maximizes

$$\sum_{t=1}^{\infty} \beta^t E(U(C_t) \mid I_0) \qquad (2\text{--}3)$$

subject to a budget constraint. *Hansen and Singleton* [1982] use the isoelastic intraperiod utility function

$$U(C_t) = \frac{1}{1-\alpha}(C_t^{1-\alpha} - 1), \qquad (2\text{--}4)$$

where C_t is real consumption at date t and $\alpha > 0$ is the reciprocal of the intertemporal elasticity of substitution (α is also the relative risk aversion coefficient for consumption in this model). The standard Euler equation for the optimization problem is

$$\frac{E[\beta C_{t+1}^{-\alpha} R_{t+1} \mid I_t]}{C_t^{-\alpha}} = 1, \qquad (2\text{--}5)$$

where R_{t+1} is the gross real return of any asset. The observed C_t they use is obviously nonstationary, although the specific form of nonstationarity is not clear (difference stationary or trend stationary, for example). Hansen and Singleton use C_{t+1}/C_t in their econometric formulation, which is assumed to be stationary. Then let $\theta = (\beta, \alpha)$, $w_t = (C_{t+1}/C_t, R_{t+1})'$ and $h(w_t, \theta) = \beta(C_{t+1}/C_t)^{-\alpha}R_{t+1} - 1$ in the notations for the NLIV model in Section 2.1 above. Any stationary variables in I_t can be used for instrumental variables z_t, and *Hansen and Singleton* [1982] use the lagged values of w_t.

In this case, u_t is in I_{t+1} because C_{t+1} and R_{t+1} are observed in period $t + 1$, and hence u_t is serially uncorrelated. *Hansen and Singleton* [1984] find that the Chi–square test for the overidentifying restrictions rejects their model especially when nominal risk free bond returns and stock returns are used simultaneously. Their finding is consistent with *Mehra and Prescott's* [1985] equity premium puzzle. When the model is rejected, the Chi-square test statistic does not provide much guidance as to what causes the rejection.

2.3.2 Habit Formation

Many researchers have considered effects of time–nonseparability in preferences on asset pricing. Replace (2–4) by

$$U(C_t, C_{t-1}, C_{t-2}, \ldots) = \frac{1}{1-\alpha}(S_t^{1-\alpha} - 1), \qquad (2\text{–}6)$$

where S_t is service flow from consumption purchases. Purchases of consumption and service flows are related by

$$S_t = a_0 C_t + a_1 C_{t-1} + a_2 C_{t-2} + \ldots . \qquad (2\text{–}7)$$

Depending on the values of the a a_τ's, this model leads to a model with habit formation and/or durability. *Constantinides* [1990] argues that habit formation could help solve the equity premium puzzle. He shows how the intertemporal elasticity of substitution and the relative risk aversion coefficient depend on the a a_τ and α parameters in a habit formation model.)

In this section, I will discuss applications by *Ferson and Constantinides* [1991], *Cooley and Ogaki* [1996], and *Ogaki and Park* [1998] to illustrate econometric formulations. In their models, it is assumed that a $a_\tau = 0$ for $\tau \geq 2$ and a_0 is normalized to be one, so that $\theta = (\beta, \alpha, a_1)$. The asset pricing equation takes the form

$$\frac{E[\beta\{S_{t+1}^{-\alpha} + \beta a_1 S_{t+2}^{-\alpha}\} R_{t+1} \mid I_t]}{E[S_t^{-\alpha} + \beta a_1 S_{t+1}^{-\alpha} \mid I_t]} = 1. \tag{2-8}$$

Then let $e_t^0 = \beta(S_{t+1}^{-\alpha} + \beta a_1 S_{t+2}^{-\alpha}) R_{t+1} - (S_t^{-\alpha} + \beta a_1 S_{t+1}^{-\alpha})$. Though Euler equation (2-8) implies that $E(e_t^0 \mid I_t) = 0$, this cannot be used as the disturbance for GMM because both of the two regularity assumptions discussed in Section 2.5 of the present paper are violated. These violations are caused by the nonstationarity of C_t and by the three sets of trivial solutions, $\alpha = 0$ and $1 + \beta a_1 = 0$; $\beta = 0$ and $\alpha = \infty$; and $\beta = 0$ and $a_1 = \infty$ with α positive. *Ferson and Constantinides* [1991] solve both of these problems by defining $e_t = e_t^0 / S_t^{-\alpha}$. Since $S_t^{-\alpha}$ is in I_t, $E(e_t \mid I_t) = 0$. The disturbance is a function of $S_{t+\tau}/S_t$ $(\tau = 1, 2)$ and R_{t+1}. When C_{t+1}/C_t and R_t are assumed to be stationary, $S_{t+\tau}/S_t$ and the disturbance can be written as a function of stationary variables.

One problem that researchers have encountered in these applications is that $C_{t+1} + a_1 C_t$ may be negative when a_1 is close to minus one. In a nonlinear search for b_T or in calculating numerical derivatives, a GMM computer program will stall if it tries a value of a_1 that makes $C_{t+1} + a_1 C_t$ negative for any t. *Atkeson and Ogaki* [1991] have encountered similar problems in estimating fixed subsistence levels from panel data. One way to avoid this problem is to program the function $f(x_t, \theta)$, so that the program returns very large numbers as the values of $f(x_t, \theta)$, when non–admissible parameter values are used. However, it is necessary to ignore these large values of $f(x_t, \theta)$, when calculating numerical derivatives. This can be done by suitably modifying programs that calculate numerical derivatives.[3]

Let z_t be a vector of instrumental variables, which are in I_t. Because e_t and the GMM disturbance $u_t = z_t e_t$ are in I_{t+2} in this model, e_t has a moving average of order 1 structure. Hence, $V = \sum_{j=-1}^{1} E(u_t u_{t-j}')$ in this case.

---

[3] *Ogaki* [1998] explains these modifications for Hansen/Heaton/Ogaki GMM package.

2.3.3 Linear Rational Expectations Models

Hansen and Sargent [1980] develops a method to apply GMM to linear rational expectations models with stationary variables, which impose the restrictions implied by linear rational expectations models. Section 2.4 discusses how to modify Hansen and Sargent's method in the presence of nonstationary variables.

Many linear rational expectations models have an implication that an economic variable depends on a geometrically declining weighted sum of expected future values of another variable

$$Y_t = aE(\sum_{i=1}^{\infty} b^i X_{t+i} \mid I_t) + c'Z_t, \tag{2–9}$$

where a and b are constants, c is a vector of constants, Y_t and X_t are random variables, and Z_t is a random vector. This implication imposes nonlinear restrictions on the VAR representation of Y_t, X_t, and Z_t as shown by *Hansen and Sargent* [1980].

Consider *West's* [1987] model as an example of linear rational expectations model. Let p_t be the real stock price (after the dividend is paid) in period t and d_t be the real dividend paid to the owner of the stock at the beginning of period t. Then the arbitrage condition is

$$p_t = E[b(p_{t+1} + d_{t+1}) \mid I_t], \tag{2–10}$$

where b is the constant real discount rate, I_t is the information set available to economic agents in period t. Solving (2–9) forward and imposing the no bubble condition, we obtain the present value formula:

$$p_t = E(\sum_{i=1}^{\infty} b^i d_{t+1} \mid I_t). \tag{2–11}$$

We now derive restrictions for p_t and d_t implied by (2–11). Many linear rational expectations models imply that a variable is the expectation of a discounted infinite sum conditional on an information set. Hence similar restrictions can be derived for these rational expectations models.

Assume that d_t is covariance stationary with mean zero (imagine that data are demeaned), so that it has a Wold moving average representation

$$d_t = \alpha(L)\nu_t,$$

where $\alpha(L) = 1 + \alpha_1 L + \alpha_2 L^2 \ldots$ and where

$$\nu_t = d_t - \text{Proj}(d_t \mid H_{t-1}).$$

Here, $\text{Proj}(\cdot \mid Ht)$ is the linear projection operator onto the information set $H_t = \{d_t, d_{t-1}, d_{t-2}, \ldots\}$. We assume that the econometrician uses the information set H_t, which may be much smaller than the economic agents' information set, I_t. Assuming that $\alpha(L)$ is invertible,

$$\phi(L)d_t = \nu_t,$$

where $\phi(L) = 1 - \phi_1 L - \phi_2 L^2 \ldots$

Using (2–11) and the law of iterated projections, we obtain

$$p_t = \text{Proj}(\sum_{i=1}^{\infty} b^i d_{t+i} \mid H_t) + w_t, \qquad (2\text{–}12)$$

where

$$w_t = E(\sum_{i=1}^{\infty} b^i d_{t+i} \mid I_t) - \text{Proj}(\sum_{i=1}^{\infty} b^i d_{t+i} \mid H_t),$$

and $\text{Proj}(w_t \mid Ht) = 0$. Because $\text{Proj}(\cdot \mid H_t)$ is the linear projection operator onto H_t,

$$E(\sum_{i=1}^{\infty} b^i d_{t+i} \mid H_t) = \delta(L)d_t,$$

here $\delta(L) = \delta_1 + \delta_2 L \ldots$. Following *Hansen and Sargent* [1980, Appendix A], we obtain the restrictions imposed by (2–11) on $\delta(L)$ and $\phi(L)$:

$$\delta(L) = \frac{bL^{-1}(\alpha(L) - \alpha(b))}{1 - bL^{-1}}\phi(L) = \frac{bL^{-1}(1 - \phi^{-1}(b)\phi(L))}{1 - bL^{-1}}. \quad (2\text{–}13)$$

We now parameterize $\phi(L)$ as a q–th order polynomial:

$$d_{t+1} = \phi_1 d_t + \ldots + \phi_q d_{t-q+1} + v_{t+1}.$$

Then (2–13) can be used to show that $\delta(L)$ is a finite order polynomial and to give a explicit formula for the coefficients for $\delta(L)$ (see *West* [1987] for the formula, which is based on *Hansen and Sargent* [1980] and on *West* [1988] for for deterministic terms when $d(t)$ has a nonzero mean.) Thus

$$p_t = \delta_1 d_t + \ldots + \delta_q d_{t-q+1} + w_t,$$

where δ_i's are functions of b and ϕ_i's:

$$\delta_0 = \{1 - \phi(b)\}^{-1}$$
$$\delta_j = \delta\gamma(b)\{1 - \delta\phi(b)\}^{-1} + (\phi_{j+1} + b\phi_{j+2} + \ldots + b^p) \qquad (2\text{--}14)$$
$$\text{for} \quad j = 1, \ldots p.$$

These are the nonlinear restrictions which Equation (2–11) implies.

Let z_{1t} be a vector of random variables in H_t. For example, $z_{1t} = (d_t, \ldots, d_{t-q+1})$. The unknown parameters b and ϕ_i's can be estimated by applying the GMM to moment conditions $E(z_{1t}\nu_{t+1}) = 0$ and $E(z_{1t}w_{t+1}) = 0$.

Let z_{2t} be a random variab le in I_t, say d_t, and

$$p_t = b(p_{t+1} + d_{t+1}) + u_{t+1}.$$

Then (2–9) implies another set of moment conditions $E(z_{2t}u_{t+1}) = 0$, which can be used to estimate b.

Hansen and Sargent's method is to use three sets of the moment conditions, $E(z_{1t}\nu_{t+1}) = 0$, $E(z_{1t}w_{t+1}) = 0$, and $E(z_{2t}u_{t+1}) = 0$, simultaneously to form a GMM estimator for the unknown parameters b and ϕ_i's with the restrictions (2–14) imposed.

Because u_t is in I_{t+1} and ν_t is in H_{t+1}, u_t and ν_t are serially uncorrelated. It should be noted, however, w_t is not necessarily in H_{t+1}. Hence w_t has an unknown order of serial correlation. The estimation of the long–run covariance matrix of the GMM disturbance must allow for an unknown order of serial correlation.

2.4 GMM in the Presence of Nonstationary Variables

This section illustrates applications of GMM to structural economic models in the presence of nonstationary variables. First, *Cooley and Ogaki's* [1996] cointegration–Euler equation approach is described. Then applications of GMM to structural error correction models (ECMs) are explained. When some of the random variables in the system are unit root nonstationary and are cointegrated, then Error Correction Models (ECM) are widely used. As *Engle and Granger* [1987] show, an ECM representation exists when the variables are cointegrated and vice versa. The standard ECMs are reduced form models just as VAR models are as pointed out by *Urbain* [1992] and *Boswijk* [1994], [1995].

2.4.1 The Cointegration–Euler Equation Approach

This section explains *Cooley and Ogaki's* [1996] cointegration–Euler Equation approach, which combines *Ogaki and Park's* [1998] cointegration approach to estimating preference parameters with *Hansen and Singleton's* [1982] Euler equation approach based on GMM. In the first step of this approach, a cointegrating regression is applied to an intratemporal first order condition for the household's maximization problem to estimate some preference parameters. In the second step, GMM is applied to an Euler equation after plugging in point estimates from the cointegrating regression in the first step. Because of the first step estimators are super consistent, asymptotic properties of the GMM estimators in the second step are not affected by the first step estimation.

Cooley and Ogaki's method is applicable when the system consists of cointegrated nonstationary variables and stationary variables with nonlinear moment conditions. *Kitamura and Phillips* [1997] provide a general asymptotic theory for linear GMM with both stationary and nonstationary variables. The results in *Park and Phillips* [1997] should make it possible to develop a general asymptotic theory for nonlinear GMM with nonstationary variables.

This section explains Cooley and Ogaki's application of the approach on consumption–leisure choice model for time nonseparable preferences which are additively separable for consumption and leisure. *Ogaki, Ostry, and Reinhart* [1996] and *Ogaki and Reinhart* [1998] apply the approach to estimate the intertemporal elasticity of substitution.

Consider a simple intraperiod utility function that is assumed to be time- and state–separable and separable in nondurable consumption, durable consumption, and leisure

$$u(t) = \frac{C(t)^{1-\alpha} - 1}{1 - \alpha} + \nu(\iota(t)),$$

where $\nu(\cdot)$ is a continuously differentiable concave function, $C(t)$ is nondurable consumption, and $\iota(t)$ is leisure. Time nonseparable preferences can be treated relatively easily with the cointegration approach as in *Cooley and Ogaki* [1996].

The usual first order condition for a household that equates the real wage rate with the marginal rate of substitution between leisure and consumption is

$$W(t) = \frac{\nu'(\iota(t))}{C(t)^{-\alpha}} \, ,$$

where $W(t)$ is the real wage rate. We assume that the stochastic process of leisure is (strictly) stationary in the equilibrium as in Eichenbaum, Hansen, and Singleton and that the random variables used to form the conditional expectations for stationary variables are stationary. Then an implication of the first order condition is that $\ln(W(t)) - \alpha \ln(C(t)) = \ln(\nu'(\iota(t))$ is stationary. When we assume that the log of consumption is difference stationary, this implies that the log of the real wage rate and the log of consumption are cointegrated with a cointegrating vector $(1, -\alpha)$. The cointegration–Euler equation approach exploits this cointegration restriction to identify the curvature parameter α from cointegrating regressions.

In the first step, a cointegration regression is used to estimate α from the stationarity restriction. Because the log real wage rate and the log consumption are cointegrated, either variable can be used as a regressand. In finite samples, the empirical results will be different depending on the choice of the regressand. However, the results should be approximately the same as long as cointegration holds and the sample size is large enough.

In the second step, the GMM procedure is applied to the asset pricing equation with the estimate of α from the cointegrating regression is plugged into the asset pricing equation. This two step procedure does not alter the asymptotic distribution of GMM estimators and test statistics because the cointegrating regression estimator is super consistent and converges at a rate faster than $T^{\frac{1}{2}}$.

2.4.2 Structural Error Correction Models

In this section, we discuss the relationship between structural models and Error Correction Models (ECMs). Following *Ogaki and Yang* [1997], we adopt a slightly more general definition of structural ECMs than *Urbain* [1992] and *Boswijk* [1994], [1995]. Let $Y(t)$ be an n-dimensional vector of first difference stationary random variables. We assume that there exist ρ linearly independent cointegrating vectors, so that $A'Y(t)$ is stationary, where A' is a $(\rho \times n)$ matrix of real numbers whose rows are linearly independent cointegrating vectors. Consider a standard ECM

$$\Delta Y(t+1) = k + GA'Y(t) + F_1\Delta Y(t) + F_2\Delta Y(t-1) + \\ \dots + F_pY(t-p+1) + v(t+1), \tag{2–15}$$

where k is a $(n \times 1)$ vector, G is a $n \times \rho$ matrix of real numbers, $v(t)$ is a stationary n-dimensional vector of random variables with $\mathrm{Proj}(v(t+1) \mid H_{t-\tau}) = 0$. In many applications $\tau = 0$, but we will give examples of applications in which $\tau > 0$.[4] There exist many ways to estimate (2–15). For example, Engle and Granger's two step method or Johansen's Maximum Likelihood methods can be used.

In many applications of standard ECMs, elements in G are given structural interpretations as parameters of the speed of adjustment toward the long–run equilibrium represented by $A'Y(t)$. It is of interest to study conditions under which the elements in G can be given such a structural interpretation. In the model of the previous section, the domestic price level gradually adjusts to its PPP level with a speed of adjustment b. We will investigate conditions under which b can be estimated as an element in G (2–15).

The standard ECM, (2–15), is a reduced form model. A class of structural models can be written in the following form of a structural ECM:

$$C_0\Delta Y(t+1) = d + BA'Y(t) + C_1\Delta Y(t) + C_2\Delta Y(t-1) + \\ \dots + C_p\Delta Y(t-p+1) + u(t+1), \tag{2–16}$$

---

[4]   We will treat more general cases in which the expectation of $v(t+1)$ conditional on the economic agents' information is not zero, but the linear projection of $v(t+1)$ onto an econometrician's information set (which is smaller than the economic agents' information set) is zero.

where C_i is a $(n \times n)$ matrix, d is a $(n \times 1)$ vector, and B is a $(n \times \rho)$ matrix of real numbers. Here C_0 is a nonsingular matrix of real numbers with ones along its principal diagonal, $u(t)$ is a stationary n-dimensional vector of random variables with $\widehat{E}[u(t+1) \mid H_{t-\tau}] = 0$. Even though cointegrating vectors are not unique, we assume that there is a normalization that uniquely determines A, so that parameters in B have structural meanings.

In order to see the relationship between the standard ECM and the structural ECM, we premultiply both sides of (15.2) by C_0^{-1} to obtain the standard ECM (2–15), where $k = C_0^{-1}d$, $G = C_0^{-1}B$, $F_i = C_0^{-1}C_i$, and $v(t) = C_0^{-1}u(t)$. Thus the standard ECM estimated by Engle and Granger's two step method or *Johansen's* [1988] Maximum Likelihood methods is a reduced form model. Hence it cannot be used to recover structural parameters in B, nor can the impulse–response functions based on $v(t)$ be interpreted in a structural way unless some restrictions are imposed on C_0.

As in a VAR, various restrictions are possible for C_0. One example is to assume that C_0 is lower triangular. If C_0 is lower triangular, then the first row of G is equal to the first row of B, and structural parameters in the first row of B are estimated by the standard methods to estimate an ECM.

2.4.3 An Exchange Rate Model with Sticky Prices

This section presents a simple exchange rate model in which the domestic price adjusts slowly toward the long–run equilibrium level implied by Purchasing Power Parity (PPP), which is used by *Ogaki and Yang* [1997] to motivate a particular form of a structural ECM in the next section. This model' two main components are a slow adjustment equation and a rational expectations equation for the exchange rate. The single equation method proposed in Section 2.4 is only based on the slow adjustment equation. The system method utilizes both the slow adjustment and rational expectations equations.

Let $p(t)$ be the log domestic price level, $p^*(t)$ be the log foreign price level, and $e(t)$ be the log nominal exchange rate (the price of one unit of the foreign currency in terms of the domestic currency). We assume that these variables are first difference stationary. We also assume that PPP holds in the long run, so that the real exchange rate, $p(t) - p^*(t) - e(t)$ is stationary, or $y(t) = (p(t), e(t), p^*(t))'$ is cointegrated with a cointegrating vector $(1, -1, -1)$. Let $\mu = E(p(t) - p^*(t) - e(t))$, then μ can be nonzero when different units are used to measure prices in the two countries.

Using a one–good version of *Mussa's* [1982] model, the domestic price level is assumed to adjust slowly to the PPP level

$$\Delta p(t+1) = b[\mu + p^*(t) + e(t) - p(t)] + E_t[p^*(t+1) + e(t+1)] - [p^*(t) + e(t)],$$

$$(2\text{–}17)$$

where $\Delta x(t+1) = x(t+1) - x(t)$ or any variable $x(t)$, $E(\cdot \mid I_t)$ is the expectation operator conditional on I_t, the information available to the economic agents at time t, and a positive constant $b < 1$ is an adjustment coefficient. The idea behind Equation (2–17) is that the domestic price level slowly adjusts toward its long–run PPP level of $p^*(t) + e(t)$. The adjustment speed is slow when b is close to zero, and the adjustment speed is fast when b is close to one.

From Equation (2–17), we obtain

$$\Delta p(t+1) = d + b[p^*(t) + e(t) - p(t)] + \Delta p^*(t+1) + \Delta e(t+1) + \varepsilon(t+1),$$

$$(2\text{–}18)$$

where $d = b\mu$, $\varepsilon(t+1) = E_t[p^*(t+1) + e(t+1)] - [p^*(t+1) + e(t+1)]$. Hence $\varepsilon(t+1)$ is a one–period ahead forecasting error, and $E[\varepsilon(t+1) \mid I_t] = 0$.

Equation (2–18) motivates the form of the structural ECM used in the next section. The single equation method described in the next section is based only on (2–18), and can be applied to any model with a slow adjustment equation like (2–17).

We close the model by adding the money demand equation and the Uncovered Interest Parity condition. Let

$$m(t) = \theta_m + p(t) - hi(t) \qquad (2\text{–}19)$$

$$i(t) = i^*(t) + E[e(t+1) \mid I_t] - e(t), \qquad (2\text{–}20)$$

where $m(t)$ is the log nominal money supply minus the log real national income, $i(t)$ is the nominal interest rate in the domestic country, and $i^*(t)$ is the nominal interest rate in the foreign country.

Here, we are assuming that the income elasticity of money is one. From (2–19) and (2–20), we obtain

$$E[e(t+1) \mid I_t] - e(t) = (1/h)[-\theta_m + p(t) - w(t)$$
$$- h\{E[p^*(t+1) - p^*(t)] \mid I_t\}], \tag{2-21}$$

where

$$w(t) = m(t) + hr^*(t),$$

and $r^*(t)$ is the foreign real interest rate:

$$r^*(t) = i^*(t) - E[p^*(t+1) \mid I_t] + p^*(t).$$

Following Mussa, solving (2–20) and (2–21) as a system of stochastic difference equation for $E[p(t+j) \mid I_t]$ and $E[e(t+j) \mid I_t]$ for fixed t results in

$$p(t) = E[F(t) \mid I_{t-1}] - \sum_{j=0}^{\infty}(1-b)^j\{E[F(t-j) \mid I_{t-j}] \tag{2-22}$$
$$- E[F(t-j) \mid I_{t-j-1}]\}$$

$$e(t) = \frac{bh-1}{bh}E[F(t) \mid I_t] - p^*(t) + \frac{1}{bh}p(t), \tag{2-23}$$

where

$$F(t) = (1 - (\delta))\sum_{j=0}^{\infty}\delta^j w(t+j),$$

and $\delta = h/(1+h)$.

We assume that $w(t)$ is first difference stationary. Since δ is a positive constant that is smaller than one, this implies that $F(t)$ is also first difference stationary. From (2–22) and (2–23),

$$e(t) + p^*(t) - p(t) =$$
$$\sum_{j=0}^{\infty}(1-b)^j\{E[F(t-j) \mid I_{t-j}] - E[F(t-j) \mid I_{t-j-1}]\}.$$

Since the right hand side of this equation is stationary,[5] $e(t) + p^*(t) - p(t)$ is stationary. Hence $(p(t), e(t), p^*(t))$ is cointegrated with a cointegrating vector $(1, -1, -1)$.

In order to obtain a structural ECM representation from the exchange rate model, we use *Hansen and Sargent's* [1980], [1982]

---

[5] This assumes that $E_t[F(t)] - E_{t-1}[F(t)]$ is stationary, which is true for a large class of first difference stationary variable $F(t)$ and information sets.

formula for linear rational expectations models. From (2–23), we obtain

$$\Delta e(t+1) = \frac{bh-1}{bh}(1-\delta)E[\sum_{j=0}^{\infty}\delta^j\Delta\omega(t+j+1)\mid I_t]$$

$$+\frac{1}{bh}\Delta p(t+1) - \Delta p^*(t+1) + \varepsilon_e(t+1), \qquad (2\text{–}24)$$

where $\varepsilon_e(t+1) = \frac{bh-1}{bh}\{E[F_{t+1}\mid I_{t+1}] - E[F_{t+1}\mid I_t]\}$, so that the law of iterated expectations implies $E[\varepsilon_e(t+1)\mid I_t] = 0$. Because this equation involves a discounted sum of expected future values of $\Delta\omega(t)$, the system method in the next section is applicable.

Hansen and Sargent [1982] proposes to project the conditional expectation of the discounted sum, $E[\sum\delta^j\Delta\omega(t+j+1)\mid I_t]$, onto an information set H_t, which is a subset of I_t, the economic agents' information set. Let $\widehat{E}(\cdot\mid H_t)$ be the linear projection operator conditional on an information set H_t which is a subset of I_t.

We take the econometrician's information set at t, H_t, to be the one generated by the linear functions of the current and past values of $\Delta p^*(t)$. Then replacing the best forecast of the economic agents, $E[\sum\delta^j\Delta\omega(t+j+1)\mid I_t]$, by the econometrician's linear forecast based on $H(t)$ in Equation (2–24), we obtain

$$\Delta e(t+1) = \frac{bh-1}{bh}(1-\delta)\widehat{E}[\sum_{j=0}^{\infty}\delta^j\Delta\omega(t+j+1)\mid H(t)]$$

$$+\frac{1}{bh}\Delta p(t+1) - \Delta p^*(t+1) + u_2(t+1),$$

where

$$u_2(t+1) = \varepsilon_e(t+1) + \frac{bh-1}{bh}(1-\delta)\,E_t\{[\sum\delta^j\Delta\omega(t+j+1)]$$

$$-\ \text{Proj}\ [\sum\delta^j\Delta\omega(t+j+1\mid H(t)]\}.$$

Because H_t is a subset of I_t, we obtain $\widehat{E}[u_2(t+1)\mid H_t] = 0$.

Since $\widehat{E}[\cdot\mid H_t]$ is the linear projection operator onto H_t, there exist possibly infinite order lag polynomials $\beta(L)$, $\gamma(L)$, and $\xi(L)$ such that

$$\widehat{E}[\Delta p^*(t+1)\mid H(t)] = \beta(L)\Delta p^*(t)$$

$$\widehat{E}[\Delta\omega(t+1)\mid H(t)] = \gamma(L)\Delta p^*(t)$$

$$\widehat{E}[\sum_{j=0}^{\infty}\delta^j\Delta\omega(t+j+1)\mid H(t)] = \xi(L)\Delta p^*(t).$$

Then following *Hansen and Sargent* [1980, Appendix A], we obtain the restrictions imposed by (2–24) on $\xi(L)$:

$$\xi(L) = \frac{\gamma(L) - \delta L^{-1}\gamma(\delta)\{1 - \delta\beta(\delta)\}^{-1}\{1 - L\beta(L)\}}{1 - \delta L^{-1}}. \qquad (2\text{--}25)$$

Assume that linear projections of $\Delta p^*(t+1)$ and $\Delta\omega(t+1)$ onto $H(t)$ have only finite number of $\Delta p^*(t)$ terms:

$$\widehat{E}[\Delta p^*(t+1) \mid H(t)] =$$
$$\beta_1 \Delta p^*(t) + \beta_2 \Delta p^*(t-1) + \ldots + \beta_p \Delta p^*(t-p+1) \qquad (2\text{--}26)$$

$$\widehat{E}[\Delta\omega(t+1) \mid H(t)] =$$
$$\gamma_1 \Delta p^*(t) + \gamma_2 \Delta p^*(t-1) + \ldots + \gamma_{p-1} \Delta p^*(t-p+2) \qquad (2\text{--}27)$$

Here we assume $\beta(L)$ is of order p and $\gamma(L)$ is of order $p-1$ in order to simplify the exposition, but we do not lose generality because any of β_i and γ_i can be zero. Then as in *Hansen and Sargent* [1982], (2–25) implies that $\xi(L)(\xi_0 + \xi_1 L + \ldots + \xi_p L^p$, where

$$\xi_0 = \gamma(\delta)\{1 - \delta\beta(\delta)\}^{-1}$$
$$\xi_j = \delta\gamma(\delta)\{1 - \delta\beta(\delta)\}^{-1}(\beta_{j+1} + \delta\beta_{j+2} + \ldots + \delta^{p-j}\beta_p) \qquad (2\text{--}28)$$
$$+ (\gamma_j + \delta\gamma_j + \ldots + \delta^{p-j}\gamma_p) \qquad \text{for} \quad j = 1, \ldots, p.$$

Thus

$$\text{Proj}[\sum_{j=0}^{\infty} \delta^j \Delta\omega(t+j+1) \mid H(t)] = \qquad (2\text{--}29)$$
$$\xi_1 \Delta p^*(t) + \xi_2 \Delta p^*(t-1) + \ldots + \xi_p \Delta p^*(t-p+1).$$

Using (2–18), (2–24), (2–26) and (2–27) we obtain a system of four equations

$$\Delta p(t+1) = d + \Delta p^*(t+1) + \Delta e(t+1) - b[p(t) - p^*(t) - e(t)]$$
$$+ u_1(t+1)$$

$$\Delta e(t+1) = \frac{1}{bh}\Delta p(t+1) - \Delta p^*(t+1) +$$
$$\alpha\xi_1\Delta p^*(t) + \alpha\xi_2\Delta p^*(t-1) + \ldots + \alpha\xi_p\Delta p^*(t-p+1) + u_2(t+1)$$
$$\Delta p^*(t+1) = \beta_1\Delta p^*(t) + \beta_2\Delta p^*(t-1) + \ldots$$
$$+ \beta_p\Delta p^*(t-p+1) + u_3(t+1)$$
$$\Delta\omega(t+1) = \gamma_1\Delta p^*(t) + \gamma_2\Delta p^*(t-1) + \ldots$$
$$+ \gamma_{p-1}\Delta p^*(t-p+2) + u_4(t+1)$$

$$(2\text{--}30)$$

where $\alpha = \frac{bh-1}{bh}(1 - \delta)$ and $u_1(t + 1) = \varepsilon(t + 1)$. Given the data for $[\Delta p(t+1), \Delta e(t+1). \Delta p^*(t+1), \Delta \omega(t+1)]'$, GMM can be applied to these four equations as will be discussed in the next section.

The exchange rate model can be written in the SECM form (2–16) as in the system of equations (2–30): we have $y(t) = [\Delta p(t + 1), \Delta e(t + 1), \Delta p^*(t + 1), \Delta \omega(t + 1)]'$, $B = [-b, 0, 0, 0]'$, $A = [1, -1, -1, 0]'$,

$$C_0 = \begin{bmatrix} 1 & -1 & -1 & 0 \\ -(1/bh) & 1 & 1 & 0 \\ 0 & 0 & 1 & 0 \\ 0 & 0 & 0 & 1 \end{bmatrix}, \tag{2–31}$$

and

$$C_j = \begin{bmatrix} 0 & 0 & 0 & 0 \\ 0 & 0 & \alpha\xi_i & 0 \\ 0 & 0 & \beta_j & 0 \\ 0 & 0 & \gamma_j & 0 \end{bmatrix}$$

for $j = 1, \ldots, p$. Note that for any nonzero constant Ψ, $\Psi(1, -1, -1)'$ is also a cointegrating vector. However, the first row of B is b only when Ψ is normalized to one.

It is instructive to observe the relationship between the structural ECM and the reduced form ECM in the exchange rate model. Because

$$C_0^{-1} = \begin{bmatrix} bh/(bh - 1) & bh/(bh - 1) & 0 & 0 \\ 1/(bh - 1) & bh/(bh - 1) & -1 & 0 \\ 0 & 0 & 1 & 0 \\ 0 & 0 & 0 & 1 \end{bmatrix},$$

$G = C_0^{-1}B = [-b^2h/(bh - 1), -b/(bh - 1), 0, 0]'$. Comparing G and B, observe the way in which the contemporaneous interactions between the domestic price and the exchange rate affect the speed of adjustment coefficients. The speed of adjustment coefficient for the domestic price is b in the structural model, while it is $b^2h/(bh-1)$ in the reduced form model. The error correction term does not appear in the second equation for the exchange rate in the structural ECM, while it appears with the speed of adjustment coefficient of $b/(bh - 1)$ in the reduced form model.

In the exchange rate model, b is a structural parameter of interest. For the purpose of estimating b in the model, the restriction that C_0 is lower triangular is not attractive. However, as is clear from Equation (2–30), the structural ECM from the one–good version of the exchange rate model does not satisfy the restriction that C_0 is lower triangular for any ordering of the variables. Even though some structural models may be written in lower triangular form, this example suggests that many structural models cannot be written in that particular form.

2.4.4 The Instrumental Variables Methods

Because standard methods of estimating Equation (2–15) may not recover the structural parameters of interest in B, *Ogaki and Yang* [1997] propose two instrumental variables methods, which does not require restrictions on C_0.

First, we consider a single equation method, which applies an IV method to a slow adjustment equation. Imagine that we are interested in estimating the first row of Equation (2–16). In some applications, the cointegrating vectors are known, and thus the values of A are known. In other applications, the values of A are unknown. In the case of the unknown cointegrating vectors, a two step method that is similar to *Engle and Granger's* [1987] and *Cooley and Ogaki's* [1996] methods can be used. In this two–step method, the cointegrating vectors are estimated in the first step.

In the first step, we estimate A, using a method to consistently estimate cointegrating vectors. There exist many methods to estimate cointegrating vectors. Johansen's Maximum Likelihood (ML) Estimators for Equation (2–15) can be used for this purpose. If ρ is equal to one, estimators based on regressions that are as efficient as Johansen's ML estimators such as *Phillips and Hansen's* [1990] Fully Modified Estimation Method, *Park's* [1992] Canonical Cointegrating Regression, and *Stock and Watson's* [1993] estimators can be used. Ordinary Least Squares estimators are also consistent when ρ is equal to one, but not as efficient as these estimators. We assume that A_T is the first step estimator, where T is the sample size, and that A_T converges to A at a faster rate than $T^{\frac{1}{2}}$.[6]

---

[6] Usually, A_T converges at the rate of T, but there are cases where A_T converges at the rate of $T^{\frac{3}{2}}$ (see *West* [1988]).

In the single equation method, an IV method is applied to

$$\Delta y_1(t+1) = d_1 - c_{02}^1 \Delta y_2(t+1) - \ldots - c_{0n}^{-1} \Delta y_n(t+1) + b_1 A' y(t)$$
$$+ c_1^1 \Delta y(t) + c_2^1 \Delta y(t-1) + \ldots + c_p^1 \Delta y(t-p+1) + u_1(t+1),$$

$$(2\text{--}32)$$

where $y_i(t)$ is the i-th element of $y(t)$ d_1 is the first element in d, c_{0i}^1 is the i-th element of the first row of C_0, b_1 is the first row of B, c_i^1 is the first row of C_i, and $u_1(t)$ is the first element of $u(t)$. When $\widehat{E}[u_1(t+1) \mid H_{t-\tau}] = 0$, any stationary variable in the information set available at time $t - \tau$ that is correlated with variables in the right hand side of Equation (2–32) can be used as an instrumental variable.

The system method combines the single equation method with *Hansen and Sargent's* [1982] procedure to impose nonlinear restrictions implied by rational expectations models.

Let $y(t) = (y_1(t), \; y_2(t), \; y_3(t), \; y_4(t))'$ be a 4×1 vector of random variables with an structural ECM representation (2–16) and only one linearly independent cointegrating vector A such that $A'y(t)$ is stationary. In the following, $y(t)$ is partitioned into four subvectors, and each subvector is given a different role. For expositional simplicity, we assume that each subvector is one dimensional so that $y(t)$ is a 4×1 vector, and that $y(t)$ has only one cointegrating vector.

The first element of $y(t)$ represents a slow adjustment as in Equation (2–18), with nonzero b_1 where $\widehat{E}[u_1(t+1) \mid H_{t-\tau}] = 0$. We assume that the second element of $y(t)$ is related to a discounted sum of expected future values of the fourth element in the following form:

$$\Delta y_2(t+1) = d_2 - c_{01}^2 \Delta y_1(t+1) - c_{03}^2 \Delta y_3(t+1) - c_{04}^2 \Delta y_4(t+1)$$

$$+ \alpha E[\sum_{j=0}^{\infty} \delta^j \Delta y_4(t+j+1) \mid I_t] + \varepsilon_e(t+1) \,,$$

$$(2\text{--}33)$$

where δ is a positive constant that is smaller than one, and α is a constant. As pointed out by Hansen and Sargent, many linear rational expectations models imply that one variable is a geometrically declining weighted sum of expected future values of other variables.

Hansen and Sargent's [1982] methodology is to project the conditional expectation of the discounted sum, $E[\sum \delta^j \Delta y_4(t+j+1) \mid$

$I_t]$, onto an information set H_t, which is a subset of I_t, the economic agents' information set. Let $\widehat{E}(\cdot \mid H_t)$ be the linear projection operator conditional on an information set H_t which is a subset of I_t. Replacing the conditional expectation by the linear projection gives

$$\Delta y_2(t+1) = d_2 - c_{01}^2 \Delta y_1(t+1) - c_{03}^2 \Delta y_3(t+1) - c_{04}^2 \Delta y_4(t+1)$$
$$+ \alpha \widehat{E}[\sum_{j=0}^{\infty} \delta^j \Delta y_4(t+j+1) \mid H_t] + u_2(t+1),$$

$$(2\text{--}34)$$

where

$$u_2(t+1) = \varepsilon_e(t+1) + E[\sum_{j=1}^{\infty} \delta^j \Delta y_4(t+j+1) \mid I_t]$$
$$- \widehat{E}[\sum_{j=1}^{\infty} \delta^j \Delta y_4(t+j+1) \mid H_t].$$

Because H_t is a subset of I_t, we obtain $\widehat{E}[u_2(t+1) \mid H_t] = 0$.

The current and past values of the first difference of the third element of $y(t)$ are used to form the econometrician's information set H_t. Since Proj $[\cdot \mid H_t]$ is the linear projection operator onto H_t, there exist possibly infinite order lag polynomials $\beta(L)$, $\gamma(L)$, and $\xi(L)$. such that

$$\widehat{E}[\Delta y_3(t+1) \mid H(t)] = \beta(L)\Delta y_3(t) \qquad (2\text{--}35)$$

$$\widehat{E}[\Delta y_4(t+1) \mid H(t)] = \gamma(L)\Delta y_3(t) \qquad (2\text{--}36)$$

$$\widehat{E}[\sum_{j=0}^{\infty} \delta^j \Delta y_4(t+j+1) \mid H(t)] = \xi(L)\Delta y_3(t). \qquad (2\text{--}37)$$

Then following *Hansen and Sargent* [1980, Appendix A], we obtain the restrictions imposed on $\xi(L)$:

$$\xi(L) = \frac{\gamma(L) - \delta L^{-1}\gamma(\delta)\{1 - \delta\beta(\delta)\}^{-1}\{1 - L\beta(L)\}}{1 - \delta L^{-1}}. \qquad (2\text{--}38)$$

Substituting (2–37) into (2–34) gives the equation

$$\Delta y_2(t+1) = d_2 - c_{01}^2 \Delta y_1(t+1) - c_{03}^2 \Delta y_3(t+1) - c_{04}^2 \Delta y_4(t+1)$$
$$+ \alpha \xi(L)\Delta y_3(t) + u_2(t+1),$$

$$(2\text{--}39)$$

where $\xi(L)$ is given by (2–38). We now make an additional assumption that the lag polynomials $\beta(L)$ and $\gamma(L)$ are finite order polynomials, so that

$$\Delta y_3(t+1) = \beta_1 \Delta y_3(t) + \beta_2 \Delta y_3(t-1) + \ldots + \beta_p \Delta y_3(t-p+1) + u_3(t+1) \tag{2–40}$$

$$\Delta y_4(t+1) = \gamma_1 \Delta y_3(t) + \gamma_2 \Delta y_3(t-1) + \ldots + \gamma_{p-1} y_3(t-p+2) + u_4(t+1) \tag{2–41}$$

where $\text{Proj}\,[u_i(t+1) \mid H_t] = 0$ for $i = 3, 4$. Here we assume $\beta(L)$ is of order p and $\gamma(L)$ is of order $p - 1$ in order to simplify the exposition, but we do not lose generality because any of β_i and γ_i can be zero. Then as in *Hansen and Sargent* [1982], (2–38) implies

$$\xi_0 = \gamma(\delta)\{1 - \delta\beta(\delta)\}^{-1}$$

$$\xi_j = \delta\gamma(\delta)\{1 - \delta\beta(\delta)\}^{-1}(\beta_{j+1} + \delta\beta_{j+2} + \ldots + \delta^{p-j}\beta_p) \tag{2–42}$$

$$+ (\gamma_j + \delta\gamma_j + \ldots + \delta^{p-j}\gamma_p) \quad \text{for} \quad j = 1, \ldots, p.$$

In the SECM form, we have $B = [-b, 0, 0, 0]'$, $A = [1, -1, -1, 0]'$,

$$C_0 = \begin{bmatrix} 1 & c_{02}^1 & c_{03}^1 & c_{04}^1 \\ c_{01}^2 & 1 & c_{03}^2 & c_{04}^2 \\ 0 & 0 & 1 & 0 \\ 0 & 0 & 0 & 1 \end{bmatrix},$$

and

$$C_j = \begin{bmatrix} c_{j1}^1 & c_{j2}^1 & c_{j3}^1 & c_{j4}^1 \\ 0 & 0 & \alpha\xi_j & 0 \\ 0 & 0 & \beta_j & 0 \\ 0 & 0 & \gamma_j & 0 \end{bmatrix},$$

for $j = 1, \ldots, p$, where $\gamma_p = 0$.

We have now obtained a system of four equations that consist of (2–32) (2–39), (2–40), and (2–41). Because $E(u_1(t) \mid I_{t-\tau}) = 0$ and $\widehat{E}(u_i(t) \mid H_t) = 0$, we can obtain a vector of instrumental variables $z_1(t)$ in $I_{t-\tau}$ for $u_1(t)$ and $z_i(t)$ in H_t for $u_i(t)$ ($i = 2, 3, 4$).

Because the speed of adjustment b for $y_1(t)$ affects dynamics of other variables,[7] there will be cross–equation restrictions involving b in many applications in addition to the restrictions in (2–42). Using the moment conditions $E[z_i(t)u_i(t)] = 0$ for $i = 1, \ldots, 4$, we form a GMM estimator, imposing the restrictions (2–42) and the other cross–equation restrictions implied by the model.

---

[7] Note that only $y_1(t)$ adjusts slowly, but b affects dynamics of other variables because of interactions of $y_1(t)$ and those variables.

Given estimates of cointegrating vectors from the first step, this system method provides more efficient estimators than the single equation method as long as the restrictions implied by the model are true. On the other hand, the single equation two step method estimators are more robust because misspecification in other equations does not affect their consistency.

2.5 Some Aspects of GMM Estimation

2.5.1 Numerical Optimization

For nonlinear models, it is usually necessary to apply a numerical optimization method to compute a GMM estimator by numerically minimizing the criterion function, $Q_T(\theta)$. The Newton–Raphson method (see, *e.g., Hamilton* [1994, Chapter 5] is often used with an approximation method to calculate the hessian matrix. A problem with the Newton–Raphson method and other practical numerical optimization methods is that global optimization is not guaranteed. The GMM estimator is defined as a global minimizer of a GMM criterion function, and the proof of its asymptotic properties depend on this assumption. Therefore, the use of a local optimization method can result in an estimator that is not necessarily consistent and asymptotically normal.

If the criterion function and parameter space are convex, then the criterion function has a unique local minimum, which also is the global minimum. In this case, a local optimization algorithm started at any parameter values should be able to reach an approximate global minimum.

For nonconvex problems, however, there can be many local minima. For such problems, an algorithm called multi–start is often used for GMM applications. In this algorithm, one starts a local optimization algorithm from initial values of the parameters to converge to a local minimum, and then one repeats the process a number of times with different initial values. The estimator is taken to be the parameter values that correspond to the small value of the criterion function obtained during the multi–start process.

It should be noted that this multi–start algorithm is used for a given distance matrix. When the two stage or iterative GMM estimators are used, a different distance matrix is used in each stage, and hence a different criterion function is minimized. In most GMM programs, one need to save the distance matrix in a file in order to apply the multi–start algorithm in each stage.

A problem with the multi–start algorithm, however, is that it does not necessarily find the global optimum. Therefore, the estimator it delivers is not necessarily consistent and asymptotically normal. *Andrews* [1997] proposes a simple stopping–rule procedure that overcomes this difficulty.

2.5.2 The Choice of Instrumental Variables

In the NLIV model discussed in Section 2.2, there are infinitely many possible instrumental variables because any variable in I_t can be used as an instrument.

Nelson and Startz [1990] perform Monte Carlo simulations to investigate small sample properties of linear instrumental variables regressions. They show that instrumental variables estimators have poor sample properties of the instrumental variables estimators when the instruments are weakly correlated with explanatory variables. In particular, they find that the Chi–square test tends to reject the null too frequently compared with its asymptotic distribution, and that t–ratios tend to be too large when the instrument is poor. Their results for t–ratios may seem counterintuitive because one might expect that the consequence of having a poor instrument would be a large standard error and a low t–ratio. Their results may be expected to carry over to NLIV estimation. *Pagan and Jung* [1993] provide practical recommendations for checking whether or not instrumental variables are valid in the context of GMM and other instrumental variables estimation.

Hansen [1985] characterizes an efficiency bound (that is, a greatest lower bound) for the asymptotic covariance matrices of the alternative GMM estimators and optimal instruments that attain the bound. Since it can be time consuming to obtain optimal instruments, an econometrician may wish to compute an estimate of the efficiency bound to assess efficiency losses from using ad hoc instruments. *Hansen* [1985] also provides a method for calculating this bound for models with conditionally homoskedastic disturbance terms with an invertible MA representation.[8] *Hansen, Heaton, and Ogaki* [1988] extend this method to models with conditionally heteroskedastic disturbances and models with an MA representation that is not invertible.[9] *Hansen and Singleton* [1996] calculate these bounds and optimal instruments for a continuous time financial economic model. *Chamberlain* [1987] and *Hansen* [1993] show that the GMM efficiency bound coincides with the semi-parametric efficiency bound for finite parameter maximum likelihood estimators.

Tauchen [1986] and *Hansen and Singleton* [1996] find that the GMM estimators with *Hansen's* [1985] optimal instruments often show poor small sample properties when they are applied to the C–CAPM. *West and Wilcox* [1996], however, find that the GMM estimators with optimal instruments are substantially more efficient in small samples for an inventory model with plausible data generation processes.

2.5.3 Normalization

In the habit formation model, the GMM disturbance term is normalized to avoid the trivial solutions of the sample counterpart of the moment conditions as explained in Section 3.2. In some applications, the GMM disturbance is normalized to incorporate a priori information about parameters. An extreme example of a priori information is that some parameter values are not admissible. Another example is that certain parameter values are not very plausible. This section discusses some issues regarding normalizations.

Consider a GMM estimator is based on moment restrictions of the form (2–1). Let $\phi(\theta)$ be a real valued function. Then one can define a new function $f^*(X_t, \theta) = f(X_t, \theta)\phi(\theta)$, and we still have moment restrictions

$$E(f^*(X_t, \theta_0)) = 0.$$

---

[8]   *Hayashi and Sim's* [1983] estimator is applicable to this example.
[9]   *Heaton and Ogaki* [1991] provide an algorithm to calculate efficiency bounds for a continuous time financial economic model based on *Hansen, Heaton, and Ogaki's* [1988] method.

One can apply GMM to these moment restrictions instead of applying to (2–1)

In NLIV estimation in Section 2.2, even random variables can be used to normalize the GMM disturbance function. If y_t is a vector of random variables in I_t and if $\phi(y_t, \theta)$ is a (measurable) real valued function, then one can define a new function $h^*(x_t, \theta) = h(x_t, \theta)\phi(y_t, \theta)$. Because $\phi(y_t, \theta)$ is in I_t, $h^*(x_t, \theta_0)$ still satisfies conditional moment conditions $E[h^*(x_t, \theta) \mid I_t] = 0$. Thus the GMM estimation can be applied to $h^*(x_t, \theta)$.

These ideas are now illustrated for the habit formation model in Section 3.2. In the model, the Euler equation implies $E(e_t \mid I_t) = 0$, where $e_t = \{\delta(S_{t+1}^\alpha + \delta a_1 S_{t+2}^\alpha)R_{t+1} - (S_t^{-\alpha} + \delta a_1 S_{t+1}^{-\alpha})\}/\{S_t^{-\alpha}[1 + \delta a_1]\}$.[10]

One problem that researchers have encountered in these applications is that $C_t + a_1 C_{t-1}$ may be negative when a a_1 is close to minus one. The values of a_1 which makes $C_t + a_1 C_{t-1}$ negative are not admissible. In order to incorporate this a priori information, one can program the procedure which define $h(x_t, \theta)$, so that very large numbers are returned as the values of $h(x_t, \theta)$ when a_1 falls to the nonadmissible region.[11]

When a_1 is positive and is greater than one, we can obtain a well behaved utility function. However, one may argue that it is not plausible for a_1 to be greater than one: why is the previous period's consumption more important than this period's consumption for this period's utility level? One way to incorporate this type of a priori information is to use a Bayesian method. Another way is to penalize such implausible parameter values in defining the GMM disturbance. Let $f(X_t, \theta)$ be the original GMM disturbance function, where $\theta = (\delta, a_1, \alpha)$. Then define

$$\phi(\theta) = \begin{cases} 1 & \text{if } a_1 \le 1 \\ (a_1 - 1)^2 + 1 & \text{if } a_1 \le 1 \end{cases} \qquad (2\text{-}43)$$

and $f^*(X_t, \theta) = f(X_t, \theta)\phi(\theta)$. Now $f^* = (X_t, \theta)$ can be used as the new GMM disturbance. Here the function ϕ is designed so that it is

---

[10] In Hansen–Heaton–Ogaki GMM package, the GMMHF.EXP file (Appendix C), which is a minor modification of a program used by *Cooley and Ogaki* [1996], is included to give an example of programing.

[11] It is necessary to modify the numerical derivative procedure in order to prevent these fictitious large numbers are used to calculate numerical derivatives. Hansen–Heaton–Ogaki package provides an example in GRADQG.PRC, which is used by GMMHF.EXP.

differentiable at $a_1 = 1$ and it does not affect the function f when $a_1 \leq 1$. The latter feature is important because of small sample considerations.

One might argue that the curvature parameter α, which will be close to the Relative Risk Aversion parameter as explained by Ferson and Constantinides under some circumstances, is not likely to be greater than ten (see *Mehra and Prescott* [1985]). This restriction can be incorporated by a normalization similar to (3).

Even though any differentiable function can be used as the normalization function ϕ without disturbing the consistency of the GMM estimator, the small sample properties of GMM estimator will be affected by normalizations. It is thus desirable not to disturb the GMM function for the parameter region where we do not have any a priori information. This idea is incorporated in the function given in (2–43). When different normalizations give very different results, it is recommended that *Hansen, Heaton, and Yaron's* [1996] continuous updating estimator, which is not affected by normalizations.

References

Altonji, J.G. and Segal, L.M. [**1996**]: Small-Sample Bias in GMM Estimation of Covariance Structures; *Journal of Business and Economic Statistics,* 14, 353-366.

Amemiya, T. [**1974**]: The Nonlinear Two-Stage Least–Squares Estimator; *Journal of Econometrics,* 2, 105-110.

Andrews, D.K. [**1997**]: A Stopping Rule for the Computation of Generalized Method of Moments Estimators; *Econometrica,* 65, 913–931.

Andrews, D.K. and McDermott, C.J. [**1995**]: Nonlinear Econometric Models with Deterministically Trending Variables; *Review of Economic Studies,* 62, 343–360.

Atkeson, A. and Ogaki, M. [**1996**]: Wealth-Varying Intertemporal Elasticities of Substitution: Evidence from Panel and Aggregate Data; *Journal of Monetary Economics;* 38, 507-534.

Boswijk, H.P. [**1994**]: Conditional and Structural Error Correction Models; *Journal of Econometrics,* 69, 159–171.

Boswijk, H.P. [**1995**]: Efficient Inference on Cointegration Parameters in Structural Error Correction Models; *Journal of Econometrics,* 69, 133–158.

Burnside, C. and Eichenbaum, M. [1996]: Small Sample Properties of GMM-Based Wald Tests; *Journal of Business and Economic Statistics,* 14, 294-308.

Chamberlain, G. [1987]: Asymptotic Efficiency in Estimation with Conditional Moment Restrictions; *Journal of Econometrics,* 34, 305-334.

Christiano, L.J. and den Haan, W.J. [1996]: Small Sample Properties for Business-Cycle Analysis; *Journal of Business and Economic Statistics,* 14, 294-308.

Constantinides, G.M. [1990]: Habit Formation: A Resolution of the Equity Premium Puzzle; *Journal of Political Economy,* 98, 519-543.

Cooley, T.F. and Ogaki, M. [1996]: A Time Series Analysis of Real Wages, Consumption, and Asset Returns: A Cointegration–Euler Equation Approach; *Journal of Applied Econometrics,* 11, 119–134.

Dwyer, M. [1995]: *Essays in Nonlinear, Nonstationary, Time Series Econometrics;* Ph.D. dissertation, University of Rochester.

Engle, R.F. and Granger, C.W.J. [1987]: Co–Integration and Error Correction: Representation, Estimation, and Testing; *Econometrica,* 55, 251–276.

Ferson, W.E. and Constantinides, G.M. [1991]: *Habit Formation and Durability in Aggregate Consumption: Empirical Tests;* Journal of Financial Economics, 29, 199-240.

Gallant, A.R. [1977]: Three-stage Least-squares Estimation for a System of Simultaneous, Nonlinear Implicit Equations; *Journal of Econometrics,* 5, 71-88.

Gallant, A.R. [1987]: *Nonlinear Statistical Models;* John Wiley and Sons, New York.

Gallant, A.R. and White, H. [1988]: *A Unified Theory of Estimation and Inference for Nonlinear Dynamic Models;* New York: Basil Blackwell.

Hamilton, J.D. [1994]: *Time-Series Analysis;* Princeton University Press, Princeton, New Jersey.

Hansen, L.P. [1982]: Large Sample Properties of Generalized Method of Moments Estimators; *Econometrica,* 50, 1029–1054.

Hansen, L.P. [1985]: A Method of Calculating Bounds on the Asymptotic Variance-Covariance Matrices of Generalized Method of Moments Estimators; *Journal of Econometrics,* 30, 203-228.

Hansen, L.P. [1993]: *Semiparametric Efficiency Bound for Linear Time-Series Models;* In Models, Methods, and Applications of Econometrics: Essays in Honor of A.R. Bergstrom, ed. by P.C.B. Phillips. Oxford: Blackwell.

Hansen, L.P., and T.J. Sargent [1980]: Formulating and Estimating Dynamic Linear Rational Expectations Models; *Journal of Economic Dynamics and Control,* 2, 7–46.

Hansen, L.P., and T.J. Sargent [1982]: Instrumental Variables Procedures for Estimating Linear Rational Expectations Models; *Journal of Monetary Economics,* 9, 263–296.

Hansen, L.P., and Singleton, K.J. [**1982**]: Generalized Instrumental Variable Estimation of Nonlinear Rational Expectations Models; *Econometrica,* 50, 1269–1286.

Hansen, L.P., Heaton, J.C. and Ogaki, M. [**1988**]: Efficiency Bounds Implied by Multiperiod Conditional Moment Restrictions; *Journal of the American Statistical Association,* 83, 863-871.

Hansen, L.P., and Singleton, K.J. [**1996**]: Efficient Estimation of Linear Asset–Pricing Models with Moving Average Errors; *Journal of Business and Economics Statistics,* 14, 53–68.

Hansen, L.P., Heaton, J.C. and Yaron, A. [**1996**]: Finite–Sample Properties of Some Alternative GMM Estimators; *Journal of Business and Economic Statistics,* 14, 262–280.

Hayashi, F. and Sims, C.A. [**1983**]: Nearly Efficient Estimation of Time Series Models with Predetermined, but Not Exogenous Instruments; *Econometrica,* 51, 783-798.

Heaton, J.C. and Ogaki, M. [**1991**]: Efficiency Bound Calculations for a Time Series Model with Conditional Heteroskedasticity; *Economics Letters,* 35, 167-171.

Imbens, G.W. [**1997**]: One-Step Estimators for Over-Identified Generalized Method of Moments Models; *Review of Economic Studies* 64, 359-383.

Imbens, G.W., Spady, R.H., and Johnson, P. [**1998**]: Information Theoretic Approaches to Inference in Moment Condition Models; *Econometrica,* (forthcoming).

Johansen, S. [**1988**]: Statistical Analysis of Cointegrating Vectors; *Journal of Economic Dynamics and Control,* 12, 231–254.

Jorgenson, D.W., and Laffont, J. [**1974**]: Efficient Estimation of Nonlinear Simultaneous Equations With Additive Disturbances; *Annals of Economic and Social Measurement,* 3, 615-640.

Kitamura, Y. and Stutzer, M. [**1997**]: An Information-Theoretic Alternative to Generalized Method of Moments; *Econometrica,* 65, 861-874.

Kitamura, Y. and Phillips, P.C.B. [**1997**]: Fully Modified IV, GIVE and GMM Estimation with Possibly Non-stationary Regressors and Instruments; *Journal of Econometrics,* 80, 85-123.

Kocherlakota, N.R. [**1990**]: On Tests of Representative Consumer Asset Pricing Models; *Journal of Monetary Economics,* 26, 285–304.

Mehra R. and Prescott, E.C. [**1985**]: The Equity Premium: a Puzzle; *Journal of Monetary Economics,* 15, 145-161.

Mussa, M. [**1982**]: A Model of Exchange Rate Dynamics; *Journal of Political Economy,* 90, 74–104.

Nelson, C. and Startz, R. [**1990**]: The Distribution of the Instrumental Variables Estimator and Its t-ratio When the Instrument Is a Poor One; *Journal of Business,* 63, S125-S140.

Ni, S. [**1997**]: Scaling Factors in Estimation of Time-Nonseparable Utility Functions; *Review of Economics and Statistics,* 79, 234-240.

Ogaki, M. [1993a]: Generalized Method of Moments: Econometric Applications, In Handbook of Statistics, *Vol. 11: Econometrics* , ed. by G.S. Maddala, C.R. Rao, and H.D. Vinod. Amsterdam: North–Holland (a)

Ogaki, M. [1993b]: *GMM: A User Guide;* Working Paper no. 348. Rochester, N.Y.: University of Rochester, Center Econ. Res. (b)

Ogaki, M. [1998]: *Sructural Econometrics for Macroeconomists;* manuscript, Ohio State University.

Ogaki, M. and Min–Seok Y. [1997]: *Structural Error Correction Models: An Application to an Exchange Rate Model;* manuscrip.

Ogaki, M., and Park, J.Y. [1998]: A Cointegration Approach to Estimating Preference Parameters, *Journal of Econometrics,* 82, 107–134.

Ogaki, M. and Reinhart, C.M. [1998]: Measuring Intertemporal Substitution: The Role of Durables; *Journal of Political Economy,* (forthcoming).

Ogaki, M., Ostry, J.D., and Reinhart, C.M. [1996]: Saving Behavior in Low– and Middle–Income Developing Countries; *IMF Staff Papers,* 43, 38–71.

Pagan, A.R. and Y. Jung [1993]: *Understanding Some Failures of Instrumental Variable Estimators;* manuscript, Australian National University.

Park, J.Y. [1992]: Canonical Cointegrating Regressions; *Econometrica,* 60, 119–43.

Park, J.Y. and Phillips, P.C.B. [1997]: *Asymptotics for Nonlinear Transformations of Integrated Time Series;* manuscript, Seoul National University and Yale University.

Phillips, P.C.B., and Hansen, B.E. [1990]: Statistical Inference in Instrumental Variables Regression with I(1) Processes; *Review of Economic Studies,* 57, 99-125.

Stock, J.H. and M.W. Watson. [1988]: A Simple Estimator of Cointegrating Vectors in Higher Order Integrated Systems; *Econometrica,* 61, 783–820.

Tauchen, G. [1986]: Statistical Properties of Generalized–Method–of–Moments Estimators of Structural Parameters Obtained from Financial Market Data; *Journal of Business and Economic Statistics,* 4, 397–425.

Urbain, J.-P. [1992]: On Weak Exogeneity in Error Correction Models; *Oxford Bulletin of Economics and Statistics,* 54, 187–207.

West, K.D. [1987]: A Specification Test for Speculative Bubbles; *Quarterly Journal of Economics,* CII, 553-580.

West, K.D. [1988]: Asymptotic Normality, When Regressors Have a Unit Root, *Econometrica,* 56, 1397-1417.

West, K.D. and Wilcox, D.W. [1996]: A Comparison of Alternative Instrumental Variable Estimators of a Dynamic Linear Model; *Journal of Business and Economic Statistics,* 14, 281-293.

Chapter 3

COVARIANCE MATRIX ESTIMATION

Matthew J. Cushing and Mary G. McGarvey

This chapter focuses on estimating the covariance matrix resulting from GMM estimation. A consistent estimate of the covariance matrix is necessary for both statistical inference and efficient parameter estimation. In the spirit of GMM estimation we focus attention on robust estimation techniques. Because the resulting covariance matrix estimates are consistent for general classes of possibly heterogeneously distributed, autocorrelated error processes, these heteroskedastic, autocorrelation consistent (HAC) covariance estimators have a wide range of applications beyond GMM.

In this chapter we consider both asymptotic results and small sample properties of covariances matrix estimators arising from GMM estimation.

3.1 Preliminary Results

Our ultimate goal is to perform statistical inference on some $p \times 1$ parameter vector θ_0. Recall from Chapter 1, Definition 1.2, that the GMM estimator of θ_0 is defined as

$$\widehat{\theta}_T = \operatorname{argmin}_\theta Q_T(\theta),$$

where the criterion function is $Q_T(\theta) = f_T(\theta)' A_T f_T(\theta)$. Sufficient conditions for the estimator's consistency and asymptotic normality are discussed in Chapter 1. Here we are interested in developing estimators of the asymptotic covariance matrix,

$$\left(\bar{F}_T' \bar{A}_T \bar{F}_T \right)^{-1} \bar{F}_T' \bar{A}_T \bar{V}_T \bar{A}_T \bar{F}_T \left(\bar{F}_T' \bar{A}_T \bar{F}_T \right)^{-1}.$$

Notice that the asymptotic covariance matrix (as defined by *White* [1984]) of the GMM estimator depends on the sample size. This is because we do not require that $f(x_t, \theta_0)$ be a stationary process or that the weighting matrices A_T and F_T converge to a constant matrix independent of T. Stationarity is not necessary for the consistency or asymptotic normality of the GMM estimator $\widehat{\theta}_T$ nor is it necessary for the consistency of many of the covariance matrix estimators discussed in this chapter.

Constructing $\bar{F}_T$ typically presents few problems. The sample analogue to $F_T(\theta)$, $F_T(\widehat{\theta})$ will ordinarily suffice. Similarly, estimates of A_T satisfying Assumption 1.3 are readily constructed. In the case where the parameters are exactly identified $(p = q)$, the weighting matrix A_T is inconsequential both in the construction of the GMM estimator and its asymptotic variance. In the case where there are more moment conditions than parameters $(q > p)$, the asymptotic variance of $\widehat{\theta}_T$ can be minimized by choosing A_T to be a consistent estimator of $\bar{V}_T^{-1}$ (see Lemma 1.1).

The critical component of the expression for the asymptotic variance is $\bar{V}_T$. We require a consistent estimator of $\bar{V}_T$, *i.e.*, we require a $\widehat{V}_T$, such that $\widehat{V}_T - \bar{V}_T \xrightarrow{p} 0$. The rest of this chapter is devoted to this task.

3.2 The Estimand

We are interested in consistent and possibly efficient estimators of

$$\bar{V}_T = T \, var \, (f_T(\theta_0)) = T^{-1} \sum_{t=1}^{T} \sum_{s=1}^{T} E(f(x_t, \theta_0)f(x_s, \theta_0)'),$$

the average of the autocovariances of the process $f(x_t, \theta_0)$. It is useful to rewrite $\bar{V}_T$ in terms of a general autocovariance function of $f(x_t, \theta_0)$.

$$\bar{V}_T = \sum_{j=-(T-1)}^{T-1} \Omega_T(j), \quad \text{where}$$

$$\Omega_T(j) = \begin{cases} T^{-1} \sum\limits_{t=j+1}^{T} E(f_t f_{t-j}'), & j \geq 0 \\ T^{-1} \sum\limits_{t=-(j-1)}^{T} E(f_{j+t} f_t'), & j < 0 \end{cases}$$

and $f_t = f(x_t, \theta_0)$. The stochastic structure of the f_t process determines the optimal choice of estimator. If the structure of the f_t process is known, the estimation problem simplifies dramatically. Before describing the general case, we present some familiar examples.

EXAMPLE 3.1

Consider a scalar linear regression model, $y_t = x_t'\beta_0 + u_t$, where $E(f_t) = E(x_t u_t) = 0$. Suppose that x_t and u_t are covariance stationary processes. $E(u_t \mid u_{t-1}, x_t, u_{t-2}, x_{t-1}, \ldots) = 0$ and

$$E(u_t u_t' \mid u_{t-1}, x_t, u_{t-2}, x_{t-1}, \ldots) = \sigma_u^2$$

so that u_t is serially uncorrelated and conditionally homoskedastic. Then $\bar{V}_T$ reduces to

$$\bar{V}_T = \Omega_T(0) = T^{-1}\sum_{t=1}^{T} E(x_t u_t u_t x_t') = \sigma_u^2 E(x_t x_t').$$

This is the standard OLS covariance matrix. The Method of Moments (MM) estimator of $\bar{V}_T$, constructed from sample analogues to population moments, is

$$\widehat{V}_T = \widehat{\sigma}_u^2 T^{-1}\sum_{t=1}^{T} x_t x_t',$$

where $\widehat{\sigma}_u^2 = T^{-1}\sum_{t=1}^{T} \widehat{u}_t^2$ and $\widehat{u}_t = y_t - x_t'\widehat{\beta}_T$. This is, of course, the standard maximum likelihood estimate of the covariance matrix.

∎

EXAMPLE 3.2

Consider again the standard linear model. Assume now that the true error is serially uncorrelated,

$$E(u_t \mid u_{t-1}, x_t, u_{t-2}, x_{t-1}, \ldots) = 0$$

but that

$$E(u_t u_t' \mid u_{t-1}, x_t, u_{t-2}, x_{t-1}, \ldots) = \sigma_t^2$$

so that the regression error u_t may be conditionally heteroskedastic. Then $\bar{V}_T$ reduces to

$$\bar{V}_T = \Omega_T(0) = T^{-1} \sum_{t=1}^{T} E(x_t u_t u_t x_t').$$

This matrix can be consistently estimated by sample analogues,

$$\widehat{V}_T = T^{-1} \sum_{t=1}^{T} x_t \widehat{u}_t \widehat{u}_t x_t',$$

which is that heteroskedasticity consistent estimator proposed by *White* [1980] and provided as a standard option in most econometric software packages.

■

EXAMPLE 3.3

Finally, if $f_t = x_t u_t$ is a linearly regular, covariance stationary process and $\Omega_T(j) = 0$ for $j > m$, then $\bar{V}_T$ is

$$\bar{V}_T = \sum_{j=-m}^{m} \Omega_T(j).$$

Again, we may use sample analogues to estimate the Ω's,

$$\widehat{\Omega}_T(j) = \begin{cases} T^{-1} \sum_{t=j+1}^{T} x_t \widehat{u}_t x_{t-j}' \widehat{u}_{t-j}, & j \geq 0 \\ T^{-1} \sum_{t=-(j-1)}^{T} x_{t+j} \widehat{u}_{t+j} x_t' \widehat{u}_t, & j < 0 \end{cases}.$$

The sample analogue to $\bar{V}_T$,

$$\widehat{V}_T = \sum_{j=-m}^{m} \widehat{\Omega}_T,$$

provides a consistent (but not necessarily desirable) estimator.

■

In the spirit of GMM estimation, most practitioners wish to avoid the strong distributional assumptions employed in the above examples. It is tempting to follow the MM approach and construct an estimator for $\bar{V}_T$ by simply replacing all of the population auto-covariances with their sample analogues. The resulting estimator, $\widehat{V}_{MM}$, would be,

$$\widehat{V}_{MM} = \sum_{j=-(T-1)}^{T-1} \widehat{\Omega}_T(j), \text{where}$$

$$\widehat{\Omega}_T(j) = \begin{cases} T^{-1} \sum\limits_{t=j+1}^{T} \widehat{f}_t \widehat{f}'_{t-j}, & j \geq 0 \\ T^{-1} \sum\limits_{t=-(j-1)}^{T} \widehat{f}_{t+j} \widehat{f}'_t, & j < 0 \end{cases}$$

and $\widehat{f}_t = f_t(x_t, \widehat{\theta}_T)$.

Unfortunately, this MM estimator, $\widehat{V}_{MM}$, is wholly unsatisfactory. The problem, asymptotically, is that the number of estimated autocovariances grows at the same rate as the sample size. As we show in the next section, $\widehat{V}_{MM}$ is, under suitable regularity conditions, asymptotically unbiased, but, because the variance does not approach zero, it is not consistent in the mean squared error sense. The finite sample properties of $\widehat{V}_{MM}$ are even more problematic. To see this, rewrite $\widehat{V}_{MM}$ as,

$$\widehat{V}_{MM} = T^{-1} \sum_{r=1}^{T} \sum_{s=1}^{T} \widehat{f}_r \widehat{f}'_s.$$

In the exactly identified case, the sample moment conditions are exactly satisfied. But this implies that $\widehat{V}_{MM}$ is identically zero for all T! The next section presents a class of estimators that circumvents some of these problems.

3.3 Kernel Estimators of $\bar{V}_T$

Suppose f_t is a stationary process with spectral density given by,

$$S_f(\lambda) = (2\pi)^{-1} \sum_{j=-\infty}^{\infty} \Omega(j) e^{-i\lambda j},$$

where $i = \sqrt{-1}$. Then, as *Hansen* [1982] pointed out, the limit of $\bar{V}_T$ as T approaches infinity is 2π times the spectral density matrix of f_t evaluated at the zero frequency. This relationship between the estimand, $\bar{V}_T$, and the spectral density matrix of the f_t process suggests that standard methods for estimating spectral densities would be appropriate. This observation has motivated much of the research in this area and most of the results on estimating $\bar{V}_T$ have direct counterparts in the spectral density literature. Some differences, however, should be noted. The spectral density literature typically assumes stationarity and focuses on estimating over frequency *bands*. The econometrics literature often allows for departures from stationarity and focuses on estimating the spectral density at a particular point (the zero frequency). In addition, the spectral density literature typically takes the f_t process, perhaps after a mean correction, as primitive, whereas the econometric literature pays more attention to the finite sample problems inherent in using the observable $\hat{f}_t$ process in place of the unobservable f_t process.

3.3.1 Weighted Autocovariance Estimators

The most widely used estimators of $\bar{V}_T$ can be written as a weighted average of sample autocovariance matrices,

$$\widehat{V}_T = \sum_{s=-(T-1)}^{T-1} w_s \widehat{\Omega}_T(s),$$

where Parzen termed the sequence of weights, $\{w_s\}$, the *"lag window"*. These estimators correspond to a class of kernel spectral density estimators evaluated at frequency zero. This class of estimators is closely related to the method of moments estimator, $\widehat{V}_{MM}$. The MM estimator uses the lag window, $w_s = 1, \forall s$. The strategy to obtain a consistent estimator here is to choose a lag window in a way that the sequence of weights approaches unity rapidly enough to obtain asymptotic unbiasedness but slowly enough to ensure that the variance converges to zero.

We concentrate on a particular class of lag windows, *scale parameter windows*, where the lag window can be expressed as $w_s = k(s/m_T)$. Here m_T simply "stretches" or "contracts" the distribution and hence acts as a scale parameter. The function $k(z)$ is referred to as the *"lag window generator"*.

ASSUMPTION 3.1

The function $k(\cdot) : R \to [-1, 1]$, satisfies $k(0) = 1$, $k(z) = k(-z) \forall z \in R$, $\int_{-\infty}^{\infty} |k(z)| \, dz < \infty$, and $k(\cdot)$ is continuous at 0 and at all but a finite number of other points.

∎

When the value of the kernel is zero for $z > 1$, m_T is called the *"lag truncation parameter"* because autocovariances corresponding to lags greater than m_T are given zero weight. The scalar m_T is often referred to as the *"bandwidth parameter"* or simply the *"scale parameter"*.

Table 3.1 lists the properties of a number of popular kernel estimators. The first and simplest is the *"truncated window"* studied in this context by *White* [1984]. This kernel weights the autocovariances equally but truncates the distribution at lag m_T. *Newey and West* [1987], observing that the truncated window does not guarantee a positive semi–definite estimate, suggested the *Bartlett* window as an alternative. The Bartlett–Newey–West window has linearly declining weights and provides a positive semi–definite estimate by construction. The *Parzen* window, suggested by *Gallant* [1987], is a standard choice in the spectral density literature and is also positive semi–definite.

The forms of the last three windows, the *Daniell, Quadratic Spectrum* and *Tent*, are based on frequency domain considerations, to which we now turn.

3.3.2 Weighted Periodogram Estimators

The properties of lag windows are most easily revealed by examining the finite Fourier transform of the lag window,

$$W(\lambda, m_T) = \frac{1}{2\pi} \sum_{s=-(T-1)}^{(T-1)} w_s e^{-is\lambda}.$$

Parzen termed this function the *"spectral window"*. Standard kernel estimators can be expressed as weighted integrals of periodogram ordinates,

$$\widehat{V}_T = \int_{-\pi}^{\pi} W(\lambda, m_T) \widehat{I}_T(\lambda) d\lambda,$$

Table 3.1: Spectral Windows

	$k(z)$	r	k_r	$\int_{-\infty}^{\infty} k^2(z)$	$W(\lambda)$
Truncated	1 for $\|z\|\le 1$, 0 otherwise,	∞	0	2	$\frac{1}{2\pi}\left\{\frac{\sin[(m_T+\frac{1}{2}\lambda]}{\sin(\lambda/2)}\right\}$
Bartlett	$1-\|z\|$ for $\|z\|\le 1$, 0 otherwise,	1	1	$2/3$	$\frac{1}{2\pi m_t}\left(\frac{\sin(m_T\lambda/2)}{\lambda/2}\right)^2$
Parzen	$1-6z^2+6\|z\|^3$ for $0\le\|z\|\le 1/2$, $2(1-\|z\|)^3$ for $1/2\le\|z\|\le 1$, 0 otherwise	2	6	$.151/280$	$\frac{3}{8\pi m_T^3}\left(\frac{\sin(m_T\lambda/4)}{\frac{1}{2}\sin(\lambda/2)}\right)^4$
Quadratic	$\frac{25}{12\pi^2 z^2}\left[\frac{\sin(6\pi z/5)}{6\pi z/5}-\cos(6\pi z/5)\right]$	2	$\pi^2/10$	$6/5$	$\frac{3m_T}{4\pi}\left\{1-\left(\frac{m_T\lambda}{\pi}\right)^2\right\}\cdot\ \|\lambda\|\le\pi/m_T$, $0,\quad \|\lambda\|>\pi/m_T$
Daniell	$(\sin\pi z)/\pi z$	2	$\pi^2/6$	1	$m_T/2\pi,\ \|\lambda\|\le=m_T$, otherwise, $0,$
Tent	$\frac{2(1-\cos(sz))}{z^2}$	2	$1/12$	4	$\frac{m_T}{\pi}(1-\frac{\|\lambda\|}{m_T}),\ \|\lambda\|\le\pi/m_T$, $0,\quad$ otherwise.

where $\widehat{I}_T(\lambda)$ is the periodogram or sample spectral density,

$$\widehat{I}_T(\lambda) = (2\pi T)^{-1} \sum_{s=-(T-1)}^{(T-1)} \widehat{\Omega}_s e^{i\lambda s},$$

and $W(\lambda, m_T)$ is the averaging kernel. Because $W(\lambda, m_T)$ is typically concentrated about zero, we may think of $\widehat{V}_T$ as a 'view' of the periodogram though a narrow 'window.' With these preliminaries, we may discuss the three spectral windows provided in Table 3.1.

The simplest spectral window is the *"rectangular"* window proposed by *Daniell* [1946]. The Daniell estimator is a simple average of the periodogram ordinates over a band of width $2\pi/m_T$, and thus the Daniell window can be thought of as the dual of the truncated window. The 'truncated' estimator weights *autocovariances* equally up to some truncation point, whereas the Daniell estimator weights the *periodogram ordinates* equally up to some truncation point.

The *tent* window which (along with the rectangular) has been advocated by *Doan and Litterman* [1995], assigns linearly declining weights to periodogram ordinates in a band of $(\pm\pi/m_T)$ about zero. The tent window can be thought of as the dual to the Bartlett window. The 'tent' assigns linearly declining weights to periodogram ordinates, whereas the Bartlett assigns linearly declining weights to the autocovariances.

The final spectral window considered here, the Quadratic Spectral window, has a more complex form. This estimator was originally derived by *Priestly* [1981], as the kernel which minimizes the average mean squared error. *Andrews* [1991] shows that this form also minimizes the mean squared error at the zero frequency.

3.3.3 Computational Considerations

At one time, the spectral approach was considered computationally burdensome. After all, the three 'time–domain' kernels in Table 3.1 require only that the first m_T autocovariances be computed whereas the three spectral estimators require all T autocovariances. Widespread use of the fast Fourier transform (FFT) algorithm for computing finite Fourier transforms has largely changed this assessment.

Define the finite (or discrete) Fourier transform of $\widehat{f}_t$ as,

$$\zeta(\lambda_p) = \frac{1}{\sqrt{2\pi T}} \sum_{t=1}^{T} \widehat{f}_t e^{i\lambda_p t}.$$

If N is highly composite (*i.e.*, can be factored into small primes) the fast Fourier transform algorithm permits rapid digital calculation of the above expression. The periodogram matrix can then be computed at the Fourier frequencies $\lambda_p = 2\pi p/T$, $p = 1,\ldots,T/2$, as the conjugate square of the finite Fourier transform,

$$\widehat{I}_T(\lambda_p) = \zeta(\lambda_p)\zeta(\lambda_p)'.$$

A good approximation to the integrals above can then be obtained from

$$\widehat{V}_T \approx \frac{2\pi}{T} \sum_{p=-[T/2]}^{[T/2]} \widehat{I}_T(\lambda_p) W(\lambda_p, m_T).$$

This approximation turns out to be exact for scale parameter families with truncation parameter $m_T \leq (T+1)/2$.

The approximation can be avoided, and exact estimates can be obtained from the spectral approach by summing over $P \geq (2T-1)$ periodogram ordinates. The exact spectral estimator can be obtained from,

$$\widehat{V}_T = \frac{2\pi}{2T-1} \sum_{p=-(T-1)}^{(T-1)} \widehat{I}_T(\lambda_p') W(\lambda_p', m_T),$$

where $\lambda_p' = 2\pi p/(2T-1)$. The periodogram at these frequencies can be obtained by 'padding' $\{\widehat{f}_t\}$ with zeros at either end and proceeding as above.

3.3.4 Spectral Interpretation

Apart from any computational advantages (or disadvantages) the spectral representation of kernel estimators provides a number of immediate insights into the estimation problem. First, because the periodogram matrix is known to be positive semi–definite by construction, a necessary and sufficient condition to guarantee a positive semi–definite estimate of $\bar{V}_T$ is that $W(\lambda, m_T)$ be everywhere non–negative. It is clear that this condition is satisfied for all of the kernels listed in Table 3.1, apart from the truncated estimator. The truncated estimator has negative 'side-lobes' (*i.e.*, gives negative weight to periodogram ordinates removed from the zero frequency) and hence, depending on the shape of the periodogram, need not be positive semi–definite. In particular, the estimate may fail to be positive semi–definite if the periodogram has a relative minimum in the neighborhood of the zero frequency.

The spectral approach clarifies the nature of the estimation problem. For stationary processes, the periodogram matrix at a particular frequency is well known to be an asymptotically unbiased estimator of the spectral density at that frequency. However, because the variance of periodogram ordinates does not approach zero, the periodogram is not a consistent estimator. To achieve consistency, we average periodogram ordinates in some band about the zero frequency. Because the elements of the periodogram matrix evaluated at the Fourier frequencies, $\lambda_p = 2\pi p/N, p = 1, \ldots, N/2$, are asymptotically independent, this averaging process dampens the variance. To achieve consistency, a) the number of independent frequencies must grow large, b) the underlying spectral density must be sufficiently smooth in the neighborhood of zero and c) the width of the frequency band must shrink.

In finite samples, the choice of a bandwidth confronts us with a trade–off between bias reduction and variance reduction. If we choose a wide bandwidth (choose a small value for m_T) our estimator averages a large number of periodogram ordinates and hence has low variance. Because this estimator uses frequencies far removed from zero, however, it may be badly biased if the true spectral density is not constant across frequencies. If we choose a narrow bandwidth (choose a large value for m_T) the bias falls but, because we employ fewer independent periodogram ordinates, the variance of the estimator grows large.

3.3.5 Asymptotic Properties of Scale Parameter Estimators

We now establish the asymptotic behavior of scale parameter windows estimators of $\bar{V}_T$. We establish the order of convergence of these estimators and their asymptotic bias, variance and mean squared error. The results of this section rely heavily on *Andrew's* [1991] treatment of the problem.

As is evident from the discussion above, the behavior of window estimators will depend on the smoothness of the underlying spectral density and on the band width of the averaging kernel. Let r be the largest integer such that

$$k_r = \lim_{z \to 0} \frac{1 - k(z)}{|z|^r}$$

is finite and non–zero. Parzen calls r the *"characteristic exponent"* of the function $k(z)$. If k_r is finite for some r_0 then it is zero for $r < r_0$. The quantity k_r may be thought of as a measure of the smoothness of the lag window and a measure of the bandwidth of the spectral window. Table 3.1 presents values of r and k_r for the six representative kernels.

A useful measure of smoothness of the spectral density function in the neighborhood of zero is $S^{(r)}$, defined as

$$S^{(r)} = (2\pi)^{-1} \sum_{j=-\infty}^{\infty} |j|^r \Omega(j).$$

Parzen terms this measure the *"generalized r^{th} derivative"* of $S_f(\lambda)$. For $r = 2$, this is simply the second (ordinary) derivative of $S_f(\lambda)$ with respect to λ evaluated at $\lambda = 0$.

To reduce the problem to one of scalars we consider a linear combination of the elements of $\widehat{V}_T$ given by $\text{vec}(\widehat{V}_T - \bar{V}_T)' B_T \text{vec}(\widehat{V}_T - \bar{V}_T)$ where B_T is a $q^2 \times q^2$ (possibly) random weighting matrix. Because occasionally we encounter GMM parameter estimators that do not possess second moments, we establish the asymptotic *truncated* mean squared error of our estimators.

DEFINITION 3.1 **Truncated Mean Squared Error**

$$MSE_h[(T/m_T), \widehat{V}_T, B_T]$$

$$= E \min \left\{ \left| \frac{T}{m_T} \text{vec}(\widehat{V}_T - \bar{V}_T)' B_T \text{vec}(\widehat{V}_T - \bar{V}_T) \right|, h \right\}.$$

∎

Following *Andrews* [1991] we employ the following additional assumptions on the $\{f_t\}$ process.

ASSUMPTION 3.2

   (i) $\{f_t\}$ is a mean zero, eight order stationary sequence of rv's with $\sum \|\Omega(j)\| < \infty$ and

$$\sum_{j_1=-\infty}^{\infty} \sum_{j_2=-\infty}^{\infty} \cdots \sum_{j_7=-\infty}^{\infty} \kappa_{a_1 \cdots a_8}(0, j_1, \ldots, j_7) < \infty,$$

       where $\kappa_{a_1 \ldots a_8}$ is the eighth order cumulant of $(f_{a_1 t}, \ldots, f_{a_8 t})$ and f_{it} is the ith element of f_t.

  (ii) vec $\left(\frac{\partial}{\partial \theta'} f_t - E \frac{\partial}{\partial \theta'} f_t\right)'$ is a mean zero, fourth order stationary sequence

$$\sum_{j=-\infty}^{\infty} \sum_{m=-\infty}^{\infty} \sum_{n=-\infty}^{\infty} \kappa_{abcd}(0, j, m, n) < \infty \; \forall \, a, b, c, d.$$

 (iii) $\sqrt{T}(\hat{\theta} - \theta_0) = O_p(1)$.
 (iv) $\sup_{t \geq 1} E \|f_t\|^2 < \infty$.
 (v) $\sup_{t \geq 1} E \sup_{\theta \in \Theta} \|F_T\|^2 < \infty$.
 (vi) $\sup_{t \geq 1} E \sup_{\theta \in \Theta} \|(\partial/\partial \theta') F_T\|^2 < \infty$.

                                              ■

The cumulant conditions, (i) and (ii), are standard in the spectral density literature. Andrews shows that they are also implied by a strong mixing condition and a moment condition. Part (iii) is implied by asymptotic normality and parts (iv), (v) and (vi) are commonly used to obtain asymptotic normality of GMM estimates.

THEOREM 3.1

    Suppose $m_T \to \infty$ and $B_T \overset{p}{\longrightarrow} B$, then we have (i) If $m_T^2/T \to 0$, then $\hat{V}_T - \bar{V}_T \overset{p}{\longrightarrow} 0$. (ii) If $m_T^{2r+1}/T \to \gamma \in (0, \infty)$ for some $r \in [0, \infty)$ for which $k_r, \|S^{(r)}\| < \infty$, then $\sqrt{T/m_T}(\hat{V}_T - \bar{V}_T) = O_p(1)$. (iii) Under the conditions of part (ii),

$$\lim_{h \to \infty} \lim_{T \to \infty} MSE_h(T/m_T), \hat{V}_T, B_T)$$

$$= 4\pi^2 \left(k_r^2 (\text{vec} S^{(r)})' B \text{vec} S^{(r)}/\gamma \right.$$

$$\left. + \int_{-\infty}^{\infty} k^2(z) dz \, tr(B)(I + B_{qq}) S_f(0) \otimes S_f(0) \right)$$

    where B_{qq} is defined as $\sum_{i=1}^{q} \sum_{j=1}^{q} e_i e_j' \otimes e_j e_i'$ and e_i is the q element zero vector with unity as the ith element.

■

Part (i) establishes the consistency of scale parameter covariance estimators for bandwidth parameter sequences that grow at rate $o(T^{\frac{1}{2}})$, part (ii) gives the rate of convergence for these estimators and part (iii) gives the asymptotic truncated MSE of scale parameter covariance estimators.

Theorem 3.1 was proved by *Andrews* [1991] under the assumptions given here. Newey and West, Andrews and others show, however, that under certain regularity conditions, Theorem 3.1 holds even if f_t is a nonstationary process without a well-defined spectral density. Theorem 3.1 establishes a class of consistent estimators of $\bar{V}_T$ which can be used to construct asymptotically valid GMM test statistics and to calculate an asymptotically efficient estimator in over–identified systems.

Theorem 3.1 also can be used to establish the asymptotic mean and variance of individual elements of $\widehat{V}_T$. The jth diagonal element of $\widehat{V}_T$ has asymptotic bias, $-m_T^{-r}k_r2\pi\, S_{j,j}^{(r)}$ and asymptotic variance

$$(m_T/T)8\pi^2 S_{j,j}^{(2)} \int_{-\infty}^{\infty} k^2(z)dz.$$

EXAMPLE 3.4

Consider the $p = 1$ case so that $\bar{V}_T$, $\widehat{V}_T$ and S_f are scalars. Suppose further that $\{f_t\}$ is homoskedastic and follows an AR(1) with coefficient $\rho = .80$ and variance $\sigma_f^2 = 1$. Then our estimand $\bar{V}_T = 2\pi\, S_f(0) = \sum_{j=-\infty}^{\infty} |\rho|^j = (1 + \rho)(1 - \rho)^{-1} = 9.0$. We also have that $2\pi S_f^{(1)} = 2\rho(1 - \rho)^{-2}$ and $2\pi S_f^{(2)} = 2\rho(1 + \rho)(1 - \rho)^{-3}$. (i) For a Newey–West–Bartlett window we have $r = 1$, $k_1 = 1$ and $\int k^2 = \frac{2}{3}$. The asymptotic bias is

$$-m_T^{-1}2\rho(1 - \rho)^{-2} = -40m_T^{-1},$$

the asymptotic variance is

$$(\frac{m_T}{T})(\frac{2}{3})(2)[(1 + \rho)/(1 - \rho)]^2 = 108(\frac{m_T}{T}),$$

and the asymptotic mean squared error is

$$1600m_T^{-2} + 108(\frac{m_T}{T}).$$

(ii) For a Tent Window we have $r = 2$, $k_2 = \frac{1}{12}$ and $\int k^2 = 4$. The asymptotic bias is

$$-m_T^{-2}(\frac{1}{12})\rho(1+\rho)(1-\rho)^{-3} = -15m_T^{-2},$$

the asymptotic variance is

$$(\frac{m_T}{T})(4)(2)[(1+\rho)/(1-\rho)]^2 = 648(\frac{m_T}{T})$$

and the asymptotic mean squared error is

$$225m_T^{-4} + 648(\frac{m_T}{T}).$$

■

3.4 Optimal Choice of Covariance Estimator

Theorem 3.1 establishes the consistency of a wide class of kernel estimators. The result, however, provides no guidance on which particular kernel estimator to choose, nor how to choose the bandwidth parameter. Further, kernel estimators are only one of a number of plausible estimation strategies. In this section we attempt to provide some guidance for the choice of estimator.

3.4.1 Optimal Choice of Scale Parameter Window

One generally accepted criterion for discriminating among covariance matrix estimators is that the estimator should always deliver positive semi–definite estimates. Negative variance estimates are clearly not sensible. More importantly, many iterative techniques for calculating the optimal GMM estimator require a positive definite $\hat{V}_T$ in each iteration. Restricting attention to positive semi–definite estimators eliminates the truncated window, but leaves a large class from which to choose.

The asymptotic results of Theorem 3.1 suggest that, all else equal, we should prefer estimators with a large r. The variance of these kernel estimators is of order $\frac{m_T}{T}$ and the bias is of order m_T^{-r}. Asymptotically then, estimators with larger r will tend to dominate according to a MSE criterion. On the other hand, no kernel estimator with $r > 2$ can be positive semi–definite. (See *Priestley* [1981, p. 568.]) This suggests that we restrict attention to estimators with $r = 2$ which rules out the Bartlett and truncated kernels.

Within the class of scale parameter windows with $r = 2$, Priestley shows that the Quadratic Spectral window minimizes the maximum relative mean square error across the spectral density. *Andrews* [1992] shows that the Quadratic Spectral window also minimizes the truncated mean square error at the zero frequency. Thus, according to the MSE criterion, the Quadratic Spectral window appears to be a good choice.

It should be noted, however, that the optimality of the spectral window is not as clear-cut as the above results appear. The asymptotic optimality need not obtain in finite samples and, as we discuss below, the MSE criterion is not terribly compelling in this context. *Newey and West's* [1994] Monte Carlo work finds only minor differences between the performance of the Quadratic Spectral window and their preferred estimator. The choice of a scale parameter turns out to be of much greater importance, in practice, than the form of the window.

3.4.2 Optimal Choice of Scale Parameter

Theorem 3.1 tells us that, from an asymptotic MSE criterion, the scale parameter should be $O(T^{\frac{1}{(2r+1)}})$. This suggests that a form, $m_T = \gamma T^{\frac{1}{(2r+1)}}$, may be appropriate. *Hannan* [1970] notes that this suggestion is 'obviously' useless because we do not know the value of γ. Unfortunately, statistical inference is often very sensitive to the choice of m_T. Some *method* of selecting m_T is clearly desirable, but ultimately, the appropriate choice requires some prior knowledge or additional restrictions on the underlying process, $\{f_t\}$.

Several 'judgmental' approaches for selecting the scale parameter have been suggested. For kernel estimators of the truncated sort (the truncated, Bartlett and Parzen), Priestly suggests a visual examination of the autocovariance function may be helpful. The idea is that because m_T is the highest order autocorrelation considered, we should use for m_T the value such that $\Omega(s) \sim 0$, where

$|s| > m_T$. This approach has a number of obvious drawbacks. One problem is that the number of moment conditions, q, may be large. Visually inspecting the q autocorrelation functions at each iteration of each estimation does not appear to be practical. In addition, the approach is only consistent for the truncated kernel. For the Bartlett and Parzen, m_T must grow large, even if the true autocorrelation function is truncated at some known, finite point.

Andrews [1991] suggests an approach that avoids a purely judgmental strategy. Suppose we are interested in minimizing the MSE of some linear combination of the elements of $\widehat{V}_T$, B vec$(\widehat{V}_T)$, where B is a $q^2 \times q^2$ non–stochastic matrix. The optimal scale parameter can be obtained by letting m_T grow at the optimal rate and then differentiating the result of Theorem 3.1 with respect to γ and setting the result equal to zero.. This yields,

$$m_T^* = \left(qk_r^2\alpha(q)T/\int k^2(z)dz \right)^{\frac{1}{(2r+1)}},$$

where

$$\alpha(r) = \frac{2(\text{vec}S^{(r)})'B\,\text{vec}S^{(r)}}{tr\,B(I + B_{pp})S_f(0) \otimes S_f(0)},$$

and B_{qq} is the $q^2 \times q^2$ commutation matrix of B.

The problem, of course, is that $S_f(0)$ and $S^{(r)}$ are unknown. Andrews' suggestion is to estimate $S_f(0)$ and $S^{(r)}$ using a simple parametric model, say a low order VAR and then using the estimated values to obtain an estimate of the optimal m_T. He shows that under suitable regularity conditions, this two–step procedure is asymptotically efficient, even if the parametric model is misspecified.

Newey and West [1996] suggest a similar approach, but they suggest a nonparametric technique for estimating S and $S^{(r)}$. They point out that S and $S^{(r)}$ can be estimated using a kernel estimator and they propose the simple, truncated estimator for this first–round estimation. Of course, their suggestion requires choosing some scale parameter, say 'n', to obtain the first–round estimates. They suggest exercising some 'judgement' on the sensitivity of results to the choice of n by increasing or decreasing the parameter and they conjecture that statistical inference will be less sensitive to the choice of 'n' than to the choice of m_T.

The great advantage of the approaches suggested by Andrews and by Newey and West is that they remove *some* of the judgmental aspects of selecting the scale parameter. Some method of preventing researchers from selecting the value of m_T that best supports their case is clearly desirable.

The optimality of the Andrews and the Newey–West procedures, however, should not be overemphasized. The choice of a low–order parametric model (Andrews) and the choice of a particular first–round scale parameter (Newey–West) implicitly imposes strong priors on the smoothness of the underlying spectral density. In addition, the MSE criterion for selecting m_T, though standard in the spectral density estimation literature, is not terribly compelling in the present context. After all, we are rarely interested in estimates of the covariance matrix per se. Instead, we are interested in the behavior of test statistics that use this estimated covariance matrix. It is by no means clear that the one–for–one trade–off between squared bias and variance, implicit in the MSE criterion, is appropriate. Indeed, Monte Carlo studies suggest that the behavior of t–statistics is far more unfavorably affected by bias than by variance in estimated covariance matrices.

3.4.3 Other Estimation Strategies

The estimators we have reviewed so far are weighted averages of the autocovariances or, equivalently weighted averages of the periodogram ordinates. As such, they are quadratic functions of the underlying observations. Quadratic estimators represent but a small class of possible estimation strategies.

den Haan and Levin [1996] advocate applying a purely parametric approach to estimating $\bar{V}_T$. Their suggestion, in essence, is simply to use the estimates derived from *Andrews'* [1991] first–round parametric estimation. That is, they suggest estimating $S(0)$ and hence $\bar{V}_T$ directly from a low order VAR or a sequence of univariate ARMA models. This approach can by made "automatic" by fitting a VAR and choosing the order according to some lag length selection criterion. In the spectral literature, this approach has been advocated by *Akaike* [1969] and *Parzen* [1974].

The relationship between the parametric approach and the kernel estimators is best understood by noting that fitting ARMA models in the time domain can be interpreted as fitting a rational polynomial in $e^{-i\lambda}$ to the periodogram ordinates in the frequency domain, see *Hannan* [1969]. Thus the parametric approach involves globally smoothing the periodogram ordinates using a rational polynomial whereas the kernel or window approach involves local smoothing with linear filters. Global smoothing by rational polynomials relies on the prior belief that the underlying spectral density has a particular shape, so that high frequency components of the periodogram provide information about the value at the zero frequency.

The 'prewhitening technique' developed by *Press and Tukey* [1956] and advocated in the present context by *Andrews and Monahan* [1992] is an appealing compromise between parametric and nonparametric approaches. The first step calls for fitting a parametric model as above. For a n-th order VAR, this step calls for estimating the model,

$$\widehat{f}_t = \Phi_1 \widehat{f}_{t-1} + \Phi_2 \widehat{f}_{t-2} + \ldots + \Phi_n \widehat{f}_{t-n}.$$

Because the VAR is only an approximation, the residuals from this regression, $\widehat{e}_t$, need not be white noise. The next step is to estimate $S_{\widehat{e}}$, the spectral density matrix of the residual process at the zero frequency. This may be accomplished by any of the kernel estimation approaches discussed above. The benefit of this approach is that we may apply a fairly wide bandwidth kernel estimator. This wide bandwidth estimator has low variance and, because the prewhitening technique has approximately flattened the spectral density, may have small bias. The final estimate can then be obtained by 'recoloring' using the estimated coefficients from the VAR,

$$\widehat{V}_{PW} = \left\{ [I_n - \widehat{\Phi}_1 - \widehat{\Phi}_2 - \cdots - \widehat{\Phi}_n] \right\}^{-1} S_{\widehat{e}}.$$

The Monte Carlo results in *Andrews and Monahan* [1992] suggest that this prewhitening estimator is robust to different underlying error structures and generally outperforms standard kernel estimators.

3.5 Finite Sample Properties of HAC Estimators

In this section we examine the finite sample properties of HAC estimators in scalar linear regression models. The appeal of using these estimators in the construction of OLS test statistics is, of course, their robustness to heteroskedastic and autocorrelated errors of unknown form. Unfortunately, although inference based on the resulting test statistics is asymptotically valid, Monte Carlo evidence suggests that the actual size of the test statistic is often far above its nominal size. We present some Monte Carlo results which show the poor small sample performance of HAC estimators and then present some small sample corrections which can substantially improve this performance.

3.5.1 Monte Carlo Evidence

We conduct seven experiments to give the reader a flavor of the finite sample properties of HAC estimators used in linear regression models. The population models are based on those used by *Andrews* [1991], where the population regression in each case contains a constant and three explanatory variables with an independently distributed mean zero error term. The vector of explanatory variables is a mean zero AR(1) normally distributed process with identity covariance matrix. In six of the seven experiments, the error is also an AR(1): in three of the six cases, its variance is one, and in the other three cases, the AR(1) unit variance process is multiplied by the absolute value of the second explanatory variable so that the error is heteroskedastic. We follow Andrews and use the same values of ρ (the AR parameter equals 0, .5, and .9) for the error and explanatory variables so that, in the homoskedastic error case, the process $(x_{it}u_t)$ is an AR(1) with parameter ρ_2. The seventh experiment generates an AR(2) unit variance error process with AR parameters, 1 and -.8. In this population the AR parameter for the explanatory variables is .9 so that the spectral density of $(x_{it}u_t)$ is not concentrated at the zero frequency. In each experiment we calculate the covariance estimate of the OLS coefficient estimator and the z–statistic of the coefficient on x_2. The tables report the mean and MSE of the variance point estimate (scaled by the sample size) as well as the confidence levels of the test statistic under the true null that the coefficient on x_2 is zero. We use the standard White heteroskedastic consistent covariance estimator (White), the Newey–West estimator (NW) with the bandwidth $3.62 \ (= 4(T/100)^{2/9})$, NW with Andrews' automatic bandwidth (NW-A), and the prewhitened estimator based on a VAR(1) using a quadratic spectral estimator with Andrews' bandwidth (PW-Q-A).

The results in the Tables 3.2–3.8 show that the true confidence levels associated with the test statistics are almost always lower than their nominal levels. The difference between the nominal and actual levels increases as the degree of positive autocorrelation in the error process increases, with the actual confidence levels being lowest when the error is heteroskedastic as well as highly positively autocorrelated.

Table 3.2: Monte Carlo Results With $T = 64$
Homoskedastic Errors, $\rho = 0$; $T V(\widehat{\beta}_{2T}) = 1.078$
$(y_t = \beta_0 + \sum_{i=1}^{3} \beta_i x_{it} + u_t, \ u_t = \rho u_{t-1} + \varepsilon_t, \ x_{it} = \rho x_{it-1} + \eta_{it})$

	Confidence levels			$E(T\widehat{V}(\widehat{\beta}_{2T}))$	$MSE(T\widehat{V}(\widehat{\beta}_{2T}))$
	.90	.95	.99		
White	.867	.925	.978	.972	.669
NW	.853	.911	.969	.927	.167
NW-A	.863	.921	.976	.963	.134
PW-Q-A	.859	.918	.972	.975	.186

Because our ultimate goal is to conduct (reliable) inference on θ_0, we would like to find a way to adjust the estimated OLS test statistic for finite sample bias in $\widehat{V}_T$ or to calculate a finite sample size correction. In the special case of iid normally distributed errors, the finite sample bias in $\widehat{V}_T$ is removed by the correction factor $\frac{T}{(T-p)}$, and the exact finite sample distribution of the test statistic is known to be $F(p, T - p)$. Correcting for finite sample bias or finding the exact finite sample distribution of the OLS test statistic is more difficult, however, under more general assumptions on the error term. For this reason, a more common approach has been to adjust $\widehat{V}_T$ for small sample bias and hope that the OLS test statistic calculated with this bias-adjusted estimate will more closely approximate its asymptotic distribution.

Table 3.3: Monte Carlo Results With $T = 64$
Homoskedastic Errors, $\rho = .5$; $TV(\hat{\beta}_{2T}) = 1.722$
$(y_t = \beta_0 + \sum_{i=1}^{3} \beta_i x_{it} + u_t,\ u_t = \rho u_{t-1} + \varepsilon_t,\ x_{it} = \rho x_{it-1} + \eta_{it})$

	Confidence levels				
	.90	.95	.99	$E(T\hat{V}(\hat{\beta}_{2T}))$	$MSE(T\hat{V}(\hat{\beta}_{2T}))$
White	.761	.838	.932	.960	1.377
NW	.796	.867	.945	1.171	.653
NW-A	.796	.867	.945	1.174	.671
PW-Q-A	.838	.897	.962	1.493	.847

Table 3.4: Monte Carlo Results With $T = 64$
Homoskedastic Errors, $\rho = .9$; $TV(\hat{\beta}_{2T}) = 7.1136$
$(y_t = \beta_0 + \sum_{i=1}^{3} \beta_i x_{it} + u_t,\ u_t = \rho u_{t-1} + \varepsilon_t,\ x_{it} = \rho x_{it-1} + \eta_{it})$

	Confidence levels				
	.90	.95	.99	$E(T\hat{V}(\hat{\beta}_{2T}))$	$MSE(T\hat{V}(\hat{\beta}_{2T}))$
White	.421	.494	.610	.948	43.328
NW	.554	.636	.751	1.895	29.888
NW-A	.570	.649	.765	2.870	29.184
PW-Q-A	.765	.827	.899	*	*

Note: * The moments of the quadratic spectrum covariance estimator do not exist in this case because the prewhitening filter was estimated from an unrestricted VAR(1) and the population AR(1) parameter is close to one.

Table 3.5: Monte Carlo Results With $T = 64$
Heteroskedastic Errors, $u_t = v_t |x_{2t}|$, $\rho = .9$; $TV(\hat{\beta}_{2T}) = 15.810$
$(y_t = \beta_0 + \sum_{i=1}^{3} \beta_i x_{it} + u_t,\ v_t = \rho v_{t-1} + \varepsilon_t,\ x_{it} = \rho x_{it-1} + \eta_{it})$

	Confidence levels				
	.90	.95	.99	$E(T\hat{V}(\hat{\beta}_{2T}))$	$MSE(T\hat{V}(\hat{\beta}_{2T}))$
White	.375	.438	.557	1.565	204.59
NW	.490	.568	.699	3.080	170.10
NW-A	.509	.586	.714	3.525	164.58
PW-Q-A	.648	.721	.824	*	*

Note: As above.

Table 3.6: Monte Carlo Results With $T = 64$
Heteroskedastic Errors, $u_t = v_t|x_{2t}|$, $\rho = 0$; $TV(\hat{\beta}_{2T}) = 2.9176$
$(y_t = \beta_0 + \sum_{i=1}^{3} \beta_i x_{it} + u_t, \; v_t = \rho v_{t-1} + \varepsilon_t, \; x_{it} = \rho x_{it-1} + \eta_{it})$

	Confidence levels			$E(T\hat{V}(\hat{\beta}_{2T}))$	$MSE(T\hat{V}(\hat{\beta}_{2T}))$
	.90	.95	.99		
White	.841	.903	.967	2.442	1.736
NW	.826	.889	.961	2.339	2.334
NW-A	.835	.898	.965	2.409	2.157
PW-Q-A	.832	.894	.963	2.433	2.389

Table 3.7: Monte Carlo Results With $T = 64$
Heteroskedastic Errors, $u_t = v_t|x_{2t}|$, $\rho = .5$; $TV(\hat{\beta}_{2T}) = 4.535$
$(y_t = \beta_0 + \sum_{i=1}^{3} \beta_i x_{it} + u_t, \; v_t = \rho v_{t-1} + \varepsilon_t, \; x_{it} = \rho x_{it-1} + \eta_{it})$

	Confidence levels			$E(T\hat{V}(\hat{\beta}_{2T}))$	$MSE(T\hat{V}(\hat{\beta}_{2T}))$
	.90	.95	.99		
White	.738	.816	.917	2.265	6.044
NW	.765	.837	.927	2.752	6.495
NW-A	.766	.842	.930	2.763	6.390
PW-Q-A	.795	.863	.941	3.474	120.050

Table 3.8: Monte Carlo Results With $T = 64$
Homoskedastic Errors, $\rho = .9$; $TV(\hat{\beta}_{2T}) = 2.079$
$(y_t = \beta_0 + \sum_{i=1}^{3} \beta_i x_{it} + u_t, \; u_t = u_{t-1} - .8u_{t-2} + \varepsilon_t, \; x_{it} = \rho x_{it-1} + \eta_{it})$

	Confidence levels			$E(T\hat{V}(\hat{\beta}_{2T}))$	$MSE(T\hat{V}(\hat{\beta}_{2T}))$
	.90	.95	.99		
White	.881	.930	.980	1.952	5.836
NW	.917	.955	.988	2.514	3.501
NW-A	.890	.937	.982	2.165	3.073
PW-Q-A	.958	.981	.996	3.916	41.928

3.5.2 Regression Model

Suppose we wish to estimate the $p \times 1$ parameter vector β in the following model:

$$y_t = x_t'\beta + u_t,$$

where u_t is a mean zero stationary random variable. We assume that $\{x_t\}$, $t = 1, 2, \ldots, T$, are fixed in repeated samples. (Alternatively, we could condition on the observed values of x_t.) The parameter vector, β, is identified by the following $q(= p)$ moment conditions:

$$E(x_t u_t) = E(f_t) = 0, \quad t = 1, 2, \ldots, T$$

The OLS estimator $\widehat{\beta}_T$ satisfies the sample moment conditions $\sum_{t=1}^{T} x_t \widehat{u}_t = 0$ so that $\widehat{\beta}_T = (X'X)^{-1}X'y$, where X and y are the observation matrices stacked in the usual way and rank$(X) = p$. Asymptotic inference on β is based on

$$\sqrt{T}(\widehat{\beta}_T - \beta) \xrightarrow{d} N(0, M_x^{-1}\bar{V}M_x^{-1})$$

where $\bar{V} = \lim_{T \to \infty} T^{-1} \sum_{t=1}^{T} \sum_{s=1}^{T} x_t E(u_t u_s) x_s' = \sum_{j=-\infty}^{\infty} E(f_t f_{t-j}')$ is 2π times the spectral density of the process $f_t = x_t u_t$, evaluated at the zero frequency and plim$(X'X/T) = X'X/T = M_x$.

We will consider small sample corrections for estimates of $\bar{V}$ under three different assumptions on the properties of the error term in the above regression model. The first case is a heteroskedastic model with uncorrelated errors, the second case allows autocorrelation but no heteroskedasticity, and the third case allows both autocorrelation and heteroskedasticity. Each case will imply a specific form for $\bar{V}$ which will guide the choice of consistent estimator.

3.5.3 Heteroskedastic but Serially

Uncorrelated Errors

Many times it is reasonable to assume that the error term in a cross-sectional regression model is conditionally heteroskedastic, but is uncorrelated across observations. That is, suppose that $E(u_t u_s) = 0$, for $t \neq s$, and $E(u_t u_s) = \sigma(x_t) = \sigma_t^2$ for $t = s$. In this case $\bar{V} = T^{-1} \sum_{t=1}^{T} x_t \sigma_t^2 x_t'$ which is typically estimated by *White's* [1980] heteroskedasticity consistent estimator, $\widehat{V}_T = T^{-1} \sum_{t=1}^{T} x_t \widehat{u}_t^2 x_t' \equiv$

HC_T. MacKinnon and White [1985] propose three asymptotically equivalent estimators of $\bar{V}$ which adjust HC_T for its use of residuals instead of the true errors. The authors then compare the behavior of test statistics using the adjusted covariance estimates to that of the traditional OLS test statistic and the test statistic using HC_T.

The first small sample adjustment MacKinnon and White consider is the standard degrees of freedom correction, $T/(T-p)$. They define the corrected estimator as

$$HC1_T = (T/(T-p))HC_T$$

Under homoskedasticity ($\sigma_t^2 = \sigma^2$ for all t), when the estimand is σ^2, the scale factor $T/(T-p)$ corrects the estimator $\widehat{\sigma}_T^2 = T^{-1}\sum_{t=1}^{T} \widehat{u}_t^2$ for bias. When the estimand is $\bar{V} = T^{-1}\sum_{t=1}^{T} x_t\sigma^2 x_t'$, however, the scale factor $T/(T-p)$ usually does not eliminate the small sample bias of HC_T.

Substituting $\widehat{u}_t = (u_t - x_t'(X'X)^{-1}X'u)$ for the OLS residual we see that, under homoskedasticity,

$$E(\widehat{u}_t^2) = \sigma^2(1 - x_t'(X'X)^{-1}x_t) = \sigma^2(1 - p_{tt}),$$

where p_{tt} is the t'th diagonal element of $X(X'X)^{-1}X'$. So the corrected estimator $HC1_T$ is unbiased only if $p_{tt} = p$.

This result suggests a second bias-adjustment to HC_T which Horn, Horn and Duncan [1975] propose and MacKinnon and White define as,

$$HC2_T = T^{-1}\sum_{t=1}^{T} x_t\widetilde{u}_t^2 x_t',$$

where $\widetilde{u}_t^2 = \widehat{u}_t^2/(1 - p_{tt})$. This estimator is, of course, unbiased under homoskedasticity.

MacKinnon and White note that each of the three estimators of $\bar{V}$, when pre- and post–multiplied by $(X'X/T)^{-1}$, is a type of jack-knife estimator of the covariance matrix of $\sqrt{T}\widehat{\beta}_T$. They therefore suggest as their final estimator that part of the ordinary jackknife estimator (see *Efron* [1982]) which corresponds to an estimate of $\bar{V}$. They define this estimator as,

$$HC3_T = \frac{T-1}{T}\left[\sum_{t=1}^{T} x_t u_t^{*2} x_t' - T^{-1}X'u^*u^{*'}X\right],$$

where $u_t^* = \widehat{u}_t/(1 - p_{tt})$.

MacKinnon and White perform Monte Carlo experiments to compare rejection frequencies of quasi t–statistics calculated using

$HC1_T$, $HC2_T$, and $HC3_T$ in a three parameter regression model under both homoskedasticity and two types of heteroskedasticity. The estimated rejection frequencies show that $HC3_T$ dominates the other two heteroskedasticity consistent estimators of The Monte Carlo results also indicate that the standard OLS test statistic substantially over rejects the null hypothesis when the error is heteroskedastic; in these cases, the test statistics using $HC3_T$ also over reject, but by a smaller amount. In the case of homoskedastic errors, the standard OLS test statistic performs the best, although the actual size of test statistics calculated using $HC3_T$ is not far from its asymptotic size.

3.5.4 Autocorrelated but Homoskedastic Errors

It is often reasonable to assume when estimating a regression model with time series data that the error term is autocorrelated but conditionally homoskedastic. In our notation, this assumption can be stated as $E(u_t u_s) = \sigma_{t-s}$, for $t \neq s$, and $E(u_t u_s) = \sigma^2$, for $t = s$. In this case the estimand of interest becomes $\bar{V} = 2\pi \int_{-\pi}^{\pi} \left[\lim_{T \to \infty} T^{-1} \left| \sum_{t=1}^{T} x_t e^{i\lambda t} \right|^2 \right] S_u(\lambda) d\lambda$, a weighted integral of the spectral density of u_t, where $\left| \sum_{t=1}^{T} x_t e^{i\lambda t} \right|^2 = \sum_{t=1}^{T} \sum_{s=1}^{T} x_t x_s' e^{i\lambda(t-s)}$. With the explanatory variables fixed in repeated samples (or, conditioning on the sample observations), the weight in the integral becomes $T^{-1} \left| \sum_{t=1}^{T} x_t e^{i\lambda t} \right|^2$, a known, finite $p \times p$ nonsingular matrix.

The assumption of homoskedasticity greatly simplifies the estimation of $\bar{V}$. Because the estimand is a weighted integral of the spectral density of u_t and the weights are finite, the weighted sum of the periodogram ordinates of the OLS residuals provides a consistent estimator of $\bar{V}$. One need not use a kernel spectral density estimator of $S_u(\lambda)$ to form a consistent estimator of $\bar{V}$. *Cushing and McGarvey* [1997b] examine the finite sample properties of test statistics based on this type of autocorrelation consistent, weighted periodogram estimator of $\bar{V}$. We consider both an unadjusted and a bias-adjusted weighted periodogram estimator.

The unadjusted autocorrelation consistent estimator of $\bar{V}$ is

$$AC1_T = 2\pi \int_{-\pi}^{\pi} \left[T^{-1} \sum_{t=1}^{T} |x_t e^{i\lambda t}|^2 \right] \widehat{I}_{u,T}(\lambda) d\lambda,$$

where $\widehat{I}_{u,T}(\lambda) = (2\pi T)^{-1} \left| \sum_{t=1}^{T} \widehat{u}_t e^{i\lambda t} \right|^2$. To find an approximate bias adjustment factor for this estimator we consider the case in which the OLS estimator $\widehat{\beta}_T$ is an asymptotically efficient estimator of β. Anderson [1971] gives the asymptotic bias of the periodogram ordinates based on OLS residuals in this special case.

$$\lim_{T \to \infty} E(\widehat{I}_{u,T}(\lambda)) - S_u(\lambda) = -S_u(\lambda) \widetilde{x}'_t(\lambda) (X'X)^{-1} \widetilde{x}_t(\lambda),$$

where $\widetilde{x}_T(\lambda) = \sum_{t=1}^{T} x_t e^{-i\lambda t}$ and transposition also denote complex conjugation.

The above result suggests a simple bias adjustment to the estimated periodogram. The adjusted autocorrelation consistent estimator is

$$AC2_T = 2\pi \int_{-\pi}^{\pi} \sum_{\lambda=\lambda_1}^{\lambda_T} \left[T^{-1} \sum_{t=1}^{T} |x_T e^{i\lambda t}|^2 \right] \widehat{I}_{u,T}(\lambda) /$$

$$(1 - \widetilde{x}'_T(\lambda)(X'X)^{-1} \widetilde{x}_t(\lambda)) d\lambda.$$

Cushing and McGarvey perform a small scale Monte Carlo study to compare the rejection frequencies of OLS test statistics based on covariance estimates using $AC1_T$ and $AC2_T$ to test statistics based on the Newey–West estimator and to the standard OLS test statistic. Our preliminary results suggest that when u_t is homoskedastic and u_t and x_t are positively autocorrelated, one is better off using either of the autocorrelation consistent estimators $AC1_T$ and $AC2_T$ than the HAC Newey–West estimator. Using the bias adjusted estimator, $AC2_T$, to construct test statistics appears to substantially reduce the discrepancy between the test's actual and nominal size. For example, in a model with $p = 5$, $T = 128$, and both x_t and u_t with first–order autocorrelation coefficient of .9, testing at a nominal level of .05 results in an actual size of .49 using the standard OLS test statistic. Using the Newey–West estimator to calculate the test statistic reduces the rejection frequency to .29 and using the correct parametric estimator reduces the size further to .14. The test statistic based on our adjusted autocorrelation consistent estimator, however, rejects the true null 12% of the

time, even closer to the nominal 5% level than that found using
the parametric estimator.

More extensive Monte Carlo analysis is needed before we can
reach general conclusions about the benefits of using autocorrelation consistent estimators such as $AC1_T$ and $AC2_T$. In particular,
a comparison of these test statistics' finite sample performance
needs to be made under heteroskedasticity. Our preliminary results
suggest, however, that if the model is homoskedastic, a covariance
estimator which incorporates that assumption will outperform a
more robust HAC estimator in finite samples.

3.5.5 Autocorrelated and Heteroskedastic Errors

The final case we consider is the general stationary error, which
is conditionally heteroskedastic, $E(u_t u_s) = \sigma(x_t) = \sigma_t^2$ for $t = s$,
and autocorrelated, $E(u_t u_s) = \sigma_{t-s}$, for $t \neq s$. This is the case
for which kernel spectral density estimators of $\bar{V}$ are ideally suited.
The estimand is unrestricted; it is merely 2π times the spectral
density matrix of $x_t u_t$ evaluated at the zero frequency.

It is well known that the kernel spectral density estimator,
$\widehat{V}_T$, is a biased estimator of the spectral density of $x_t u_t$ evaluated
at frequency zero and that test statistics based on this estimator
suffer from size distortions. As discussed earlier, *Andrews* [1991]
and *Andrews and Monahan* [1992] suggest using an estimate of the
optimal lag truncation parameter and prewhitening the residuals to
both reduce the mean-squared-error of the covariance estimates and
to improve the performance of confidence intervals. Neither of these
suggestions, however, explicitly takes into account the estimator's
use of residuals instead of true errors. *Cushing and McGarvey*
[1997a] attempt to correct $\widehat{V}_T$ for bias due to its use of residuals
and suggest a degrees of freedom adjustment to the resulting test
statistic.

To see the problem introduced by using residuals, recall that
the HAC estimator of $\bar{V}$ is a weighted integral of the estimated
periodogram of $x_t u_t$,

$$\widehat{V}_T = \int_{-\pi}^{\pi} W(\lambda, m_T)\widehat{I}_T(\lambda)d\lambda,$$

where $\widehat{I}_T(\lambda) = (2\pi T)^{-1} \sum_{t=1}^{T} \sum_{s=1}^{T} x_t \widehat{u}_t \widehat{u}_s x_s' e^{i\lambda(t-s)}$. Because the OLS estimator satisfies the sample moment conditions, $\sum_{t=1}^{T} x_t \widehat{u}_t = 0$, the estimated periodogram is constrained to be identically zero at the zero frequency. Thus, even asymptotically, there is a bias in the periodogram estimates from using residuals.

To calculate the bias in $\widehat{V}_T$ due to using residuals instead of the true errors, we assume the regression error is conditionally homoskedastic and uncorrelated across observations. In this case,

$$E(\widehat{I}_T(\lambda)) = E(I_T(\lambda)) - D_T(\lambda, E(I_T(0))),$$

where $I_T(\lambda)$ is the periodogram of $\{x_t u_t\}$ and the difference $D_T(\lambda, E(I_T(0))$ is

$$D_T(\lambda, I_T(0)) = \sum_{t=1}^{T} \sum_{s=1}^{T} x_t x_t' (X'X)^{-1} I_T(0) (X'X)^{-1} x_s x_s'.$$

Note that there is no asymptotic bias in the periodogram estimates from using residuals except, of course, at the zero frequency, for $\lim_{T \to \infty} E(\widehat{I}_T(\lambda) - I_T(\lambda)) = -S_{xu}(\lambda)$, for $\lambda = 0$ and $= 0$, for $\lambda \neq 0$. Since as $T \to \infty$, the point estimator $\widehat{V}_T$ is a weighted average of $\widehat{I}_T(\lambda)$ over the entire interval $-\pi$ to π, using residuals to estimate $S_{xu}(0)$ is asymptotically equivalent to using the true errors. In sample sizes typical of economic quarterly data, however, $E(\widehat{I}_T(\lambda) - I_T(\lambda))$ will be large at frequencies close to zero if x_t is positively autocorrelated and, because $\widehat{V}_T$ is a weighted average of a finite number of frequencies, in practice this difference can create a large bias in $\widehat{V}_T$.

Our adjusted HAC estimator, based on the result above, reduces the bias in $\widehat{V}_T$ due to using residuals and eliminates this bias when the regression error is white noise. The adjusted estimator is

$$\text{vec}\widehat{V}_T^A = (I_{p^2} - A)^{-1} \cdot \text{vec}\widehat{V}_T,$$

where

$$A = \int_{-\pi}^{\pi} W(\lambda, m_T) \sum_{t=1}^{T} \sum_{s=1}^{T} e^{i\lambda(t-s)} (x_t x_t' (X'X)^{-1})$$
$$\otimes ((X'X)^{-1} x_s x_s') d\lambda.$$

This estimator exists if the eigenvalues of A are less than one in absolute value, a condition which can be checked easily. If this condition is true, then

$$\mathrm{vec}\widehat{V}_T^A = \left[\sum_{j=0}^{\infty} A^j\right] \cdot \mathrm{vec}\widehat{V}_T.$$

If we restrict $\widehat{V}_T$ to be a positive semidefinite HAC kernel estimator, then each term in the above summation is the vectorization of a positive semidefinite matrix. Thus, the bias–adjusted estimator, $\widehat{V}_T^A$, is positive semidefinite.

Cushing and McGarvey use a small scale Monte Carlo study to compare the effects of correcting the Bartlett–Newey–West estimator by the standard bias correction $T/(T-p)$ to correcting by the method given above. The experiments paralleled those performed by *Andrews* [1991] with a five parameter, orthogonal regressor model with x_t and u_t having identical first–order autocorrelation coefficient, ρ, equal to 0, .5, .7, .9 and .95, and $T = 128$. We find that using $\widehat{V}_T^A$ rather than $(T/T-p) \cdot \widehat{V}_T$ to estimate the variance of an element of $\widehat{\beta}$ results in a smaller bias and MSE across *all window widths* considered. When comparing the two estimators' MSEs across only *optimal window widths*, our bias adjusted version of the Newey–West estimator provides between a 16 % and 27 % lower MSE than the uncorrected version.

More relevant than the bias and MSE of the estimated variance of $\widehat{\beta}_i$ is the behavior of the quasi t–statistic and estimated confidence intervals for β. The Monte Carlo results of Andrews and others suggest that, even if one adjusts $\widehat{V}_T$ by $(T/T-p)$ to calculate standard errors for $\widehat{\beta}_i$, with highly autocorrelated x_t and u_t, the actual confidence levels are much smaller than their nominal levels. One reason that the standard degrees of freedom correction, $T/(T-p)$, does not eliminate the bias in $\widehat{V}_T$ due to using residuals is that, when estimating the spectral density at zero, it is not p, the number of estimated parameters, which is relevant, but rather m_T, the number of covariances included in the weighted estimator. Therefore, we suggest not only using $\widehat{V}_T^A$ to calculate the standard error of $\widehat{\beta}_i$ but also basing confidence intervals and hypotheses tests on the t distribution with degrees–of–freedom adjusted for using residuals.

To calculate the adjusted degrees of freedom, we first note that the ith diagonal element of the Bartlett estimator of $S_{xu}(0)$ using the *true errors* is asymptotically Chi–squared. We approximate its degrees of freedom by $1.5(T/m_T)$, two times the ratio of the estimator's asymptotic mean to its asymptotic variance, where the variance is calculated under the assumption that $x_t u_t$ is white noise. We then scale $1.5(T/m_T)$ by the inverse of CR, our bias adjustment factor, where $CR = \text{trace}(\widehat{V}_T^A)/\text{trace}(\widehat{V}_T)$. Our degrees of freedom adjusted confidence interval thus uses $\widehat{V}_T^A$ to calculate the standard error of $\widehat{\beta}_i$ and the t value corresponding to degrees of freedom, $CR^{-1} \cdot 1.5(T/m_T)$.

In our Monte Carlo experiments we calculated confidence intervals based on $\widehat{V}_T^A$ and the degrees of freedom corrected t value as well as standard confidence intervals using $\widehat{V}_T \cdot T/(T-p)$ and the z value. Our adjusted confidence intervals work remarkably well compared to the standard procedure. The improvement is most dramatic for moderately to highly autocorrelated $x_t u_t$ just as is the improvement in bias and MSE. For example, with $\rho = .95$, the true confidence level corresponding to a nominal 95 % interval using the standard procedure was estimated to be 62 %. Using our procedure it was estimated to be 94 %. With $\rho = 0$, however, both methods produced correct confidence levels.

3.5.6 Summary

Monte Carlo evidence indicates that the standard HAC kernel spectral density estimators of $\bar{V}_T$ are severely downwardly biased in the presence of positive autocorrelation. Moreover, quasi t–statistics appear to reject a true null far more often then their nominal size. The results reviewed in Section 3.5 suggest that one can reduce this bias and improve the finite sample performance of test statistics in linear regression models by adjusting the estimate of $\bar{V}_T$ for small sample bias. These adjustments alone appear to work very well if one can reasonably assume a model with either heteroskedasticity with no autocorrelation or autocorrelation with no heteroskedasticity. The first assumption is common in cross section regression models and the second is often made in time series regression models.

In the more general case of both conditionally heteroskedastic and autocorrelated errors, it appears that a bias correction to $\widehat{V}_T$ alone will not sufficiently improve the behavior of estimated test statistics or confidence intervals on β. Two approaches suggested in the literature appear promising in this case. *Andrews and Monahan* [1991] examine the behavior of estimated confidence intervals in regression models using $\widehat{V}_T$ where the optimal value of m_T is estimated after pre- whitening the $x_t\, u_t$ process. Their Monte Carlo evidence suggests this method can substantially improve the behavior of the resulting test statistics. The second approach is that suggested by *Cushing and McGarvey* [1997]. Our preliminary results suggest that using a bias adjusted version of $\widehat{V}_T$ in conjunction with a degrees of freedom corrected t critical value has the potential to dramatically improve finite sample inference.

References

Akaike, H. [**1969**]: Fitting Autoregressive Models for Prediction; *Annals of the Institute of Statistical Mathematics*, 21, 243-247.

Andrews, Donald W. K. [**1991**]: Heteroskedasticity and Autocorrelation Consistent Covariance Matrix Estimation; *Econometrica*, 59, 817-858.

Andrews, D.W.K. and J. Christopher Monahan [**1992**]: An Improved Heteroskedasticity and Autocorrelation Consistent Covariance Matrix Estimator; *Econometrica*, 60, 953-966.

Cushing, M.J. and M.G. McGarvey [**1997a**]: *Degrees of Freedom Correction for Heteroskedasticity and Autocorrelation Consistent Covariance Estimators*; unpublished manuscript.

Cushing, M.J. and M. McGarvey [**1997b**]: *A Bias-Corrected Autocorrelation Consistent Least Squares Covariance Estimator*; unpublished manuscript.

Daniell, P.J. [**1946**]: Discussion on "Symposium on Autocorrelation in Time Series"; *Journal of the Royal Statistical Society*, Supplement, 8, 88–90.

Doan, T. and R. Litterman [**1995**]: *Regression Analysis for Time Series*; Users Manual, Version 4.2.

den Haan, W. and A. Levin [**1996**]: *Inferences from Parametric and Non-Parametric Covariance Matrix Estimation Procedures*; unpublished manuscript.

Efron, B. [**1982**]: *The Jackknife, the Bootstrap and Other Resampling Plans*; Philadelphia: Society for Industrial and Applied Mathematics.

Gallant, R. [**1987**]: *Nonlinear Statistical Models*; New York: Wiley.

Hannan, E.J. [**1970**]: *Multiple Time Series*; New York: Wiley.

Hansen, L.P. [**1982**]: Large Sample Properties of Generalized Method of Moments Estimators; *Econometrica*, 50, 1029-1054.

Horn, S.D., Horn, R.A. and D.B. Duncan [**1975**]: Estimating Heteroskedastic Variances in Linear Models; *Journal of the American Statistical Association*, 70, 380-385.

MacKinnon, J.G. and H. White [**1985**]: Some Heteroskedasticity Consistent Covariance Matrix Estimators with Improved Finite Sample Properties; *Journal of Econometrics*, 29, 305-325.

Newey, W.K. and K.D. West [**1987**]: A Simple Positive Definite, Heteroskedasticity and Autocorrelation Consistent Covariance Matrix; *Econometrica*, 55, 703-708.

Newey, W.K. and K.D. West [**1994**]: Automatic Lag Selection in Covariance Estimation; *Review of Economic Studies*, 61, 631-653.

Parzen, E. [**1974**]: Some Recent Advances in Time Series Modeling; *IEEE Transactions on Automatic control*, AC-19, 723-730.

Press, H. and J.W. Tukey [**1956**]: *Power Spectral Methods of Analysis and their Applications to Problems in Airplane Dynamics*; Bell Systems Monographs 2602.

Priestly, M.B. [**1981**]: *Spectral Analysis and Time Series*; Volumes I and II London: Academic Press.

White, H. [**1980**]: A Heteroscedasticity Consistent Covariance Matrix Estimator and a Direct Test for Heteroscedasticity; *Econometrica*, 48, 817–838.

White, H. [**1984**]: *Asymptotic Theory for Econometricians*; Academic Press, New York.

Chapter 4

HYPOTHESIS TESTING IN MODELS

ESTIMATED BY GMM

Alastair R. Hall

Since its introduction the Generalized Method of Moments (GMM) has had considerable impact on the theory and practice of econometrics. For theoreticians, the main advantage is that GMM provides a very general framework for considering issues of statistical inference because it encompasses many estimators of interest in econometrics. For applied researchers, it provides a computationally convenient method of estimating nonlinear dynamic models without complete knowledge of the probability distribution of the data.[1] All these applications have a common structure. An economic and/or statistical model implies a vector of observed variables, x_t, and an unknown parameter vector, θ_0, satisfy a vector of population moment conditions,

$$E[f(x_t, \theta_0)] = 0. \qquad (4\text{--}1)$$

For the model to be of practical use, it is necessary to find a suitable value for the parameter vector. GMM provides a simple framework by which the information in (4–1) can be combined with a sample on x_t to provide an estimate of θ_0. Within this general structure, three broad questions naturally arise: Is the estimation based upon correct information? Does the parameter vector satisfy a set of restrictions implied by economic theory? Which of two competing models is correct? This chapter reviews various hypothesis testing techniques which have been designed to answer these questions.

---

[1] See *Hall* [1993] and *Ogaki* [1993] for an overview of these applications.

The population moment condition must possess certain properties for GMM estimation to be feasible. At this stage, we need only note the requirement that q, the dimension of the population moment condition, is at least as large as p, the dimension of the parameter vector. In nearly all the applications refered to above, q exceeds p and we shall maintain this assumption for most of our discussion because this introduces the unique features of the GMM framework. By its very nature, GMM induces a fundamental relationship between the parameter estimates and the population moment conditions upon which they are based. This relationship limits the types of hypotheses which can be tested, and also implies certain important properties which play a crucial role in the analysis of the various statistics discussed below. Therefore in Section 4.1, we briefly describe the basic structure of GMM estimation. Particular attention is paid to the decomposition of the population moment condition into the *identifying restrictions* and the *overidentifying restrictions*. The identifying restrictions represent the part of the population moment condition which actually goes into parameter estimation; the overidentifying restrictions are just the remainder. In the sample, the analog to the identifying restrictions are satisfied at the estimator, $\hat{\theta}_T$, and so it is not possible to test whether the identifying restrictions hold at the true parameter value. However, the sample analog to the overidentifying restrictions are not imposed and so it is possible to test whether these restrictions hold in the population. Most importantly, the two components of this decomposition are orthogonal and this property plays an important role in the discussion.

In practice, it is prudent to begin by testing the overidentifying restrictions because if this hypothesis is rejected then this indicates the model is misspecified. In such an eventuality, the natural course is to re–examine the specification rather than proceed to examine other types of hypotheses within the current model. Therefore our review begins in Section 4.2 with a description of a statistic for testing the overidentifying restrictions and a discussion of its properties. If the null is rejected, then it is useful to diagnose the source of the problem and Section 4.3 describes statistics for testing hypotheses about a subset of the moment conditions. Section 4.4 discusses methods for testing the hypothesis that the parameter vector satisfies a set of nonlinear restrictions of the form $r(\theta_0) = 0$. These types of restrictions naturally arise in many economic models and so test results can often provide useful insights about the underlying economic structure. It is shown that these hypotheses can be expressed in terms of the identifying restrictions and this perspective provides a useful interpretation of this type of test.

One of the main assumptions behind GMM is that the population moment condition in (4–1) holds throughout the entire sample; in other words the model is assumed to be structurally stable. A natural concern is that (4–1) may only hold for part of the sample and so the model exhibits structural instability. Section 4.5 describes various methods for testing structural stability. The differences between the tests are most easily understood by considering their sensitivity to instability of identifying and overidentifying restrictions separately. It is also shown how this decomposition can be exploited to develop tests which can distinguish between instability in the parameters alone and instability of a more general form.

In most cases, a number of models have been proposed to explain a particular economic phenomenon. In some cases, one model is nested within another and so it is possible to assess which is more appropriate using the types of procedure described in Sections 4.2 through 4.4. However, in other cases the competing models are not nested in this fashion, and so alternative procedures must be developed. As will be seen, this type of question is much harder to address within the GMM framework without further restrictions. Section 4.6 discusses the difficulties and describes various procedures which have been proposed for testing non–nested hypotheses.

Inevitably, this type of review must be selective. We have chosen to focus on inference procedures which highlight the unique aspects of the GMM framework. This choice is guided by the types of problems that arise in applications in economics and finance. Obvious omissions are hypothesis tesing procedures originally proposed for specific examples of GMM such as maximum likelihood or least squares.[2] In our opinion, this omission is justified because little insight is typically gained by reinterpreting these tests from a GMM perspective. However, there are some exceptions, such as conditional moment and Hausman tests, and so these are briefly discussed in Section 4.7. It is also beyond the scope of this chapter

---

[2]   *Engle* [1984] provides a comprehensive review of these techniques.

to provide an introduction to the general theory of statistical hypothesis testing; the interested reader is refered to *Lehmann* [1959] or *Cox and Hinckley* [1974]. Finally, it should be noted that we concentrate purely on the asymptotic properties of the tests and leave a review of their finite sample behavior to Chapter 5.

We conclude this introduction by stating certain conventions which are maintained throughout to enable us to focus more clearly on the issues associated with hypothesis testing. The data $\{x_t; t = 1, 2, \ldots T\}$ are assumed to be a realization from a stationary and ergodic process. In most cases, it is desired to perform inference based on the GMM estimator calculated with the optimal weighting matrix and so we restrict attention to this case. Accordingly, $\hat{\theta}_T$ is defined to be the value of θ which minimizes

$$Q_T(\theta) = f_T(\theta)' \, V_T^{-1} \, f_T(\theta) \,,$$

where $f_T(\theta) = T^{-1} \sum_{t=1}^{T} f(x_t, \theta)$ and V_T is a consistent estimator of $V = \lim_{T \to \infty} Var[T^{1/2} f_T(\theta_0)]$; see Chapter 3. All the procedures are based on asymptotic theory and so it is assumed that the necessary regularity conditions apply; see Chapter 1.[3] The symbol $\overset{A}{\sim}$ denotes "asymptotically distributed as"; $N(\mu, \Sigma)$ denotes a multivariate normal distribution with mean μ and covariance matrix Σ; $\chi_a^2(b)$ denotes a non–central χ^2 distribution with a degrees of freedom and non–centrality parameter b but the latter is omitted if $b = 0$.

4.1 Identifying and Overidentifying Restrictions

We begin with a description of the decomposition of the population moment condition into identifying and overidentifying restrictions. This framework was first explicitly characterized by *Sowell* [1996a], although its existence was clearly exploited implicitly in earlier work such as *Newey* [1985a].

The decomposition stems from the set of first order conditions associated with the minimization of $Q_T(\theta)$,

$$\partial Q_T(\hat{\theta}_T)/\partial \theta = F_T(\hat{\theta}_T)' V_T^{-1} f_T(\hat{\theta}_T) = 0 \,. \tag{4-2}$$

---

[3] Also see *Hansen* [1982], *Gallant and White* [1988].

Sowell [1996a] observes that since $\widehat{\theta}_T$ satisfies (4–2) it must also satisfy

$$\widehat{P}\,V_T^{-1/2}f_T(\widehat{\theta}_T) = 0\,, \tag{4–3}$$

where $\widehat{P} = \widehat{M}(\widehat{M}'\widehat{M})^{-1}\widehat{M}'$, $\widehat{M} = V_T^{-1/2}F_T(\widehat{\theta}_T)$ and $F_T(\theta) = \partial f_T(\theta)/\partial\theta'$. Therefore, although we began with the information in (4–1), GMM estimation is actually based on the population analog to (4–3), namely

$$P\,V^{-1/2}E[f(x_t,\theta_0)] = 0\,, \tag{4–4}$$

where $P = M(M'M)^{-1}M'$, $M = V^{-1/2}E[F_t(\theta_0)]$ and $F_t(\theta) = \partial f(x_t,\theta)/\partial\theta'$. *Sowell* [1996a] termed the elements of (4–4) the *identifying restrictions* for θ_0, if θ_0 is identified then. The projection matrix P is of rank p and so these restrictions set only p unique linear combinations of the $(q \times 1)$ vector $E[f(x_t,\theta_0)]$ to zero. Since $q > p$, this does not necessarily imply (4–1), and so clearly a part of the original moment condition is unused in estimation. By definition this remainder is

$$(I_q - P)V^{-1/2}E[f(x_t,\theta_0)] = 0 \tag{4–5}$$

and this equation contains what Hansen termed the *overidentifying restrictions* in his original article.

This decomposition has fundamental implications for two statistics which play a central role in hypothesis testing. By definition, the identifying restrictions are imposed in the sample to obtain $\widehat{\theta}_T$. It is therefore not surprising that the function of the data in these restrictions determines the asymptotic distribution of the estimator. It can be shown that

$$T^{1/2}(\widehat{\theta}_T - \theta_0) = -(M'M)^{-1}M'V^{-1/2}T^{1/2}f_T(\theta_0) + o_p(1) \tag{4–6}$$

and so $MT^{1/2}(\widehat{\theta}-\theta_0)$ is asymptotically equivalent to $-PV^{-1/2}T^{1/2}f_T(\theta_0)$. Notice also that (4–6) implies

$$T^{1/2}(\widehat{\theta} - \theta_0) \overset{\text{d}}{\to} N\left(0,(M'M)^{-1}\right)\,.$$

The other statistic of interest is the sample moment condition, $f_T(\widehat{\theta}_T)$. These sample moments are in fact the the sample analog to the function of the data in the overidentifying restrictions because using (4–3) we have

$$(I_q - \widehat{P})V_T^{-1/2}f_T(\widehat{\theta}_T) = V_T^{-1/2}f_T(\widehat{\theta}_T)\,. \tag{4–7}$$

This means that $Q_T(\widehat{\theta}_T)$ measures how far the data are from satisfying the overidentifying restrictions in the sample. Given this structure it is not surprising to discover that the asymptotic distribution of these sample moments is determined by the function of the data in the overidentifying restrictions. Since $\widehat{P}$ converges in probability to P, it follows that from (4–7)

$$V_T^{-1/2} T^{1/2} f_T(\widehat{\theta}_T) = (I_q - P) V^{-1/2} T^{1/2} f_T(\theta_0) + o_p(1) \qquad (4\text{–}8)$$

and so

$$V_T^{-1/2} T^{1/2} f_T(\widehat{\theta}_T) \xrightarrow{d} N(0, I_q - P). \qquad (4\text{–}9)$$

One final aspect needs to be noted: the decomposition is orthogonal because of the projection matrix structure. This implies the asymptotic covariance of the two statistics is zero because from (4–6) and (4–8)

$$\lim_{T \to \infty} Cov[T^{1/2}(\widehat{\theta}_T - \theta_0), T^{1/2} f_T(\widehat{\theta}_T)] = (M'M)^{-1} M'(I_q - P) = 0 \qquad (4\text{–}10)$$

and hence the two statistics are asymptotically independent. This property plays an important role in our discussion.

4.2 Testing Hypotheses About $E[f(x_t, \theta_0)]$

The population moment condition in (4–1) is derived from the set of assumptions which make up the underlying economic and or statistical model. By their nature, these assumptions may or may not be correct, and so it is important to assess whether (4–1) is consistent with the data. For reasons that will become apparent, it is most convenient to state this hypothesis formally as[4]

$$H_0 : V^{-1/2} E[f(x_t, \theta_0)] = 0. \qquad (4\text{–}11)$$

Using the decomposition described above it is clear that $H_0 = H_0^I \cap H_0^O$, where

$$H_0^I : P V^{-1/2} E[f(x_t, \theta_0)] = 0$$
$$H_0^O : (I_q - P) V^{-1/2} E[f(x_t, \theta_0)] = 0.$$

---

[4] Since V is positive definite by assumption, $V^{-1/2}$ is nonsingular and hence (4–1) and (4–11) are equivalent.

Our earlier discussion implies that it is not possible to test H_0^I because the sample analog to the identifying restrictions are automatically satisfied by the estimated sample moments. However, H_0^O can be tested because the overidentifying restrictions are not imposed during estimation. *Hansen* [1982] proposes testing this null hypothesis using the statistic

$$J_T = T\, Q_T(\widehat{\theta}_T)$$

and shows that it converges to a χ^2_{q-p} distribution under H_0^O. This result can be derived heuristically by using (4–1) and (4–11) to deduce that

$$J_T \overset{A}{\sim} z_q'(I_q - P)'(I_q - P)z_q = z_q'(I - P)z_q, \qquad (4\text{–}12)$$

where $z_q \sim N(0, I_q)$. The quoted distribution then follows directly from (4–12), for example, see *Judge et al.* [1985, p. 943.].

This statistic is known as the "overidentifying restrictions test". It has become a standard diagnostic for models estimated by GMM and is routinely calculated in most computer packages. Its name reflects the focus of the statistic and it is instructive to investigate its properties more formally using a local power analysis. To this end, we introduce the following sequences of local alternatives to H_0^I and H_0^O

$$H_A^I : P V^{-1/2} E[f(x_t, \theta_0)] = T^{-1/2} P\, \eta_I = T^{-1/2}\mu_I$$
$$H_A^O :[I_q - P]V^{-1/2} E[f(x_t, \theta_0)] = T^{-1/2}[I_q - P]\eta_O = T^{-1/2}\mu_O$$

in which $\mu_I \neq 0, \mu_O \neq 0$. Notice that it is always possible to decompose $V^{-1/2}E[f(x_t, \theta_0)]$ into

$$V^{-1/2}E[f(x_t, \theta_0)] =$$
$$P V^{-1/2}E[f(x_t, \theta_0)] + (I_q - P)V^{-1/2}E[f(x_t, \theta_0)] \tag{4–13}$$

and so, using (4–13), H_A^I and H_A^O translate directly into sequences of alternatives to $V^{-1/2}E[f(x_t, \theta_0)] = 0$.

First, we verify that J_T has power against violations of the overidentifying restrictions. It is pedagogically convenient to treat the two types of violations separately and so we also assume that the identifying restrictions are satisfied for this part of the discussion, *i.e.*, the data satisfy $H_0^I \cap H_A^O$. In this case it follows from (4–13) that

$$T^{1/2} f_T(\widehat{\theta}_T) \overset{d}{\to} N\big((I_q - P)\eta_O, I_q - P \big)$$

and so

$$J_T \overset{A}{\sim} (z_q + \eta_O)'(I_q - P)(z_q + \eta_O) = \chi^2_{q-p}(\mu'_O \mu_O).$$

Since $\mu'_O \mu_O > 0$, J_T has power against this alternative. Now consider what happens if the overidentifying restrictions are satisfied but the identifying restrictions are not, *i.e.*, $H^I_A \cap H^O_0$. Under this sequence of alternatives, it follows from (4–8) and (4–13) that

$$T^{1/2} f_T(\widehat{\theta}_T) \overset{A}{\sim} N\left((I_q - P)P\eta_I,\ I_q - P\right).$$

However, since $(I_q - P)P = 0$, the mean of this limiting distribution is zero and so J_T converges to a χ^2_{q-p} distribution. This means the statistic has the same distribution under H^O_0 regardless of whether H^I_0 or H^I_A holds, and so has no power to discriminate between the latter two hypotheses.

If H^O_0 can be rejected then the more general hypothesis H_0 can also be rejected. However, as we have just seen, the failure to reject H^O_0 does not imply the validity of H_0 because H^I_0 may be violated. In view of this structure, it is important to understand more about the consequences of violations of H^I_0.[5] Given their nature, it would be anticipated that violations of the identifying restrictions effect the parameter estimator in some way. In fact, using similar analysis to before, it follows from (4–6) that under $H^I_A \cap H^O_0$

$$T^{1/2}(\widehat{\theta} - \theta_0) \overset{A}{\sim} N\left(-(M'M)^{-1}M'\eta_I, (M'M)^{-1}\right)$$

and so the asymptotic distribution of $\widehat{\theta}_T$ is biased away from θ_0.[6] It is easily verified using (4–6) that the asymptotic distribution in of $\widehat{\theta}_T$ is uneffected by whether the data satisfy H^O_0 or H^O_A; so it is only local violations of the identifying restrictions which cause this bias. In one sense, these are the types of violation which are of most concern because they effect inferences about the parameters. However, it is an inevitable consequence of their imposition during estimation that they cannot be tested. The only hope is to examine the overidentifying restrictions for any evidence of model misspecification, but clearly caution must be exercised in the interpretation of an insignificant statistic.

---

[5] Many of the points made in this paragraph are qualitatively similar to those made by *Newey* [1985a]. However, Newey does not explicitly invoke the decomposition into identifying and overidentifying restrictions.

[6] However note that the sequence of alternatives is carefully constructed so that $\widehat{\theta}_T$ is still consistent for θ_0.

If (4–1) can be rejected, then this may be because some or all of the elements of $E[f(x_t, \theta_0)]$ are nonzero. In many cases different elements of (4–1) refer to different aspects of the model, and in some cases there may be a priori information which indicates the misspecification is confined to certain elements of (4–1). In these circumstances it may be useful to test whether the data are consistent with this pattern of misspecification. This is the topic of the next section.

4.3 Testing Hypotheses About Subsets of $E[f(x_t, \theta_0)]$

To present methods for testing hypotheses about subsets of the population moment condition, it is useful to define the following partitions of θ_0 and $f(.)$. Let $\theta_0' = (\theta_{01}', \theta_{02}')$ where θ_{0i} is $(p_i \times 1)$, and $f(x_t, \theta_0)' = [f_1(x_t, \theta_{01})', f_2(x_t, \theta_0)']$ where $f_i(.)$ is $(q_i \times 1)$.

As with the previous section, we begin with a formal statement of the null and alternative hypotheses, and then consider the extent to which various statistics achieve this goal. This null hypothesis is

$$H_0^S : \ E[f_1(x_t, \theta_{01})] = 0 \quad \text{and} \quad E[f_2(x_t, \theta_0)] = 0$$

and the alternative is

$$H_A^S : \ E[f_1(x_t, \theta_{01})] = 0 \quad \text{and} \quad E[f_2(x_t, \theta_0)] = T^{-1/2}\mu_2 \,,$$

where for convenience we have stated the H_A^S as a local alternative. Two features of this specification should be noted. First, the veracity of $E[f_1(x_t, \theta_{01})] = 0$ is maintained under both null and alternative; so the potential misspecification is confined to $E[f_2(x_t, \theta_0)]$. Second, this framework allows for the possibility that the maintained moment conditions, $E[f_1(x_t, \theta_{01})] = 0$, only depend on part of the parameter vector.

Using the decomposition described in Section 4.1, it is seen that a violation of $E[f_2(x_t, \theta_0)] = 0$ can impact on the identifying and/or overidentifying restrictions. In fact, all the statistics proposed for testing H_0^S versus H_A^S are actually based on just one of these components. We begin by considering tests which focus on the overidentifying restrictions. To motivate these statistics, it is useful to briefly abstract to a world in which θ_0 is known. If $f_T(.)$ is partitioned in the same way as $f(.)$ then it follows from the Central Limit Theorem that its asymptotic distribution under H_A^S is

$$\begin{bmatrix} T^{1/2} f_{T1}(\theta_{01}) \\ T^{1/2} f_{T2}(\theta_0) \end{bmatrix} \xrightarrow{d} N\left(\begin{bmatrix} 0_{q_1} \\ \mu_2 \end{bmatrix}, \begin{bmatrix} V_{11} & V_{12} \\ V_{21} & V_{22} \end{bmatrix} \right),$$

where 0_{q_1} is a $(q_1 \times 1)$ vector of zeros and V_{ij} define the obvious partition of V. This implies the conditional distribution of $T^{1/2} f_{T2}(\theta_0)$ given $T^{1/2} f_{T1}(\theta_{01})$ is also normal and can be most conveniently expressed as

$$T^{1/2} f_{T2}(\theta_0) - V_{21} V_{11}^{-1} T^{1/2} f_{T1}(\theta_{01}) \xrightarrow{d} N\left(\mu_2, V_{22} - V_{21} V_{11}^{-1} V_{12} \right).$$
(4–14)

If θ_0 was known then the statistic on the left hand side of (4–14) is the obvious function of the data to use for inference because its mean is zero under H_0^S and μ_2 under H_A^S. However, θ_0 is unknown in practice, and so some adjustment needs to be made. *Newey* [1985a] proposes substituting $\hat{\theta}_T$ for θ_0 and then basing inference on

$$n_T = T^{1/2} f_{T2}(\hat{\theta}_T) - \hat{V}_{21} \hat{V}_{11}^{-1} T^{1/2} f_{T1}(\hat{\theta}_{T1}),$$

where $\hat{\theta}_T = (\hat{\theta}'_{T1}, \hat{\theta}'_{T2})$ has been partitioned conformably with θ_0 and $\hat{V}_{ij}$ is a consistent estimator of V_{ij}. The test statistic is

$$N_T = n_T' \hat{Q}_T^- n_T,$$

where $\hat{Q}_T$ is a consistent estimator of $Q = L(I_q - P)L'$, $L = [-V_{21} V_{11}^{-1}, I_{q_2}] V^{1/2}$ and A^- denotes a generalized inverse of a matrix A.[7] *Newey* [1985a] shows that N_T converges in distribution to χ_ν^2 distribution under H_0^S where $\nu_1 = rank(Q)$ and *Ahn* [1995] shows that $\nu_1 = q_2 - p_2$. Notice that ν_1 equals the degree to which θ_{02} is overidentified by $E[f_2(x_t, \theta_0)] = 0$ if θ_{01} is known.

In the previous section, it was shown that $T^{1/2} f_T(\hat{\theta}_T)$ actually captures the information in the overidentifying restrictions. Therefore, since N_T is based on this statistic, the implicit null hypothesis of N_T must involve only the overidentifying restrictions and not the population moment condition *per se*. This intuition can be more formally justified by observing that n_T can be rewritten as

$$n_T = [-\hat{V}_{21} \hat{V}_{11}^{-1}, I_{q_2}] T^{1/2} f_T(\hat{\theta}_T)$$

---

[7] There are many ways of constructing a generalized inverse but not all possess the property that $p \lim_{T \to \infty} \hat{Q}^- = Q^-$. *Newey* [1985a] discusses conditions under which this property holds and these are assumed to apply here.

and so under both H_0^S and H_A^S it follows that

$$n_T = L[I_q - P]V^{-1/2}T^{1/2}f_T(\theta_0) + o_p(1).$$

Therefore, the implicit null hypothesis of the test is

$$Q^- L[I_q - P]V^{-1/2}E[f(x_t, \theta_0)] = 0, \qquad (4\text{--}15)$$

which clearly involves a linear combination of the overidentifying restrictions. Although perhaps not readily apparent from (4–15), it can be shown after a lot of algebra that this implicit null hypothesis is violated by any sequence of alternatives in H_A^S which also violate H_0^O; see *Ahn* [1995]. However, it is clear from (4–15) that the statistic has no power against alternatives which violate the identifying restrictions alone.

The form of the statistic, N_T, is very useful for developing the intuition behind the tests but is a little cumbersome to construct in practice. Fortunately, *Ahn* [1995] shows this statistic is asymptotically equivalent to a more convenient statistic which had been independently proposed by *Eichenbaum, Hansen, and Singleton* [1988]. This statistic involves two estimations and is similar in spirit to the likelihood ratio statistic from maximum likelihood theory. The first estimation is based on the full set of moment conditions in (4–1). The second involves the estimation based on only the population moment conditions which are maintained to be true under both H_0^S and H_A^S. *Eichenbaum, Hansen, and Singleton's* [1988] statistic is then T times the difference in these two estimated GMM minimands, namely

$$C_T = T\{Q_T(\hat{\theta}_T) - Q_{1T}(\tilde{\theta}_{1T})\},$$

where $\tilde{\theta}_{1T}$ is the value of θ_1 which minimizes

$$Q_{1T} = f_{T1}(\theta_1)'\hat{V}_{11}^{-1}f_{T1}(\theta_1).$$

The asymptotic equivalence of C_T and N_T holds under both H_0^S and H_A^S, and so the previous comments about the implicit null hypothesis of N_T apply equally to C_T.[8]

The statistics N_T and C_T offer a method for the detection of $E[f_2(x_t, \theta_0)] \neq 0$ via its impact on the overidentifying restrictions.

---

[8] *Newey* [1985a] also proposes another asymptotically equivalent version of these statistics which can be used if $p_2 = 0$. It is similar in construction to N_T but is evaluated at $\tilde{\theta}_{1T}$. However for brevity, we refer the interested reader to *Newey* [1985a] for the exact details.

It would clearly be desirable to develop complementary statistics for testing H_0^S which are sensitive to violations in the identifying restrictions. In view of our earlier comments, this might seem impossible, but there is a crucial difference here which makes it possible under certain conditions. To motivate these conditions, we briefly reconsider testing H_0^I against H_A^I. The problem there was that we tried to test the information upon which estimation was based using the estimator obtained from that information; and this cannot be done because of the fundamental relationship between the two. However, if $p_2 = 0$ and $q_1 \geq p$ then we can use $E[f_1(x_t, \theta_0)] = 0$ to provide an alternative estimator of θ_0, $\tilde{\theta}_T$ say, which does not satisfy the identifying restrictions in (4–3) by construction. Inference can then be based on

$$\tilde{I}_T = \tilde{P} f_T(\tilde{\theta}_T), \qquad (4\text{–}16)$$

where $\tilde{P} = \widetilde{M}(\widetilde{M}'\widetilde{M})^{-1}\widetilde{M}$ and $\widetilde{M} = \tilde{V}_T^{-1/2} F_T(\tilde{\theta}_T)$ and $\tilde{V}_T$ is a consistent estimator of V based on $\tilde{\theta}_T$. Intuition suggests that if H_0^S is satisfied then $\tilde{I}_T$ should be zero allowing for sampling error. The null hypothesis of such a test is[9]

$$H_0^{SI} : \; PV^{-1/2}E[f(x_t, \theta_0)] - M(M_1'M_1)^{-1}M_1'V_{11}^{-1/2}E[f_1(x_t, \theta_0)] = 0,$$

where $M_1 = V_{11}^{-1/2}F_1$ and $F_1 = E[\partial f_1(x_t, \theta_0)/\partial \theta']$. Therefore if $E[f_1(x_t, \theta_0)] = 0$ then the test is clearly sensitive to alternatives which satisfy both H_A^S and H_A^I. Rather than formally derive a statistic based directly on $\tilde{I}_T$, it is more convenient to develop a transformed version which can be conveniently expressed in terms of the parameter estimators from two separate estimations. To do this, notice that the projection matrix structure implies the information in $\tilde{I}_T$ is equivalent to the information in

$$h_T = (\tilde{F}_T'\tilde{V}_T^{-1}\tilde{F}_T)^{-1}\tilde{F}_T'\tilde{V}_T^{-1}f_T(\tilde{\theta}_T).$$

Newey [1985a] shows $h_T = T^{1/2}(\hat{\theta}_T - \tilde{\theta}_T) + o_p(1)$ under both H_0^S and H_A^S and so it is possible to test H_0^{SI} using the *Hausman* [1978] type statistic

$$H_T = T(\hat{\theta}_T - \tilde{\theta}_T)\,\widehat{V}_h^-\,(\hat{\theta}_T - \tilde{\theta}_T),$$

where $\widehat{V}_h$ is a consistent estimator of

$$V_h = (F_1'V_{11}^{-1}F_1)^{-1} - (F'V^{-1}F)^{-1}.$$

---

[9] This follows from an application of the Mean Value Theorem to $f_T(\tilde{\theta}_T)$ around θ_0 in (4–16) and using an analogous expression to (4–7) for $\tilde{\theta} - \theta_0$.

Newey [1985a] proves that H_T converges to a $\chi^2_{\nu_2}$ distribution under H_0^S where $\nu_2 = rank(V_h)$. In most cases, this rank is equal to p and so the generalized inverse can be replaced by the inverse; however this need not always be the case.

One final comment is in order. All the statistics in this section are designed to test for violations of $E[f_2(x_t, \theta_0)] = 0$ conditional on the validity of $E[f_1(x_t, \theta_0)] = 0$. However, if the latter is untrue, then this may cause the statistic in question to be significant even though $E[f_2(x_t, \theta_0)]$ is actually zero.

4.4   Testing Hypotheses About the Parameter Vector

It is often the case that a particular aspect of an economic theory translates into a set of restrictions on the parameter vector of the econometric model. So the veracity of the theory can be assessed by testing whether the restrictions in question are satisfied by the data. This section describes various methods for performing this type of inference.

We adopt the general framework in which it is desired to test

$$H_0^R : \ r(\theta_0) = 0 \qquad \text{versus} \qquad H_A^R : \ r(\theta_0) = T^{-1/2}\mu_R,$$

where $r(.)$ is a $(s \times 1)$ vector of continuous differentiable functions denoted by $R(\theta) = \partial r(\theta)/\partial \theta'$. Once again, we have expressed the alternative in a local form for brevity; it is assumed that $\mu_R \neq 0$. The mapping $r : \Re^p \to \Re^s$ must also satisfy certain other restrictions. First, the number of restrictions, s, cannot exceed the number of parameters.[10] Second, the restrictions must form a coherent set of equations so that given the value of $p - s$ elements of θ_0 it is possible to solve uniquely for the remaining s values using $r(\theta_0) = 0$. This property is guaranteed by the Implicit Function Theorem if the rank of $R(\theta_0)$ is s, for example see *Apostol* [1974, p. 374].

Newey and West [1987] develop the theory for testing this type of null hypothesis. They propose three main statistics which

---

[10] It takes at most p unique restrictions to define the the value of the p parameters. So if, $s > p$ then either certain restrictions are redundant or the system $r(\theta_0) = 0$ is inconsistent and hence has no solution for θ_0.

can be viewed as extensions to the GMM framework of the Wald, Likelihood Ratio (LR) and Lagrange Multiplier (LM) tests from maximum likelihood theory.[11] To facilitate the presentation, it is useful to define unrestricted and restricted estimators of θ_0. The unrestricted estimator is just $\widehat{\theta}_T$ defined earlier. The restricted estimator is the value of θ which minimizes $Q_T(\theta)$ subject to $r(\theta) = 0$; this is denoted $\bar{\theta}_T$. It is assumed that both these minimizations use the weighting matrix V_T^{-1}. We now introduce the three statistics in turn.

The *Wald* test examines whether the unrestricted estimator, $\widehat{\theta}_T$, satisfies the restrictions with due allowance for sampling error. The statistic is

$$W_T = Tr(\widehat{\theta}_T)' \left[R(\widehat{\theta}_T)\,(\widehat{M'M})^{-1} R(\widehat{\theta}_T)' \right]^{-1} r(\widehat{\theta}_T)\,.$$

The D or *LR-type* test examines the impact on the GMM minimand of the imposition of the restrictions. This statistic is

$$D = T[Q_T(\bar{\theta}_T) - Q_T(\widehat{\theta}_T)]\,.$$

Finally, the *LM* test examines whether the restricted estimator, $\bar{\theta}_T$, satisfies the first order conditions from the unrestricted estimation. This statistic is:

$$LM_T = T\, f_T(\bar{\theta}_T)' V_T^{-1/2'} \, \bar{P}\, V_T^{-1/2} f_T(\bar{\theta}_T)\,,$$

where $\bar{P} = \bar{M}(\bar{M}'\bar{M})^{-1}\bar{M}'$ and $\bar{M} = V_T^{-1/2} F_T(\bar{\theta}_T)$.

Newey and West [1987] show that all three statistics are asymptotically equivalent under both H_0^R and H_A^R: under H_0^R the statistics converge to a χ_s^2 distribution and under H_A^R to a $\chi_s^2(\delta_R)$ where

$$\delta_R = \mu_R' \left(R(\theta_0)(M'M)^{-1} R(\theta_0)) \right)^{-1} \mu_R > 0\,.$$

So the statistics have power against the alternative for which they are designed. In view of their equivalence, some other criteria must be used to choose between the three. One such criterion is computational burden, although this is less of a concern now than it once was. The D statistic is more burdensome because it requires two estimations, whereas the Wald and LM only require one. Sometimes the unrestricted estimation is easier and sometimes not, it all depends on the model in question and the nature of $r(.)$.

---

[11] *Newey and West* [1987] also analyze a minimum Chi–squared statistic, but this is rarely used and so is omitted here.

However, the Wald test has two disadvantages which should be mentioned. First, it is not invariant to a reparameterization of the model or the restrictions. This means that it is possible to rewrite the model and restrictions in a logically consistent way, but end up with a different Wald statistic.[12] Neither of the other two tests have this problem.[13] The second disadvantage is that the Wald statistic tends to be less well approximated by the χ_s^2 distribution in finite samples than the other two statistics, see, for example, simulation evidence reported in *Gallant* [1987].

It is possible to re–express this hypothesis in terms of the identifying restrictions associated with GMM estimation and thereby gain useful insights into the interpretation of a significant statistic. To set up this analysis it is useful to return to the identifying restrictions for the unrestricted estimation given in (4–4). *Sowell* [1996a] observes that these restrictions state that the projection of $V^{-1/2}E[f(x_t, \theta_0)]$ onto the column space of M, $C(\mathcal{M})$, is zero. We now show that H_0^R can be interpreted as a hypothesis about a sub–space of $C(\mathcal{M})$. To do this notice that if H_0^R is true then the Implicit Function Theorem implies that the population moment condition can be written as

$$E[f(x_t, g(\psi_0))] = 0 \qquad (4\text{--}17)$$

where ψ_0 is a $p-s$ vector which satisfies $\theta_0 = g(\psi_0)$. Now, if (4–17) is treated as a basis for GMM estimation of ψ_0 then the associated identifying restrictions imply the projection of $V^{-1/2}E[f(x_t, \theta_0)]$ onto the columnspace of $M_\psi = V^{-1/2}E[\partial f(x_t, g(\psi_0))/\partial \psi']$ is zero. However, since

$$M_\psi = M\left\{\partial g(\psi_0)/\partial \psi'\right\},$$

it follows that the column space of M_ψ, $C(\mathcal{M}_\psi)$, is of dimension $p-s$ and $C(\mathcal{M}_\psi) \subset C(\mathcal{M})$.

This interpretation is useful because it emphasizes an important aspect of H_0^R: it is a hypothesis about the projection of $V^{-1/2}E[f(x_t, \theta_0)]$ onto $C(\mathcal{M}_\psi)$ conditional on its projection onto $\mathcal{C}$ being zero. So the hypothesis may be rejected because the identifying restrictions are satisfied at θ_0 but $r(\theta_0) \neq 0$ – or it may be rejected when $r(\theta_0) = 0$ because the identifying restrictions

---

[12] For example the restriction $\theta_{0i} = 0$ can also be rewritten as $\theta_{0i}^k = 0$ for any finite positive integer k.

[13] See *Davidson and MacKinnon* [1993 p.467-469] for a useful discussion of this issue and some examples.

are not satisfied at the true parameter value, θ_0. This emphasizes the importance of using the tests in Sections 4.2 and 4.3 to assess the model specification before performing inference about the parameters. It also highlights that W_T, D_T and LM_T are functions of the identifying restrictions and so from (4–10) are asymptotically independent of the previous statistics based on the overidentifying restrictions under H_0 or any of the local alternatives considered above.

4.5 Testing Hypotheses About Structural Stability

So far, it has been assumed that if (4–1) is violated then the value of $E[f(x_t, \theta_0)]$ is the same for all t. This property is refered to as *structural stability*. However, (4–1) is also violated if $E[f(x_t, \theta_0)] \neq 0$ for only part of the sample; such behavior is termed *structural instability*. This section reviews various methods for testing structural stability based on GMM estimators.

The null hypothesis for structural stability tests is very simple: it states that some aspect of the model has remained constant over the sample. The alternative is more difficult, however, because it must specify how the model changes. In the GMM literature, attention has focused almost exclusively on the case where the instability involves a discrete change at a single point in the sample known as the "breakpoint".[14] To present the null and alternative hypotheses, it is necessary to introduce the following notation. Let π be a constant defined on $(0, 1)$ and let πT denote the potential breakpoint at which some aspect of the model changes. For our purposes here, it is convenient to divide the original sample into two sub–samples. Sub-sample 1 consists of the observations before the breakpoint, namely $T_1 = \{1, 2, \ldots, [\pi T]\}$, where [.] denotes the integer part, and sub–sample 2 consists of the observations after the breakpoint, $T_2 = \{[\pi T] + 1, \ldots T\}$. This breakpoint may be treated as known or unknown in the construction of the tests. If it is known, then the breakpoint is specified a priori by the researcher and it

---

[14] *Sowell* [1996a] provides a general framework for considering the design of tests for structural stability. We briefly discuss other forms of instability at the end of this section.

is only desired to test for instability at this point alone.[15] If the breakpoint is unknown, then the null is the broader hypothesis that there is no instability at any point in the sample. It is easily imagined that tests for the two cases are closely related. We begin our discussion with the simpler case in which the breakpoint is known because this provides a more convenient setting for introducing the statistics and contrasting their properties. We then consider the extension of these techniques to the unknown breakpoint case.

Andrews and Fair [1988] propose tests for "parameter variation". Their statistics are most easily presented by introducing the augmented population moment condition:

$$E[g(x_t, \phi_0)] = \begin{bmatrix} d_t(\pi)f(x_t, \theta_1) \\ (1 - d_t(\pi))f(x_t, \theta_2) \end{bmatrix} = 0 \qquad (4\text{--}18)$$

where $d_t(\pi)$ is a dummy variable which equals one when $t \leq \pi T$ and $\phi_0' = (\theta_1', \theta_2')$. This population moment condition is more general than (4–1) because it allows for the possibility that $E[f(x_t, \theta)] = 0$ is satisfied at different parameter values before and after the breakpoint. However, it also contains (4–1) as a special case because if $\theta_1 = \theta_2$ then the moment condition is satisfied at the same parameter value throughout the sample. This restriction is most easily tested by using (4–18) as a basis for GMM estimation of ϕ_0 and then calculating the Wald, LR– or LM–type statistics from the previous section for the hypothesis: $[I_p, -I_p]\phi_0 = 0_p$. Whichever version is chosen, it has a limiting χ_p^2 distribution if the restriction holds. For example, this route yields the Wald statistic

$$W_T(\pi) = T\left(\widehat{\theta}_1(\pi) - \widehat{\theta}_2(\pi)\right) \widehat{V}_W(\pi)^{-1} \left(\widehat{\theta}_1(\pi) - \widehat{\theta}_2(\pi)\right),$$

where $\widehat{\theta}_i(\pi)$ is the two step GMM estimator based on the sub–sample T_i,

$$\widehat{V}_W(\pi) = [\widehat{M}_1(\pi)'\widehat{M}_1(\pi)]^{-1}/\pi + [\widehat{M}_2(\pi)'\widehat{M}_2(\pi)]^{-1}/(1 - \pi),$$

$\widehat{M}_i(\pi) = \widehat{V}_i(\pi)^{-1/2} \sum_{t \in T_i} \partial f(x_t, \widehat{\theta}_i(\pi))/\partial \theta'$ and $\widehat{V}_i(\pi)$ is a consistent estimator of V based on T_i.

Ghysels and Hall [1990b] take a different approach. They focus on testing the null hypothesis

$$H_0 : E[f(x_t, \theta_0)] = 0 \qquad t \in T_1 \cap T_2$$

---

[15] For example, *Ghysels and Hall* [1990a] investigate whether the change in operating procedures by the Federal Reserve in October 1978 caused instability in certain asset pricing models.

against the (local) alternative

$$H_A^1 : E[f(x_t, \theta_0)] = 0 \quad t \in T_1 \quad \text{and}$$
$$E[f(x_t, \theta_0)] = T^{-1/2}\mu_2 \quad t \in T_2,$$

where $\mu_2 \neq 0$. Their statistic is based on evaluating the sample moments from T_2 at $\hat{\theta}_1(\pi)$. Under H_0, this estimated sample moment should converge in probablity to zero. This approach leads to the Predictive test statistic

$$PR_T(\pi) = T^{-1/2} \sum_{t \in T_2} f(x_t, \hat{\theta}(\pi))' \, \hat{V}_{PR}^{-1} T^{-1/2} \sum_{t \in T_2} f(x_t, \hat{\theta}(\pi)),$$

where $\hat{V}_{PR}$ is a covariance matrix defined in *Ghysels and Hall* [1990b]. *Ghysels and Hall* [1990b] show that this statistic converges to a χ_q^2 distribution under H_0.[16] This limiting distribution has more degrees of freedom than $W_T(\pi)$ and so $PR_T(\pi)$ is clearly testing something more than parameter variation.

The difference between the two types of tests is best understood by recasting the hypotheses in terms of the identifying and overidentifying restrictions. Since the identifying restrictions are imposed in estimation, there are always parameter values which satisfy them in each of the two-subsamples. So the identifying restrictions are structurally stable if they are satisfied by the same parameter value in each sub–sample. This null is formally stated as

$$H_0^I(\pi) : P V^{-1/2} E[f(x_t, \theta_0)] = 0, \qquad t \in T_1$$
$$P V^{-1/2} E[f(x_t, \theta_0)] = 0, \qquad t \in T_2.$$

The overidentifying restrictions are stable if they hold before and after the breakpoint. This is formally stated as $H_0^O(\pi) = H_0^{O1}(\pi) \cap H_0^{O2}(\pi)$ where

$$H_0^{O1}(\pi) : [I_q - P_1] V_1^{-1/2} E[f(x_t, \theta_1)] = 0, \qquad t \in T_1$$
$$H_0^{O2}(\pi) : [I_q - P_2] V_2^{-1/2} E[f(x_t, \theta_2)] = 0, \qquad t \in T_2,$$

where $P_i = M_i(M_i'M_i)^{-1}M_i'$, $M_i = V_i^{-1/2}E[F_t(\theta_i)]$ and V_i is the analog to V defined on T_i for $i = 1, 2$. Notice that $H_0^{O1}(\pi)$ and $H_0^{O2}(\pi)$ allow for the possibility that the overidentifying restrictions are satisfied at different values. By the very nature of the

---

[16] *Ghysels and Hall* [1990a] propose a structural stability test based along a similar principle to the *Eichenbaum, Hansen, and Singleton* [1988] statistic in the previous section, but *Ahn* [1995] shows this is asymptotically equivalent to the Predictive test; however their finite sample properties may be different.

decomposition, it is clear that any instability must be reflected in a violation of at least one of the three hypotheses: $H_0^I(\pi)$, $H_0^{O1}(\pi)$ or $H_0^{O2}(\pi)$. Therefore these three hypotheses provide a framework for contrasting the properties of the above tests. It is easily seen that $H_0^I(\pi)$ is equivalent to the null hypothesis of no parameter variation and so the Wald, LR– or LM–type statistics are testing this hypothesis. However, the orthogonality between the identifying and overidentifying restrictions means that these statistics have no power against local alternatives to either $H_0^{O1}(\pi)$ or $H_0^{O2}(\pi)$. In contrast *Ghysels, Guay, and Hall* [1997] show that the Predictive test has power against local alternatives to both $H_0^I(\pi)$ and $H_0^{O2}(\pi)$, and this accounts for the difference in the degrees of freedom mentioned above.

Since instability can manifest itself in a violation of any one these three components, it is clear that both the parameter variation and Predictive tests have important weaknesses as general diagnostics for structural instability. To address these problems, *Hall and Sen* [1996a] propose testing the stability of the identifying and overidentifying restrictions separately. As we have seen, the Wald test[17] can be used to test $H_0^I(\pi)$. The stability of the overidentifying restrictions can be tested using

$$O_T(\pi) \;=\; O1_T(\pi) \,+\, O2_T(\pi)\,,$$

where $O1_T(\pi)$ and $O2_T(\pi)$ are the overidentifying restrictions tests based on the sub–samples T_1 and T_2 respectively. *Hall and Sen* [1996a] show that under $O_T(\pi)$ converges to a $\chi^2_{2(q-p)}$ under this null hypothesis. The orthogonality of the decomposition ensures the tests have some useful properties. *Hall and Sen* [1996a] show that $W_T(\pi)$ has power against local alternatives to $H_0^I(\pi)$, denoted $H_A^I(\pi)$, but none against local alternatives to $H_0^O(\pi)$, denoted $H_A^O(\pi)$. Whereas, $O_T(\pi)$ has power against $H_A^O(\pi)$ but none against $H_A^I(\pi)$. Furthermore these two statistics are asymptotically independent and so can be used together to diagnose the source of the instability. This approach clearly remedies the weakness of using the Wald test alone or the Predictive test. *Hall and Sen* [1996a] show that it has the added advantage of allowing the researcher to distinguish between two scenarios of interest. The first is one in which the instability is confined to the parameters alone; this case

---

[17] The LR– or LM–type statistics can also be used without effecting any of following discussion.

is consistent with a violation of $H_0^I(\pi)$ but the validity of $H_0^O(\pi)$. The second scenario is one in which the instability is not confined to the parameters alone but effects other aspects of the model; this would imply a violation of $H_0^O(\pi)$ and most likely $H_0^I(\pi)$ as well.

We now consider the extension of these methods to the unknown breakpoint case. Once again, it is beneficial to treat the hypotheses about the stability of the identifying and overidentifying restrictions separately.[18] So we begin by describing statistics for testing the composite null hypothesis that $H_0^I(\pi)$ for all $\pi \in \Pi \subset (0,1)$.[19] The construction is a natural extension of the fixed breakpoint methods. Now $W_T(\pi)$ is calculated for each possible π to produce a sequence of statistics indexed by π, and inference is based on some function of this sequence. This function is chosen to maximize power against a local alternative in which a weighting distribution is used to indicate the relative importance of departures from $H_0^I(\pi)$ in different directions at different breakpoints. A general framework for the derivation of these optimal tests is provided by *Andrews and Ploberger* [1994] in the context of maximum likelihood estimators and this is generalized to the GMM framework by *Sowell* [1996a]. One drawback with this approach is that a different choice of weighting distribution leads to a different optimal statistic; however, three choices have received particular attention. To facilitate their presentation, we define the following local alternative to $H_0^I(\pi)$,

$$H_A^I(\pi) : PV^{-1/2}E[f(x_t, \theta_0)] = T^{-1/2}\mu_{I1}, \qquad t \in T_1$$
$$PV^{-1/2}E[f(x_t, \theta_0)] = T^{-1/2}\mu_{I2}, \qquad t \in T_2.$$

It is assumed that $\mu_{I1} = 0$ and a weighting distribution is specified for (μ_{I2}, π).[20] If the conditional distribution of μ_{I2} given π is of the form $rL(\pi)U$ where r is a scalar, $L(\pi)$ is a particular matrix and U is the uniform distribution on the unit sphere in $\Re^p$ then *Andrews*

---

[18] *Ghysels, Guay, and Hall* [1997] develop similar extensions for the Predictive test but in view of our previous comments about its weaknesses, we do not describe these here.

[19] In applications it is desireable for Π to be as wide as possible, but at the same time not too wide that asymptotic theory is a poor approximation in the sub–samples. For example, in applications to models of economic time series, it has become customary for $\Pi = (0.15, 0.85)$.

[20] For these tests of parameter variation, the roles of μ_{I1}, μ_{I2} can be interchanged.

and *Ploberger* [1995] show that for r sufficiently large the optimal statistic is

$$\text{Sup}\, W_T \;=\; \sup_{\pi \in \Pi}\{\, W_T(\pi)\,\}\,.$$

This statistic had been proposed earlier by *Andrews* [1993] who derives and tabulates the non–standard limiting distribution. The other two choices arise from a specification for the conditional distribution of η_{I2} given π as $N(0, c\Sigma_\pi)$, for some constant c. *Andrews and Ploberger* [1994] and *Sowell* [1996a] show that for a particular choice of Σ_π, the optimal statistic only depends on c and not Σ_π. So for convenience this choice is made and then attention has focussed on two values of c. If $c = 0$ then the optimal statistic takes the form

$$\text{Av}\, W_T \;=\; \int_\Pi W_T(\pi)\, dJ(\pi)\,,$$

where $J(\pi)$ defines the weighting distribution for the breakpoint over Π. If $c = \infty$ then the optimal statistic takes the form

$$\exp W_T \;=\; \log\left\{\int_\Pi \exp[0.5 W_T(\pi)]\, dJ(\pi)\right\}\,.$$

Andrews and Ploberger [1994] derive and tabulate the non–standard limiting distributions of $Av W_T$ and $\exp W_T$ under the assumption that $J(\pi)$ is a uniform distribution on Π.[21]

The same ideas can be used to construct tests of the null hypothesis that $H_0^O(\pi)$ holds for all $\pi \in \Pi$. However, this time the exact nature of the alternative is crucial. To show how, we must specify the following sequences of alternatives:

$$H_A^{O1}(\pi) : [I_q - P_1]\, V_1^{-1/2} E[f(x_t, \theta_1)] = T^{-1/2}\mu_{O1}, \qquad t \in T_1$$
$$H_A^{O2}(\pi) : [I_q - P_2]\, V_2^{-1/2} E[f(x_t, \theta_2)] = T^{-1/2}\mu_{O2}, \qquad t \in T_2\,.$$

Sowell [1996b] derives optimal tests for testing this null against an alternative in which the overidentifying restrictions are violated before but not after the breakpoint, *i.e.*, $H_A^{O1}(\pi) \cap H_0^{O2}(\pi)$, $\pi \in \Pi$. These statistics are based on the forward moving partial sums, $G_t^1 = T^{-1}\sum_{i=1}^t f(x_t, \hat{\theta}_T)$. Using similar kinds of weighting distributions on μ_{O1} to those described above, *Sowell* [1996b] derives statistics which involve the same types of functional. However, *Hall and Sen* [1996b] show that these statistics are sub–optimal against

---

[21] *Hansen* [1997] reports response surfaces which can be used to calculate p–values for all three versions of these tests.

an alternative in which the overidentifying restrictions are violated after instead of before the breakpoint, *i.e.,* $H_0^{O1}(\pi) \cap H_A^{O2}(\pi)$. *Hall and Sen* [1996b] derive the optimal tests in this case and they involve similar functionals but are based on the backward moving partial sums $G_t^2 = T^{-1} \sum_{i=t+1}^{T} f(x_t, \hat{\theta}_T)$. Typically, a researcher does not wish to pick either of these particular alternatives but is interested in the more general alternative in which the overidentifying restrictions may be violated before or after the breakpoint, *i.e.,* $\{H_A^{O1}(\pi) \cap H_0^{O2}(\pi)\} \cup \{H_0^{O1}(\pi) \cap H_A^{O2}(\pi)\}$ $\pi \in \Pi$. *Hall and Sen* [1996a] propose testing this hypothesis using the statistics

$$\text{Sup} \, O_T = \sup_{\pi \in \Pi} \{ O_T(\pi) \}$$

$$\text{Av} \, O_T = \int_{\Pi} O_T(\pi) \, dJ(\pi),$$

$$\exp O_T = \log \left\{ \int_{\Pi} \exp[0.5 O_T(\pi)] \, dJ(\pi) \right\}$$

and derive their limiting distributions under $H_0^O(\pi), \pi \in \Pi$; they also tabulate these distributions for the case where $J(\pi)$ is a uniform distribution.[22] *Hall and Sen* [1997a] simulate the distributions of all the above statistics for testing the stability of the overidentifying restrictions. This evidence indicates that the statistics based on $O_T(\pi)$ are more powerful unless there is strong *a priori* information about the side of the breakpoint on which the violation occurs.

Although these statistics are designed to test for a discrete change at a single point in the sample, they can all be shown to have non–trivial power against other forms of instability. One other specific case is briefly worth mentioning; this is where the true value of the parameter changes continually via a martingale difference sequence. In this case, *Hansen* [1990] shows that the LM statistic for parameter constancy is well approximated by AvW_T and so this statistic is likely have good power properties against this alternative as well.[23]

Finally, it should be noted that all these procedures rely on asymptotically large samples and so are unlikely to have good power properties against instability at the very beginning or end of the

---

[22] *Hall and Sen* [1997b] provide response surfaces for calculating *p*–values for all the unknown breakpoint versions of the test based on $O_T(\pi)$.

[23] *Hansen* [1990] also proposes a variation on this statistic. His analysis is motivated by earleir work due to *Nyblom* [1989] in the context of maximum likelihood estimators.

sample. *Dufour, Ghysels, and Hall* [1994] propose a Generalized Predictive test which can be applied in this situation. The null and alternative hypothesis are the same as the Predictive test except this time only T_1 need be asymptotically large and T_2 may be as small as one observation. The statistic is based on $\{f(x_t, \widehat{\theta}_1(\pi)),\ t \in T_2\}$ and not the sub–sample average. Since the focus is now the individual observations, it is not possible to use a conventional asymptotic analysis to deduce the distribution. One solution is to make a distributional assumption, but this is unattractive in most GMM settings. Therefore *Dufour, Ghysels, and Hall* [1994] consider various distribution free methods of approximating or bounding the p–value of their statistics.

4.6 Testing Non–nested Hypotheses

So far, we have concentrated on methods for testing hypotheses about population moment conditions or parameters within a particular model. However, in many cases more than one model has been advanced to explain a particular economic phenomenon and so it may become necessary to choose between them. Sometimes, one model is nested within the other in the sense that it can be obtained by imposing certain parameter restrictions. In this case the choice between them amounts to testing whether the data support the restrictions in question using the methods described in Section 4.4. Other times, one model is not a special case of the other and so they are said to be *non–nested*. There have been two main approaches to developing tests between non–nested models. One is based on creating a more general model which nests both candidate models as a special case; the other examines whether one model is capable of explaining the results in the other. Most of this literature has focused on regression models or models estimated by maximum likelihood. While these situations technically fall within the GMM framework, they do not possess its distinctive features and so are not covered here.[24] Instead, we focus on methods for discriminating between two non–nested Euler equation models. These models involve partially specified systems and so involve aspects unique to the GMM in its most general form.

---

[24] These techniques are well described in the recent comprehensive review by *Gourieroux and Monfort* [1994].

We consider the case where there are two competing models denoted $M1$ and $M2$. If $M1$ is true then the parameter vector and θ_1 and the data satisfy the Euler equation

$$E_1[u_1(x_t, \theta_1)|\Omega_{t-1}] = 0, \qquad (4\text{--}19)$$

where Ω_{t-1} is the information available at time $t-1$ and $E_1[.]$ denotes expectations under the assumption $M1$ is correct. For our purposes, it is sufficient to assume the Euler equation residual $u_1(x_t, \theta_1)$ is a scalar. From (4–19) it follows that the residual is orthogonal to any $(q_1 \times 1)$ vector $z_{1t} \in \Omega_{t-1}$, and this yields the population moment condition

$$E_1[z_{1t}u_1(x_t, \theta_1)] = 0. \qquad (4\text{--}20)$$

Using analogous definitions, $M2$ leads to the $(q_2 \times 1)$ population moment condition

$$E_2[z_{2t}u_2(x_t, \theta_2)] = 0, \qquad (4\text{--}21)$$

where again the Euler equation residual is taken to be a scalar. It is assumed that the two models are globally non–nested in the sense that one model is not a special case of the other.[25] Since both models can be subjected to the tests in Sections 4.2–4.4, there can only be a need to discriminate between them if both models pass all these diagnostics; so we assume this is the case.

As mentioned above there are two main strategies to developing non–nested hypothesis tests and each has been applied within the context of Euler equation models. *Singleton* [1985] proposes nesting the Euler equations of $M1$ and $M2$ within the Euler equation of a more general model. *Ghysels and Hall* [1990c] propose tests of whether one model can explain the results in another. We now describe these in turn.

Singleton's [1985] analysis begins with the observation that if $M1$ is false and its overidentifying restrictions test is insignificant then it must be because the test has poor power properties when $M2$ is true. Therefore, he proposes choosing the linear combination of the overidentifying restrictions which has the most power in the direction of $M2$. The problem is how to characterize this direction. *Singleton* [1985] solves this issue by introducing a more general

---

[25] See *Pesaran* [1987] for a formal definition of nested, partially non–nested and globally non–nested models. The distinction between the last two can be important but need not concern us here.

Euler condition which is the following convex combination those from $M1$ and $M2$,

$$E_G[e_t(\theta_1, \theta_2, \omega)|\Omega_{t-1}] = 0, \qquad (4\text{--}22)$$

where

$$e_t(\theta_1, \theta_2, \omega) = \omega u_1(x_t, \theta_1) + (1 - \omega) u_2(x_t, \theta_2),$$

where $0 \leq \omega \leq 1$ and $E_G[.]$ taken with respect to the true distribution of the data under this more general model. Notice that $\omega = 1$ implies $M1$ is correct, and $\omega = 0$ implies $M2$ is correct. The other values of ω imply a continuum of residual processes which lie between those implied by $M1$ and $M2$ in some sense. If ω is replaced by a suitabley defined sequence ω_T which converges to one from below at rate $T^{1/2}$ and $z_{1t} = z_{2t} = z_t$, then

$$E_G[z_t e_t(\theta_1, \theta_2, \omega)] = 0$$

defines a sequence of local alternatives to (4–20) in the direction of (4–21) *Singleton* [1985] shows that the linear combination of the overidentifying restrictions in $M1$ which maximizes power against this local alternative is

$$A_T = V_{1T}^{-1} \left(f_{1T}(\widehat{\theta}_{1T}) - f_{2T}(\widehat{\theta}_{2T}) \right),$$

where $f_{iT}(\widehat{\theta}_{iT}) = T^{-1} \sum_{t=1}^{T} z_t u_1(x_t, \widehat{\theta}_1)$, V_{1T} is a consistent estimator of $\lim_{T\to\infty} \mathrm{Var}[T^{1/2} f_{1T}(\theta_1)]$ and $\widehat{\theta}_{1T}$ is the GMM estimator of θ_i. This leads to the test statistic

$$NN_T(1,2) = T f_{1T}(\widehat{\theta}_{1T})' A_T \left(A_T' \Sigma_{1T}^{-1} A_T \right)^{-1} A_T' f_{1T}(\widehat{\theta}_{1T}),$$

where

$$\Sigma_{i1T} = V_{1T} - \widehat{F}_{1T}(\widehat{F}_{1T}' V_{1T}^{-1} \widehat{F}_{1T})^{-1} \widehat{F}_{1T}' \quad \text{and} \quad \widehat{F}_{1T} = \partial f_{1T}(\widehat{\theta}_{1T})/\partial \theta'.$$

Singleton [1985] shows that if $M1$ is correct then $NN_T(1,2)$ converges to a χ_1^2 distribution. The roles of $M1$ and $M2$ can be reversed to produce the analogous statistic $NN_T(2,1)$ which would be asymptotically χ_1^2 if $M2$ is correct. In fact, the test should be performed both ways and so there are four possible outcomes: $NN_T(1,2)$ is significant but $NN_T(2,1)$ is not and so $M2$ is chosen; $NN_T(2,1)$ is significant but $NN_T(1,2)$ is not and so $M1$ is chosen; both $NN_T(1,2)$ and $NN_T(2,1)$ are significant and so both models can be rejected; both $NN_T(1,2)$ and $NN_T(2,1)$ are insignificant and so it is not possible to choose between them in this way.

This approach is relatively simple to implement because it does not require any additional assumptions or computations beyond those already involved for the estimation of $M1$ and $M2$. Its weakness is that the convex combination of the Euler equations from $M1$ and $M2$ may not be the Euler equation of a well defined economic model.[26] In such cases, it is unclear how a significant statistic should be interpreted. The only way to avoid this problem is to consider sequences of local alternatives to the data generation process implied by $M1$ which are in the direction of the data generation process implied by $M2$. However, this involves making the type of distributional assumption which the use of GMM was designed to avoid.

Ghysels and Hall [1990c] propose an alternative approach to testing based on whether one model can explain the results in the other.[27] More specifically, the data are said to support $M1$ if

$$T^{-1} \sum_{t=1}^{T} z_{2t} u_2(x_t, \widehat{\theta}_{2T}) \; - \; E_1[z_{2t} u_2(x_t, \widehat{\theta}_{2T})] \tag{4--23}$$

is zero allowing for sampling error. To implement the test it is necessary to know or be able to estimate the expectation term in (4–23). Unfortunately, this will typically involve specifying the conditional distribution of x_t and so is unattractive for the reason mentioned above.[28] *Ghysels and Hall* [1990c] develop a test based on approximating the expectation using quadrature based methods, but we omit the details here.

Both these statistics are clearly focusing on the overidentifying restrictions alone. It is possible to extend *Ghysels and Hall's* [1990c] approach to tests of whether $M1$ can explain the identifying restrictions in $M2$. Such a test would focus on whether the solution to the identifying restrictions in $M2$ is equal to the value predicted by $M1$. In other words, it would examine

$$\widehat{\theta}_{2T} \; - \; E_1[\widehat{\theta}_{2T}].$$

---

[26] For example, *Ghysels and Hall* [1990c] show that a model constructed by taking a convex combination of the data generating processes for x_t implied by $M1$ and $M2$ does not typically possess an Euler equation of the form in (4–21).

[27] This general approach is often refered to as the encompassing test principle; see *Mizon and Richard* [1986].

[28] Furthermore *Ghysels and Hall* [1990c] show that a misspecification of this distribution can cause their statistic to be significant.

However, it would suffer from the same drawbacks as mentioned above and so we do not pursue such a test here.

Neither of these approaches is really satisfactory. *Singleton's* [1985] test is only really appropriate in the limited setting where (4–21) is the Euler condition of a meaningful model. *Ghysels and Hall's* [1990c] test is always appropriate but requires additional assumptions about the distribution, and once these are made, it is more efficient to use maximum likelihood estimation.[29] This contrasts with the more successful treatments of the hypotheses in Sections 4.2–4.5. In these earlier cases, the partial specification caused no problems, but it clearly does for non–nested hypotheses. In one sense, these results are more important because they illustrate the the potential limits to inference based on a partially specified model.

4.7 Conditional Moment and Hausman Tests

In sections 4.2, 4.3 and 4.5 it is assumed that it is desired to test hypotheses about the population moment conditions upon which estimation is based. This mirrors the majority of empirical applications mentioned in the introduction. In these types of application, the model is only partially specfied and so it is desireable to base estimation on as much relevant information as possible. Therefore all available moment conditions tend to be used in estimation.[30] However, if the distribution of the data is known then the most asymptotically efficient estimates are obtained by using maximum likelihood. From a GMM perspective, maximum likelihood amounts to estimation based on the score function of the data. So, in this case there is no advantage to including any other moment conditions implied by the model. These other moment conditions are not redundant because they can be used to test whether the specification of the model is correct. In this section we describe two approaches to constructing this type of test; these

---

[29] Although, full information maximum likelihood may be more computationally burdensome; see *Ghysels and Hall* [1990c].

[30] The choice of moment conditions may be limited by other factors such as data availability or computational constraints.

are conditional moment tests and Hausman tests. We examine each in turn. Our aim here is to contrast these tests with those described earlier, and not to provide a comprehensive review.

4.7.1 Conditional Moment Tests

Newey [1985b] and *Tauchen* [1985] independently introduce a general framework for conditional moment testing based on maximum likelihood estimators. To illustrate this framework, suppose that the conditional probability density of x_t given $\{x_{t-1}, x_{t-2}, \ldots x_1\}$ is $p_t(x_t; \theta_0)$, and so the score function is

$$E[L_t(\theta_0)] = 0,$$

where $L_t(\theta_0) = \partial \log(p_t(x_t; \theta_0))/\partial\theta$. As mentioned above this is moment condition upon which estimation is based. Now assume that if this model is correctly specfied then the data also satisfy the $(q \times 1)$ population moment condition $E[g(x_t, \theta_0)] = 0$. Therefore one way to assess the validity of the model is to test

$$H_0: \; E[g(x_t, \theta_0)] = 0$$

against the alternative

$$H_A: \; E[g(x_t, \theta_0)] \neq 0.$$

This hypothesis can be tested using the statistic

$$CM_T = T^{-1} \sum_{t=1}^{T} h_t(\widehat{\theta}_T)' Q_T^{-1} \sum_{t=1}^{T} h_t(\widehat{\theta}_T), \qquad (4\text{–}24)$$

where

$$h_t(\theta) = (g(x_t, \theta)', L_t(\theta)')',$$

Q_T is a consistent estimator of $\lim_{T \to \infty} Var[h_t(\theta_0)]$ and $\widehat{\theta}_T$ is the maximum liklihood estimator. Under H_0, CM_T converges to a χ_q^2 distribution. The statistic has a similar structure to the overidentifying restrictions test but there is an important difference. Since $E[g(x_t, \theta_0)] = 0$ is not used in estimation, the statistic has power against any violations of H_0; see *Newey* [1985b]. In spite of this, some caution is needed in the interpretation of the results. While a rejection of H_0 implies the model is misspecified, a failure to reject only implies that the assumed distribution exhibits this particular characteristic of the true distribution.

The choice of $g(.)$ varies from model to model. For example, in the normal linear regression model, $g(.)$ often involves the third and fourth moments of the error process; see *Bowman and Shenton* [1975]. *White* [1982] suggests that one generally applicable choice is to base $g(.)$ on the information matrix identity,

$$E[L_t(\theta_0)L_t(\theta_0)'] = -E[\partial L_t(\theta_0)/\partial\theta']$$

because if the the null hypothesis cannot be rejected then conventional formulae for Wald, LR and LM statistics are valid. Consequently, this approach has been explored in many settings; see, for example, *Chesher* [1984] and *Hall* [1987]. Various other examples are provided by *Newey* [1985b] and *Tauchen* [1985].

4.7.2 Hausman Tests

We have already encountered the *Hausman* [1978] test principle in testing hypotheses about subset of moment conditions. However, the basic idea is more widely applicable and we now briefly discuss its use in the context of maximum likelihood estimation. As we have seen, the test compares two estimates of the parameter vector: one is consistent under the null hypothesis that the model is correctly specified – this is the maximum likelihood estimator (MLE) in our context – and the other is consistent under both null and the alternative. The exact nature of this alternative will become apparent below. Let $\widehat{\theta}_T$ once again denote the MLE and $\widetilde{\theta}_T$ be the GMM estimator of θ_0 based on $E[f(x_t,\theta_0)] = 0$. The Hausman test statistic is

$$H_T = T\left(\widehat{\theta}_T - \widetilde{\theta}_T\right)\left(\widehat{V}_T - \widetilde{V}_T\right)^{-1}\left(\widehat{\theta}_T - \widetilde{\theta}_T\right),$$

where $\widehat{V}_T$ and $\widetilde{V}_T$ are consistent estimators of the asymptotic covariance of $\widehat{\theta}_T$ and $\widetilde{\theta}_T$ respectively. Under the null hypothesis that maximum likelihood is based on the correct model and $E[f(x_t,\theta_0)] = 0$ then *Hausman* [1978] shows that H_T converges to a χ^2_p distribution. The alternative hypothesis is that the model is not correctly specified but nevertheless $E[f(x_t,\theta_0)] = 0$. Just as in Section 4.3, this statistic can be interpreted in terms of the identifying restrictions.

White [1982] shows that H_T is asymptotically equivalent to a statistic based on $T^{-1/2} \sum_{t=1}^{T} L_t(\widetilde{\theta}_T)$. Since $L_t(.)$ is $(p \times 1)$ it follows that $T^{-1/2} \sum_{t=1}^{T} L_t(\widetilde{\theta}_T)$ contains exactly the same information as

$$\widetilde{P} \, \widetilde{V}_L^{-1/2} T^{-1/2} \sum_{t=1}^{T} L_t(\widetilde{\theta}_T) \,, \tag{4-25}$$

where $\widetilde{P} = \widetilde{M}(\widetilde{M}'\widetilde{M})^{-1}\widetilde{M}'$, $\widetilde{M} = \widetilde{V}^{-1/2}T^{-1}\partial L_T(\widetilde{\theta}_T)/\partial \theta'$, $L_T(\theta) = \sum_{t=1}^{T} L_t(\theta)$ and $\widetilde{V}_L = T^{-1} \sum_{t=1}^{T} L_t(\widetilde{\theta}_T)L_t(\widetilde{\theta}_T)$. A comparison of (4–24) with (4–3) indicates that the Hausman statistic is using the information in $E[f(x_t, \theta_0)] = 0$ to test the validity of the identifying restrictions for maximum likelihood estimation.

References

Ahn, S.C. [**1995**]: *Model specification testing based on root-T consistent estimators,* Discussion paper, Department of Economics, Arizona State University, Tempe, AZ.

Andrews, D.W.K. [**1993**]: Tests for parameter instability and structural change with unknown change point, *Econometrica,* 61: 821-856.

Andrews, D.W.K., and Fair, R. [**1988**]: Inference in econometric models with structural change, *Review of Economic Studies,* 55: 615-640.

Andrews, D.W.K., and Ploberger, W. [**1994**]: Optimal tests when a nuisance parameter is present only under the alternative, *Econometrica,* 62: 1383-1414.

Andrews, D.W.K., and Ploberber, W. [**1995**]: Admissibility of the Likelihood Ratio test when a nuisance parameter is present only under the alternative, *Annals of Statistics,* 23: 1609-1629.

Apostol, T.M. [**1974**]: *Mathematical Analysis.* Addison-Wesley, Reading, MA, second edn.

Bowman, K.O., and Shenton, L.R. [**1975**]: Omnibus contours for departures from normality based on b_1 and b_2, *Biometrika,* 62: 243-250.

Chesher, A. [**1984**]: Testing for neglected heterogeneity, *Econometrica,* 52: 865-872.

Chow, G.C. [**1960**]: Tests of equality between sets of coefficients in two linear regressions, *Econometrica,* 28: 591-605.

Cox, D.R., and Hinckley, D.V. [**1974**]: *Theoretical Statistics.* Chapman and Hall, London

Davidson, R., and MacKinnon, J.G. [**1993**]: *Estimation and Inference in Econometrics.* Oxford University Press, Oxford.

Dufour, J.-M., Ghysels, E., and Hall, A.R. [**1994**]: Generalized predictive tests and structural change analysis in econometrics, *International Economic Review,* 35: 199-229.

Eichenbaum, M., Hansen, L.P., and Singleton, K.S. [**1988**]: A time series analysis of representative agent models of consumption and leisure under uncertainty, *Quarterly Journal of Economics,* 103: 51-78.

Gallant, A.R. [**1987**]: *Nonlinear Statistical Models.* Wiley, New York.

Gallant, A.R., and White, H. [**1988**]: *A Unified Theory of Estimation and Inference in Nonlinear Models.* Basil Blackwell, Oxford.

Ghysels, E., Guay, A., and Hall, A.R. [**1997**]: Predictive test for structural change with unknown breakpoint, *Journal of Econometrics,* 82, 209–233.

Ghysels, E., and Hall, A.R. [**1990a**]: Are consumption based intertemporal asset pricing models structural? *Journal of Econometrics,* 45: 121-139.

Ghysels, E., and Hall, A.R. [**1990b**]: A test for structural stability of Euler condition parameters estimated via the Generalized Method of Moments, *International Economic Review,* 31: 355-364.

Ghysels, E., and Hall, A.R. [**1990c**]: Testing non-nested Euler conditions with quadrature based methods of approximation, *Journal of Econometrics,* 46: 273-308.

Gourieroux, C., and Monfort, A. [**1994**]: Testing non-nested hypotheses, in R.F. Engle and D.L. McFadden (eds.), *Handbook of Econometrics,* vol. 4, pp. 2583-2637. Elsevier Science Publishers, Amsterdam, The Netherlands.

Hall, A.R. [**1987**]: The information matrix test for the linear model, *Review of Economic Studies,* 54: 257-263.

Hall, A.R. [**1993**]: Some aspects of Generalized Method of Moments estimation, in G.S.Maddala, C.R. Rao, and H.D. Vinod (eds.), *Handbook of Statistics,* vol, 11, pp. 393-417. Elsevier Science Publishers, Amsterdam, The Netherlands.

Hall, A.R., and Sen, A. [**1996a**]: *Structural stability testing in models estimated by Generalized Method of Moments,* Discussion paper, Department of Economics, North Carolina State University, Raleigh, NC.

Hall, A.R., and Sen, A. [**1996b**]: *On the interpretation of optimality in certain tests of structural stability,* Discussion paper, Department of Economics, North Carolina State University, Raleigh, NC.

Hall, A.R., and Sen, A. [**1997a**]: *Approximate p-values for new tests of structural stability,* Discussion paper, Department of Economics, North Carolina State University, Raleigh, NC.

Hall, A.R., and Sen, A. [**1997b**]: *Structural stability testing in models estimated by Generalized Method of Moments,* Discussion paper, Department of Economics, North Carolina State University, Raleigh, NC.

Hansen, B.E. [**1990**]: *Lagrange multiplier tests for parameter instability in non-linear models,* Discussion paper, Department of Economics, University of Rochester, Rochester, NY.

Hansen, B.E. [1997]: Approximate asymptotic p-values for structural change tests, *Journal of Business and Economic Statistics,* 15: 60-67.

Hansen, L.P. [1982]: Large sample properties of Generalized Method of Moments estimators, *Econometrica,* 50: 1029-1054.

Hausman, J. [1978]: Specification tests in econometrics, *Econometrica,* 46: 1251-1271.

Holly, A. [1982]: A remark on Hausman's specification test, *Econometrica,* 50: 749-759.

Judge, G.G., Griffiths, W.E., Hill, R.C., Lutkepohl, H., and Lee, T.-C. [1985]: *Theory and Practice of Econometrics.* Wiley, New York, second edn.

Lehmann, E.L. [1959]: *Testing Statistical Hypotheses.* Wiley, New York.

Mizon, G.E., and Richard, J.F. [1986]: The encompassing principle and its application to testing non-nested hypotheses, *Econometrica,* 54: 657-678.

Newey, W.K. [1985a]: Generalized Method of Moments specification testing, *Journal of Econometrics,* 29: 229-256.

Newey, W.K. [1985b]: Maximum likelihood specification testing and instrumented score tests *Econometrica,* 53: 1047-1070.

Newey, W.K., and West, K. [1987]: Hypothesis testing with efficient method of moments testing, *International Economic Review,* 28: 777-787.

Nyblom, J. [1989]: Testing for the constancy of parameters over time, *Journal of the American Statistical Association,* 84: 223-230.

Ogaki, M. [1993]: Generalized Method of Moments: econometric applications, in G.S. Maddala, C.R.Rao, and H.D.Vinod (eds.), *Handbook of Statistics,* vol. 11, pp. 455-488. Elsevier Science Publishers, Amsterdam, The Netherlands.

Pesaran, M.H. [1987]: Global and partial non-nested hypotheses and asymptotic local power, *Econometric Theory,* 3: 69-97.

Singleton, K.J. [1985]: Testing specifications of economic agents intertemporal optimum problems in the prescence of alternative models, *Journal of Econometrics,* 30: 391-413.

Sowell, F. [1996a]: Optimal tests for parameter instability in the Generalized Method of Moments framework, *Econometrica,* 64: 1085-1108.

Sowell, F. [1996b]: *Test for violations of moment conditions,* Discussion paper, Graduate School of Administration, Carnegie Mellon University, Pittsburgh, PA.

Tauchen, G. [1985]: Diagnostic testing and evaluation of maximum likelihood models, *Journal of Econometrics,* 30: 415-443.

White, H. [1982]: Maximum likelihood estimation of misspecified models, *Econometrica,* 50: 1-26.

Chapter 5

FINITE SAMPLE PROPERTIES OF

GMM ESTIMATORS AND TESTS

Jan M. Podivinsky

Although GMM estimators are consistent and asymptotically normally distributed under general regularity conditions, it has long been recognized that this first–order asymptotic distribution may provide a poor approximation to the finite sample distribution. In particular, GMM estimators may be badly biased, and asymptotic tests based on these estimators may have true sizes substantially different from presumed nominal sizes.

This chapter reviews these finite sample properties, from both the theoretical perspective, and from simulation evidence of Monte Carlo studies. The theoretical literature on the finite sample behavior of instrumental variables estimators and tests is seen to provide valuable insights into the finite sample behavior of GMM estimators and tests.

The chapter then considers Monte Carlo simulation evidence of the finite sample performance of GMM techniques. Such studies have often focussed on applications of GMM to estimating particular models in economics and finance, *e.g.,* business cycle models, inventory models, asset pricing models, and stochastic volatility models. This survey reviews and summarizes the lessons from this simulation evidence.

The final section examines how this knowledge of the finite sample behavior might be used to conduct improved inference. For example, bias corrected estimators may be obtained. Also, properly implemented bootstrap techniques can deliver modified critical values or improved test statistics with rather better finite sample behavior. Alternatively, analytical techniques might be used to obtain corrected test statistics.

5.1 Related Theoretical Literature

It is well recognized that the GMM estimator can be considered as an instrumental variables (IV) estimator. For, example, *Hall's* [1993] comprehensive introduction to GMM proceeds by first outlining the (asymptotic) properties of the IV estimator in the (static) linear regression model, and then extending the analysis to the properties of GMM in dynamic nonlinear models. Since the conventional IV estimator is a special case of GMM, this suggests that the extensive literature (see *Phillips* [1983] for an early survey) on the theoretical properties of IV techniques may be a useful guide to understanding the properties of GMM.

One aspect of this theoretical literature is a comparison of IV based methods (including Two Stage Least Squares (2SLS) and Generalized Instrumental Variables Estimator (GIVE)) and maximum likelihood based methods (Limited Information Maximum Likelihood (LIML) and Full Information Maximum Likelihood (FIML)). In the context of single equation estimation, one disadvantage of 2SLS relative to LIML is that the 2SLS estimator is not invariant to normalisation. *Hillier* [1990] demonstrated that the 2SLS estimator is identified only with respect to its direction, and not its magnitude, and then argued that this feature is responsible for distorting the finite sample behavior of 2SLS. We will see later how this argument might be used to suggest an alternative GMM estimator.

Recently, there has been considerable interest in examining the consequences of IV estimators when the instruments are "weak", *i.e.,* poorly correlated with the endogenous regressors. *Nelson and Startz* [1990b] evaluated the exact small sample distribution of the IV estimator in a simple leading case of a linear regression framework. Among their findings, they find that the central tendency of the IV estimator is biased away from the true value, and suggest

that the asymptotic distribution of IV is a rather poor approximation to the exact distribution when an instrument is only weakly
correlated with the endogenous regressor, and when the number of
observations is small. They also find that the IV estimator may
be bimodal, but *Maddala and Jeong* [1992] emphasize that this is
primarily a consequence of *Nelson and Startz's* [1990b] covariance
matrix design, and not entirely due to the weak instrument problem. This evidence of the importance of the "quality" (*i.e.,* degree
of correlation with endogenous regressors) of the instruments in
IV estimation suggests that similar considerations are likely to be
important with GMM estimation.

Staiger and Stock [1997] undertake a rather more extensive
analysis of this "weak" instruments problem. They develop an asymptotic framework alternative to conventional asymptotics (both
first–order and higher–order) to approximate the distributions of
statistics in single equation IV linear models. Staiger and Stock find
that their results provide guidance as to which of several alternative
tests have greatest power and least size distortions in the case of
weak instruments. In addition, they provide several alternative
methods for forming confidence intervals that are asymptotically
valid with weak instruments. Although they confine themselves to
considering only the linear IV framework, it would be constructive
to extend their analysis to the GMM framework. *Stock and Wright*
[1996], in a related contribution, develop a similar asymptotic distribution theory framework applied to GMM, and suggest that it
can help explain the non–normal finite sample distributions that
they uncover.

In a related study, *Pagan and Jung* [1993] explore the consequences for IV and GMM estimation of the weak instruments
problem, by focussing on particular measures or indices (including
but not restricted to the degree of correlation between instruments
and regressors) that usefully explain the performance of these estimators. They use their suggested framework to analyse three particular examples, and argue that their indices, considered jointly,
are useful in highlighting problems of estimators in these examples.

In a Monte Carlo study arising out of *Nelson and Startz's*
[1990b] analysis, *Nelson and Startz* [1990a] investigate the properties of t–ratios and the chi-squared test for the overidentifying restrictions in the context of linear instrumental variables regressions,
under weak instrument conditions. When the instruments are only

weakly correlated with the endogenous regressors, they find that the overidentification chi-square test tends to reject the null too frequently compared with its asymptotic chi-squared distribution, and that coefficient t–ratios tend to be too large. *Ogaki* [1993] has argued that *Nelson and Startz's* [1990a] results for t–ratios seem to be counterintuitive because an anticipated consequence of poor instruments would be a large equation standard error in estimation, and hence (ceteris paribus) a low t–ratio. Nevertheless (Ogaki argues), *Nelson and Startz's* [1990a] results may be expected to carry over to tests based upon nonlinear IV estimation, rather closer to the framework of GMM estimation and testing.

5.2 Simulation Evidence

In recent years, there has been a small but growing literature on the small sample behavior of GMM estimators and tests, partly reversing the state of affairs recently summarized by *Ogaki* [1993, p. 480] statement:

"Unfortunately there has not been much work done on the small sample properties of GMM estimators."

Here we consider this evidence (primarily simulation–based in nature) with respect to several main classes of models which have seen extensive empirical applications of GMM.

We consider the following general notation. We denote the $q \times 1$ vector of population moment conditions:

$$E[f(x_t, \theta_0)] = 0,$$

where θ_0 denotes the (unknown) true value of the $p \times 1$ vector of parameters, where $q \geq p$. The $q \times 1$ vector of empirical moment conditions based upon a sample of T observations on the data vector x_t is:

$$f_T(\theta) = \frac{1}{T} \sum_{t=1}^{T} f(x_t, \theta).$$

The standard GMM approach is to minimize the criterion function:

$$Q_T(\theta) = f_T(\theta)' W_T f_T(\theta)$$

(depending upon a $q \times q$ positive-definite weighting matrix W_T) by an appropriate choice of θ, leading to the GMM estimator:

$$\widehat{\theta}_T = \operatorname{argmin}_\theta Q_T(\theta) \,.$$

Provided $q > p$, we can test the validity of $(q - p)$ overidentifying restrictions using the statistic:

$$J = T f_T(\widehat{\theta_T^*})' \widehat{W_T^*} f_T(\widehat{\theta_T^*}) \,,$$

where $\widehat{\theta_T^*}$ denotes the asymptotically efficient GMM estimator of θ (based upon an appropriate choice of weighting matrix W_T), and $\widehat{W_T^*}$ denotes an estimate of the optimal weighting matrix. Under the null hypothesis that $E[f(x_t, \theta_0)] = 0$, the goodness of fit J test statistic is asymptotically distributed as a $\chi^2(q - p)$ random variable.

5.2.1 Asset Pricing Models

The earliest, and perhaps the most extensive, area of application of GMM techniques is that of asset pricing models, motivated by the original papers of *Hansen* [1982] and especially *Hansen and Singleton* [1982]. In the first published simulation based studies of the small sample behavior of GMM techniques, *Tauchen* [1986] and *Kocherlakota* [1990] examine applications to data generated from artificial nonlinear consumption based asset pricing models. *Tauchen* [1986] applied the so–called *two–step GMM estimator.* This starts with a sub–optimal choice (an identity matrix, perhaps) of the weighting matrix W_T to provide an estimate (by minimizing the appropriate criterion function) of θ, and thus an estimate of the optimal weighting matrix. These are then used in the second stage to provide (again by minimizing the criterion function) the asymptotically efficient estimator $\widehat{\theta_T^*}$ of θ. He concluded that the GMM estimators and test statistics he considered have reasonable small sample properties for data produced by simulations for a consumption based capital asset pricing model (C-CAPM). These findings related to a relatively small sample size (either 50 or 75 observations). *Tauchen* [1986] also investigated the small sample properties of (asymptotically) optimal instrumental variables GMM estimators. He finds that the optimal estimators based upon the optimal selection of instruments often do not perform as well in small samples as GMM estimators using an arbitrary selection of instruments.

Kocherlakota [1990] considers artificial data from a model very similar to that used by *Tauchen* [1986], but allows for multiple assets and different sets of instruments. However, instead of using the two stage GMM estimator his analysis uses the *iterated GMM estimator*, obtained by iterating between estimates of the parameter vector θ and the weighting matrix W_T until convergence is attained. For a sample size of 90 observations, Kocherlakota finds that GMM performs worse with larger instrument sets, leading to downward biases in coefficient estimates, and confidence intervals that are too narrow. In addition, he finds evidence that the chi-squared J test for overidentifying restrictions tends to reject the null too frequently compared with its asymptotic size. The apparent discrepancy between some of the findings of *Kocherlakota* [1990] and *Tauchen* [1986] may be related to the problem of poor "quality" instruments discussed previously in the context of IV estimation. Based upon this evidence, it seems sensible to recommend using a relatively small number of instruments rather than the often large number of instruments arising out of the use of an arbitrary selection of instruments.

Ferson and Foerster [1994] examine models for differing numbers of asset returns using financial data (of between 60 and 720 observations), and subject to nonlinear, cross-equation restrictions. They study both the two stage and iterated GMM estimators. They find that the two stage GMM approach produces goodness of fit test statistics that over–reject the restrictions. In contrast, the iterated GMM estimator has superior finite sample properties, producing coefficient estimates that are approximately unbiased in simple models. However, the estimated coefficients' asymptotic standard errors are underestimated. This can be at least partially corrected by using simple scalar degrees-of-freedom adjustment factors for the estimated standard errors. In more complex models (*e.g.*, as the number of assets increases), however, they find that both the estimated coefficients and their standard errors can be highly unreliable. Tests of a single premium model have higher power against a two premium, fixed beta alternative than against a C-CAPM alternative with time varying betas. Low power in the direction of some alternatives is seen as an inevitable consequence of the generality of the GMM approach to inference. Finally, the previously documented over-rejection of the J test of overidentifying restrictions is confirmed when using the two stage GMM estimator, but when using the iterated GMM estimator the J test tends to under-reject marginally relative to its nominal size.

Hansen, Heaton and Yaron [1996] consider (*inter alia*) both the two stage and iterated GMM estimators in a framework similar to that used by *Tauchen* [1986] and *Kocherlakota* [1990], together with alternative choices of the weighting matrix W_T. They find that both the two stage and iterated GMM estimators have small sample distributions that can be greatly distorted (even for a sample as large as 400 observations), resulting in over-rejections of the J test of overidentifying restrictions, and unreliable hypothesis testing and confidence-interval coverage. Based upon this evidence, they recommend an alternative form of GMM estimator, to be considered later.

5.2.2 Business Cycle Models

Christiano and den Haan [1996] conduct a Monte Carlo simulation investigation of the finite sample properties of GMM procedures for conducting inference about statistics that are of interest in the business cycle literature. Such statistics (based upon GMM estimators) include the second moments of data filtered using either the first difference or Hodrick–Prescott filters, and include statistics for evaluating model fit. Both types of statistics are commonly used in business cycle studies. In their investigation they take care to use what they consider as empirically plausible data generating processes (DGPs) for their data. Examples include a four–variable vector autoregression (VAR) in (the logarithms of) consumption, employment, output and investment. Their results indicate that in a sample the size ($T = 120$) of quarterly postwar U.S. data, the existing asymptotic distribution theory is not a reliable guide to the behavior of the procedures considered.

In an assessment of the small sample properties of GMM based Wald statistics, *Burnside and Eichenbaum* [1996] consider as alternative DGPs both a vector white noise process, and an equilibrium business cycle model. With $T = 100$ observations, they find that in many cases the small sample size of the Wald test exceeds its asymptotic size and increases sharply with the number of hypotheses being tested jointly. *Burnside and Eichenbaum* [1996] argue that this is mostly due to difficulty in estimating the spectral density matrix of the residuals, and conclude that they are very skeptical that the problem can be resolved by using any of the alternative nonparametric estimators of this matrix that have recently been discussed in the literature (see Chapter 3). This evidence of the importance of correctly estimating the spectral density matrix of the residuals mirrors similar findings by *Christiano and den Haan* [1996]. However, the properties of Wald statistics can be improved, often substantially, by using estimators of this spectral density matrix that impose prior information embodied in restrictions implied by either the model or the null hypothesis.

Finally, *Gregory and Smith* [1996] present two applications to US post–war data of business cycles that may be defined or measured by parametrizing detrending filters to maximize the ability of a business cycle model to match the moments of the remaining cycles. In this way a business cycle theory can be used to guide business cycle measurement. In one application, these cycles are measured with a standard real business cycle model, and in the second, they are measured using information on capacity utilization and unemployment rates. *Gregory and Smith* [1996] then use simulation methods to describe the properties of the GMM estimators and to conduct exact inference.

5.2.3 Stochastic Volatility Models

Changes over time in the variance or volatility of some financial asset return can be modelled using the class of stochastic volatility (SV) models. This approach is based on treating the volatility σ_t of returns y_t as an unobserved variable, for instance:

$$y_t = \sigma_t v_t \quad v_t \sim i.i.d.N(0,1)$$

the logarithm of which is modelled as a linear stochastic process, usually an autoregression, *e.g.*,

$$\log \sigma_t^2 = \beta_0 + \beta_1 \log \sigma_{t-1}^2 + u_t,$$

where $u_t \sim i.i.d.N(0, \sigma_u^2)$ independent of v_t. Note that this lognormal parameterisation is commonly employed because it is consistent with evidence of excess kurtosis or "heavy tails" in the unconditional distribution of returns.

Ruiz [1994] analysed the asymptotic and finite sample properties of a Quasi–Maximum Likelihood (QML) estimator (based on the Kalman filter) of such an SV model, and applied this to an exchange rate model. Although based upon normality, the QML estimator can still be employed when the SV model is generalized to allow for distributions with heavier tails than the normal. Initial evidence by *Ruiz* [1994] appeared to suggest that this QML estimator displayed considerable advantages relative to the GMM estimator. In particular, the relative efficiency of the QML estimator when compared with estimators based on the GMM appeared to be quite high for parameter values often found in empirical applications. However, *Andersen and Sørensen* [1997] [see also *Ruiz* [1997]] point out a flaw in *Ruiz's* [1994] calculations of the asymptotic standard errors of the GMM estimator. *Andersen and Sørensen* [1997] describe a practical procedure for arbitrarily precise calculation of the GMM asymptotic standard errors, and apply this to correct *Ruiz's* [1994] calculations. In some cases they find the correct results are some orders of magnitude different from Ruiz's previously published figures; this places the relative efficiencies of GMM and QML estimators on a more even footing.

Jacquier, Polson and Rossi [1994] develop alternative Bayesian techniques for the analysis of stochastic volatility models in which the logarithm of conditional variance follows an autoregressive model. They use a cyclic Metropolis algorithm to construct a Markov chain simulation tool. Simulations from this Markov chain can be shown to converge in distribution to draws from the posterior distribution, thus enabling exact finite sample inference. One convenient byproduct of their Markov chain simulation method is the exact solution to the filtering/smoothing problem of inference about the unobserved variance states. In addition, their method means that multistep–ahead predictive densities can be constructed that reflect both inherent model variability and parameter uncertainty. After illustrating their method to analyzing daily and weekly data on stock returns and exchange rates, *Jacquier, Polson and Rossi* [1994] conduct sampling experiments to compare the performance of their Bayes estimators to both GMM and QML estimators. They conclude that for both parameter estimation and filtering, the Bayes estimators outperform both alternative approaches, and GMM weakly dominates QML.

Andersen and Sørensen [1996] examine alternative GMM procedures for estimation of a stochastic autoregressive volatility model by Monte Carlo simulation methods. To maintain comparability with *Jacquier, Polson and Rossi's* [1994] evidence, they use an experimental design similar to that used by *Jacquier, Polson and Rossi* [1994], but extended by allowing larger sample sizes ($T =$ 500, 1000, 2000, 4000 and 10000) more representative of those often used in applications of GMM to high–frequency financial data. *Andersen and Sørensen* [1996] find a clear trade–off between the number of moments, or the amount of information, included in estimation and the quality, or precision, of the objective function used for estimation. Generally, they find it is not optimal to use many moments in estimation if the sample size is relatively limited. Also, their results suggest that using less volatile and lower–order moments dominates using more volatile and higher–order moments. Furthermore, Andersen and Sørensen use an approximation to the optimal weighting matrix to explore the impact of the weighting matrix W_T for estimation, specification testing and inference procedures. Provided these guidelines concerning choice of moments relative to sample size are followed, the chi–squared J test for overidentifying restrictions is reasonably well behaved. While Andersen and Sørensen indicate many further finite sample issues that deserve attention, they argue that their results provide guidelines that help achieve desirable small sample properties in a wide range of economic settings characterized by strong conditional heteroskedasticity and correlation among the moments.

Dahlquist [1996] includes a simulation analysis of the small sample properties of the GMM estimators in his application of alternative interest rate processes estimated for Denmark, Germany, Sweden, and the UK, using the GMM estimator. In line with previous evidence from the study by *Chan, Karolyi, Longstaff, and Sanders* [1992] on US data, there seems to be a positive relation between interest rate level and volatility for some countries. However, Dahlquist finds that mean–reversion plays an important role for the specification of the interest rate dynamics. He finds that these results seem to be robust to the use of different moment conditions, and simulations of the estimated models reveal that they are also reasonably successful at capturing non–fitted moments as well.

Flesaker [1993] provides empirical tests of two commonly used models for pricing fixed-income derivative securities, using the constant volatility version of the Heath, Jarrow, and Morton model, which is also the continuous time limit of the Ho and Lee model. He finds that this model can be rejected using a GMM test for most subperiods of three years of daily data for Eurodollar futures and futures options. He also conducts a limited simulation analysis of the small sample properties and power of the GMM framework.

5.2.4 Inventory Models

Fuhrer, Moore and Schuh [1995] compare GMM and maximum likelihood (ML) estimators of the parameters of a linear–quadratic inventory model using both US nondurable manufacturing data and Monte Carlo simulations. GMM estimates for five normalizations vary widely, but generally reject the model, while the ML estimates differ, generally supporting the model. Their Monte Carlo simulation experiments reveal a possible explanation for this difference. They find that the GMM estimates are often biased, statistically insignificant, economically implausible, and dynamically unstable, while the ML estimates are generally unbiased (even in misspecified models), statistically significant, economically plausible, and dynamically stable. They attribute the poor performance of GMM to the weak instrument problem. However, in findings reminiscent of those of *Ruiz* [1994], they find that asymptotic standard errors for ML are 3 to 15 times smaller than for GMM, which suggests that *Andersen and Sørensen's* [1997] method for arbitrarily precise calculation of GMM asymptotic standard errors might usefully be employed.

West and Wilcox [1996] consider IV (and GMM) estimation of a scalar dynamic linear equation with a conditionally homoskedastic moving average disturbance. Such equations arise regularly in empirical work on inventory data (see *West* [1996], and *West and Wilcox* [1994]). They compare two parameterizations of a commonly used IV estimator to one that is asymptotically optimal in a class of estimators that includes the conventional one. Based upon some plausible DGPs (including that used in *West and Wilcox* [1994]), the optimal estimator is found to be more efficient asymptotically, and they recommend this estimator. Their simulations indicate that in samples of size typically available ($T = 100$ or 300), asymptotic theory describes the distribution of the parameter estimates reasonably well but that test statistics occasionally are poorly sized.

5.2.5 Models of Covariance Structures

Models of covariance structures cover a variety of different areas of empirical applications. These include studies of contract models, consumption, and the effects of individual endowments on earnings and education. In such models of covariance structures, when GMM minimizes the weighted distance between a vector m of sample second moments and the vector $f(\theta)$ of population second moments, it is commonly known as the optimal minimum distance (OMD) estimator:

$$\widehat{\theta}_{OMD} = \mathrm{argmin}_\theta (m - f(\theta))'\widehat{\Omega}^{-1}(m - f(\theta)),$$

where $\widehat{\Omega}$ denotes the estimated covariance matrix of m.

Altonji and Segal [1996] examine the small sample properties of the OMD (*i.e.*, GMM) estimator applied to models of covariance structures, and find that the OMD estimator $\widehat{\theta}_{OMD}$ is almost always biased downwards in absolute value. This bias arises because sampling errors in the second moments are correlated with sampling errors in the weighting matrix used by OMD. Furthermore, they find that OMD is usually dominated by the equally weighted minimum distance (EWMD) estimator:

$$\widehat{\theta}_{EWMD} = \mathrm{argmin}_\theta (m - f(\theta))'(m - f(\theta)).$$

Altonji and Segal [1996] also propose an alternative estimator that is unbiased and asymptotically equivalent to OMD, but their Monte Carlo simulation evidence indicates, however, that it, too, is usually dominated by EWMD.

Clark's [1996] study examines the small sample properties of GMM and maximum likelihood (ML) estimators of nonlinear models of covariance structure, thus extending the work of *Altonji and Segal* [1996]. Clark considers the properties of GMM and ML estimates for both a single factor model (the *Hall and Mishkin* [1982] model of consumption and income), and a simple structural VAR–type error model. His simulation analysis based upon either

100 or 200 observations shows that optimally weighted GMM estimation can yield biased parameter estimates. In addition, a model specification test based on GMM estimation exhibits size substantially greater than the asymptotic size. Finally, these problems are reduced when the number of overidentifying restrictions in a model is reduced.

5.2.6 Other Applications of GMM

Finally, we consider a range of other applications of GMM which include some evidence of small sample behavior of GMM estimators and tests. We omit any consideration of various studies of small sample properties of GMM statistics in panel data models, as these are covered separately in Chapter 8.

Ni [1997] investigates the consequences for GMM estimation of scaling factors are often used to restore stationarity in Euler equation residuals, when data exhibit exponential trends. He demonstrates that finite sample estimates are sensitive to the scaling factors, and even seemingly plausible scaling factors may produce quite spurious estimates. One suggestion might be to choose scaling factors such that the scaled marginal utility remains roughly constant. Ni illustrates this by estimating a representative agent's time nonseparable utility function, using both artificial data, and aggregate consumption and asset returns.

Lee and Lee [1997] applied GMM estimation to the truncated or censored regression model. In a typical limited dependent variable regression, the conditional mean of the error distribution is no longer zero, so this cannot be used as a moment condition in GMM estimation. However, by appropriate symmetric trimming of the error distribution, we can obtain a zero conditional mean, and hence obtain the moment or orthogonality conditions required for GMM estimation. In an application of this symmetrically trimmed GMM estimator to a model of recreational demand, the bootstrap is used to simulate the finite sample distribution of this estimator.

The consistency of the GLS estimator in static models with pooled cross section time series data is often tested by a Hausman test. *Ahn and Low* [1996] reformulate the Hausman test based on a GMM approach and find that it incorporates and tests only a limited set of moment restrictions. They also consider an alternative GMM statistic incorporating additional restrictions, which has power toward additional sources of model misspecification. Their Monte Carlo simulations demonstrate that while both the Hausman test and their alternative test have good power detecting endogenous regressors, the alternative dominates the Hausman test if coefficients of regressors are nonstationary.

Non–parametric tests for duration dependence are considered by *Mudambi and Taylor* [1995]. Using finite sample critical values obtained by Monte Carlo methods, their results applied to UK business cycle data for 1854-1992 are remarkably consistent, for tests based on the method of moments, GMM, and a statistic whose null distribution probability limit is zero. However, they find that the null distribution of the GMM test statistic for samples of the size considered is distinctly non–normal, so that asymptotic critical values give erroneous results.

5.3 Extensions of Standard GMM

Since the evidence summarized in the previous section indicates that often there can be problems with the behavior of standard GMM statistics in small samples, this has motivated researchers to develop and investigate various refinements or extensions to standard GMM techniques. This section examines some of the most promising extensions, initially discussing estimation, and then testing.

5.3.1 Estimation

Hansen, Heaton and Yaron's [1996] analysis of two stage and iterated GMM estimators applied to asset pricing models was considered in the previous section. Because they (and others) find that these two standard GMM estimators often exhibit poor small sample properties, they introduce and examine an alternative GMM estimator, namely the *continuous updating GMM estimator*.

Both the two stage and iterated GMM estimators take the weighting matrix W_T as fixed in each stage of the estimation procedure (*i.e.*, when minimizing the GMM criterion function). The continuous updating GMM estimator changes this weighting matrix as θ is changed within the minimization. Thus the continuous updating GMM estimator is defined as:

$$\widehat{\theta}_T^c = \mathrm{argmin}_\theta f_T(\theta)' W_T(\theta) f_T(\theta),$$

where the weighting matrix $W_T(\theta)$ now varies with θ. Thus the first–order conditions for this minimization problem with respect to θ now have an additional term arising from the weighting matrix $W_T(\theta)$, thus adding to the complexity of the numerical optimisation. However, this does not alter the limiting distribution of the estimator. *Hansen, Heaton and Yaron* [1996] refer to *Pakes and Pollard* [1989] for a formal justification of the asymptotic properties of this continuous updating GMM estimator, and point out that it has the added advantage of being invariant to scaling of the moment conditions (see the related discussion of *Ni* [1997] in the previous section.

An added advantage of this continuous updating GMM estimator is that it matches the recommendations of *Magdalinos* [1994] with respect to dominance of methods that change weighting matrices to embody restrictions. This is because the continuous updating GMM estimator is analagous to the LIML estimator, whereas the two stage and iterated estimators are closer to 2SLS: as we pointed out earlier, LIML has various advantages over 2SLS.

Hansen, Heaton and Yaron [1996] investigate the small sample properties of this continuous updating GMM estimator, and find that it typically dominates the two stage and iterated GMM estimators (at least within the asset pricing model framework they consider). However, they caution that large sample inferences occasionally are unreliable. This is related to the finding that the continuous updating GMM estimator is often approximately median unbiased (like the LIML estimator), but sometimes exhibits extreme outlier behavior. They conclude that this estimator should be useful in many applications of GMM where standard GMM methods have been found to be deficient.

Since the small sample performance optimally weighted GMM estimators has been found to be poor in some applications (despite its desirable asymptotic properties), *Kitamura and Stutzer* [1997] propose a computationally simple alternative, for weakly dependent DGPs, based on minimizing the Kullback–Leibler Information Criterion. They derive conditions under which the asynptotic properties of this estimator are similar to GMM (*i.e.,* consistency, asymptotic normality, and the same asymptotic covariance matrix as GMM). They also suggest tests of overidentifying and parametric restrictions as alternatives to analogous GMM test procedures. Although they report no small sample evidence, they identify this as an important topic for further research.

Imbens [1997] proposes other alternatives to standard GMM estimators, and shows that they have several advantages. An initial estimate of the weighting matrix is no longer required, and it becomes straightforward to derive the distribution of the estimator under general misspecification. Some of the alternative estimators he proposes turn out to have appealing information–theoretic interpretations, and have distributions that can be approximate by saddlepoint approximations. The principal disadvantage is that of computation: the system of equations that has to be solved is of greater dimension than the number of parameters of interest.

In a related paper, *Smith* [1997] examines alternative semi–parametric quasi-likelihood approaches to GMM. These embed sample versions of the moment conditions used in GMM into a non–parametric quasi–likelihood function by use of additional parameters associated with these moment conditions. It is possible to define both specification and misspecification tests which are similar to classical tests and are first–order equivalent to the corresponding GMM test statistics. He explores the structure of this semi-parametric quasi-maximum likelihood estimator for models estimated by instrumental variables.

Finally, it is worth mentioning *Kitamura and Phillips'* [1995] development of a limit theory for instrumental variables (IV) estimation that allows for possibly nonstationary processes. They derive fully modified (FM) versions of several estimators, including GMM and the generalized instrumental variables estimator (GIVE). They investigate by simulation methods the small sample properties of the following estimation procedures: ordinary least squares, crude (conventional) IV, FM–IV, FM–GMM, and FM–GIVE. They find that among FM–IV, FM–GMM, and FM–GIVE, when applied to the stationary coefficients, FM–GIVE generally outperforms FM–IV and FM–GMM by a wide margin, whereas the difference between FM–IV and FM–GMM is quite small whenever the autoregressive roots of the stationary processes are quite large. However, when applied to the nonstationary coefficients, the three estimators are numerically very close.

5.3.2 Testing

Smith [1992] proposed non–nested tests for competing models estimated by GMM, based upon the Cox and encompassing principles. His results apply to non–nested linear regression models with heteroskedasticity and serial correlation of unknown form and differing instrument validity assumptions. *Arkonac and Higgins* [1995] examine the finite sample properties of these tests using Monte Carlo simulations. The size and power of the tests are found to depend upon the degree of heteroskedasticity, the degree of correlation between regressors and instrumental variables, the error distribution, the sample size and the number of regressors.

Since various simulation experiments suggest that tests based on GMM estimators and their asymptotic critical values often have true sizes that differ greatly from their nominal sizes, *Hall and Horowitz* [1996] investigate conditions under which the bootstrap provides asymptotic refinements to the critical values of t-tests and tests of overidentifying restrictions, particular in the case of dependent data. Their simulation results show that the bootstrap usually reduces the errors in size that occur when critical values based on first–order asymptotic theory are used. The bootstrap also provides an indication of the accuracy of critical values obtained from first–order asymptotic theory.

Zhou [1994] proposed alternative GMM tests that are analytically solvable in many econometric models. In particular, this provides analytical GMM tests for asset pricing models with time–varying risk premiums. He provides simulation evidence showing that the proposed tests have good finite sample properties and that their asymptotic distribution is reliable for the sample size commonly used.

5.4 Concluding Comments

The literature surveyed in this chapter demonstrates two key features. First, there is considerable evidence that the finite sample properties of GMM estimators and test are often not well approximated by conventional asymptotics. This conclusion holds over the wide range of different models, and areas of economics and finance, that have seen application of GMM techniques. Second, there is a lively and important current literature suggesting and investigating extended GMM procedures for estimation and testing. Many of these new developments have yet to be fully evaluated, either in practice or with respect to their finite sample behavior. We can expect to see important contributions to this topic of research.

References

Ahn, S.C., and S. Low [1996]: A Reformulation of the Hausman Test for Regression Models with Pooled Cross Section-Time Series Data; *Journal of Econometrics*, 71(1-2), 309-319.

A., J.G. and L.M. Segal [1996]: Small-Sample Bias in GMM Estimation of Covariance Structure; *Journal of Business & Economic Statistics*, 14(3), 353-366.

Andersen, T.G., and B.E. Sørensen [1996]: GMM Estimation of a Stochastic Volatility Model: A Monte Carlo Study; *Journal of Business & Economic Statistics*, 14(3), 328-352.

Andersen, T.G. and B.E. Sørensen [1997]: GMM and QML Asymptotic Standard Deviations in Stochastic Volatility Models: A Comment on Ruiz (1994); *Journal of Econometrics*, 76(1-2), 397-403.

Arkonac, S.Z. and M.L. Higgins [1995]: A Monte Carlo Study of Tests for Nonnested Models Estimated by Generalized Method of Moments; *Communications in Statistics - Simulation and Computation*, 24(3), 745-763.

Burnside, C. and M. Eichenbaum [1996]: Small-Sample Properties of GMM-Based Wald Tests; *Journal of Business & Economic Statistics*, 14(3), 294-308.

Chan, K., G. Karolyi, F. Longstaff and A. Sanders [1992]: An Empirical Comparison of Some Alternative Models of the Short-Term Interest Rate, Journal of Finance, 47(3), 1209-1227.

Christiano, L.J. and W.J. den Haan [1996]: Small-Sample Properties of GMM for Business-Cycle Analysis; *Journal of Business & Economic Statistics*, 14(3), 309-327.

Clark, T.E. [1996]: Small-Sample Properties of Estimators of Nonlinear Models of Covariance Structure; *Journal of Business & Economic Statistics*, 14(3), 367-373.

Dahlquist, M. [1996]: On Alternative Interest Rate Processes; *Journal of Banking and Finance*, 20(6), 1093-1119.

Ferson, W.E. and S.R. Foerster [1994]: Finite-Sample Properties of the Generalized Method of Moments in Tests of Conditional Asset Pricing Models; *Journal of Financial Economics*, 36(1), 29-55.

Flesaker, B. [1993]: Testing the Heath-Jarrow-Morton/Ho-Lee Model of Interest Rate Contingent Claims Pricing; *Journal of Financial and Quantitative Analysis*, 28(4), 483-495.

Fuhrer, J.C., G.R. Moore and S.D. Schuh [1995]: Estimating the Linear-Quadratic Inventory Model: Maximum Likelihood versus Generalized Method of Moments; *Journal of Monetary Economics*, 35(1), 115-157.

Gregory, A.W. and G.W. Smith [1996]: Measuring Business Cycles with Business Cycle Models; *Journal of Economic Dynamics and Control*, 20(6-7), 1007-1025.

Hall, A. [1993]: *Some Aspects of Generalized Method of Moments Estimation*; Ch. 15 (pp. 393-417) in G.S. Maddala, C.R. Rao and H.D. Vinod (eds.), Handbook of Statistics, Vol. 11, Amsterdam: North-Holland.

Hall, P. and J.L. Horowitz [1996]: Bootstrap Critical Values for Tests Based on Generalized Method of Moments Estimators; *Econometrica*, 64(4), 891-916.

Hall, R.E. and F.S. Mishkin [1982]: The Sensitivity of Consumption to Transitory Income: Estimates from Panel Data on Households; *Econometrica*, 50(2), 462-480.

Hansen, L.P. [1982]: Large Sample Properties of Generalized Method of Moments Estimator; *Econometrica*, 50(4), 1029-1054.

Hansen, L.P. and K. Singleton [1982]: Generalized Instrumental Variable Estimation of Nonlinear Rational Expectations Models; *Econometrica*, 50(5), 1269-1286.

Hansen, L.P., J. Heaton and A. Yaron [1996]: Finite-Sample Properties of Some Alternative GMM Estimators; *Journal of Business & Economic Statistics*, 14(3), 262-280.

Hillier, G.H. [1990]: On the Normalization of Structural Equations: Properties of Direction Estimators; *Econometrica*, 58(5), 1181-1194.

Imbens, G.W. [1997]: One-Step Estimators for Over-Identified Generalized Method of Moments Models; *Review of Economic Studies*, 64(3), 359-383.

Jacquier, E., N.G. Polson and P.E. Rossi [1994]: Bayesian Analysis of Stochastic Volatility Models; *Journal of Business & Economic Statistics*, 12(4), 371-389.

Kitamura, Y., and P.C.B. Phillips [1995]: Efficient IV Estimation in Non-stationary Regression - An Overview and Simulation Study; *Econometric Theory*, 11(5), 1095-1130.

Kitamura, Y. and M. Stutzer [1997]: An Information-Theoretic Alternative to Generalized Method of Moments Estimation; *Econometrica*, 65(4), 861-874.

Kocherlakota, N.R. [1990]: On Tests of Representative Consumer Asset Pricing Models; *Journal of Monetary Economics*, 26(2), 285-304.

Lee, B.J., and M.J. Lee [1997]: Generalized Method of Moment Estimation of Truncated or Censored Regression; *Applied Economics Letters*, 4(6), 365-368.

Maddala, G.S. and J. Jeong [1992]: On the Exact Small Sample Distribution of the Instrumental Variable Estimator; *Econometrica*, 60(1), 181-183.

Magdalinos, M.A. [1994]: Testing Instrument Admissability: Some Refined Asymptotic Results; *Econometrica*, 62(2), 373-405.

Mudambi, R. and L.W. Taylor [1995]: Some Nonparametric Tests for Duration Dependence: An Application to UK Business Cycle Data; *Journal of Applied Statistics*, 22(1), 163-177.

Nelson, C.R. and R. Startz [1990a]: The Distribution of the Instrumental Variable Estimator and Its t–Ratio When the Instrument is a Poor One; *Journal of Business*, 63(1), 125-163.

Nelson, C.R. and R. Startz [1990b]: Some Further Results on the Exact Small Sample Properties of the Instrumental Variables Estimator; *Econometrica*, 58(4), 967-976.

Ni, S. [1997]: Scaling Factors in Estimation of Time-Separable Utility Functions; *Review of Economics and Statistics*, 79(2), 234-240.

Ogaki, M. [1993]: *Generalized Method of Moments: Econometric Applications*; Ch. 17 (pp. 455-488) in G.S. Maddala, C.R. Rao and H.D. Vinod (eds.), Handbook of Statistics, Vol. 11, Amsterdam: North-Holland.

Pagan, A.R. and Y. Jung [1993]: *Understanding Some Failures of Instrumental Variable Estimators*; mimeo, Australian National University.

Pakes, A., and D. Pollard [1989]: Simulation and the Asymptotics of Optimization Estimators; *Econometrica*, 57(5), 1027-1057.

Phillips, P.C.B. [1983]: *Exact Small Sample Theory in the Simultaneous Equations Model*; Ch. 7 (pp. 449-516) in Z. Griliches and M.D. Intriligator (eds.), Handbook of Econometrics, Vol. 1, Amsterdam: North Holland.

Ruiz, E. [1994]: Quasi-Maximum Likelihood Estimation of Stochastic Volatility Models; *Journal of Econometrics*, 63(1), 289-903.

Ruiz, E. [1997]: QML and GMM Estimators of Stochastic Volatility Models: Response to Andersen and Sørensen; *Journal of Econometrics*, 76(1-2), 405.

Smith, R.J. [1992]: Non-Nested Tests for Competing Models Estimated by Generalized Method of Moments; *Econometrica*, 60(4), 973-980.

Smith, R.J. [1997]: Alternative Semi-parametric Likelihood Approaches to Generalised Method of Moments Estimation; *Economic Journal*, 107(441), 503-519.

Staiger, D. and J.H. Stock [**1997**]: Instrumental Variables Regression with Weak Instruments; *Econometrica*, 65(3), 557-586.

Stock, J.H. and J. Wright [**1996**]: *Asymptotics for GMM Estimators with Weak Instruments*; Technical Working Paper No. 198, NBER.

Tauchen, G. [**1986**]: Statistical Properties of Generalized Method-of-Moments Estimators of Structural Parameters Obtained from Financial Market Data; *Journal of Business & Economic Statistics*, 4, 397-425.

West, K.D. [**1996**]: *Inventory Models*; in M.H. Pesaran and M.R. Wickens (eds.), Handbook of Applied Econometrics, Vol. 1, Oxford: Basil Blackwell.

West, K.D. and D.W. Wilcox [**1994**]: *Some Evidence on Finite Sample Distributions of Instrumental Variables Estimators of the Linear Quadratic Inventory Model*; pp. 253-282 in R. Fiorito (ed.), Inventory Cycles and Monetary Policy, Berlin: Springer-Verlag.

West, K.D. and D.W. Wilcox [**1996**]: A Comparison of Alternative Instrumental Variables Estimators of a Dynamic Linear Model; *Journal of Business & Economic Statistics*, 14(3), 281-293.

Zhou, G.F. [**1994**]: Analytical GMM Tests: Asset Pricing with Time-Varying Risk; *Review of Financial Studies*, 7(4), 687-709.

Chapter 6

GMM ESTIMATION OF TIME SERIES MODELS

David Harris

In time series analysis, the basic univariate model is the autoregressive moving average (ARMA) one. The estimation of ARMA models has been the subject of a vast literature over many years. If a pure autoregressive (AR) model is considered then ordinary least squares (OLS) estimation is appropriate and is asymptotically equivalent to maximum likelihood when the errors are normally distributed. However, the introduction of moving average (MA) components to the model complicates the estimation problem because the least squares criterion is no longer linear in the parameters. Both least squares and maximum likelihood estimation for models involving MA terms involves numerical optimisation and is relatively computationally difficult. As a result, a variety of techniques for the estimation of models with MA terms have been suggested that do not involve numerical optimisation. These techniques have generally made use (implicitly or explicitly) of moment conditions implied by the ARMA model, and therefore fall within the class of GMM estimators. This chapter has two aims. The first is to provide an introduction to some of these moments–based estimators. The second is a pedagogic one to illustrate the general theory of GMM presented in Chapter 1 as applied to a relatively simple time series model.

An outline of the chapter is as follows. In Section 6.1 we discuss the estimation of pure MA models. For simplicity we focus mostly on first order MA models, and indicate how extensions to higher order models follow. In Section 6.2, we consider the estimation of ARMA models, with particular emphasis on the estimation of AR coefficients by instrumental variables methods. The result is a computationally simple moments–based estimation procedure for ARMA models. In Section 6.3 we investigate how these methods can be applied to testing for unit roots.

6.1 Estimation of Moving Average Models

In this section we discuss the estimation of pure moving average models of the form

$$y_t = \varepsilon_t + \theta_1 \varepsilon_{t-1} + \ldots + \theta_q \varepsilon_{t-q},$$

where ε_t is an i.i.d. zero mean error process with variance σ_0^2 and fourth order cumulant κ_4. With the extra assumption that ε_t is normally distributed, maximum likelihood estimation of $\theta_1, \ldots, \theta_q$ is possible, but requires numerical maximization of the likelihood. For this reason, there has been considerable interest in finding simpler estimators that have properties approaching those of maximum likelihood, and some of these simpler estimators can be put in the GMM framework.

In the following section, we give a simple estimator derived directly from the moments implied by an MA(1) model, but we show that it generally has poor properties. We then describe a popular approach to the estimation of moving average models which makes use of approximate autoregressive models that can be estimated by OLS regression. The properties of these estimators can be very good. Finally, we indicate how the methods can be extended to moving average models of general order.

6.1.1 A Simple Estimator of an MA(1) Model

We consider the estimation of θ_0 in the model

$$y_t = \varepsilon_t + \theta_0 \varepsilon_{t-1}, \tag{6-1}$$

where we assume that $\varepsilon_t \sim$ i.i.d.$(0, \sigma_0^2)$ and $|\theta_0| < 1$. It is straightforward to show that the first order autocorrelation implied by this model is

$$\rho_0 = \frac{E(y_t y_{t-1})}{E(y_t^2)} = \frac{\theta_0}{1 + \theta_0^2}. \tag{6-2}$$

It is also the case that all higher order autocorrelations are zero, but these additional moment conditions are not used here. If we define the sample first order autocorrelation

$$\widehat{\rho}_T = \frac{\sum_{t=2}^{T} y_t y_{t-1}}{\sum_{t=1}^{T} y_t^2},$$

then the replacement of unknown parameters by sample estimators in Equation (6-2) suggests we solve the quadratic

$$\widehat{\theta}_T^2 - \widehat{\rho}_T^{-1} \widehat{\theta}_T + 1 = 0$$

to obtain the estimator $\widehat{\theta}_T$. In order for the solution of this quadratic to be real we require $|\widehat{\rho}_T| \leq 0.5$, and it is also the case that the true first order autocorrelation satisfies $|\rho_0| < 0.5$. Thus, given the consistency of $\widehat{\rho}_T$, it follows that $\Pr(|\widehat{\rho}_T| \leq 0.5) \to 1$. However, in a finite sample it is possible that $|\widehat{\rho}_T| > 0.5$, particularly if $|\theta_0|$ is near one. To provide an estimator of θ_0 that is always real valued we could define

$$\widetilde{\rho}_T = \begin{cases} -0.5, & \text{if } \widehat{\rho}_T < -0.5, \\ \widehat{\rho}_T, & \text{if } |\widehat{\rho}_T| < 0.5, \\ 0.5, & \text{if } \widehat{\rho}_T > 0.5, \end{cases}$$

and $\widetilde{\theta}_T$ to be the quadratic solution

$$\widetilde{\theta}_T = \frac{1 - \sqrt{1 - 4\widehat{\rho}_T^2}}{2\widehat{\rho}_T}.$$

It can be seen that the finite sample distribution of $\widetilde{\theta}_T$ consists of a mixture of two discrete probability masses at ± 1 (which disappear as $T \to \infty$) and a continuous distribution for $-1 < \widetilde{\theta}_T < 1$.

An estimator for σ_0^2 can then be found from the relationship

$$E(y_t^2) = \sigma_0^2 (1 + \theta_0^2). \tag{6-3}$$

Using appropriate sample quantities we have

$$\widetilde{\sigma}_T^2 = \frac{T^{-1} \sum_{t=1}^{T} y_t^2}{1 + \widetilde{\theta}_T^2}.$$

We can put this estimator into the GMM framework defined in Chapter 1. If we let the parameter vector be $\eta = (\theta, \sigma^2)'$ and define

$$f(y_t, \eta) = \begin{pmatrix} y_t y_{t-1} - \sigma^2 \theta \\ y_t^2 - \sigma^2(1 + \theta^2) \end{pmatrix},$$

then it follows from (6–2) and (6–3) that $Ef(y_t, \eta_0) = 0$. The sample moments are

$$f_T(\eta) = T^{-1} \sum_{t=1}^{T} f(y_t, \eta) = \begin{pmatrix} T^{-1} \sum_{t=1}^{T} y_t y_{t-1} - \sigma^2 \theta \\ T^{-1} \sum_{t=1}^{T} y_t^2 - \sigma^2(1 + \theta^2) \end{pmatrix},$$

and solving the exactly identified equation $f_T(\widehat{\eta}_T) = 0$ for $\widehat{\eta}_T$ gives the estimator $\widehat{\theta}_T$ defined above, and $\widehat{\sigma}_\varepsilon^2$ defined analogously to $\widetilde{\sigma}_\varepsilon^2$. We can also define $\widetilde{\eta}_T = (\widetilde{\theta}_T, \widetilde{\sigma}_\varepsilon^2)'$.

The asymptotic properties of these estimators are summarized in the following theorem, the proof of which is given in the Appendix of this chapter.

THEOREM 6.1

Both $\widehat{\eta}_T$ and $\widetilde{\eta}_T$ are consistent and both $\sqrt{T}(\widehat{\eta}_T - \eta_0)$ and $\sqrt{T}(\widetilde{\eta}_T - \eta_0)$ is asymptotically normal with mean 0 and asymptotic covariance matrix

$$\frac{1}{(1 - \theta_0^2)^2} \begin{pmatrix} 1 + \theta_0^2 + 4\theta_0^4 + \theta_0^6 + \theta_0^8 & -2\sigma_\varepsilon^2 \theta_0^3 (2 + \theta_0^2 + \theta_0^4) \\ -2\sigma_\varepsilon^2 \theta_0^3 (2 + \theta_0^2 + \theta_0^4) & 2\sigma_\varepsilon^4 (1 - 2\theta_0^2 + 3\theta_0^4 + 2\theta_0^6) \end{pmatrix}$$
$$+ \begin{pmatrix} 0 & 0 \\ 0 & \kappa_4. \end{pmatrix}$$

∎

It is of interest to consider the asymptotic efficiency of $\widehat{\theta}_T$ in particular. Its asymptotic variance is

$$\frac{1 + \theta_0^2 + 4\theta_0^4 + \theta_0^6 + \theta_0^8}{(1 - \theta_0^2)^2},$$

as compared to the asymptotic variance of the maximum likelihood estimator under the normality assumption, which is $1 - \theta_0^2$. If $\theta_0 = 0$ then it can be seen that $\widehat{\theta}_T$ is as asymptotically efficient as the maximum likelihood estimator, but as θ_0 departs from zero $\widehat{\theta}_T$ rapidly becomes less efficient than maximum likelihood. This estimator and its generally poor properties appear in *Hannan* [1960],

(p. 47–48), see also *Hannan* [1970], (p. 373–374). This provides a simple example of the fact that (G)MM can provide quite inefficient estimators, and it is important to examine the properties of any new estimator derived.

6.1.2 Estimation by Autoregressive Approximation

A commonly used method for the estimation of MA(1) models (and, more generally, ARMA models) is to use an AR model to approximate the time series and derive estimates of the MA(1) model from the estimates of the AR model. The idea was suggested by *Durbin* [1959] and many modifications and extensions have since been made.

In the case of the invertible MA(1) model (6–1), we have the AR representation

$$y_t = \sum_{j=1}^{\infty} \alpha_j\,(\theta_0)\,y_{t-j} + \varepsilon_t, \qquad (6\text{–}4)$$

where

$$\alpha_j(\theta) = -\,(-\theta)^j, \quad j = 1, 2, \ldots \qquad (6\text{–}5)$$

for any θ. We use the notation $\alpha_j(\theta)$ to show explicitly that the autoregressive coefficients are functions of θ. Since (6–4) is of infinite order, it is necessary in practice to approximate it by an AR(k) model

$$y_t = \sum_{j=1}^{k} \alpha_j(\theta_0) y_{t-j} + \varepsilon_{kt}, \qquad (6\text{–}6)$$

in order to obtain any estimates. Note that the error term $\varepsilon_{kt} = \varepsilon_t + \sum_{j=k+1}^{\infty} \alpha_j(\theta_0) y_{t-j} = \varepsilon_t + (-1)^{k+1}\theta_0^{k+1}\varepsilon_{t-k-1}$ in (6–6) is different from that in (6–4), reflecting the extra error made by approximating the AR(∞) by an AR(k). However, since $|\theta_0| < 1$, this error decreases as k increases. For the asymptotic results that follow, it is necessary to assume that k is chosen in such a way that $k \to \infty$ as $T \to \infty$, so that (6–6) approximates (6–4) increasingly well as the sample size increases.

In order to put these ideas into the GMM framework, we regard (6–1) as a structural model and (6–6) as a reduced form model whose role is to summarize the moments of the MA(1) process. In particular, the structural model has implications for the second moments of y_t (*i.e.*, the autocovariances) and the AR model captures these moments. That is, we use an AR model to summarize the second order properties of y_t instead of (the first element of) the autocovariance function as in the previous section. The connection between the parameter of interest θ_0 and the reduced form parameters $\alpha_j(\theta_0)$ is given by (6–5), and these relations can be used to define estimators for θ_0 based on estimators for $\alpha_j(\theta_0)$.

For any θ, we define a $k \times 1$ vector

$$A_k(\theta) = \begin{pmatrix} \alpha_1(\theta) \\ \vdots \\ \alpha_k(\theta) \end{pmatrix},$$

with $\alpha_j(\theta)$ given by (6–5). The vector of true autoregressive coefficients in (6–6) may therefore be written $A_k(\theta_0)$. Similarly, let $\widehat{A}_k$ represent the $k \times 1$ vector of OLS estimators $\widehat{\alpha}_1, \ldots, \widehat{\alpha}_k$ in (6–6). The estimation strategy is, for some value of k, to choose $\widehat{\theta}_{Tk}$ to be the value of θ that minimizes the difference between $\widehat{A}_k$ and $A_k(\theta)$. That is, we can define

$$\widehat{\theta}_{Tk} = \text{argmin}_{\theta \in \Theta} \left(\widehat{A}_k - A_k(\theta) \right)' V_{Tk} \left(\widehat{A}_k - A_k(\theta) \right), \qquad (6\text{–}7)$$

where $\Theta = (-1, 1)$ and V_{Tk} is a $k \times k$ weighting matrix. For a given k, different estimators can be constructed by using different sub–vectors of $\left(\widehat{A}_k - A_k(\theta) \right)$, and more generally, by choosing different weighting matrices. The following well known estimators are of the form of (6–7).

6.1.2.1 The Durbin Estimator

Durbin [1959] suggested an estimator that follows naturally from a re–arranged form of (6–5). We can write (6–5) as

$$\alpha_j(\theta) = -\theta \alpha_{j-1}(\theta), \quad j = 1, 2, \ldots$$

with $\alpha_0(\theta) = -1$. This may be interpreted as an exact autoregressive relationship for $\alpha_j(\theta)$. Hence we could estimate θ_0 by regressing the estimates $(\widehat{\alpha}_1, \ldots, \widehat{\alpha}_k)'$ from (6–6) on a "lag" of themselves, *i.e.*, $(1, \widehat{\alpha}_1, \ldots, \widehat{\alpha}_{k-1})'$. The estimator is thus

$$\widehat{\theta}_D = - \left(\sum_{j=1}^{k} \widehat{\alpha}_j \widehat{\alpha}_{j-1} \right) \Big/ \left(\sum_{j=1}^{k} \widehat{\alpha}_{j-1}^2 \right),$$

with $\hat{\alpha}_0 = 1$. *Durbin* [1959] showed that $\hat{\theta}_D$ is consistent and asymptotically normal with asymptotic variance $(1-\theta_0^2)$. Hence this estimator is asymptotically as efficient as the maximum likelihood estimator.

To express $\hat{\theta}_D$ in terms of (6–7), let $B_k(\theta) = I_k + \theta L_k$, where L_k is a $k \times k$ matrix with ones on the first lower off–diagonal and zeros elsewhere. Then $\hat{\theta}_D$ results from (6–7) when $V_{Tk} = B_k(\theta)' B_k(\theta)$.

6.1.2.2 The Galbraith and Zinde-Walsh Estimator

Galbraith and Zinde-Walsh [1994] made use of autoregressive approximations to estimate MA models of any order. For the first order case, their approach is to make use of relationship (6–5) only for $j = 1$. That is, they choose $\hat{\theta}_{GZW}$ to minimize the difference between $\hat{\alpha}_1$ and $\alpha_1(\theta) = \theta$, which results in the estimator

$$\hat{\theta}_{GZW} = \hat{\alpha}_1.$$

In terms of (6–7), this implies that V_{Tk} is chosen to be a $k \times k$ matrix of zeros except for element $(1, 1)$, which is set to one. This results in a very simple estimator, but one which is not always asymptotically efficient. It is shown by *Galbraith and Zinde-Walsh* [1994] that the asymptotic variance of $\hat{\theta}_{GZW}$ is one for any θ_0. Thus $\hat{\theta}_{GZW}$ is asymptotically efficient for $\theta_0 = 0$, but loses efficiency relative to $\hat{\theta}_D$ and maximum likelihood as θ_0 departs from zero. The loss of asymptotic efficiency relative to $\hat{\theta}_D$ may have been expected because only 1 of k possible moment conditions are used in constructing $\hat{\theta}_{GZW}$.

6.1.3 A Finite Order Autoregressive Approximation

The equations (6–5) apply to the infinite order autoregressive representation (6–4). In practice we must use the finite order autoregressive approximation (6–6), and rely on the assumption that $k \to \infty$ as $T \to \infty$ to claim that (6–5) will provide an accurate relationship between the autoregressive and moving average parameters. An alternative approach, suggested by *Ghysels, Khalaf and Vodounou* [1994] is to replace (6–5) by equations derived by *Galbraith and*

Zinde-Walsh [1994], (equation 10) assuming a fixed and finite lag length k. That is, we use

$$\alpha_j(\theta) = -(-\theta)^j \frac{1 - \theta^{2(k-j+1)}}{1 - \theta^{2(k+1)}} \tag{6-8}$$

to construct $A_k(\theta)$, and $\widehat{\theta}_{Tk}$ be found from (6–7). Clearly (6–8) converges to (6–5) if k is let to go to infinity. It is possible that the inclusion of the additional terms in (6–8) that are functions of k will improve the finite sample performance of the estimator by explicitly acknowledging the finite order autoregression used. A disadvantage of the approach is additional computational complexity compared to the Galbraith and Zinde-Walsh and Durbin estimators above. If we follow the Galbraith and Zinde-Walsh approach and estimate θ_0 using only the first autoregressive coefficient, then the sample version of (6–8) with $j = 1$ rearranges to give

$$\widehat{\alpha}_1 \widehat{\theta}^{2(k+1)} - \widehat{\theta}^{2k+1} + \widehat{\theta} - \widehat{\alpha}_1 = 0.$$

That is, it is necessary to solve a $2(k + 1)$ order polynomial to obtain the estimator, making the approach less convenient than those above.

6.1.4 Higher Order MA Models

The first order moving average estimators of the previous sections can be extended to higher order MA models with little conceptual difficulty. Given the poor properties of the estimator in Section 6.1.1 we only consider estimators based on autoregressive approximations.

We consider the MA(m) model

$$y_t = \varepsilon_t + \theta_{10}\varepsilon_{t-1} + \ldots + \theta_{m0}\varepsilon_{t-m},$$

and its infinite autoregressive representation (6–4) where $\theta_0 = (\theta_{10}, \ldots, \theta_{m0})'$ and the relationships between $\alpha_j(\theta)$ and θ are given by (see *Galbraith and Zinde-Walsh* [1994])

$$\alpha_j(\theta) = - \sum_{i=1}^{\min(j,m)} \theta_i \alpha_{j-i}(\theta), \quad j = 1, 2, \ldots. \tag{6-9}$$

We again make use of the approximate AR(k) model (6–6) with $k \to \infty$ as $T \to \infty$. It is necessary that k be at least as large as m in any application in order to identify θ.

The *Galbraith and Zinde-Walsh* [1994] approach takes the first m equations in (6–9), replaces the parameters with sample estimators and solves for the $m \times 1$ vector $\widehat{\theta}_{GZW}$. For a given k, it is straightforward to obtain formulae for the elements of $\widehat{\theta}_{GZW}$. For example, for an MA(3) model we have

$$\widehat{\theta}_{GZW1} = \widehat{\alpha}_1,$$
$$\widehat{\theta}_{GZW2} = \widehat{\alpha}_2 + \widehat{\alpha}_1^2,$$
$$\widehat{\theta}_{GZW3} = \widehat{\alpha}_3 + 2\widehat{\alpha}_1\widehat{\alpha}_2 + \widehat{\alpha}_1^3.$$

In general, $\widehat{\theta}_{GZW}$ is not asymptotically efficient because it uses only a fixed number of an expanding number of moment conditions.

The *Durbin* [1959] approach uses all of $\widehat{\alpha}_1, \ldots, \widehat{\alpha}_k$. Sample counterparts to the equations (6–9) are available for $j = 1, \ldots, k$. These equations imply the m order autoregression in $\widehat{\alpha}_j$

$$\widehat{\alpha}_j = -\widehat{\theta}_1\widehat{\alpha}_{j-1} - \ldots - \widehat{\theta}_m\widehat{\alpha}_{j-m}$$

estimated by OLS over $j = 1, \ldots, k$ with $\widehat{\alpha}_j = 0$ for $j < 0$. The resulting coefficient vector $\widehat{\theta}_D = (\widehat{\theta}_{D1}, \ldots, \widehat{\theta}_{Dm})'$ is an asymptotically efficient estimator of θ_0.

6.2 Estimation of ARMA Models

We now consider the estimation of ARMA models. We first discuss the estimation of the AR coefficients of an ARMA model by instrumental variables methods. These estimators clearly fall into the class of GMM estimators.

6.2.1 IV Estimation of AR Coefficients

In some applications, the estimation of the AR coefficients of an ARMA model may be of primary interest, and the MA coefficients may be nuisance parameters. For example, suppose a first order autoregressive signal is observed with an additive white noise measurement error:

$$y_t = \phi_t + u_t$$
$$\phi_t = \alpha\phi_{t-1} + v_t,$$

where u_t and v_t are independent i.i.d. processes. These equations can be combined to give

$$y_t - \alpha y_{t-1} = u_t + v_t - \alpha v_{t-1},$$

which is equivalent in its moments to an ARMA(1,1) model with the MA coefficient being a function of α and the variances of u_t and v_t. In this case we are only interested in the autoregressive parameter α and the moving average parameter is a nuisance parameter reflecting the presence of the measurement error. This type of application arises in engineering system identification, see *Stoica, Soderstrom and Friedlander* [1985] for example. Useful application of the following methods can also be made in unit root testing as discussed in Section 6.3 and also as part of a method of estimating the full ARMA model as discussed in Section 6.2.3.

6.2.2 The ARMA(1,1) Model

For clarity, we treat the ARMA(1,1) model in some detail. The model is

$$y_t = \beta_0 y_{t-1} + \varepsilon_t + \theta_0 \varepsilon_{t-1}, \qquad (6\text{–}10)$$

and we assume that $\beta_0 \neq -\theta_0$ and that y_t is stationary and invertible (that is $|\beta_0| < 1$ and $|\theta_0| < 1$). For now, we are concerned only with the estimation of β_0. We view the model as a regression

$$y_t = \beta_0 y_{t-1} + u_t, \qquad (6\text{–}11)$$

where u_t is the autocorrelated error term

$$u_t = \varepsilon_t + \theta_0 \varepsilon_{t-1}.$$

Note that the OLS estimator of β_0 in (6–11) (ignoring the moving average structure of u_t) is inconsistent because $E(u_t y_{t-1}) \neq 0$. That is, the regressor is correlated with the error term. This can be seen by noting that

$$y_t = \sum_{j=0}^{\infty} \beta_0^j u_{t-j} \qquad (6\text{–}12)$$

by back substitution in (6–11). Then $E(u_t y_{t-1}) = E(u_t u_{t-1}) = \sigma_\varepsilon^2 \theta_0$. Therefore, we consider the instrumental variables estimation of (6–11).

6.2.2.1 A Simple IV Estimator

Note that the MA(1) structure of u_t implies that $E(u_t u_{t-j}) = 0$ for all $j \geq 2$. Furthermore, (6–12) implies that

$$E(u_t y_{t-j}) = 0 \text{ for all } j \geq 2. \tag{6–13}$$

These moment conditions can be used to identify and consistently estimate β_0. Just one of these moment conditions is sufficient to identify β_0, and the natural one to choose is $E(u_t y_{t-2}) = 0$. We then have the moment conditions $E f(y_t, \beta_0) = 0$, where

$$f(y_t, \beta) = (y_t - \beta y_{t-1}) y_{t-2}.$$

Then $f_T(\beta) = T^{-1} \sum_{t=3}^{T} (y_t - \beta y_{t-1}) y_{t-2}$ and solving $f_T(\widehat{\beta}_T) = 0$ for $\widehat{\beta}_T$ yields

$$\widehat{\beta}_T = \left(\sum_{t=3}^{T} y_{t-2} y_{t-1} \right)^{-1} \sum_{t=3}^{T} y_{t-2} y_t.$$

Of course, this is just the simple IV estimator of (6–11) using y_{t-2} as an instrumental variable for y_{t-1}.

We have the following asymptotic properties.

THEOREM 6.2

> $\widehat{\beta}_T$ is consistent and $\sqrt{T} \left(\widehat{\beta}_T - \beta_0 \right)$ is asymptotically normally distributed with mean 0 and variance
>
> $$\frac{(1 - \beta_0^2)}{(1 + \beta_0 \theta_0)^2 (\beta_0 + \theta_0)^2} \left(1 + 4\theta_0^2 + 4\beta_0 \theta_0 + 4\beta_0 \theta_0^3 + 2\beta_0^2 \theta_0^2 + \theta_0^4 \right).$$

■

Notice that the asymptotic variance of $\widehat{\beta}_T$ becomes infinite when $\beta_0 = -\theta_0$. If $\beta_0 = -\theta_0$ then y_t is equivalent to a white noise process and both β_0 and θ_0 are not identified. This possibility is excluded by our assumptions, but the asymptotic distribution suggests that if β_0 is near $-\theta_0$ then $\widehat{\beta}_T$ may have a large variance.

For the purposes of comparison, the asymptotic distribution of the maximum likelihood estimator of the autoregressive parameter in an ARMA(1,1) model with normally distributed errors is

$$\sqrt{T} \left(\widehat{\beta}_{MLE} - \beta_0 \right) \xrightarrow{d} N \left(0, \frac{(1 + \beta_0 \theta_0)^2 (1 - \beta_0^2)}{(\beta_0 + \theta_0)^2} \right),$$

(see *Brockwell and Davis* [1993], (p. 260) for example). As would be expected, the asymptotic variance of $\widehat{\beta}_{MLE}$ is smaller than that of $\widehat{\beta}_T$. For values of β_0 and θ_0 near zero, $\widehat{\beta}_T$ is almost as asymptotically efficient as $\widehat{\beta}_{MLE}$. However, for larger values of β_0 and θ_0, $\widehat{\beta}_{MLE}$ is considerably more asymptotically efficient (especially if β_0 is close to $-\theta_0$ and close to one in magnitude). Note that $\widehat{\beta}_{MLE}$ may also have a large variance if β_0 is close to $-\theta_0$.

6.2.2.2 Optimal IV Estimation

In the preceding section we used y_{t-2} as an instrument for y_{t-1}. It is possible to use any one of y_{t-j}, $j = 2, 3, \ldots$ as an admissable instrument for y_{t-1}, and to construct estimators

$$\widehat{\beta}_{Tj} = \left(\sum_{t=j+1}^{T} y_{t-1} y_{t-j} \right)^{-1} \sum_{t=j+1}^{T} y_t y_{t-j}$$

for various values of $j \geq 2$. However, it is shown by *Dolado* [1990] that $\widehat{\beta}_{Tj}$ has asymptotic variance equal to $\beta_0^{-2(j-2)}$ times the asymptotic variance given in Theorem 1.2 above. Since $|\beta_0| < 1$ by assumption, it follows that $\widehat{\beta}_{T2}$ is the most asymptotically efficient of all of the estimators $\widehat{\beta}_{Tj}$. Intuitively, this result is expected. In general, the asymptotic efficiency of an **IV** estimator is positively related to the correlation between the stochastic regressor (y_{t-1} in this case) and its instrumental variable (y_{t-j}). Since y_t is a stationary ARMA process, it follows that the correlation between y_{t-1} and y_{t-j} decreases as j increases, so it is preferable to choose j as small as is admissable, that is $j = 2$.

We can also consider estimators that make use of more than one instrument for y_{t-1} implied by the moment conditions (6–13). This was considered for the estimation of ARMA models of any order by *Stoica, Soderstrom and Friedlander* [1985]. Suppose we make use of the first q consecutive moment conditions implied by (6–13):

$$E f (y_t, \beta_0) = 0,$$

where now

$$f (y_t, \beta) = Y_{q,t-2} (y_t - \beta y_{t-1})$$

is a $q \times 1$ vector of moments and $Y_{q,t} = (y_t, \ldots, y_{t-m+1})'$ is a $q \times 1$ vector of instrumental variables. Following Definition 1.2, we define

$$\widehat{\beta}_{Tq} = \text{argmin}_\beta Q_T(\beta),$$

where
$$Q_T(\beta) = f_T(\beta)' A_{Tq} f_T(\beta),$$
and A_{Tq} is a positive definite $O_p(1)$ weighting matrix. This leads to

$$\widehat{\beta}_{Tq} = \left(\sum_{t=q+2}^{T} y_{t-1} Y'_{q,t-2} A_{Tq} \sum_{t=q+2}^{T} Y_{q,t-2} y_{t-1} \right)^{-1} \times$$

$$\sum_{t=q+2}^{T} y_{t-1} Y'_{q,t-2} A_{Tq} \sum_{t=q+2}^{T} Y_{q,t-2} y_t.$$

The admissability of $Y_{q,t-2}$ as a set of instruments for y_{t-1} guarantees the consistency of $\widehat{\beta}_{Tq}$. In order to give the asymptotic distribution of $\widehat{\beta}_{Tq}$, we define the $q \times 1$ vector $R_q = E\left(Y_{q,t-2} y_{t-1}\right)$. The jth element of R_q is

$$\sigma_\varepsilon^2 \beta_0^{j-1} \frac{(1 + \beta_0 \theta_0)(\beta_0 + \theta_0)}{(1 - \beta_0^2)},$$

and $T^{-1} \sum_{t=q+2}^{T} Y_{q,t-2} y_{t-1} \xrightarrow{p} R_q$. The asymptotic distribution of $\widehat{\beta}_{Tq}$ is shown by *Stoica, Soderstrom and Friedlander* [1983] to be

$$\sqrt{T}\left(\widehat{\beta}_{Tq} - \beta_0\right) \xrightarrow{d} N\left(0, \sigma_\varepsilon^2 (R'_q A_q R_q)^{-1} R'_q A_q V_q A_q R_q (R'_q A_q R_q)^{-1}\right),$$

where
$$V_q = \lim_{T \to \infty} T \mathrm{var} f_T(\beta_0).$$

The asymptotic efficiency of $\widehat{\beta}_{Tq}$ is a function of the choice of the number of instruments (q) and the weighting matrix A_{Tq}. The optimal choice of A_{Tq} for a given q is such that $A_{Tq} \xrightarrow{p} V_q^{-1}$. Then

$$\sqrt{T}\left(\widehat{\beta}_{Tq} - \beta_0\right) \xrightarrow{d} N\left(0, \sigma_\varepsilon^2 (R'_q V_q^{-1} R_q)^{-1}\right).$$

Stoica, Soderstrom and Friedlander also show that the term $(R'_q V_q^{-1} R_q)^{-1}$ is a monotonically decreasing function of q and converges to a finite non–zero limit, and hence maximum asymptotic efficiency is achieved by letting $q \to \infty$ as $T \to \infty$.

6.3 Applications to Unit Root Testing

Instrumental variables estimation methods have been used in the construction of tests for autoregressive unit roots, and we show that they can also be applied in the construction of tests for moving average unit roots.

6.3.1 Testing for an Autoregressive Unit Root

Pantula and Hall [1991] consider the problem of testing for an autoregressive unit root in an ARMA model of known order. *Said and Dickey* [1985] suggested a test based on nonlinear least squares estimation of the model, so the instrumental variables approach provides a computationally simpler approach that does not require numerical optimisation. Other popular methods for testing for autoregressive unit roots such as those of *Said and Dickey* [1984] and *Phillips* [1987] use semi–parametric approximations to the ARMA model and therefore do not exploit the knowledge of the order of the ARMA model. Of course, in practice the model order is the result of a model selection procedure and the approximate nature of the semi–parametric approaches may be less of a disadvantage.

The model we consider is

$$\Delta y_t = \alpha y_{t-1} + \sum_{j=1}^{m} \beta_j \Delta y_{t-j} + u_t, \qquad (6\text{--}14)$$

where u_t is a moving average error of order n:

$$u_t = \varepsilon_t + \sum_{j=1}^{n} \theta_j \varepsilon_{t-j}. \qquad (6\text{--}15)$$

We assume that the autoregressive lag polynomial $\beta(L) = 1 - \sum_{j=1}^{m} \beta_j L^j$ is stationary and that the moving average lag polynomial $\theta(L) = 1 + \sum_{j=1}^{n} \theta_j L^j$ is invertible. The aim is to test the null hypothesis that $\alpha = 0$, in which case y_t follows an ARIMA$(m, 1, n)$ model. The alternative hypothesis is that $\alpha < 0$, which implies that y_t follows a stationary ARIMA$(m + 1, 0, n)$ model. The estimation theory for (6–14) is given under the null hypothesis so that the null distributions of tests of $\alpha = 0$ can be found.

If we were to estimate (6–14) by OLS ignoring the MA structure of u_t, then the asymptotic distribution of the resulting $\widehat{\alpha}$ would be a function of nuisance parameters reflecting the autocorrelation in the error term and the correlation between the regressors and error term (see *Phillips* [1987] for example). *Hall* [1989] in the pure MA case ($m = 0$) and *Pantula and Hall* [1991] in the ARMA model given above suggest using instrumental variables for y_{t-1} and $X_{t-1} = (\Delta y_{t-1}, \ldots, \Delta y_{t-m})'$. They suggest using y_{t-k} and X_{t-k} as instruments for y_{t-1} and X_{t-1} respectively. These are admissible instruments if $k > n$. Standard instrumental variables regression on

$$\Delta y_t = \alpha y_{t-1} + X'_{t-1}\beta + u_t$$

using these instruments gives

$$\begin{pmatrix} \widehat{\alpha}_k \\ \widehat{\beta}_k \end{pmatrix} = \begin{pmatrix} \sum y_{t-k}y_{t-1} & \sum y_{t-k}X_{t-1} \\ \sum X_{t-k}y_{t-1} & \sum X_{t-k}X_{t-1} \end{pmatrix}^{-1} \begin{pmatrix} \sum y_{t-k}\Delta y_t \\ \sum X_{t-k}\Delta y_t \end{pmatrix}.$$

Tests of $\alpha = 0$ are based on $\widehat{\alpha}_k$ and the asymptotic properties derived by *Pantula and Hall* [1991] given in Theorem 1.3 below. To present these results we require some notation. Let $W(r)$ denote a standard Brownian motion defined on $0 \leq r \leq 1$, and, following *Pantula and Hall* [1991], define the random variables

$$\Gamma = \int_0^1 W(r)^2 dr,$$

and

$$\xi = \frac{1}{2}\left(W(1)^2 - 1\right).$$

Also, let $B = 1 - \sum_{j=1}^m \beta_j$ denote the sum of the autoregressive coefficients in (6–14), and let $A_k = E(X_{t-k}X_{t-1})$.

THEOREM 6.3

If $\alpha = 0$ in (6–14), $k > q$ and A_k is non–singular then

$$T\widehat{\alpha}_k \overset{d}{\to} B\Gamma^{-1}\xi,$$

and

$$\widehat{\beta}_k \overset{p}{\to} \beta.$$

∎

The consistency of $\widehat{\beta}_k$ follows from the admissability of the instruments ($k > q$). Since β is a nuisance parameter vector when testing α, it follows that a consistent estimator is all that will be required. However, it is possible that more efficient estimators of

β derived from larger sets of instruments for X_{t-1} (for example, $Z_{l,t-k} = (\Delta y_{t-k}, \ldots, \Delta y_{t-k-l})'$ for some $l > m$) may result in improved finite sample properties for $\widehat{\alpha}_k$.

It is the asymptotic distribution of $\widehat{\alpha}_k$ that is of interest. Note that the random variable $\Gamma^{-1}\xi$ has the Dickey–Fuller distribution first given by *Fuller* [1976] for the case where u_t is i.i.d.. The sum of the autoregressive coefficients (B) enters this distribution as a nuisance parameter. However, using the consistent estimator $\widehat{\beta}_k$, B can easily be removed from the asymptotic distribution to give a coefficient test of $\alpha = 0$. Define $\widehat{B} = 1 - \sum_{j=1}^{m} \widehat{\beta}_{k,j}$. Then the test statistic $T\widehat{\alpha}_k/\widehat{B}$ converges in distribution to $\Gamma^{-1}\xi$ when $\alpha = 0$, and hence critical values can be obtained from the usual tables, see Table 10.A.1 of *Fuller* [1996].

It is also possible to construct a t statistic for testing $\alpha = 0$. A t statistic can be defined as

$$t_k = \widehat{\sigma}_u^{-1} \left(\sum_{t=k+1}^{T} y_{t-k}y_{t-1} \right)^{1/2} \widehat{\alpha}_k,$$

where

$$\widehat{\sigma}_u^2 = T^{-1} \sum_{t=k+1}^{T} \widehat{u}_t^2,$$

and

$$\widehat{u}_t = \Delta y_t - \widehat{\alpha}_k y_{t-1} - \sum_{j=1}^{m} \widehat{\beta}_{j,k} \Delta y_{t-j}.$$

The asymptotic distribution of t_k is not free of nuisance parameters because it ignores the autocorrelation in u_t. The statistic must be modified using the long run variance of u_t which, given its $\text{MA}(n)$ structure, is given by

$$\omega_u^2 = \sigma_\varepsilon^2 \left(1 + \sum_{j=1}^{n} \theta_j \right)^2. \tag{6–16}$$

A consistent estimator of ω_u^2 can easily be constructed if we can replace σ_ε^2 and θ_j, $j = 1, \ldots, n$ in (6–16) by consistent estimators. *Pantula and Hall* [1991] do not take this option because consistent estimation of θ_j requires an inconvenient nonlinear least squares estimation. However, we can make use of the more convenient moving average estimators in section 6.1 to obtain estimators. Either the *Galbriath and Zinde-Walsh* [1994] or the *Durbin* [1959] methods can be applied to $\hat{u}_t$ to obtain $\hat{\theta}_{k,j}$ and $\hat{\sigma}_\varepsilon^2$ and hence $\hat{\omega}_u^2$. It can then be shown that when $\alpha = 0$

$$\tilde{t}_k = \frac{\hat{\sigma}_u}{\hat{\omega}_u} t_k \xrightarrow{d} \Gamma^{-1/2}\xi.$$

That is $\tilde{t}_k$ has the same asymptotic null distribution as a Said–Dickey or Phillips–Perron test and the usual critical values can be used, see Table 10.A.2 of *Fuller* [1996] for example.

One difficulty with implementing a test based on $\tilde{t}_k$ is that $\sum_{t=k+1}^{T} y_{t-k}y_{t-1}$ is not necessarily positive, and hence its square root may not be real. *Li* [1995] suggests replacing this term with the asymptotically equivalent term $\sum_{t=2}^{T} y_{t-1}^2$, which is always positive. An alternative, based on the IV formulae in Chapter 1, is to replace

$$\sum_{t=k+1}^{T} y_{t-k}y_{t-1} \qquad \text{with} \qquad \left(\sum_{t=k+1}^{T} y_{t-k}y_{t-1}\right)^2 \bigg/ \sum_{t=2}^{T} y_{t-k}^2,$$

which is also asymptotically equivalent.

6.3.2 Testing for a Moving Average Unit Root

We can also consider the problem of testing for a unit root in the moving average lag polynomial of a time series. Such a test can also be used as a test of the null hypothesis that a time series is stationary against the alternative that it has an autoregressive unit root. Many papers have been written on this testing problem. We consider here the ARIMA$(m, 1, 1)$ model of *Leybourne and McCabe* [1994]

$$\Delta y_t = x_t,$$

$$x_t = \sum_{j=1}^{m} \beta_j x_{t-j} + u_t,$$

$$u_t = \varepsilon_t + \theta\varepsilon_{t-1},$$

where $\beta(L) = 1 - \sum_{j=1}^{m} \beta_j L^j$ is a stationary autoregressive lag polynomial and $|\theta| \leq 1$. We are interested in testing the null hypothesis that $\theta = 1$. If $\theta = 1$ then x_t has a moving average unit root, and it follows that y_t is $I(0)$. If $|\theta| < 1$ then x_t is a stationary and invertible ARMA$(m, 1)$ process and hence y_t is $I(1)$. Therefore a test of $\theta = 1$ is a test that y_t has been over–differenced.

The test procedure proposed by *Leybourne and McCabe* [1994] involves the estimation of β_j, $j = 1, \ldots, m$ and construction of the filtered series

$$y_t^* = y_t - \sum_{j=1}^{m} \widehat{\beta}_j y_{t-j}.$$

This filtered series is regressed on an intercept and time trend (if required) to obtain residuals e_t. The test statistic is then

$$s = \frac{\sum_{t=1}^{T} \left(\sum_{j=1}^{t} e_j \right)^2}{T \sum_{t=1}^{T} e_t^2}.$$

The asymptotic null distribution of this test statistic has the general form

$$s \xrightarrow{d} \int_0^1 U(r)^2 dr,$$

where $U(r)$ is a function of the standard Brownian motion $W(r)$ that varies depending on the form of de-meaning or de-trending carried out on y_t^*. For example, if y_t^* is de-meaned then $U(r) = W(r) - rW(1)$ is a Brownian bridge. Critical values for these tests are given in *Kwiatkowski et al.* [1992].

Our interest in this testing procedure lies in the estimation of β_j, $j = 1, \ldots, m$. Leybourne and McCabe [1994] suggest maximum likelihood estimation of the ARIMA$(m, 1, 1)$ model

$$\Delta y_t = \sum_{j=1}^{m} \beta_j \Delta y_{t-j} + \varepsilon_t + \theta \varepsilon_{t-1} \qquad (6\text{--}17)$$

to obtain $\widehat{\beta}_j$. However, we do not require an estimate of θ to construct the test statistic and we only require consistent estimation of β_j for the asymptotic theory to hold. Therefore, for convenience, we could use the instrumental variables estimators of Section 6.2 to estimate (6–17). That is, denoting $X_{t-1} = (\Delta y_{t-1}, \ldots, \Delta y_{t-m})'$ and $\beta = (\beta_1, \ldots, \beta_m)'$, we could use

$$\widehat{\beta} = \left(\sum_{t=m+3}^{T} X_{t-2} X_{t-1}' \right)^{-1} \sum_{t=m+3}^{T} X_{t-2} \Delta y_t.$$

In this case, we are using X_{t-2} as a set of instrumental variables for X_{t-1}, and one could experiment with larger vectors of instruments.

Appendix: Proof of Theorem 6.1

We first consider the consistency of $\hat{\eta}_T$. To do this, we check that Assumptions 1.1 and 1.2 in Chapter 1 are satisfied. We need not check Assumption 1.3 because the weighting matrix A_T specified for the general form of the GMM estimator is not required in the exactly identified case. We could work with the explicit formulae, but the proof is presented in this way for the purpose of examining these general assumptions in a simple example.

For Assumption 1.1, we have

$$
\begin{aligned}
g(\eta) &= E f(y_t, \theta) \\
&= \begin{pmatrix} E\left(y_t y_{t-1}\right) - \sigma^2 \theta \\ E(y_t^2) - \sigma^2\left(1 + \theta^2\right) \end{pmatrix} \\
&= \begin{pmatrix} \sigma_0^2 \theta_0 - \sigma^2 \theta \\ \sigma_0^2(1 + \theta_0^2) - \sigma^2(1 + \theta^2) \end{pmatrix}.
\end{aligned}
$$

The parameter space for this estimation problem is $\Upsilon : [-1, 1] \times (0, \infty)$. We need to show that $g(\eta)$ is solved uniquely in Υ by $\eta = \eta_0$. Setting the first element of $g(\eta)$ to zero gives

$$
\sigma^2 = \sigma_0^2 \frac{\theta_0}{\theta}.
$$

Substituting this expression for σ into the second element of $g(\eta)$ and setting to zero leads to the quadratic in θ

$$
\theta_0 \theta^2 - (1 + \theta_0^2)\theta + \theta_0 = 0.
$$

If $\theta_0 = 0$ then it can be seen that the equation is solved by $\theta = 0$. If $\theta_0 \neq 0$ then the quadratic has the solutions $\theta = \theta_0$ and $\theta = 1/\theta_0$, of which only $\theta = \theta_0$ is in Υ. With $\theta = \theta_0$ we obtain $\sigma^2 = \sigma_0^2$. Thus Assumption 1.1 is satisfied.

For Assumption 1.2, we require that $f_T(\eta)$ converges uniformly in probability to $g(\eta)$ given above. In this case, we need only verify that $T^{-1} \sum_{t=1}^{T} y_t^2 \xrightarrow{p} E(y_t^2)$ and $T^{-1} \sum_{t=2}^{T} y_t y_{t-1} \xrightarrow{p} E(y_t y_{t-1})$. These two results follow from applications of standard weak laws of large numbers for stationary time series, so Assumption 1.2 is satisfied. In this relatively simple case we do not need to resort to any more primitive assumptions in order to verify Assumption 1.2. In particular, the structure of the model is such that we do not need to restrict the parameter space to be compact.

Since these assumptions hold, we can apply Theorem 1.1 to conclude that $\hat{\eta}_T$ is consistent. To show that the real–valued estimator $\tilde{\eta}_T$ is consistent we show that $\tilde{\eta}_T - \hat{\eta}_T \overset{p}{\to} 0$. With respect to $\tilde{\theta}_T$, we see that $\tilde{\theta}_T = \hat{\theta}_T$ if $\left|\hat{\theta}_T\right| \leq 0.5$. Since $\Pr\left(\left|\hat{\theta}_T\right| \leq 0.5\right) \to 1$, we can conclude that $\tilde{\theta}_T - \hat{\theta}_T \overset{p}{\to} 0$. It is then immediate that $\tilde{\sigma}_T^2 - \hat{\sigma}_T^2 \overset{p}{\to} 0$, which shows that $\tilde{\theta}_T$ is consistent.

In order to derive the asymptotic distribution of the estimator, we consider Assumptions 1.7–1.9 from Chapter 1. The matrix of first derivatives of $f(y_t, \eta)$ with respect to η is

$$\frac{\partial f(y_t, \eta)}{\partial \eta'} = -\begin{pmatrix} \sigma^2 & \theta \\ 2\sigma^2\theta & 1+\theta^2 \end{pmatrix} = F_T(\eta).$$

Each element of this matrix is continuous with respect to θ and σ^2 on Υ, so Assumption 1.7 is satisfied.

Hence for any η_T^* such that $\eta_T^* \overset{p}{\to} \eta_0$ it follows that

$$F_T(\eta_T^*) \overset{p}{\to} -\begin{pmatrix} \sigma_0^2 & \theta_0 \\ 2\sigma_0^2\theta_0 & 1+\theta_0^2 \end{pmatrix} = F.$$

For Assumption 1.9, we require a central limit theorem for the vector

$$\sqrt{T}f_T(\eta_0) = \begin{pmatrix} T^{-1/2}\sum_{t=1}^T (y_t y_{t-1} - \sigma_0^2\theta_0) \\ T^{-1/2}\sum_{t=1}^T (y_t^2 - \sigma_0^2(1+\theta_0^2)) \end{pmatrix}.$$

That is, we require a central limit theorem for the sample variance and first order autocovariance of a first order moving average process. This is a special case of well known results for the autocovariances of a linear process (see *Anderson* [1971], Theorem 8.4.2 or *Fuller* [1996], Theorems 6.2.1 and 6.3.6 for example). We have

$$\sqrt{T}f_T(\eta_0) \overset{d}{\to} N(0, V),$$

where the form of V can be deduced from the aforementioned theorems to be

$$V = \lim_{T\to\infty} \operatorname{var}\sqrt{T}f_T(\eta_0) = \lim_{T\to\infty} T^{-1}\times$$

$$\begin{pmatrix} \operatorname{var}\left(\sum_{t=1}^T y_t^2\right) & \operatorname{cov}\left(\sum_{t=1}^T y_t^2, \sum_{t=2}^T y_t y_{t-1}\right) \\ \operatorname{cov}\left(\sum_{t=2}^T y_t y_{t-1}, \sum_{t=1}^T y_t^2\right) & \operatorname{var}\left(\sum_{t=2}^T y_t y_{t-1}\right) \end{pmatrix} =$$

$$\begin{pmatrix} 2\sigma_0^4(1+4\theta_0+\theta_0^4)+\kappa_4\theta_0^{*2} & -4\sigma_0^4\theta_0\theta_0^* - \kappa_4\theta_0\theta_0^* \\ -4\sigma_0^4\theta_0\theta_0^* - \kappa_4\theta_0\theta_0^* & \sigma_0^4(1+5\theta_0^2+\theta_0^4)+\kappa_4\theta_0^2 \end{pmatrix}$$

where $\theta_0^* = (1 + \theta_0^2)$. Then from Theorem 1.2 we have that

$$\sqrt{T}\left(\widehat{\eta}_T - \eta_0\right) \xrightarrow{d} N\left(0, F^{-1}VF^{-1\prime}\right).$$

Note that the simplified asymptotic covariance matrix is obtained because in this case θ_0 is exactly identified. We then find

$$F^{-1}VF^{-1\prime} = \frac{1}{(1 - \theta_0^2)^2} \times$$
$$\begin{pmatrix} 1 + \theta_0^2 + 4\theta_0^4 + \theta_0^6 + \theta_0^8 & 2\sigma_0^2\theta_0^3(2 + \theta_0^2 + \theta_0^4) \\ 2\sigma_0^2\theta_0^3(2 + \theta_0^2 + \theta_0^4) & 2\sigma_0^4(1 - 2\theta_0^2 + 3\theta_0^4 + 2\theta_0^6) \end{pmatrix}$$
$$+ \begin{pmatrix} 0 & 0 \\ 0 & \kappa_4 \end{pmatrix}.$$

This expression gives the asymptotic variance of both $\widehat{\eta}_T$ (which is asymptotically real with probability one) and $\widetilde{\eta}_T^2$. The additional term involving the fourth order cumulant κ_4 reflects the effect of any non–normality of ε_t on the asymptotic variance of $\widehat{\sigma}_T^2$.

References

Anderson, T.W. [**1971**]: *The Statistical Analysis of Time Series*; Wiley, New York.

Brockwell, P.J. and R.A. Davis [**1993**]: *Time Series: Theory and Methods*; 2nd ed. Springer-Verlag, New York.

Dolado, J. [**1990**]: Optimal Instrumental Variable Estimator of the AR Parameter of an ARMA(1,1) Process; *Econometric Theory*, 6, 117–119.

Durbin, J. [**1959**]: Efficient Estimation of Parameters in Moving Average Models; *Biometrika*, 46, 306–316.

Fuller, W.A. [**1976**]: *Introduction to Statistical Time Series*; Wiley, New York.

Fuller, W.A. [**1996**]: *Introduction to Statistical Time Series*; 2nd ed. Wiley, New York.

Galbraith, J.W. and V. Zinde-Walsh [**1994**]: A Simple Noniterative Estimator for Moving Average Models; *Biometrika*, 81, 143–155.

Ghysels, E., L. Khalaf and C. Vodounou [**1994**]: *Simulation Based Inference in Moving Average Models*; CIRANO Scientific Series No. 94s-11.

Hall, A. [**1989**]: Testing for a Unit Root in the Presence of Moving Average Errors; *Biometrika*, 76, 49–56.

Hannan, E.J. [**1960**]: *Time Series Analysis*; Methuen, London.

Hannan, E.J. [**1970**]: *Multiple Time Series*; Wiley, New York.

Kwiatkowski, D., P.C.B. Phillips, P. Schmidt and Y. Shin [1992]: Testing the Null Hypothesis of Stationarity Against the Alternative of a Unit Root; *Journal of Econometrics*, 54, 159–178.

Leybourne, S.J. and B.P.M. MacCabe [1994]: A Consistent Test for a Unit Root; *Journal of Business and Economic Statistics*, 12, 157–166.

Li, H. [1995]: The Power of Modified Instrumental Variables Tests for Unit Roots; *Biometrika*, 82, 660–666.

Pantula, S.G. and A. Hall [1991]: Testing for Unit Roots in Autoregressive Moving Average Models, An Instrumental Variable Approach; *Journal of Econometrics*, 48, 325–353.

Phillips, P.C.B. [1987]: Time Series Regression with a Unit Root; *Econometrica*, 55, 277–302.

Said, S.E. and D.A. Dickey [1984]: Testing for Unit Roots in Autoregressive Moving Average Models of Unknown Order; *Biometrika*, 71, 599–607.

Said, S.E. and D.A. Dickey [1985]: Hypothesis Testing in ARIMA(p,1,q) Models; *Journal of the American Statistical Association*, 80, 369–374.

Stoica, P., T. Soderstrom and B. Friedlander [1985]: Optimal Instrumental Variables Estimates of the AR Parameters of an ARMA Process; *IEEE Transactions on Automatic Control*, AC-30 11, 1066–1074.

Chapter 7

REDUCED RANK REGRESSION USING GMM

Frank Kleibergen

Since the mid eighties, alongside the literature arising on GMM, a large number of papers emerged on cointegration as well. This is due to the fact that cointegration models combine two features which many economic time series possess, *i.e.,* random walk individual behavior and stationary linear combinations of multiple series.

Cointegration models are essentially linear models with reduced rank parameters. The reduced forms of the traditional simultaneous equation models have also this reduced rank property (see *Hausman* [1983]). The estimation techniques used in cointegration and simultaneous equation models are therefore very similar. Maximum likelihood estimators for both models use, for example, canonical correlations, (see *Anderson and Rubin* [1949] and *Johansen* [1991]), and maximum likelihood reduced rank regression therefore amounts to the use of canonical correlations and vectors. This chapter shows that GMM reduced rank regression amounts to the use of two stage least squares (2SLS) estimators. The asymptotic properties of the 2SLS estimators used in simultaneous equation models are in general identical to the properties of maximum likelihood estimators (see, for example, *Phillips* [1983]). This chapter shows that this also holds for cointegration models. Furthermore, the GMM objective function has asymptotic properties which are identical to a likelihood ratio statistic for cointegration, the Johansen trace statistic (*Johansen* [1991]), and it can thus be used in a similar way. The similarities between GMM and maximum likelihood estimators in reduced rank models are therefore quite large. The GMM, however, also allows for the derivation of the asymptotic properties in the more complex reduced rank models, which is not true for the maximum likelihood estimators. We show this for cointegration models with structural breaks in the variance and cointegrating vectors. In practice, there is a need for the construction of cointegration estimators and test statistics which can be applied for these kind of models as a large number of economic time series have these properties (like heteroskedasticity and structural breaks). There is a need therefore for the development of cointegration estimators and test statistics, which can be applied for these models. The main aim of this chapter is to introduce GMM estimators for cointegration models incorporating heteroskedasticity and/or structural breaks.

The chapter is organized as follows. In Section 7.1 the relation between the GMM–2SLS estimators in cointegration and simultaneous equations models is discussed jointly with the limiting distributions of the cointegrating vector estimators for a few widely used specifications. Section 7.2 shows the limiting distribution of the GMM objective function, which can be used to test for the number of unit roots/cointegrating relationships. Section 7.3 extents the stylized model to a model where a shift of variance occurs after a predefined time period. A Generalized Least Squares approach, which assumes a priori knowledge of the variance shift moment, is used to construct the GMM cointegration estimators and statistics that allow for heteroskedasticity. Section 7.4 discusses GMM cointegration estimators and statistics that allow for a change in the cointegrating relationship and/or multiplicator. Both extensions can be further generalized to more shifts and, also, more moment conditions can be added. Finally, Section 7.5 concludes.

Note that the following definitions are used throughout this chapter; $\Rightarrow$ indicates weak convergence; integrals are taken over the unit interval unless indicated otherwise; when possible without confusion, integrals like $\int W(t)dt$ are shortly denoted as $\int W$. The theorems are derived assuming Gaussian disturbances, which can be relaxed (see, for example, *Phillips and Solo* [1992]).

7.1 GMM–2SLS Estimators in Reduced Rank Models

7.1.1 Reduced Rank Regression Models

Reduced rank regression models are characterized by the lower column or row rank of a parameter matrix. Two well known models with this property are the Error Correction Cointegration Model (ECCM) and the INcomplete Simultaneous Equations Model (INSEM). The ECCM is specified as (see *Engle and Granger* [1987] and *Johansen* [1991])

$$\Delta x_t = \alpha \beta' x_{t-1} + \varepsilon_t, \tag{7-1}$$

where $x_t : k \times 1$, $t = 1, ..., T$; $\alpha, \beta : k \times r$; $\beta' = (I_r \ \text{-} \beta'_2)$; and ε_t is Gaussian white noise with covariance matrix Σ. For simplicity higher order lags are neglected. The INSEM reads (see Chapter 1 and *Hausman* [1983])

$$\begin{aligned} y_{1t} &= \beta' y_{2t} + \gamma' x_{1t} + \varepsilon_{1t} \\ y_{2t} &= \Pi_{21} x_{1t} + \Pi_{22} x_{2t} + \varepsilon_{2t}, \end{aligned} \tag{7-2}$$

where $y_{1t} : m_1 \times 1$, $y_{2t} : m_2 \times 1$, $x_{1t} : k_1 \times 1$, $x_{2t} : k_2 \times 1$, $t = 1, ..., T$; $\beta : m_2 \times m_1$; $\gamma : k_1 \times m_1$; $\Pi_{21} : m_2 \times k_1$; $\Pi_{22} : m_2 \times k_2$. The disturbances ε_{1t} and ε_{2t} are assumed to be Gaussian white noise with covariance matrix Ω. The variables x_{1t} and x_{2t} are assumed to be (weakly) exogenous. The INSEM (7–2) is identified when the number of excluded exogenous variables from the first set of equations, k_2, is at least as large as the number of equations in the second set, m_2, $k_2 \geq m_2$.

Time series generated by ECCMs exhibit random walk patterns for individual series while the joint behavior of the series has stationary linear combinations (see *Engle and Granger* [1987]). In the case of ECCM (7–1) these stationary linear combinations are represented by $\beta' x_t$, which is why β is called the cointegrating vector. These properties are observed in many economic time series which explains the popularity of cointegration in applied work. As a traditional simultaneous equation model, INSEMs explain series which are generated simultaneously. These types of economic time series have been analysed since the late fourties, see, for example, *Anderson and Rubin* [1949].

The reduced rank property of both of these models is obtained when they are specified as restrictions of the standard linear model,

$$z_t = \Pi w_t + u_t. \tag{7-3}$$

Both the ECCM and the INSEM are restricted versions of (7–3). The ECCM is obtained when $z_t = \Delta x_t$, $\Pi = \alpha\beta' = \begin{pmatrix} \alpha_{11} & -\alpha_{11}\beta_2' \\ \alpha_{21} & -\alpha_{21}\beta_2' \end{pmatrix}$, $u_t = \varepsilon_t$, $w_t = x_{t-1}$, while the INSEM is obtained when we substitute the equation of y_{2t} in the equation of y_{1t} which then results in (7–3) with $z_t = \begin{pmatrix} y_{1t} \\ y_{2t} \end{pmatrix}$, $w_t = \begin{pmatrix} x_{1t} \\ x_{2t} \end{pmatrix}$, $u_t = \begin{pmatrix} \varepsilon_{1t} + \beta_2'\varepsilon_{2t} \\ \varepsilon_{2t} \end{pmatrix}$, $\Pi = \begin{pmatrix} \beta'\Pi_{21} + \gamma & \beta'\Pi_{22} \\ \Pi_{21} & \Pi_{22} \end{pmatrix}$. The reduced rank structure of the ECCM is obvious while the INSEM has a reduced rank structure when $\gamma = 0$ since the first set of rows of Π is a linear function of the other rows in that case. The reduced rank properties of both models are different, however, as in the ECCM the last set of columns is a linear combination of the first set, while in the INSEM the first set of rows is a linear combination of the last set. This also implies that the GMM estimators of the parameters of these two models are different.

7.1.2 GMM–2SLS Estimators

The reduced rank property of the INSEM and ECCM implies that the parameters of these models cannot be estimated using the method of moments. This results from the fact that the moment condition of model (7–3),

$$f_T(\Pi) = E(\sum_{t=1}^{T} w_t u_t') = 0, \tag{7-4}$$

does not lead to unique estimator of the parameters as the number of parameters in Π, $r(2k - r)$ in case of the ECCM and $(m-1)(k+1) + k_1$ in case of the INSEM, is less than the number of equations in (7–4), k^2 (see, also, Chapter 1). The GMM is designed to estimate the parameters of a model overidentified by the moment conditions.

Instead of the moment conditions (7–4), the GMM minimizes a quadratic form of it with respect to a weighting matrix A_T

$$Q_T(\theta) = \text{vec}(f_T(\Pi(\theta)))' A_T \text{vec}(f_T(\Pi(\theta)))$$

$$= \text{vec}(\sum_{t=1}^{T} u_t w_t')'((\sum_{t=1}^{T} w_t w_t')^{-1} \otimes \Sigma^{-1})\text{vec}(\sum_{t=1}^{T} u_t w_t') \quad (7\text{–}5)$$

$$= tr[\Sigma^{-1}(\sum_{t=1}^{T} u_t w_t')(\sum_{t=1}^{T} w_t w_t')^{-1}(\sum_{t=1}^{T} u_t w_t')'],$$

where $\theta = (\alpha, \beta_2)$ in the case of the ECCM and $\theta = (\beta, \gamma, \Pi_{21}, \Pi_{22})$ in the case of the INSEM. We choose as weighting matrix $A_T = ((\sum_{t=1}^{T} w_t w_t')^{-1} \otimes \Sigma^{-1})$, as this enables us to use $Q_T(\theta)$ as a test statistic as well to test hypotheses on θ.

To construct the first order conditions for a minimum of $Q_T(\theta)$, the specification of the first order derivatives of Π with respect to the different elements of θ, are needed. These expressions read, for the ECCM,

$$\frac{\partial \text{vec}(\Pi)}{\partial \text{vec}(\beta')'} = -(I_k \otimes \alpha),$$

$$\frac{\partial \text{vec}(\Pi)}{\partial \text{vec}(\alpha)'} = -(\beta \otimes I_k), \quad (7\text{–}6)$$

and for the INSEM,

$$\frac{\partial \text{vec}(\Pi)}{\partial \text{vec}(\beta_2')'} = -((\,\Pi_{21} \quad \Pi_{22}\,)' \otimes \begin{pmatrix} I_{m_1} \\ 0 \end{pmatrix}),$$

$$\frac{\partial \text{vec}(\Pi)}{\partial \text{vec}(\gamma_1')'} = -((\,I_{k_1} \quad 0\,)' \otimes \begin{pmatrix} I_{m_1} \\ 0 \end{pmatrix}),$$

$$\frac{\partial \text{vec}(\Pi)}{\partial \text{vec}(\Pi_{21})'} = -((\,I_{k_1} \quad 0\,)' \otimes \begin{pmatrix} \beta_2' \\ I_{m_2} \end{pmatrix}), \quad (7\text{–}7)$$

$$\frac{\partial \text{vec}(\Pi)}{\partial \text{vec}(\Pi_{22})'} = -((\,0 \quad I_{k_2}\,)' \otimes \begin{pmatrix} \beta_2' \\ I_{m_2} \end{pmatrix}).$$

These derivatives are substituted in the first order condition for a minimum of $Q_T(\theta)$,

$$\frac{\partial Q_T(\theta)}{\partial \theta'} = 0 \Leftrightarrow$$

$$\sum_{t=1}^{T} (\frac{\partial u_t}{\partial \theta'})(w_t' \otimes I_k)((\sum_{t=1}^{T} w_t w_t')^{-1} \otimes \Sigma^{-1})\text{vec}(\sum_{t=1}^{T} u_t w_t') = 0 \Leftrightarrow$$

$$(\frac{\partial \text{vec}(\Pi)}{\partial \theta'})'\text{vec}(\Sigma^{-1}\sum_{t=1}^{T} u_t w_t') = 0.$$

$$(7\text{–}8)$$

For the parameters of the ECCM these first order conditions then read,

$$(I_k \otimes \alpha)'\text{vec}(\Sigma^{-1}\sum_{t=1}^{T} u_t x_{t-1}') = 0 \Leftrightarrow$$

$$(7\text{–}9)$$

$$(\sum_{t=1}^{T} x_{t-1} x_{t-1}')^{-1}(\sum_{t=1}^{T} x_{t-1}\Delta x_t')\Sigma^{-1}\alpha(\alpha'\Sigma^{-1}\alpha)^{-1} = \beta,$$

$$(\beta \otimes I_k)'\text{vec}(\Sigma^{-1}\sum_{t=1}^{T} u_t x_{t-1}') = 0 \Leftrightarrow$$

$$(7\text{–}10)$$

$$(\sum_{t=1}^{T} \Delta x_t x_{t-1}'\beta)(\beta'\sum_{t=1}^{T} x_{t-1} x_{t-1}'\beta)^{-1} = \alpha,$$

while for the parameters of the INSEM these first order conditions read,

$$((\,\Pi_{21} \quad \Pi_{22}\,)' \otimes \begin{pmatrix} I_{m_1} \\ 0 \end{pmatrix})'\text{vec}(\Sigma^{-1}\sum_{t=1}^{T} u_t x_t') = 0 \Leftrightarrow$$

$$((\,\Pi_{21} \quad \Pi_{22}\,)\sum_{t=1}^{T} x_t y_{2t}')^{-1}(\,\Pi_{21} \quad \Pi_{22}\,)\sum_{t=1}^{T} x_t(y_{1t} - \gamma_1' x_{1t})' = \beta_2,$$

$$(7\text{–}11)$$

$$((\,I_{k_1} \quad 0\,)' \otimes \begin{pmatrix} I_{m_1} \\ 0 \end{pmatrix})'\text{vec}(\Sigma^{-1}\sum_{t=1}^{T} u_t x_t') = 0 \Leftrightarrow$$

$$(7\text{–}12)$$

$$(\sum_{t=1}^{T} x_{1t} x_{1t}')^{-1}\sum_{t=1}^{T} x_{1t}(y_{1t} - \beta_2' y_{2t})' = \gamma_1,$$

$$(I_k \otimes \begin{pmatrix} \beta_2' \\ I_{m_2} \end{pmatrix})' \mathrm{vec}(\Sigma^{-1} \sum_{t=1}^{T} u_t x_t') = 0 \Leftrightarrow$$

$$(\sum_{t=1}^{T} y_{2t} x_t')(\sum_{t=1}^{T} x_t x_t')^{-1} = \Pi_2. \tag{7-13}$$

The first order conditions for the INSEM (7–11)-(7–13) lead to the well known 2SLS estimator as (7–13) shows that Π_2 can be estimated independently from β_2 and γ_1. The resulting least squares (GMM) estimator of Π_2 is then used to construct estimators for β_2 and γ_1 (GMM–2SLS estimators, see also Chapter 1).

The first order conditions for the ECCM (7–9)-(7–10) show that the GMM estimators of α and β in the ECCM both depend on each other. As we did not restrict α and β, they are not identified. If we specify β as, $\beta = (I_r \; -\beta_2')'$, both α and β_2 are properly identified. When this specification of β is used, a consistent GMM estimator of α is,

$$\hat{\alpha} = (\sum_{t=1}^{T} \Delta x_t (1 - x_{2t-1}'(\sum_{t=1}^{T} x_{2t-1} x_{2t-1}')^{-1} x_{2t-1}) x_{1t-1}')$$

$$(\sum_{t=1}^{T} x_{1t-1}(1 - x_{2t-1}'(\sum_{t=1}^{T} x_{2t-1} x_{2t-1}')^{-1} x_{2t-1}) x_{1t-1}')^{-1}, \tag{7-14}$$

where $x_t = \begin{pmatrix} x_{1t} \\ x_{2t} \end{pmatrix}$, $x_{1t} : r \times 1$, $x_{2t} : (k-r) \times 1$. This estimator consists of the first r columns of the least squares estimator of Π in (7–3).

If $\hat{\alpha}$ is substituted in the first order conditions of the cointegrating vector β, (7–9), the resulting cointegrating vector estimator $\hat{\beta}$ automatically satisfies the identifying restrictions on β. $\hat{\beta}$ is then the GMM–2SLS estimator of the cointegrating vector β. In a Bayesian analysis this GMM–2SLS estimator equals the mean of the conditional posterior of β given α, when a diffuse prior is used (see *Kleibergen and van Dijk* [1994a]). The estimators $\hat{\alpha}$ and $\hat{\beta}$ in (7–9) and (7–10) also allow for the construction of an iterative estimation scheme which converges to the maximum likelihood estimators. Asymptotically the GMM–2SLS cointegrating vector estimator possesses the same kind of properties as the maximum likelihood estimator, *i.e.*, superconsistency and asymptotic normality. This is shown in the theorems of the following sections. Note, that the asymptotic normality of this GMM–2SLS estimator does not result from Section 1.3.2 of Chapter 1 as the data is nonstationary and Assumption 1.9 is violated.

7.1.3 Limiting Distributions for the GMM–2SLS Cointegration Estimators

As an extensive literature exists on the limiting distribution of the 2SLS estimator in the INSEM, see, for example, *Phillips* [1983], we focus on the limiting distribution of the GMM–2SLS estimators for the ECCM, which is only sparsely discussed in the literature (see, for example, *Quintos* [1994], where the case that w_t in (7–5) is uncorrelated with x_{t-1} is discussed). Theorem 7.1 states the limiting distribution of the GMM multiplicator estimator, $\widehat{\alpha}$, and the GMM–2SLS cointegrating vector estimator, $\widehat{\beta}$.

THEOREM 7.1

When the Data Generating Process (DGP) in (7–1) is such that the number of cointegrating vectors equals r ($k-r$ unit roots) and $\alpha'_\perp \beta_\perp$ is nonsingular, the GMM estimators

$$\widehat{\alpha} = (\sum_{t=1}^{T} \Delta x_t (1 - x'_{2t-1}(\sum_{t=1}^{T} x_{2t-1}x'_{2t-1})^{-1}x_{2t-1})x'_{1t-1})$$

$$(\sum_{t=1}^{T} x_{1t-1}(1 - x'_{2t-1}(\sum_{t=1}^{T} x_{2t-1}x'_{2t-1})^{-1}x_{2t-1})x'_{1t-1})^{-1}$$

(7–15)

and

$$\widehat{\beta} = (\sum_{t=1}^{T} x_{t-1}x'_{t-1})^{-1}(\sum_{t=1}^{T} x_{t-1}\Delta x'_t)\Sigma^{-1}\widehat{\alpha}(\widehat{\alpha}'\Sigma^{-1}\widehat{\alpha})^{-1} \qquad (7–16)$$

which use the same value of r, have a limiting behavior characterized by

$$\sqrt{T}(\widehat{\alpha} - \alpha) \Rightarrow N(0, \ \text{cov}(\beta'x)^{-1} \otimes \Sigma), \qquad (7–17)$$

$$T(\widehat{\beta} - \beta) \Rightarrow \begin{pmatrix} 0 \\ (\beta'_\perp\beta_\perp)^{-1}\beta'_\perp\alpha_\perp\Lambda_1^{-1'}(\int W_1W'_1)^{-1}\int W_1dW'_2\Lambda'_2 \end{pmatrix}$$

$$\Rightarrow \begin{pmatrix} 0 \\ N(0, \alpha'\Sigma^{-1}\alpha \otimes \Theta) \end{pmatrix},$$

(7–18)

where W_1, resp. W_2 are $(k - r)$, resp. r dimensional stochastically independent Brownian motions defined on the unit interval, $\Lambda_1 = (\alpha'_\perp \Sigma \alpha_\perp)^{\frac{1}{2}}$, $\Lambda_2 = (\alpha' \Sigma^{-1} \alpha)^{\frac{1}{2}}$,

$$\Theta = (\beta'_\perp \beta_\perp)^{-1} \beta'_\perp \alpha_\perp \Lambda_1^{-1'} (\int W_1 W_1')^{-1} \Lambda_1^{-1} \alpha'_\perp \beta_\perp (\beta'_\perp \beta_\perp)^{-1}$$

and Σ is estimated by the sum of squared residuals, $\widehat{\Sigma} =$

$$\tfrac{1}{T} \sum_{t=1}^{T} (\Delta x_t (1 - x'_{t-1} (\sum_{t=1}^{T} x_{t-1} x'_{t-1})^{-1} x_{t-1}) \Delta x'_t).$$

∎

For proof of the Theorem see the Appendix.

The limiting distributions of the GMM estimators in Theorem 7.1 do not result from *Hansen* [1982] as the data are generated by a nonstationary process and Assumption 1.9 from Chapter 1 is therefore violated. Asymptotic normality of the GMM cointegrating vector estimator $\widehat{\beta}$ is obtained as it consists of the projection of a standard least squares estimator of Π on a space spanned by $\widehat{\alpha}$. Johansen's Representation theorem (see *Johansen* [1991]) shows that the random walk components of the DGP resulting from an ECCM lie in a space orthogonal to α. The projection on $\widehat{\alpha}$, which is a consistent estimator of α, therefore implies that $\widehat{\beta}$ is asymptotically uncorrelated with the random walk components of the DGP. The limiting distribution of the GMM estimator $\widehat{\beta}$ therefore has the same properties as it would have in the case of a stationary DGP, *i.e.*, asymptotic normality, instead of consisting of Brownian motion functionals as in case of most random walk DGPs (see *Phillips* [1991]).

Theorem 7.1 discusses the limiting distribution of the cointegrating vector estimator for the most straightforward case, *i.e.*, no further lags in the VAR polynomial and no deterministic components, and shows that it is identical to the limiting distribution of the canonical correlation maximum likelihood estimator of Johansen (see *Johansen* [1991]). While adding lags Δx_t only changes the limiting distribution of the cointegrating vector estimator, $\widehat{\beta}$, in the sense that $\alpha'_\perp \beta_\perp$ has to be replaced by $\alpha'_\perp \Gamma(1) \beta_\perp$, where $\Gamma(L) \Delta x_t = \alpha \beta' x_{t-1} + \varepsilon_t$ and $\Gamma(L)$ is a $(p-1)$ dimensional lag polynomial in the case of a VAR(p), inclusion of deterministic components also changes the functional form of the cointegrating vector estimator (see, for example, *Johansen* [1991] and *Kleibergen and van Dijk* [1994b]). Theorem 7.2 states the GMM estimators and their limiting distributions of the multiplicator and cointegrating vector for a few commonly used specifications of the deterministic components.

THEOREM 7.2

When the DGP reads

$$\Delta x_t = \alpha(\beta' x_{t-1} + \mu') + \varepsilon_t, \tag{7-19}$$

and the number of cointegrating vectors equals r $(k - r$ unit roots), $\alpha'_\perp \beta_\perp$ nonsingular, the GMM estimators

$$\widehat{\alpha} = (\sum_{t=1}^{T} \Delta x_t (1 - \begin{pmatrix} x_{2t-1} \\ 1 \end{pmatrix}' (\sum_{t=1}^{T} \begin{pmatrix} x_{2t-1} \\ 1 \end{pmatrix} \begin{pmatrix} x_{2t-1} \\ 1 \end{pmatrix}')^{-1}$$

$$\begin{pmatrix} x_{2t-1} \\ 1 \end{pmatrix}) x'_{1t-1})(\sum_{t=1}^{T} x_{1t-1}(1 - \begin{pmatrix} x_{2t-1} \\ 1 \end{pmatrix}' (\sum_{t=1}^{T} \begin{pmatrix} x_{2t-1} \\ 1 \end{pmatrix} \tag{7-20}$$

$$\begin{pmatrix} x_{2t-1} \\ 1 \end{pmatrix}')^{-1} \begin{pmatrix} x_{2t-1} \\ 1 \end{pmatrix}) x'_{1t-1})^{-1}$$

and

$$\begin{pmatrix} \widehat{\beta} \\ \widehat{\mu} \end{pmatrix} = (\sum_{t=1}^{T} \begin{pmatrix} x_{t-1} \\ 1 \end{pmatrix} \begin{pmatrix} x_{t-1} \\ 1 \end{pmatrix}')^{-1}$$

$$(\sum_{t=1}^{T} \begin{pmatrix} x_{t-1} \\ 1 \end{pmatrix} \Delta x'_t) \Sigma^{-1} \widehat{\alpha} (\widehat{\alpha}' \Sigma^{-1} \widehat{\alpha})^{-1} \tag{7-21}$$

have a limiting behavior characterized by

$$\sqrt{T}(\widehat{\alpha} - \alpha) \Rightarrow N(0, \ \text{cov}(\beta' x - \mu')^{-1} \otimes \Sigma), \tag{7-22}$$

$$\begin{pmatrix} T I_k & 0 \\ 0 & T^{\frac{1}{2}} \end{pmatrix} \begin{pmatrix} \widehat{\beta} - \beta \\ \widehat{\mu} - \mu \end{pmatrix} \Rightarrow$$

$$\left(\begin{pmatrix} (\beta'_\perp \beta_\perp)^{-1} \beta'_\perp \alpha_\perp \Lambda_1^{-1'} & 0 \\ 0 & 1 \end{pmatrix} W_*^{-1} (\int \begin{pmatrix} W_1 \\ \iota \end{pmatrix} dW'_2) \Lambda'_2 \right) \Rightarrow$$

$$\begin{pmatrix} 0 \\ N(0, \alpha' \Sigma^{-1} \alpha \otimes \Theta_1) \end{pmatrix}, \quad \text{where}$$

$$W_* = (\int \begin{pmatrix} W_1 \\ \iota \end{pmatrix} \begin{pmatrix} W_1 \\ \iota \end{pmatrix}') \tag{7-23}$$

When the DGP

$$\Delta x_t = c + \alpha \beta' x_{t-1} + \varepsilon_t, \tag{7-24}$$

$c = \alpha\mu' + \alpha_\perp\lambda'$, and the number of cointegrating vectors equals r ($k - r$ unit roots), $\alpha_\perp'\beta_\perp$ nonsingular, the GMM estimators

$$\widehat{\alpha} = (\sum_{t=1}^{T} \Delta x_t (1 - \begin{pmatrix} x_{2t-1} \\ 1 \end{pmatrix}' (\sum_{t=1}^{T} \begin{pmatrix} x_{2t-1} \\ 1 \end{pmatrix} \begin{pmatrix} x_{2t-1} \\ 1 \end{pmatrix}')^{-1}$$

$$\begin{pmatrix} x_{2t-1} \\ 1 \end{pmatrix}) x_{1t-1}')(\sum_{t=1}^{T} x_{1t-1}(1 - \begin{pmatrix} x_{2t-1} \\ 1 \end{pmatrix}' (\sum_{t=1}^{T} \begin{pmatrix} x_{2t-1} \\ 1 \end{pmatrix} \qquad (7\text{–}25)$$

$$\begin{pmatrix} x_{2t-1} \\ 1 \end{pmatrix}')^{-1} \begin{pmatrix} x_{2t-1} \\ 1 \end{pmatrix}) x_{1t-1}')^{-1}$$

and

$$\begin{pmatrix} \widehat{\beta} \\ \widehat{\mu} \end{pmatrix} = (\sum_{t=1}^{T} \begin{pmatrix} x_{t-1} \\ 1 \end{pmatrix} \begin{pmatrix} x_{t-1} \\ 1 \end{pmatrix}')^{-1}$$

$$(\sum_{t=1}^{T} \begin{pmatrix} x_{t-1} \\ 1 \end{pmatrix} \Delta x_t') \Sigma^{-1} \widehat{\alpha} (\widehat{\alpha}' \Sigma^{-1} \widehat{\alpha})^{-1} \qquad (7\text{–}26)$$

have a limiting behavior characterized by

$$\sqrt{T}(\widehat{\alpha} - \alpha) \Rightarrow N(0, \ \text{cov}(\beta'x - \mu')^{-1} \otimes \Sigma), \qquad (7\text{–}27)$$

$$\left(\begin{pmatrix} TI_{k-r-1} & 0 \\ 0 & T^{\frac{3}{2}} \end{pmatrix} (\beta_{21}^{*\prime}\beta_{21}^{*})^{-1}\beta_{21}^{*\prime} \quad 0 \\ 0 \qquad\qquad\qquad\qquad T^{\frac{1}{2}} \right) \begin{pmatrix} \beta_2 - \widehat{\beta}_2 \\ \widehat{\mu} - \mu \end{pmatrix}$$

$$\Rightarrow \begin{pmatrix} \Lambda_3 & 0 \\ 0 & 1 \end{pmatrix}^{-1\prime} (\int \begin{pmatrix} W_{11} \\ \tau \\ \iota \end{pmatrix} \begin{pmatrix} W_{11} \\ \tau \\ \iota \end{pmatrix}')^{-1} \int \begin{pmatrix} W_{11} \\ \tau \\ \iota \end{pmatrix} dW_2'\Lambda_2'$$

$$\Rightarrow N(0, \ \alpha'\Sigma^{-1}\alpha \otimes \Theta_2). \qquad (7\text{–}28)$$

When the DGP reads

$$\Delta x_t = c + \alpha(\beta'x_{t-1} + \delta't) + \varepsilon_t, \qquad (7\text{–}29)$$

$c = \alpha\mu' + \alpha_\perp\lambda'$, and the number of cointegrating vectors equals r ($k - r$ unit roots), $\alpha_\perp'\beta_\perp$ nonsingular, the GMM estimators

$$
\widehat{\alpha} = (\sum_{t=1}^{T} \Delta x_t (1 - \begin{pmatrix} x_{2t-1} \\ 1 \\ t \end{pmatrix}' (\sum_{t=1}^{T} \begin{pmatrix} x_{2t-1} \\ 1 \\ t \end{pmatrix} \begin{pmatrix} x_{2t-1} \\ 1 \\ t \end{pmatrix}')^{-1}
$$

$$
\begin{pmatrix} x_{2t-1} \\ 1 \\ t \end{pmatrix}) x'_{1t-1}) (\sum_{t=1}^{T} x_{1t-1} (1 - \begin{pmatrix} x_{2t-1} \\ 1 \\ t \end{pmatrix}' (\sum_{t=1}^{T} \begin{pmatrix} x_{2t-1} \\ 1 \\ t \end{pmatrix})
$$

$$
\begin{pmatrix} x_{2t-1} \\ 1 \\ t \end{pmatrix}')^{-1} \begin{pmatrix} x_{2t-1} \\ 1 \\ t \end{pmatrix}) x'_{1t-1})^{-1}
$$

(7–30)

and

$$
\begin{pmatrix} \widehat{\beta} \\ \widehat{\mu} \\ \widehat{\delta} \end{pmatrix} = (\sum_{t=1}^{T} \begin{pmatrix} x_{t-1} \\ 1 \\ t \end{pmatrix} \begin{pmatrix} x_{t-1} \\ 1 \\ t \end{pmatrix}')^{-1}
$$

$$
(\sum_{t=1}^{T} \begin{pmatrix} x_{t-1} \\ 1 \\ t \end{pmatrix} \Delta x'_t) \Sigma^{-1} \widehat{\alpha} (\widehat{\alpha}' \Sigma^{-1} \widehat{\alpha})^{-1}
$$

(7–31)

have a limiting behavior characterized by

$$
\sqrt{T} (\widehat{\alpha} - \alpha) \Rightarrow N(0, \ \mathrm{cov}(\beta' x - \mu' - \delta' t)^{-1} \otimes \Sigma), \qquad (7\text{–}32)
$$

$$
\begin{pmatrix} T I_k & 0 & 0 \\ 0 & T^{\frac{1}{2}} & 0 \\ 0 & 0 & T^{\frac{3}{2}} \end{pmatrix} \begin{pmatrix} \widehat{\beta} - \beta \\ \widehat{\mu} - \mu \\ \widehat{\delta} - \delta \end{pmatrix} \Rightarrow
$$

$$
\left(\begin{pmatrix} (\beta'_\perp \beta_\perp)^{-1} \beta'_\perp \alpha_\perp \Lambda_1^{-1'} & 0 \\ 0 & I_2 \end{pmatrix} W_{**}^{-1} (\int \begin{pmatrix} W_1 \\ \iota \\ \tau \end{pmatrix}' dW'_2) \Lambda'_2 \right) \qquad (7\text{–}33)
$$

$$
\Rightarrow \begin{pmatrix} 0 \\ N(0, \alpha' \Sigma^{-1} \alpha \otimes \Theta_3) \end{pmatrix},
$$

where W_1, W_{11} and W_2 are $(k - r)$, $(k - r - 1)$ and r dimensional stochastically independent Brownian motions, the value of r used for the GMM estimators equals the value of r for the involved DGP,

$$W_{**} = (\int \begin{pmatrix} W_1 \\ \iota \\ \tau \end{pmatrix} \begin{pmatrix} W_1 \\ \iota \\ \tau \end{pmatrix}')$$

$$\Lambda_1 = (\alpha'_\perp \Sigma \alpha_\perp)^{\frac{1}{2}},$$

$$\Lambda_2 = (\alpha' \Sigma^{-1} \alpha)^{\frac{1}{2}},$$

$$\Lambda_3 = \left(\left(\frac{\lambda_\perp (\alpha'_\perp \alpha_\perp)^{-1} \alpha'_\perp \Sigma^{\frac{1}{2}}}{\lambda \lambda'} \right) \left(\frac{\lambda_\perp (\alpha'_\perp \alpha_\perp)^{-1} \alpha'_\perp \Sigma^{\frac{1}{2}}}{\lambda \lambda'} \right)' \right)^{\frac{1}{2}},$$

$$\tau(t) = t, \quad \iota(t) = 1,$$

$$0 \le t \le 1, \quad \beta = \begin{pmatrix} I_r \\ -\beta_2 \end{pmatrix},$$

$$\beta_{2\perp}^* = (\beta'_\perp \beta_\perp)^{-1} \beta'_\perp \alpha_\perp (\alpha'_\perp \alpha_\perp)^{-1} \begin{pmatrix} \lambda_\perp \\ \lambda \end{pmatrix}',$$

$$\Theta_1 = (\beta'_\perp \beta_\perp)^{-1} \beta'_\perp \alpha_\perp \Lambda_1^{-1'} W_*^{-1} \Lambda_1^{-1} \alpha'_\perp \beta_\perp (\beta'_\perp \beta_\perp)^{-1},$$

$$\Theta_2 = \begin{pmatrix} \Lambda_3 & 0 \\ 0 & 1 \end{pmatrix}^{-1'} (\int \begin{pmatrix} W_{11} \\ \tau \\ \iota \end{pmatrix} \begin{pmatrix} W_{11} \\ \tau \\ \iota \end{pmatrix}')^{-1} \begin{pmatrix} \Lambda_3 & 0 \\ 0 & 1 \end{pmatrix}^{-1},$$

$$\Theta_3 = (\beta'_\perp \beta_\perp)^{-1} \beta'_\perp \alpha_\perp \Lambda_1^{-1'} W_{**}^{-1} \Lambda_1^{-1} \alpha'_\perp \beta_\perp (\beta'_\perp \beta_\perp)^{-1}.$$

∎

PROOF OF THE THEOREM

The first and third part of the theorem are natural extensions of Theorem 7.1. The second part of the theorem is proved in the Appendix.

∎

Theorems 7.1 and 7.2 show the asymptotic normality of the GMM cointegrating vector estimator and standard (asymptotic) χ^2 tests can therefore be performed to test hypotheses on the cointegrating vectors (see *Phillips* [1991]). This extends the asymptotic normality of the GMM estimator discussed in Chapter 1 to an important class of models. The GMM not only allows for testing hypotheses on the cointegrating vectors or multiplicators but also on the number of cointegrating vectors. As discussed in the next section, the GMM objective function (7–5) can be used for this purpose.

7.2 Testing Cointegration Using GMM–2SLS Estimators

The GMM objective function (7–5) not only allows us to construct the GMM estimators but can also be used to test for the number of cointegrating vectors, unit roots (see also Chapter 6). This results as the optimal value of the objective function has a specific limiting distribution under $H_0 : r = r^*$. In Theorem 7.3, the analytical form of this objective function is presented for several specifications of the deterministic components and their limiting distributions.

THEOREM 7.3

> When (7–1) is the DGP and the number of cointegrating vectors equals r $((k - r)$ unit roots), substitution of the GMM estimators (7–15) and (7–16), using the same value of r in the GMM objective function (7–5) leads to a limiting behavior characterized by
>
> $$Q_T(\widehat{\alpha}, \widehat{\beta}) \Rightarrow tr[(\int W_1 dW_1')'(\int W_1 W_1')^{-1}(\int W_1 dW_1')]. \qquad (7\text{--}34)$$
>
> When (7–19) is the DGP and the number of cointegrating vectors equals r $((k - r)$ unit roots), substitution of the GMM estimators (7–20) and (7–26), using the same value of r in the GMM objective function (7–27) leads to a limiting behavior characterized by
>
> $$Q_T(\widehat{\alpha}, \widehat{\beta}, \widehat{\mu})$$
> $$\Rightarrow tr[(\int \begin{pmatrix} W_1 \\ \iota \end{pmatrix} dW_1')'(\int \begin{pmatrix} W_1 \\ \iota \end{pmatrix} \begin{pmatrix} W_1 \\ \iota \end{pmatrix}')^{-1}(\int \begin{pmatrix} W_1 \\ \iota \end{pmatrix} dW_1')].$$
> $$(7\text{--}35)$$
>
> When (7–24) is the DGP and the number of cointegrating vectors equals r $((k - r)$ unit roots), substitution of the GMM estimators (7–25) and (7–26), using the same value of r in the GMM objective function (7–5) leads to a limiting behavior characterized by
>
> $$Q_T(\widehat{\alpha}, \widehat{\beta}, \widehat{c}) \quad \Rightarrow \quad tr[(\int \begin{pmatrix} \bar{W}_{11} \\ \bar{\tau} \end{pmatrix} dW_1')'$$
> $$(\int \begin{pmatrix} \bar{W}_{11} \\ \bar{\tau} \end{pmatrix} \begin{pmatrix} \bar{W}_{11} \\ \bar{\tau} \end{pmatrix}')^{-1}(\int \begin{pmatrix} \bar{W}_{11} \\ \bar{\tau} \end{pmatrix} dW_1')]. \qquad (7\text{--}36)$$

When (7–29) is the DGP and the number of cointegrating vectors equals r $((k - r)$ unit roots), substitution of the GMM estimators (7–30) and (7–31), using the same value of r, in the GMM objective function (7–5) leads to a limiting behavior characterized by

$$Q_T(\widehat{\alpha}, \widehat{\beta}, \widehat{\delta}, \widehat{c})$$

$$\Rightarrow tr[(\int \begin{pmatrix} \bar{W}_1 \\ \bar{\tau} \end{pmatrix} dW_1')'(\int \begin{pmatrix} \bar{W}_1 \\ \bar{\tau} \end{pmatrix} \begin{pmatrix} \bar{W}_1 \\ \bar{\tau} \end{pmatrix}')^{-1}(\int \begin{pmatrix} \bar{W}_1 \\ \bar{\tau} \end{pmatrix} dW_1')],$$

$$(7\text{–}37)$$

where $x_t = \begin{pmatrix} x_{1t} \\ x_{2t} \end{pmatrix}$, $x_{1t} : r \times 1$, $x_{2t} : (k - r) \times 1$; $\bar{x}_{t-1} = x_{t-1} - \frac{1}{T}\sum_{t=1}^{T} x_{t-1}$, $\bar{t} = t - \frac{1}{T}\sum_{t=1}^{T} t$; W_1, W_{11} are $(k - r)$, $(k - r - 1)$ dimensional Brownian motions, $W_1 = \begin{pmatrix} W_{11} \\ w_{12} \end{pmatrix}$, $\bar{W}_1 = W_1 - \int W_1$, $\bar{W}_{11} = W_{11} - \int W_{11}$, $\tau(t) = t$, $\iota(t) = 1$, $0 \le t \le 1$, $\bar{\tau} = \tau - \int \tau$, and Σ is estimated by the residual sum of squares for the unrestricted model.

∎

Proof of the Theorem

The first part the proof is given in the Appendix, the other parts follow straightforwardly.

∎

The limiting distributions of the GMM objective function (7–5) stated in Theorem 7.3 can be used to test for the number of cointegrating vectors. By simulating from these limiting distributions, the asymptotic critical values can be determined. These values are tabulated, for example, in *Hamilton* [1994]. Q_T can then be calculated for different values of the number of cointegrating vectors $r, r = 1, ..., k$, such that the values of r can be determined for which the associated Q_T's exceed their asymptotic critical values. These values of r are then rejected to be plausible values of the number of cointegrating vectors.

Theorems 7.1 to 7.3 show that the limiting distributions using the GMM–2SLS estimators are identical to the limiting distributions when maximum likelihood estimators are used (see *Johansen* [1991]). As maximum likelihood estimators can be constructed in a straightforward way using canonical correlations, they are not computationally more difficult than GMM–2SLS estimators. Differences between these two estimators can arise though in their small sample distributions and in model extensions as maximum likelihood estimators become analytically intractable when more complicated models are analyzed.

In *Phillips* [1994], it is shown that the canonical correlation cointegrating vector estimator has a small sample distribution with Cauchy type tails such that it has no finite moments. When we neglect the dynamic property of the data and assume fixed regressors, results from *Phillips* [1983] indicate that the small sample distribution of the GMM–2SLS cointegrating vector estimator has finite moments up to the degree $(k - r)$. This degree is determined by the $\Sigma^{-1}\widehat{\alpha}(\widehat{\alpha}'\Sigma^{-1}\widehat{\alpha})^{-1}$ expression appearing in the cointegrating vector estimator $\widehat{\beta}$ (see also Chapter 5). As β is specified such that it always has rank r, rank reduction of $\alpha\beta'$ implies that α has a lower rank value. In that case $\widehat{\alpha}'\Sigma^{-1}\widehat{\alpha}$ would not be invertible leading to the fat tails in the small sample distribution. So, cointegration tests essentially test for the rank of α and can be considered as tests for the local identification of β and are, therefore, comparable with the concentration parameter in the INSEM (see *Phillips* [1983]).

The maximum likelihood cointegrating vector estimator is appealing as it has a simple expression in the standard case. The relation between maximum likelihood cointegrating vector estimators and canonical correlations is, however, lost when extensions of the model are considered. The GMM framework allows for the analytical construction of cointegrating vector estimators for a general class of models. In the next sections two kind of structural break model extensions are analyzed, *i.e.*, structural breaks in the variance (heteroskedasticity) and structural breaks in the cointegrating vector and/or multiplicator, for which the cointegrating vector maximum likelihood estimators are not of the canonical correlation type.

7.3 Cointegration in a Model with Heteroskedasticity

Assuming homoskedastic disturbances in (7–1), the maximum likelihood estimator of the cointegrating vector can be constructed using canonical correlations. This estimator has a normal limiting distribution under conditions, which are more general than strict homoskedasticity (see, for example, *Phillips and Solo* [1992], where it is shown that the weak convergence is retained in the case of conditional heteroskedasticity with constant unconditional variances). This weak convergence is, however, lost when the mean of the conditional variances changes from period to period. Furthermore, the relation between the maximum likelihood estimator and canonical correlations is lost. A GMM–2SLS cointegrating vector estimator can still, however, be constructed when the functional form of the heteroskedasticity is known. To show this, we derive GMM estimators and their limiting distributions for an example of a change of the variance after a predefined period T_1. The analyzed model thus reads,

$$\Delta x_t = \alpha \beta' x_{t-1} + \varepsilon_t, \tag{7–38}$$

where

$$\begin{aligned} \text{cov}(\varepsilon_t) &= \Sigma_1, & t &= 1, ..., T_1 \\ &= \Sigma_2. & t &= T_1 + 1, ..., T. \end{aligned} \tag{7–39}$$

In the next section, the GMM cointegrating vector estimator and cointegration test and their limiting distributions are derived using a Generalized Least Squares (GLS) framework to account for the heteroskedasticity.

7.3.1 Generalized Least Squares Cointegration Estimators

Assuming that we know the form of the heteroskedasticity, we use a different GMM objective function than (7–5) to derive the GMM estimators.

$$
Q_T(\alpha, \beta) = \text{vec}\left(\sum_{t=1}^{T_1} \Sigma_1^{-1} \varepsilon_t x_{t-1}' + \sum_{t=T_1+1}^{T} \Sigma_2^{-1} \varepsilon_t x_{t-1}'\right)'
$$

$$
\left(\sum_{t=1}^{T_1} (x_{t-1} x_{t-1}' \otimes \Sigma_1^{-1}) + \sum_{t=T_1+1}^{T} (x_{t-1} x_{t-1}' \otimes \Sigma_2^{-1})\right)^{-1}
$$

$$
\text{vec}\left(\sum_{t=1}^{T_1} \Sigma_1^{-1} \varepsilon_t x_{t-1}' + \sum_{t=T_1+1}^{T} \Sigma_2^{-1} \varepsilon_t x_{t-1}'\right).
$$

$$(7\text{--}40)$$

In the next theorem the GMM estimators and their limiting distributions jointly with the limiting distribution of the optimal value of the GMM objective function are stated. Note, that the estimators and limiting distributions of Theorem 7.4 can also be extended to more variance shifts and other moment conditions for the variances can be incorporated as well.

THEOREM 7.4

When the DGP in equations (7–38), (7–39) is such that the number of cointegrating vectors is r ($k - r$ unit roots), $\alpha_\perp' \beta_\perp$ nonsingular, the GMM estimators,

$$
\text{vec}(\widehat{\alpha}) = \left(\left(\sum_{t=1}^{T_1} x_{t-1} x_{t-1}' \otimes \widehat{\Sigma}_1^{-1}\right) + \left(\sum_{t=T_1+1}^{T} x_{t-1} x_{t-1}' \otimes \widehat{\Sigma}_2^{-1}\right)\right)_1^{-1}
$$

$$
\text{vec}\left(\sum_{t=1}^{T_1} \widehat{\Sigma}_1^{-1} \Delta x_t x_{t-1}' + \sum_{t=T_1+1}^{T} \widehat{\Sigma}_2^{-1} \Delta x_t x_{t-1}'\right),
$$

$$(7\text{--}41)$$

and

$$
\text{vec}(\widehat{\beta}') = \left(\left(\sum_{t=1}^{T_1} x_{t-1} x_{t-1}' \otimes \widehat{\alpha}' \widehat{\Sigma}_1^{-1} \widehat{\alpha}\right)\right.
$$

$$
+ \left(\sum_{t=T_1+1}^{T} x_{t-1} x_{t-1}' \otimes \widehat{\alpha}' \widehat{\Sigma}_2^{-1} \widehat{\alpha}\right)\right)^{-1} \text{vec}\left(\sum_{t=1}^{T_1} \widehat{\alpha}' \widehat{\Sigma}_1^{-1} \Delta x_t x_{t-1}' \right. \quad (7\text{--}42)
$$

$$
\left. + \sum_{t=T_1+1}^{T} \widehat{\alpha}' \widehat{\Sigma}_2^{-1} \Delta x_t x_{t-1}'\right),
$$

have a limiting behavior characterized by

$$\sqrt{T}\text{vec}(\hat{\alpha} - \alpha) \Rightarrow N(0, (w(\text{cov}(\beta'x)_1 \otimes \alpha'\Sigma_1^{-1}\alpha) \qquad (7\text{--}43)$$
$$+ (1 - w)(\text{cov}(\beta'x)_2 \otimes \alpha'\Sigma_2^{-1}\alpha))^{-1}),$$

and

$$T[\text{vec}(\beta_2 - \widehat{\beta}_2)]$$

$$\Rightarrow ((\beta'_\perp\beta_\perp)^{-1}\beta'_\perp\alpha_\perp \otimes I_r)((\Lambda_1 \int_0^w W_1W'_1\Lambda'_1 \otimes \alpha'\Sigma_1^{-1}\alpha) +$$

$$(\int_w^1 (\Lambda_2W_1(t) + \Lambda_1W_1(w))(\Lambda_2W_1(t) \qquad (7\text{--}44)$$

$$+ \Lambda_1W_1(w))'dt \otimes \alpha'\Sigma_2^{-1}\alpha))^{-1}\text{vec}[\Omega_1(\int_0^w dW_2W'_1)\Lambda'_1$$

$$+ \Omega_2(\int_w^1 dW_2(t)(\Lambda_2W_1(t) + \Lambda_1W_1(w))'dt)],$$

Assuming that the value of r used for the estimators $\hat{\alpha}$ and $\hat{\beta}$ equals the value of r of the DGP (7–38), substitution of these estimators in (7–40) leads to a limiting behavior of the resulting optimal value of the GMM objective function characterized by

$$Q_T(\hat{\alpha}, \hat{\beta}) \Rightarrow \text{vec}[\Lambda_1(\int_0^w dW_1W'_1)\Lambda'_1$$

$$+ \Lambda_2(\int_w^1 dW_1(t)(\Lambda_2W_1(t) + \Lambda_1W_1(w))'dt)]'$$

$$((\Lambda_1 \int_0^w W_1W'_1\Lambda'_1 \otimes \alpha'_\perp\Sigma_1^{-1}\alpha_\perp)$$

$$+ (\int_w^1 (\Lambda_2W_1(t) + \Lambda_1W_1(w))$$

$$(\Lambda_2W_1(t) + \Lambda_1W_1(w))'dt \otimes \alpha'_\perp\Sigma_2^{-1}\alpha_\perp))^{-1}$$

$$\text{vec}[\Lambda_1(\int_0^w dW_1 W_1')\Lambda_1'$$

$$+ \Lambda_2(\int_w^1 dW_1(t)(\Lambda_2 W_1(t) + \Lambda_1 W_1(w))'dt)], \tag{7-45}$$

where $w = \frac{T_1}{T}$, W_1 and W_2, are stochastically independent r, $(k-r)$ dimensional Brownian motions with identity covariance matrices, $\Lambda_1 = (\alpha_{\perp}' \Sigma_1^{-1} \alpha_{\perp})^{\frac{1}{2}}$, $\Lambda_2 = (\alpha_{\perp}' \Sigma_2^{-1} \alpha_{\perp})^{\frac{1}{2}}$, $\Omega_1 = (\alpha' \Sigma_1 \alpha)^{\frac{1}{2}}$, $\Omega_2 = (\alpha' \Sigma_2 \alpha)^{\frac{1}{2}}$,

$$\widehat{\Sigma}_1 = \frac{1}{T_1 - k} \sum_{t=1}^{T_1} \Delta x_t (1 - x_{t-1}'(\sum_{t=1}^{T_1} x_{t-1} x_{t-1}')^{-1} x_{t-1}) \Delta x_t',$$

$$\widehat{\Sigma}_2 = \frac{1}{T - T_1 - k}$$

$$\sum_{t=T_1+1}^{T} \Delta x_t (1 - x_{t-1}' \ (\sum_{t=T_1+1}^{T} x_{t-1} x_{t-1}')^{-1} x_{t-1}) \Delta x_t',$$

$$\text{cov}(\beta' x)_1 = \beta' \sum_{i=0}^{\infty} C_i^* \Sigma_1 C_i^{*'} \beta, \ \text{cov}(\beta' x)_2 = \beta' \sum_{i=0}^{\infty} C_i^* \Sigma_2 C_i^{*'} \beta,$$

and $(\ )_1^{-1}$ are the first kr rows of $(\ )^{-1}$.   ∎

PROOF OF THE THEOREM

The asymptotic results for subsamples using the fraction w result from *Perron* [1989]. Using these asymptotics for subsamples, the other results follow straightforwardly from the proofs of Theorems 7.1–7.3.   ∎

The cointegrating vector estimator from Theorem 7.4 is a GMM–2SLS estimator as it is constructed in two sequential steps. In the first step, we estimate Π in (7–3) using least squares and use its first r columns to construct $\widehat{\alpha}$. Furthermore, we construct $\widehat{\Sigma}_1$ and $\widehat{\Sigma}_2$ as the sum of squared residuals of the two subsamples. In the second step then we construct the GMM estimator $\widehat{\beta}$ (7–42).

Theorem 7.4 shows the asymptotic normality of the GMM cointegrating vector estimator $\widehat{\beta}$. Jointly with Theorems 7.1–7.2, this shows the elegancy of the GMM as it leads to asymptotic normality even in some models which violate the standard assumptions. When we use a cointegrating vector estimator which neglects the heteroskedasticity of the disturbances, we cannot find accurate expressions of its covariance matrix so that it is hard to test hypotheses on the cointegrating vector. The resulting estimator is not asymptotically normally distributed either.

The limiting distribution of the optimal value of the GMM objective function depends on the relative change of the covariance matrix and w, the relative time period during which the variance differs. As it is not known what the true values of these parameters are, they are typically replaced by sample estimates. The resulting distribution is, in that case, no longer the true limiting distribution but only an approximation of it. It would be interesting to investigate whether nonparametric covariance estimators, like the White (*White* [1980]) or Newey–West (*Newey and West* [1987]), see also Chapter 3, can be used to overcome these difficulties. These covariance matrix estimators can directly be used in the GMM objective function but the expressions of the resulting limiting distributions are still unknown.

7.4 Cointegration with Structural Breaks

In ECCMs with structural breaks in the value of the multiplicator or the cointegrating vector, the maximum likelihood estimators no longer have a closed analytical form. The GMM, however, still gives analytical expressions of cointegrating vector estimators even in these kinds of models. To show this, we analyze the influence of a structural break in α, the value of the multiplicator, and β the cointegrating vector, at a T_1 point. The model, therefore, reads

$$\Delta x_t = \alpha \beta' x_{t-1} + \varepsilon_t \qquad\qquad t = 1, ..., T_1,$$
$$\Delta x_t = \theta \gamma' x_{t-1} + \varepsilon_t \qquad\qquad t = T_1 + 1, ..., T,$$
$$(7\text{–}46)$$

where ε_t, $t = 1, ..., T$, are Gaussian white noise disturbances with covariance matrix Σ. The GMM objective function we use for this model reads,

$$Q_T(\alpha, \beta, \gamma, \theta) = \text{vec}(\sum_{t=1}^{T_1} \varepsilon_t x'_{t-1}, \sum_{t=T_1+1}^{T} \varepsilon_t x'_{t-1})'$$

$$\begin{pmatrix} ((\sum_{t=1}^{T_1} x_{t-1} x'_{t-1})^{-1} \otimes \Sigma^{-1}) & 0 \\ 0 & ((\sum_{t=T_1+1}^{T} x_{t-1} x'_{t-1})^{-1} \otimes \Sigma^{-1}) \end{pmatrix}$$

$$\text{vec}(\sum_{t=1}^{T_1} \varepsilon_t x'_{t-1}, \sum_{t=T_1+1}^{T} \varepsilon_t x'_{t-1}),$$

$$(7\text{–}47)$$

where $\text{vec}(A, B) = (\text{vec}(A)' \; \text{vec}(B)')'$. In Theorem 7.5, the GMM estimators of the cointegrating vector, multiplicator and their limiting distributions are presented jointly with the limiting distribution of the GMM objective function. As the cointegrating vector estimators and multiplicators all have normal limiting distribution, standard χ^2 tests can be performed to test for the equality of the parameters in each of the two periods. Theorem 7.5 also presents the estimators and their limiting distributions, which can be used when either the cointegrating vectors or multiplicators in each of the two periods are equal to each other.

THEOREM 7.5

    When the DGP in (7–46) is such that the number of cointegrating vectors is r ($k - r$ unit roots), $\alpha'_\perp \beta_\perp$ nonsingular, the estimators,

$$\hat{\alpha} = (\sum_{t=1}^{T_1} \Delta x_t (1 - x'_{2t-1}(\sum_{t=1}^{T_1} x_{2t-1} x'_{2t-1})^{-1} x_{2t-1}) x'_{1t-1})$$

$$(\sum_{t=1}^{T_1} x_{1t-1}(1 - x'_{2t-1}(\sum_{t=1}^{T_1} x_{2t-1} x'_{2t-1})^{-1} x_{2t-1}) x'_{1t-1})^{-1},$$

$$(7\text{–}48)$$

$$\hat{\theta} =$$

$$(\sum_{t=T_1+1}^{T} \Delta x_t (1 - x'_{2t-1}(\sum_{t=T_1+1}^{T} x_{2t-1} x'_{2t-1})^{-1} x_{2t-1}) x'_{1t-1})$$

$$(\sum_{t=T_1+1}^{T} x_{1t-1}(1 - x'_{2t-1}(\sum_{t=T_1+1}^{T} x_{2t-1} x'_{2t-1})^{-1} x_{2t-1}) x'_{1t-1})^{-1},$$

$$(7\text{–}49)$$

and

$$\widehat{\beta} = (\sum_{t=1}^{T_1} x_{t-1}x'_{t-1})^{-1}(\sum_{t=1}^{T_1} x_{t-1}\Delta x'_t)\Sigma_1^{-1}\widehat{a}(\widehat{a}'\Sigma_1^{-1}\widehat{a})^{-1}, \qquad (7\text{--}50)$$

$$\widehat{\gamma} =$$
$$(\sum_{t=T_1+1}^{T} x_{t-1}x'_{t-1})^{-1}(\sum_{t=T_1+1}^{T} x_{t-1}\Delta x'_t)\Sigma_2^{-1}\widehat{\theta}(\widehat{\theta}'\Sigma_2^{-1}\widehat{\theta})^{-1} \qquad (7\text{--}51)$$

have a limiting behavior characterized by

$$\sqrt{T}(\widehat{a} - a) \;\Rightarrow\; N(0,\; \mathrm{cov}(\beta'x)^{-1} \otimes w\Sigma), \qquad (7\text{--}52)$$

$$\sqrt{T}(\widehat{\theta} - \theta) \;\Rightarrow\; N(0,\; \mathrm{cov}(\gamma'x)^{-1} \otimes (1-w)\Sigma), \qquad (7\text{--}53)$$

and

$$T(\widehat{\beta} - \beta) \;\Rightarrow\;$$
$$\left(\begin{array}{c} 0 \\ (\beta'_\perp\beta_\perp)^{-1}\beta'_\perp a_\perp \Lambda_1^{-1'}(\int_0^w W_1 W'_1)^{-1}(\int_0^w W_1 dW'_2)\Omega'_1 \end{array} \right), \qquad (7\text{--}54)$$

$$T(\gamma_2 - \widehat{\gamma}_2) \;\Rightarrow\;$$
$$[(\int_w^1 (\gamma'_\perp\beta_\perp(a'_\perp\beta_\perp)^{-1}\Lambda_1 W_1(w) + \gamma'_\perp\gamma_\perp(\theta'_\perp\gamma_\perp)^{-1}\Lambda_2 W_1(t))$$
$$(\gamma'_\perp\beta_\perp(a'_\perp\beta_\perp)^{-1}\Lambda_1 W_1(w) + \gamma'_\perp\gamma_\perp(\theta'_\perp\gamma_\perp)^{-1}\Lambda_2 W_1(t))' dt)]^{-1}$$
$$\int_w^1 [\gamma'_\perp\beta_\perp(a'_\perp\beta_\perp)^{-1}\Lambda_1 W_1(w) + \gamma'_\perp\gamma_\perp(\theta'_\perp\gamma_\perp)^{-1}\Lambda_2 W_1(t))$$
$$dW_2(t)' dt]\Omega'_2. \qquad (7\text{--}55)$$

The limiting behavior of the optimal value of the objective function can be characterized by,

$$Q_T(\widehat{a}, \widehat{\beta}, \widehat{\gamma}, \widehat{\theta})$$
$$\Rightarrow \mathrm{vec}((\int_0^w W_1 dW'_1)')'((\int_0^w W_1 W'_1)^{-1} \otimes I_{k-r})\mathrm{vec}((\int_0^w W_1 dW'_1)')$$

$$+ \text{vec}(\int_w^1 [\Lambda_2^{-1}\theta'_\perp\gamma_\perp(\gamma'_\perp\gamma_\perp)^{-1}\gamma'_\perp\beta_\perp(\alpha'_\perp\beta_\perp)^{-1}\Lambda_1 W_1(w)$$

$$+ W_1(t)]dW_1(t)')'([\int_w^1 (\Lambda_2^{-1}\theta'_\perp\gamma_\perp(\gamma'_\perp\gamma_\perp)^{-1}\gamma'_\perp\beta_\perp(\alpha'_\perp\beta_\perp)^{-1}\Lambda_1$$

$$W_1(w) + W_1(t))(\Lambda_2^{-1}\theta'_\perp\gamma_\perp(\gamma'_\perp\gamma_\perp)^{-1}\gamma'_\perp\beta_\perp(\alpha'_\perp\beta_\perp)^{-1}\Lambda_1 W_1(w)$$

$$+ W_1(t))'dt]^{-1} \otimes I_{k-r})\text{vec}(\int_w^1 [\Lambda_2^{-1}\theta'_\perp\gamma_\perp(\gamma'_\perp\gamma_\perp)^{-1}\gamma'_\perp\beta_\perp(\alpha'_\perp\beta_\perp)^{-1}$$

$$\Lambda_1 W_1(w) + W_1(t)]dW_1(t)').$$

$$(7\text{--}56)$$

When the model in (7–46) is such that the cointegrating vectors are equal in the two subsamples, $\beta = \gamma$, which can be tested using an asymptotic χ^2 test, the GMM estimator for β reads (estimators for α and θ result from (7–48) and (7–49),

$$\text{vec}(\widehat{\beta}') = [(\sum_{t=1}^{T_1} x_{t-1}x'_{t-1} \otimes \widehat{\alpha}'\Sigma_1^{-1}\widehat{\alpha}))+$$

$$(\sum_{t=T_1+1}^{T} x_{t-1}x'_{t-1} \otimes \widehat{\theta}'\Sigma_2^{-1}\widehat{\theta})]^{-1}[(I_k \otimes \widehat{\alpha}'\Sigma_1^{-1})$$

$$(\text{vec}(\sum_{t=1}^{T_1} \Delta x_t x'_{t-1}) + (I_k \otimes \widehat{\theta}'\Sigma_2^{-1})(\text{vec}(\sum_{t=T_1+1}^{T} \Delta x_t x'_{t-1}))]$$

$$=\text{vec}(\begin{pmatrix} I_r \\ -\beta_2 \end{pmatrix}') + [(\sum_{t=1}^{T_1} x_{t-1}x'_{t-1} \otimes \widehat{\alpha}'\Sigma_1^{-1}\widehat{\alpha}))$$

$$+ (\sum_{t=T_1+1}^{T} x_{t-1}x'_{t-1} \otimes \widehat{\theta}'\Sigma_2^{-1}\widehat{\theta})]^{-1}[\text{vec}(\sum_{t=1}^{T_1} \widehat{\alpha}'\Sigma_1^{-1}\varepsilon_t x'_{t-1})$$

$$+ \text{vec}(\sum_{t=T_1+1}^{T} \widehat{\theta}'\Sigma_2^{-1}\varepsilon_t x'_{t-1})]$$

$$(7\text{--}57)$$

and the limiting behavior of this estimator is characterized by

$$T\text{vec}(\widehat{\beta}_2 - \beta_2)$$
$$\Rightarrow ((\beta'_\perp \beta_\perp)^{-1} \otimes I_r)[((\alpha'_\perp \beta_\perp)^{-1} \Lambda_1$$
$$(\int_0^w W_1 W_1') \Lambda_1'(\beta'_\perp \alpha_\perp)^{-1} \otimes \alpha' \Sigma^{-1} \alpha)$$

$$+ ([\int_w^1 ((\alpha'_\perp \beta_\perp)^{-1} \Lambda_1 W_1(w) + (\theta'_\perp \beta_\perp)^{-1} \Lambda_2 W_1(t))$$

$$((\alpha'_\perp \beta_\perp)^{-1} \Lambda_1 W_1(w) + (\theta'_\perp \beta_\perp)^{-1} \Lambda_2 W_1(t))' dt]$$

$$\otimes \theta' \Sigma^{-1} \theta)]^{-1} \text{vec}(\Omega_1(\int_0^w dW_2 W_1') \Lambda_1'(\beta'_\perp \alpha_\perp)^{-1}$$

$$+ \Omega_2 \int_w^1 [dW_2(t)(W_1'(w) \Lambda_1'(\beta'_\perp \alpha_\perp)^{-1} + W_1'(t) \Lambda_2'(\beta'_\perp \theta_\perp)^{-1}) dt]).$$

$$(7\text{–}58)$$

When the model in (7–46) is such that the multiplicators of the cointegrating vectors are equal in the two susbsamples, $\alpha = \theta$, which can be tested using a χ^2 test, the GMM estimator for α reads (estimators for β and γ result from (7–50) and (7–51)

$$\widehat{\alpha} = (\sum_{t=1}^{T_1} \Delta x_t x'_{t-1} \widehat{\beta} + \sum_{t=T_1+1}^{T} \Delta x_t x'_{t-1} \widehat{\gamma})^{-1} \times$$
$$(\widehat{\beta}' \sum_{t=1}^{T_1} x_{t-1} x'_{t-1} \widehat{\beta} + \widehat{\gamma}' \sum_{t=T_1+1}^{T} x_{t-1} x'_{t-1} \widehat{\gamma})^{-1}$$

$$(7\text{–}59)$$

and its limiting behavior is characterized by

$$\sqrt{T}(\widehat{\alpha} - \alpha) \Rightarrow N(0, w\text{cov}(\beta'x)_1 + (1 - w)\text{cov}(\gamma'x)_2) \qquad (7\text{–}60)$$

where $w = \frac{T_1}{T}$, W_1 and W_2, are stochastically independent r, $(k - r)$ dimensional Brownian motions with identity co-variance matrices, $\Lambda_1 = (\alpha'_\perp \Sigma^{-1} \alpha_\perp)^{\frac{1}{2}}$, $\Lambda_2 = (\theta'_\perp \Sigma^{-1} \theta_\perp)^{\frac{1}{2}}$, $\Omega_1 = (\alpha' \Sigma \alpha)^{\frac{1}{2}}$, $\Omega_2 = (\theta' \Sigma \theta)^{\frac{1}{2}}$,

$$\widehat{\Sigma}_1 = \frac{1}{T_1 - k} \sum_{t=1}^{T_1} \Delta x_t (1 - x'_{t-1} (\sum_{t=1}^{T_1} x_{t-1} x'_{t-1})^{-1} x_{t-1}) \Delta x'_t,$$

$$\widehat{\Sigma}_2 = \frac{1}{T - T_1 - k} \sum_{t=T_1+1}^{T} \Delta x_t$$

$$(1 - x'_{t-1} \left(\sum_{t=T_1+1}^{T} x_{t-1} x'_{t-1} \right)^{-1} x_{t-1}) \Delta x'_t,$$

$$\text{cov}(\beta'x)_1 = \beta' \sum_{i=0}^{\infty} C_{1i}^* \Sigma_1 C_{1i}^{*\prime} \beta, \text{cov}(\gamma'x)_2 = \beta' \sum_{i=0}^{\infty} C_{2i}^* \Sigma_2 C_{2i}^{*\prime} \beta,$$

and $C_1(L)$, $C_2(L)$ are the Vector Moving Average representations of the first and second subsets.

∎

PROOF OF THE THEOREM

Again uses asymptotics for subsamples (see *Perron* [1989]) and results from proofs of Theorems 7.1–7.3.

∎

Theorem 7.5 shows that the GMM estimators of the cointegrating vector and multiplicator have normal limiting distributions in case of structural breaks in the cointegrating vector and/or multiplicator. Similar to the limiting distribution of the optimal value of the GMM objective function in case of heteroskedasticity, the limiting distribution of the optimal value of the GMM objective function again depends on model parameters and the relative size of the subsamples. An approximation of this limiting distribution can again be constructed using the estimated values of the parameters, α, β, θ, γ and T_1. As this leads to a rather complicated testing procedure, it may be preferable to fix the number of cointegrating vectors a priori and just perform tests on the estimated cointegrated vectors and multiplicators, which are straightforward to construct. This also holds for the cointegration tests discussed in the previous section.

7.5 Conclusion

The GMM preserves many of its properties when used to construct estimators in cointegration models. Although cointegration models violate the standard assumptions used to derive the asymptotic normality of the GMM estimators, they still retain this property.

Tests on the parameters in cointegration models can therefore be conducted straightforwardly using asymptotic χ^2 critical values. Tests on the cointegration rank can be performed using the GMM objective function as it has a limiting distribution which is identical to the limiting distribution of the Johansen trace statistic. Both these asymptotic properties and the easy analytical expressions of the GMM estimators show the attractiveness of the GMM in cointegration models. These features also hold for the standard cointegration models' maximum likelihood estimators but these estimators loose a lot of their attractivity when more complex models are considered. We showed, however, that the GMM still gives tracktable analytical expressions for the estimators and allows for the derivation of the asymptotic properties even in more complicated cointegration models. In applied work, many cointegrated series, like most of the financial time series, violate the properties of the standard cointegation model and the development of estimation techniques able to deal with them is quite important.

Appendix

PROOF OF THEOREM 7.1.

In *Johansen* [1991], it is proved that the stochastic process x_t, from (7–1), can be represented by $\Delta x_t = C(L)\Sigma^{\frac{1}{2}}\xi_t$, where $\beta = (\ I_r \quad -\beta_2'\ )'$, and ξ_t is a k–variate Gaussian white noise process with zero mean and identity covariance matrix. Consequently,

$$x_t = \beta_\perp(\alpha_\perp'\beta_\perp)^{-1}\alpha_\perp'\Sigma^{\frac{1}{2}}\sum_{j=1}^{t}\xi_j + C^*(L)\Sigma^{\frac{1}{2}}\xi_t,$$

$$x_{1t} = \beta_2'(\alpha_\perp'\beta_\perp)^{-1}\alpha_\perp'\Sigma^{\frac{1}{2}}\sum_{j=1}^{t}\xi_j + \begin{pmatrix} I_r \\ 0 \end{pmatrix}C^*(L)\Sigma^{\frac{1}{2}}\xi_t,$$

$$x_{2t} = (\alpha_\perp'\beta_\perp)^{-1}\alpha_\perp'\Sigma^{\frac{1}{2}}\sum_{j=1}^{t}\xi_j + \begin{pmatrix} 0 \\ I_{k-r} \end{pmatrix}C^*(L)\Sigma^{\frac{1}{2}}\xi_t,$$

where
$$C(L) = C(1) + (1 - L)C^*(L),$$

$C^*(L) = \sum_{i=0}^{\infty} C_i^* L^i$. The least squares estimator of α, $\hat{\alpha}$, can also be expressed as

$$\hat{\alpha} - \alpha = (\sum_{t=1}^{T} u_t (1 - x'_{2t-1}(\sum_{t=1}^{T} x_{2t-1} x'_{2t-1})^{-1} x_{2t-1}) x'_{1t-1})$$

$$(\sum_{t=1}^{T} x_{1t-1}(1 - x'_{2t-1}(\sum_{t=1}^{T} x_{2t-1} x'_{2t-1})^{-1} x_{2t-1}) x'_{1t-1})^{-1}$$

$$= (\sum_{t=1}^{T} u_t (x_{1t-1} - \tilde{\beta}'_2 x_{2t-1})')$$

$$(\sum_{t=1}^{T} (x_{1t-1} - \tilde{\beta}'_2 x_{2t-1})(x_{1t-1} - \tilde{\beta}'_2 x_{2t-1})')^{-1}$$

where $\tilde{\beta}_2 = (\sum_{t=1}^{T} x_{2t-1} x'_{2t-1})^{-1} x_{2t-1} x'_{1t-1}$. $\tilde{\beta}_2$ is a super-consistent estimator of β_2 and can therefore be treated as equal to β_2 in the derivation of the limiting distribution of $\hat{\alpha}$. Since

$$\frac{1}{T} \sum_{t=1}^{T} (x_{1t-1} - \tilde{\beta}'_2 x_{2t-1})(x_{1t-1} - \tilde{\beta}'_2 x_{2t-1})' \quad \Rightarrow$$

$$\text{cov}(\beta' x) = \beta' \sum_{i=0}^{\infty} C_i^* \Sigma C_i^{*\prime} \beta,$$

and,

$$T^{-\frac{1}{2}} (\sum_{t=1}^{T} u_t (x_{1t-1} - \tilde{\beta}'_2 x_{2t-1})') \quad \Rightarrow \quad N(0, \text{cov}(\beta' x) \otimes \Sigma),$$

the limiting distribution of $\hat{\alpha}$ becomes

$$\sqrt{T}(\hat{\alpha} - \alpha) \Rightarrow N(0, \text{cov}(\beta' x)^{-1} \otimes \Sigma).$$

With respect to the cointegrating vector,

$$\hat{\beta} = (\sum_{t=1}^{T} x_{t-1} x'_{t-1})^{-1} (\sum_{t=1}^{T} x_{t-1} \Delta x'_t) \Sigma^{-1} \hat{\alpha} (\hat{\alpha}' \Sigma^{-1} \hat{\alpha})^{-1} =$$

$$\begin{pmatrix} I_r \\ (\sum_{t=1}^{T} x_{t-1} x'_{t-1})_2^{-1} (\sum_{t=1}^{T} x_{t-1}(x'_{t-1} \beta \alpha' + u'_t)) \Sigma^{-1} \hat{\alpha} (\hat{\alpha}' \Sigma^{-1} \hat{\alpha})^{-1} \end{pmatrix} =$$

$$\begin{pmatrix} I_r \\ (\sum_{t=1}^{T} x_{t-1} x'_{t-1})_2^{-1} (\sum_{t=1}^{T} x_{t-1}(x'_{t-1} \beta \alpha' + u'_t)) \Sigma^{-1} \alpha (\alpha' \Sigma^{-1} \alpha)^{-1} \end{pmatrix} =$$

$$\begin{pmatrix} I_r \\ -\beta_2 \end{pmatrix} + \begin{pmatrix} 0 \\ (\sum_{t=1}^{T} x_{t-1}x'_{t-1})_2^{-1}(\sum_{t=1}^{T} x_{t-1}u'_t)\Sigma^{-1}\alpha(\alpha'\Sigma^{-1}\alpha)^{-1} \end{pmatrix},$$

where $(\ )_2^{-1}$ indicates the last $(k-r)$ rows of $(\ )^{-1}$ and $\hat{\alpha}$ is a consistent estimator of α such that the difference between $\hat{\alpha}$ and α will only affects orders of convergence exceeding T. Furthermore $\hat{\alpha} = (\sum_{t=1}^{T} x_{t-1}x'_{t-1})_1^{-1}(\sum_{t=1}^{T} x_{t-1}\Delta x'_t)$, where $(\ )_1^{-1}$ indicates the first r rows of $(\ )^{-1}$. To analyze the limiting behavior of $\hat{\beta}$, we have to determine the limiting expressions of both $(\sum_{t=1}^{T} x_{t-1}x'_{t-1})_2^{-1}$ and $(\sum_{t=1}^{T} x_{t-1}u'_t)\Sigma^{-1}\alpha(\alpha'\Sigma^{-1}\alpha)^{-1}$. Starting with the latter expression, its limiting behavior can be analyzed using the stochastic trend specification of x_{t-1}.

$$(\sum_{t=1}^{T} x_{t-1}u'_t)\Sigma^{-1}\alpha(\alpha'\Sigma^{-1}\alpha)^{-1} =$$

$$(\sum_{t=1}^{T} \beta_\perp(\alpha'_\perp\beta_\perp)^{-1}\alpha'_\perp\Sigma^{\frac{1}{2}}(\sum_{j=1}^{t-1} \xi_j)\xi'_t\Sigma^{-\frac{1}{2}}\alpha$$

$$+ \sum_{t=1}^{T} C^*(L)\Sigma^{\frac{1}{2}}\xi_{t-1}\xi'_t\Sigma^{-\frac{1}{2}}\alpha)(\alpha'\Sigma^{-1}\alpha)^{-1}.$$

Since $\Sigma^{\frac{1}{2}}\alpha_\perp$ is orthogonal to $\Sigma^{-\frac{1}{2}}\alpha$, i.e., $(\Sigma^{\frac{1}{2}}\alpha_\perp)'\Sigma^{-\frac{1}{2}}\alpha = \alpha'_\perp\alpha = 0$, the Brownian motions appearing in the limiting expression are independent,

$$\frac{1}{T}\sum_{t=1}^{T} \alpha'_\perp\Sigma^{\frac{1}{2}}(\sum_{j=1}^{t-1} \xi_j)\xi'_t\Sigma^{-\frac{1}{2}}\alpha \Rightarrow \Lambda_1 \int W_1 dW'_2\Lambda'_2,$$

since $\frac{1}{\sqrt{T}}\alpha'_\perp\Sigma^{\frac{1}{2}}(\sum_{j=1}^{T-1} \xi_j) \Rightarrow \Lambda_1 W_1$, W_1 is a $(k-r)$ dimensional Brownian motion with covariance matrix I_{k-r} and $\Lambda_1 = (\alpha'_\perp\Sigma\alpha_\perp)^{\frac{1}{2}}$, W_2 is a r dimensional Brownian motion with covariance matrix I_r and W_2 is stochastically independent of W_1, $\Lambda_2 = (\alpha'\Sigma^{-1}\alpha)^{\frac{1}{2}}$. Also the limiting behavior of $(\sum_{t=1}^{T} x_{t-1}x'_{t-1})^{-1}$ is determined by the stochastic trend specification

$$(\sum_{t=1}^{T} x_{t-1}x_{t-1}')^{-1} =$$

$$(\beta \quad \beta_\perp)\, [(\beta \quad \beta_\perp)'\, (\sum_{t=1}^{T} x_{t-1}x_{t-1}')\, (\beta \quad \beta_\perp)]^{-1}$$

$$(\beta \quad \beta_\perp)' \, .$$

So, the limiting behavior of

$$(\beta \quad \beta_\perp)'\, (\sum_{t=1}^{T} x_{t-1}x_{t-1}')\, (\beta \quad \beta_\perp) \quad \text{is,}$$

$$(T^{-\frac{1}{2}}\beta \quad T^{-1}\beta_\perp)'\, (\sum_{t=1}^{T} x_{t-1}x_{t-1}')\, (T^{-\frac{1}{2}}\beta \quad T^{-1}\beta_\perp) \Rightarrow$$

$$\begin{pmatrix} \mathrm{cov}(\beta'x) & 0 \\ 0 & \beta'_\perp\beta_\perp(\alpha'_\perp\beta_\perp)^{-1}\Lambda_1(\int W_1 W_1')\Lambda_1'(\alpha'_\perp\beta_\perp)^{-1'}\beta'_\perp\beta_\perp \end{pmatrix}$$

as

$$T^{-1}\sum_{t=1}^{T} \beta' C^*(L)\Sigma^{\frac{1}{2}}\xi_{t-1}\xi_{t-1}'\Sigma^{\frac{1}{2}'}C^*(L)\beta \Rightarrow \mathrm{cov}(\beta'x),$$

$$T^{-2}\beta'_\perp\beta_\perp(\alpha'_\perp\beta_\perp)^{-1}\sum_{t=1}^{T}(\alpha'_\perp\Sigma^{\frac{1}{2}}\sum_{j=1}^{t-1}\xi_j)$$

$$(\sum_{j=1}^{t-1}\xi_j'\Sigma^{\frac{1}{2}'}\alpha_\perp)(\alpha'_\perp\beta_\perp)^{-1'}\beta'_\perp\beta_\perp \Rightarrow$$

$$\beta'_\perp\beta_\perp(\alpha'_\perp\beta_\perp)^{-1}\Lambda_1(\int W_1 W_1')\Lambda_1'(\alpha'_\perp\beta_\perp)^{-1'}\beta'_\perp\beta_\perp,$$

$$T^{-1\frac{1}{2}}\sum_{t=1}^{T} \beta' C^*(L)\Sigma^{\frac{1}{2}}\xi_{t-1}(\sum_{j=1}^{t-1}\xi_j'\Sigma^{\frac{1}{2}'}\alpha_\perp)(\alpha'_\perp\beta_\perp)^{-1'}\beta'_\perp\beta_\perp$$

$$\Rightarrow 0.$$

Consequently,

$$[(T^{-\frac{1}{2}}\beta \quad T^{-1}\beta_\perp)'\, (\sum_{t=1}^{T} x_{t-1}x_{t-1}')\, (T^{-\frac{1}{2}}\beta \quad T^{-1}\beta_\perp)]^{-1} \Rightarrow$$

$$\begin{pmatrix} \mathrm{cov}(\beta'x)^{-1} & 0 \\ 0 & \Theta \end{pmatrix}$$

where

$$\Theta = (\beta'_\perp \beta_\perp)^{-1} \beta'_\perp \alpha_\perp \Lambda_1^{-1'} (\int W_1 W'_1)^{-1} \Lambda_1^{-1} \alpha'_\perp \beta_\perp (\beta'_\perp \beta_\perp)^{-1}$$

and

$$(\sum_{t=1}^{T} x_{t-1} x'_{t-1})^{-1} \Rightarrow O(T)\beta \mathrm{cov}(\beta' x)^{-1} \beta' + O(T^2)$$

$$\beta_\perp (\beta'_\perp \beta_\perp)^{-1} \beta'_\perp \alpha_\perp \Lambda_1^{-1'} (\int W_1 W'_1)^{-1} \Lambda_1^{-1} \alpha'_\perp \beta_\perp (\beta'_\perp \beta_\perp)^{-1} \beta'_\perp$$

where $O(T^j)$ indicates that the limiting behavior of this part is proportional to T^j. The latter part governs the limiting behavior of $(\sum_{t=1}^{T} x_{t-1} x'_{t-1})_2^{-1}$, which can be characterized by

$$T^2 (\sum_{t=1}^{T} x_{t-1} x'_{t-1})_2^{-1} \Rightarrow$$

$$(\beta'_\perp \beta_\perp)^{-1} \beta'_\perp \alpha_\perp \Lambda_1^{-1'} (\int W_1 W'_1)^{-1} \Lambda_1^{-1} \alpha'_\perp \beta_\perp (\beta'_\perp \beta_\perp)^{-1} \beta'_\perp$$

as $\beta_\perp = \begin{pmatrix} \beta'_2 \\ I_{k-r} \end{pmatrix}$. So, the limiting expression for the cointegrating vector estimator becomes,

$$T(\hat{\beta} - \beta) \Rightarrow \begin{pmatrix} 0 \\ (\beta'_\perp \beta_\perp)^{-1} \beta'_\perp \alpha_\perp \Lambda_1^{-1'} (\int W_1 W'_1)^{-1} (\int W_1 dW'_2) \Lambda'_2 \end{pmatrix}$$

$$\Rightarrow \begin{pmatrix} 0 \\ N(0, \alpha' \Sigma^{-1} \alpha \otimes \Theta) \end{pmatrix}$$

and can be approximated by

$$(\frac{1}{T^2} \sum_{t=1}^{T} x_{2t-1} (1 - x'_{1t-1} (\sum_{t=1}^{T} x_{1t-1} x'_{1t-1})^{-1} x_{1t-1}) x'_{2t-1})^{-1}.$$

$$(\Rightarrow \Theta)$$

PROOF OF THEOREM 7.2

(Only the second part of Theorem 7.2 is proved here). When the DGP of x_t reads,

$$\Delta x_t = \alpha_\perp \lambda' + \alpha(\beta' x_{t-1} + \mu') + \varepsilon_t,$$

where $c = \alpha_\perp \lambda' + \alpha\mu'$, it has the stochastic trend representation, see *Johansen* [1991], $\Delta x_t = C(L)(c + \Sigma^{\frac{1}{2}}\xi_t)$, $\beta = (I_r \quad -\beta_2')'$, where ξ_t is a k-variate Gaussian white noise process with zero mean and identity covariance matrix. Consequently,

$$x_t = \beta_\perp(\alpha_\perp'\beta_\perp)^{-1}\alpha_\perp'(t\alpha_\perp\lambda' + \Sigma^{\frac{1}{2}}\sum_{j=1}^{t}\xi_j)$$
$$+ C^*(1)\alpha\mu' + C^*(L)\Sigma^{\frac{1}{2}}\xi_t,$$

$$x_{1t} = \beta_2'(\alpha_\perp'\beta_\perp)^{-1}\alpha_\perp'(t\alpha_\perp\lambda' + \Sigma^{\frac{1}{2}}\sum_{j=1}^{t}\xi_j)+$$
$$\begin{pmatrix} I_r \\ 0 \end{pmatrix}(C^*(1)\alpha\mu' + C^*(L)\Sigma^{\frac{1}{2}}\xi_t),$$

$$x_{2t} = (\alpha_\perp'\beta_\perp)^{-1}\alpha_\perp'(t\alpha_\perp\lambda' + \Sigma^{\frac{1}{2}}\sum_{j=1}^{t}\xi_j)$$
$$+ \begin{pmatrix} 0 \\ I_{k-r} \end{pmatrix}(C^*(1)\alpha\mu' + C^*(L)\Sigma^{\frac{1}{2}}\xi_t),$$

where

$$C(L) = C(1) + (1 - L)C^*(L),$$

$$C^*(L) = \sum_{i=0}^{\infty} C_i^* L^i, \quad \beta'C^*(1)\alpha = I_r.$$

The least squares estimator of α, $\hat{\alpha}$, can also be expressed as

$$\hat{\alpha} - \alpha =$$
$$(\sum_{t=1}^{T} u_t(1 - \begin{pmatrix} x_{2t-1} \\ 1 \end{pmatrix}'(\sum_{t=1}^{T}\begin{pmatrix} x_{2t-1} \\ 1 \end{pmatrix}\begin{pmatrix} x_{2t-1} \\ 1 \end{pmatrix}')^{-1}$$
$$\begin{pmatrix} x_{2t-1} \\ 1 \end{pmatrix})x_{1t-1}')$$

$$(\sum_{t=1}^{T} x_{1t-1}(1 - \begin{pmatrix} x_{2t-1} \\ 1 \end{pmatrix}' (\sum_{t=1}^{T} \begin{pmatrix} x_{2t-1} \\ 1 \end{pmatrix} \begin{pmatrix} x_{2t-1} \\ 1 \end{pmatrix}')^{-1}$$

$$\begin{pmatrix} x_{2t-1} \\ 1 \end{pmatrix})x_{1t-1}')^{-1}$$

$$= (\sum_{t=1}^{T} u_t(x_{1t-1} - \begin{pmatrix} \tilde{\beta}_2 \\ \tilde{\mu} \end{pmatrix}' \begin{pmatrix} x_{2t-1} \\ 1 \end{pmatrix})')(\sum_{t=1}^{T}(x_{1t-1} - \begin{pmatrix} \tilde{\beta}_2 \\ \tilde{\mu} \end{pmatrix}'$$

$$\begin{pmatrix} x_{2t-1} \\ 1 \end{pmatrix})(x_{1t-1} - \begin{pmatrix} \tilde{\beta}_2 \\ \tilde{\mu} \end{pmatrix}' \begin{pmatrix} x_{2t-1} \\ 1 \end{pmatrix}))^{-1}$$

with $\begin{pmatrix} \tilde{\beta}_2 \\ \tilde{\mu} \end{pmatrix} = (\sum_{t=1}^{T} \begin{pmatrix} x_{2t-1} \\ 1 \end{pmatrix} \begin{pmatrix} x_{2t-1} \\ 1 \end{pmatrix}')^{-1} \sum_{t=1}^{T} \begin{pmatrix} x_{2t-1} \\ 1 \end{pmatrix} x_{1t-1}'.$

$\tilde{\beta}_2$ is a superconsistent estimator of β_2. Since

$$\frac{1}{T} \sum_{t=1}^{T}(x_{1t-1} - \begin{pmatrix} \tilde{\beta}_2 \\ \tilde{\mu} \end{pmatrix}' \begin{pmatrix} x_{2t-1} \\ 1 \end{pmatrix})(x_{1t-1} - \begin{pmatrix} \tilde{\beta}_2 \\ \tilde{\mu} \end{pmatrix}' \begin{pmatrix} x_{2t-1} \\ 1 \end{pmatrix})'$$

$$\Rightarrow \text{cov}(\beta'x - \mu') = \beta' \sum_{i=0}^{\infty} C_i^* \Sigma C_i^{*\prime} \beta,$$

and,

$$T^{-\frac{1}{2}}(\sum_{t=1}^{T} u_t(x_{1t-1} - \begin{pmatrix} \tilde{\beta}_2 \\ \tilde{\mu} \end{pmatrix}' \begin{pmatrix} x_{2t-1} \\ 1 \end{pmatrix})')$$

$$\Rightarrow N(0, \text{cov}(\beta'x - \mu') \otimes \Sigma),$$

the limiting distribution of $\hat{\alpha}$ becomes

$$\sqrt{T}(\hat{\alpha} - \alpha) \Rightarrow N(0, \text{cov}(\beta'x - \mu')^{-1} \otimes \Sigma).$$

With respect to the cointegrating vector,

$$\begin{pmatrix} \hat{\beta} \\ \hat{\mu} \end{pmatrix} =$$

$$(\sum_{t=1}^{T} \begin{pmatrix} x_{t-1} \\ 1 \end{pmatrix} \begin{pmatrix} x_{t-1} \\ 1 \end{pmatrix}')^{-1} (\sum_{t=1}^{T} \begin{pmatrix} x_{t-1} \\ 1 \end{pmatrix} \Delta x_t') \Sigma^{-1} \hat{\alpha} (\hat{\alpha}' \Sigma^{-1} \hat{\alpha})^{-1}$$

$$= \begin{pmatrix} I_r \\ -\hat{\beta}_2 \\ \hat{\mu} \end{pmatrix}$$

$$
\begin{pmatrix} -\widehat{\beta}_2 \\ \widehat{\mu} \end{pmatrix} = ((\sum_{t=1}^{T} \begin{pmatrix} x_{t-1} \\ 1 \end{pmatrix} \begin{pmatrix} x_{t-1} \\ 1 \end{pmatrix}')_2^{-1} (\sum_{t=1}^{T} \begin{pmatrix} x_{t-1} \\ 1 \end{pmatrix}
$$

$$
(\begin{pmatrix} x_{t-1} \\ 1 \end{pmatrix}' \begin{pmatrix} \beta \\ \mu \end{pmatrix} \alpha' + \lambda \alpha'_{\perp} + u'_t)) \Sigma^{-1} \widehat{\alpha} (\widehat{\alpha}' \Sigma^{-1} \widehat{\alpha})^{-1}
$$

$$
= (\sum_{t=1}^{T} \begin{pmatrix} x_{t-1} \\ 1 \end{pmatrix} \begin{pmatrix} x_{t-1} \\ 1 \end{pmatrix}')_2^{-1} (\sum_{t=1}^{T} \begin{pmatrix} x_{t-1} \\ 1 \end{pmatrix}
$$

$$
(\begin{pmatrix} x_{t-1} \\ 1 \end{pmatrix}' \begin{pmatrix} \beta \\ \mu \end{pmatrix} \alpha' + u'_t)) \Sigma^{-1} \alpha (\alpha' \Sigma^{-1} \alpha)^{-1}
$$

$$
= \begin{pmatrix} -\beta_2 \\ \mu \end{pmatrix} + (\sum_{t=1}^{T} \begin{pmatrix} x_{t-1} \\ 1 \end{pmatrix} \begin{pmatrix} x_{t-1} \\ 1 \end{pmatrix}')_2^{-1}
$$

$$
(\sum_{t=1}^{T} \begin{pmatrix} x_{t-1} \\ 1 \end{pmatrix} u'_t) \Sigma^{-1} \alpha (\alpha' \Sigma^{-1} \alpha)^{-1}
$$

as $\alpha'_{\perp} \Sigma^{-1} \alpha = 0$ since $\Sigma^{-1} = P \Lambda P'$, $\Lambda = \text{diag}(\lambda_i) = \sum_{i=1}^{k} \lambda_i e_i e'_i$, $PP' = I_k$, $\alpha'_{\perp} PP' \alpha = b'_{\perp} b = 0$, $P' \alpha = b = (b'_1 ... b'_k)'$, $\alpha'_{\perp} \Sigma^{-1} \alpha = b'_{\perp} \Lambda b = \sum_{i=1}^{k} \lambda_i b'_{\perp i} b_i = 0$ as $b'_{\perp i} b_i = 0$ $\forall i$. $(\sum_{t=1}^{T} \begin{pmatrix} x_{t-1} \\ 1 \end{pmatrix} \begin{pmatrix} x_{t-1} \\ 1 \end{pmatrix}')_2^{-1}$ indicates the last $(k - r + 1)$

rows of $(\sum_{t=1}^{T} \begin{pmatrix} x_{t-1} \\ 1 \end{pmatrix} \begin{pmatrix} x_{t-1} \\ 1 \end{pmatrix}')^{-1}$ and $\widehat{\alpha}$ is a consistent estimator of α such that the difference between $\widehat{\alpha}$ and α will only affect orders of convergence exceeding T. To analyze the limiting behavior of $\widehat{\beta}$, we have to determine the limiting expressions of both $(\sum_{t=1}^{T} \begin{pmatrix} x_{t-1} \\ 1 \end{pmatrix} \begin{pmatrix} x_{t-1} \\ 1 \end{pmatrix}')_2^{-1}$

and $(\sum_{t=1}^{T} \begin{pmatrix} x_{t-1} \\ 1 \end{pmatrix} u'_t) \Sigma^{-1} \alpha (\alpha' \Sigma^{-1} \alpha)^{-1}$. Starting with the latter expression, its limiting behavior can be analyzed using the stochastic trend specification.

$$
(\sum_{t=1}^{T} \begin{pmatrix} x_{t-1} \\ 1 \end{pmatrix} u'_t) \Sigma^{-1} \alpha (\alpha' \Sigma^{-1} \alpha)^{-1}
$$

$$
= (\sum_{t=1}^{T} \begin{pmatrix} \beta_{\perp} (\alpha'_{\perp} \beta_{\perp})^{-1} \alpha'_{\perp} (t \alpha_{\perp} \lambda' + \Sigma^{\frac{1}{2}} (\sum_{j=1}^{t-1} \xi_j)) \\ 1 \end{pmatrix} \xi'_t \Sigma^{-\frac{1}{2}} \alpha
$$

$$
+ \sum_{t=1}^{T} \begin{pmatrix} C^*(1) \alpha \mu' + C^*(L) \Sigma^{\frac{1}{2}} \xi_{t-1}) \\ 0 \end{pmatrix} \xi'_t \Sigma^{-\frac{1}{2}} \alpha) (\alpha' \Sigma^{-1} \alpha)^{-1}
$$

Since $\Sigma^{\frac{1}{2}}\alpha_\perp$ is orthogonal to $\Sigma^{-\frac{1}{2}}\alpha$, *i.e.*, $(\Sigma^{\frac{1}{2}}\alpha_\perp)'\Sigma^{-\frac{1}{2}}\alpha = \alpha'_\perp\alpha = 0$, the Brownian motions appearing in the limiting expression are independent,

$$\begin{pmatrix} T^{-1}\lambda_\perp \\ T^{-\frac{3}{2}}\lambda \end{pmatrix} (\alpha'_\perp\alpha_\perp)^{-1}\alpha'_\perp \sum_{t=1}^{T}(t\alpha_\perp\lambda' + \Sigma^{\frac{1}{2}}(\sum_{j=1}^{t-1}\xi_j))\xi'_t\Sigma^{-\frac{1}{2}}\alpha)$$

$$\Rightarrow \Lambda_3 \int \begin{pmatrix} W_{11} \\ \tau \end{pmatrix} dW'_2\Lambda'_2$$

and

$$\begin{pmatrix} T^{-1}I_{k-r-1} & 0 \\ 0 & T^{-\frac{3}{2}} \end{pmatrix} \beta^{*'}_\perp(\sum_{t=1}^{T}\beta_\perp(\alpha'_\perp\beta_\perp)^{-1}\alpha'_\perp(t\alpha_\perp\lambda'$$

$$+ \Sigma^{\frac{1}{2}}(\sum_{j=1}^{t-1}\xi_j)\xi'_t\Sigma^{-\frac{1}{2}}\alpha) \quad\Rightarrow\quad \Lambda_3 \int \begin{pmatrix} W_{11} \\ \tau \end{pmatrix} dW'_2\Lambda'_2.$$

So,

$$\left(\beta^*_\perp \begin{pmatrix} T^{-1}I_{k-r-1} & 0 \\ 0 & T^{-\frac{3}{2}} \end{pmatrix} \quad 0 \\ \quad\quad\quad\quad 0 \quad\quad T^{-\frac{1}{2}} \right)' (\sum_{t=1}^{T}\begin{pmatrix} x_{t-1} \\ 1 \end{pmatrix} u'_t)\Sigma^{-1}$$

$$\alpha(\alpha'\Sigma^{-1}\alpha)^{-1} \Rightarrow \begin{pmatrix} \Lambda_3 & 0 \\ 0 & 1 \end{pmatrix} \int \begin{pmatrix} W_{11} \\ \tau \\ \iota \end{pmatrix} dW'_2\Lambda'_2,$$

where $\beta^*_\perp = \beta_\perp(\beta'_\perp\beta_\perp)^{-1}\beta'_\perp\alpha_\perp(\alpha'_\perp\alpha_\perp)^{-1}\begin{pmatrix} \lambda_\perp \\ \lambda \end{pmatrix}'$, $\lambda_\perp\lambda' = 0$, W_{11} is a $(k-r-1)$ dimensional Brownian motion with covariance matrix I_{k-r-1} and

$$\Lambda_3 = (\begin{pmatrix} \lambda_\perp(\alpha'_\perp\alpha_\perp)^{-1}\alpha'_\perp\Sigma^{\frac{1}{2}} \\ \lambda\lambda' \end{pmatrix} \begin{pmatrix} \lambda_\perp(\alpha'_\perp\alpha_\perp)^{-1}\alpha'_\perp\Sigma^{\frac{1}{2}} \\ \lambda\lambda' \end{pmatrix}')^{\frac{1}{2}},$$

w_2 is a r dimensional Brownian motion with covariance matrix I_r and W_2 is stochastically independent of W_{11}, $\Lambda_2 = (\alpha'\Sigma^{-1}\alpha)^{\frac{1}{2}}$, $\tau(t) = t$, $\iota(t) = 1$, $0 \le t \le 1$. Also the limiting behavior of $(\sum_{t=1}^{T}\begin{pmatrix} x_{t-1} \\ 1 \end{pmatrix}\begin{pmatrix} x_{t-1} \\ 1 \end{pmatrix}')^{-1}$ is determined by the stochastic trend specification:

$$
(\sum_{t=1}^{T} \binom{x_{t-1}}{1} \binom{x_{t-1}}{1}')^{-1}
$$

$$
= \begin{pmatrix} \beta & \beta_\perp^* & 0 \\ 0 & 0 & 1 \end{pmatrix} [\begin{pmatrix} \beta & \beta_\perp^* & 0 \\ 0 & 0 & 1 \end{pmatrix}' \sum_{t=1}^{T} \binom{x_{t-1}}{1} \binom{x_{t-1}}{1}')
$$

$$
\begin{pmatrix} \beta & \beta_\perp^* & 0 \\ 0 & 0 & 1 \end{pmatrix}]^{-1} \begin{pmatrix} \beta & \beta_\perp^* & 0 \\ 0 & 0 & 1 \end{pmatrix}'
$$

$$
\begin{pmatrix} T^{-\frac{1}{2}}\beta & \beta_\perp^* \begin{pmatrix} T^{-1}I_{k-r-1} & 0 \\ 0 & T^{-\frac{3}{2}} \end{pmatrix} & 0 \\ 0 & 0 & T^{-\frac{1}{2}} \end{pmatrix}' (\sum_{t=1}^{T} \binom{x_{t-1}}{1}
$$

$$
\binom{x_{t-1}}{1}') \begin{pmatrix} T^{-\frac{1}{2}}\beta & \beta_\perp^* \begin{pmatrix} T^{-1}I_{k-r-1} & 0 \\ 0 & T^{-\frac{3}{2}} \end{pmatrix} & 0 \\ 0 & 0 & T^{-\frac{1}{2}} \end{pmatrix}
$$

$$
\Rightarrow \begin{pmatrix} \operatorname{cov}(\beta'x - \mu') + \mu'\mu & 0 & \mu' \\ 0 & \Lambda_3(\int \binom{W_{11}}{\tau}\binom{W_{11}}{\tau}')\Lambda_3' & 0 \\ \mu & 0 & 1 \end{pmatrix}.
$$

Consequently,

$$
(\begin{pmatrix} T^{-\frac{1}{2}}\beta & \begin{pmatrix} T^{-1}I_{k-r-1} & 0 \\ 0 & T^{-\frac{3}{2}} \end{pmatrix}\beta_\perp^* & 0 \\ 0 & 0 & T^{-\frac{1}{2}} \end{pmatrix}' (\sum_{t=1}^{T} \binom{x_{t-1}}{1}
$$

$$
\binom{x_{t-1}}{1}') \begin{pmatrix} T^{-\frac{1}{2}}\beta & \begin{pmatrix} T^{-1}I_{k-r-1} & 0 \\ 0 & T^{-\frac{3}{2}} \end{pmatrix}\beta_\perp^* & 0 \\ 0 & 0 & T^{-\frac{1}{2}} \end{pmatrix})^{-1} \Rightarrow
$$

$$
\begin{pmatrix} \operatorname{cov}(\beta'x - \mu')^{-1} & 0 \\ 0 & \Lambda_3^{-1'}(\int \binom{W_{11}}{\tau}\binom{W_{11}}{\tau}')^{-1}\Lambda_3^{-1} \\ -\mu\operatorname{cov}(\beta'x - \mu')^{-1} & 0 \end{pmatrix}
$$

$$
\begin{pmatrix} -\operatorname{cov}(\beta'x - \mu')^{-1}\mu' \\ 0 \\ 1 + \mu\operatorname{cov}(\beta'x - \mu')^{-1}\mu' \end{pmatrix})).
$$

The limiting behavior of $(\sum\limits_{t=1}^{T} x_{t-1}x'_{t-1})_2^{-1}$ now becomes

$$
\left(\beta^*_{2\perp} \begin{pmatrix} TI_{k-r-1} & 0 \\ 0 & T^{\frac{3}{2}} \\ 0 & \end{pmatrix} \quad 0 \\ \quad T^{\frac{1}{2}} \right) \left(\sum_{t=1}^{T} \begin{pmatrix} x_{t-1} \\ 1 \end{pmatrix} \begin{pmatrix} x_{t-1} \\ 1 \end{pmatrix}' \right)_2^{-1}
$$

$$
\left(\beta^*_{\perp} \begin{pmatrix} TI_{k-r-1} & 0 \\ 0 & T^{\frac{3}{2}} \\ 0 & \end{pmatrix} \quad 0 \\ \quad T^{\frac{1}{2}} \right)
$$

$$
\Rightarrow \begin{pmatrix} \Lambda_3 & 0 \\ 0 & 1 \end{pmatrix}^{-1\prime} (\int \begin{pmatrix} W_{11} \\ \tau \\ \iota \end{pmatrix} \begin{pmatrix} W_{11} \\ \tau \\ \iota \end{pmatrix}')^{-1} \begin{pmatrix} \Lambda_3 & 0 \\ 0 & 1 \end{pmatrix}^{-1}
$$

where $\beta^*_{2\perp} = (\beta'_\perp \beta_\perp)^{-1}\beta'_\perp \alpha_\perp (\alpha'_\perp \alpha_\perp)^{-1} \begin{pmatrix} \lambda_\perp \\ \lambda \end{pmatrix}'$. So, the limiting expression for the cointegrating vector estimator becomes,

$$
\left(\begin{pmatrix} TI_{k-r-1} & 0 \\ 0 & T^{\frac{3}{2}} \\ 0 & \end{pmatrix} (\beta^{*\prime}_{2\perp}\beta^*_{2\perp})^{-1}\beta^{*\prime}_{2\perp} \quad 0 \\ \quad T^{\frac{1}{2}} \right) \begin{pmatrix} \beta_2 - \widehat{\beta}_2 \\ \widehat{\mu} - \mu \end{pmatrix}
$$

$$
\Rightarrow \begin{pmatrix} \Lambda_3 & 0 \\ 0 & 1 \end{pmatrix}^{-1\prime} (\int \begin{pmatrix} W_{11} \\ \tau \\ \iota \end{pmatrix} \begin{pmatrix} W_{11} \\ \tau \\ \iota \end{pmatrix}')^{-1} \int \begin{pmatrix} W_{11} \\ \tau \\ \iota \end{pmatrix} dW'_2 \Lambda'_2
$$

$$
\Rightarrow N(0, \; \alpha'\Sigma^{-1}\alpha \otimes \Theta_2),
$$

where

$$
\Theta_2 = \begin{pmatrix} \Lambda_3 & 0 \\ 0 & 1 \end{pmatrix}^{-1\prime} (\int \begin{pmatrix} W_{11} \\ \tau \\ \iota \end{pmatrix} \begin{pmatrix} W_{11} \\ \tau \\ \iota \end{pmatrix}')^{-1} \begin{pmatrix} \Lambda_3 & 0 \\ 0 & 1 \end{pmatrix}^{-1}.
$$

PROOF OF THEOREM 7.3

(Only the first part is proved here, the other proofs are similar) The optimal value of the GMM objective function reads

$$
Q_T(\widehat{\alpha},\widehat{\beta}) = \mathrm{vec}(\sum_{t=1}^{T} \widehat{\varepsilon}_t x'_{t-1})'((\sum_{t=1}^{T} x_{t-1}x'_{t-1})^{-1} \otimes \Sigma^{-1})
$$

$$
\mathrm{vec}(\sum_{t=1}^{T} \widehat{\varepsilon}_t x'_{t-1})
$$

$$=\text{vec}(\sum_{t=1}^{T}(\Delta x_t - \widehat{\alpha}(\widehat{\alpha}'\Sigma^{-1}\widehat{\alpha})^{-1}\widehat{\alpha}'\Sigma^{-1}(\sum_{t=1}^{T}\Delta x_t x'_{t-1})$$

$$(\sum_{t=1}^{T}x_{t-1}x'_{t-1})^{-1}\sum_{t=1}^{T}x_{t-1}x'_{t-1})'((\sum_{t=1}^{T}x_{t-1}x'_{t-1})^{-1}\otimes\Sigma^{-1})$$

$$\text{vec}(\sum_{t=1}^{T}(\Delta x_t - \widehat{\alpha}(\widehat{\alpha}'\Sigma^{-1}\widehat{\alpha})^{-1}\widehat{\alpha}'\Sigma^{-1}(\sum_{t=1}^{T}\Delta x_t x'_{t-1})$$

$$(\sum_{t=1}^{T}x_{t-1}x'_{t-1})^{-1}\sum_{t=1}^{T}x_{t-1}x'_{t-1})$$

$$=\text{vec}((\Sigma^{-1}-\Sigma^{-1}\widehat{\alpha}(\widehat{\alpha}'\Sigma^{-1}\widehat{\alpha})^{-1}\widehat{\alpha}'\Sigma^{-1})(\sum_{t=1}^{T}\Delta x_t x'_{t-1}))'$$

$$((\sum_{t=1}^{T}x_{t-1}x'_{t-1})^{-1}\otimes\Sigma)\text{vec}((\Sigma^{-1}-\Sigma^{-1}\widehat{\alpha}(\widehat{\alpha}'\Sigma^{-1}\widehat{\alpha})^{-1}$$

$$\widehat{\alpha}'\Sigma^{-1})(\sum_{t=1}^{T}\Delta x_t x'_{t-1})).$$

This functional consists of two parts, $((\sum_{t=1}^{T}x_{t-1}x'_{t-1})^{-1}\otimes\Sigma)$
and $\text{vec}((\Sigma^{-1}-\Sigma^{-1}\widehat{\alpha}(\widehat{\alpha}'\Sigma^{-1}\widehat{\alpha})^{-1}\widehat{\alpha}'\Sigma^{-1})(\sum_{t=1}^{T}\Delta x_t x'_{t-1}))$, each
of which limiting behavior is analyzed separately. Starting
with the latter expression,

$$\frac{1}{T}\text{vec}((\Sigma^{-1}-\Sigma^{-1}\widehat{\alpha}(\widehat{\alpha}'\Sigma^{-1}\widehat{\alpha})^{-1}\widehat{\alpha}'\Sigma^{-1})(\sum_{t=1}^{T}\Delta x_t x'_{t-1}))$$

$$=\frac{1}{T}\text{vec}((\widehat{\alpha}_{\perp}(\widehat{\alpha}'_{\perp}\Sigma\widehat{\alpha}_{\perp})^{-1}\widehat{\alpha}'_{\perp}(\sum_{t=1}^{T}\Delta x_t x'_{t-1}))$$

$$\Rightarrow\frac{1}{T}\text{vec}(\alpha_{\perp}(\alpha'_{\perp}\Sigma\alpha_{\perp})^{-1}\sum_{t=1}^{T}(\alpha'_{\perp}\Sigma^{\frac{1}{2}}\xi_t(\sum_{j=1}^{t-1}\xi'_j\Sigma^{\frac{1}{2}}\alpha_{\perp}(\beta'_{\perp}\alpha_{\perp})^{-1}\beta'_{\perp}))$$

$$\Rightarrow(\beta_{\perp}(\alpha'_{\perp}\beta_{\perp})^{-1}\otimes\alpha_{\perp}(\alpha'_{\perp}\Sigma\alpha_{\perp})^{-1})\text{vec}(\Lambda_1(\int W_1 dW'_1)'\Lambda'_1).$$

While

$$T^2((\sum_{t=1}^{T}x_{t-1}x'_{t-1})^{-1}\otimes\Sigma)\Rightarrow$$

$$(\beta_{\perp}(\beta'_{\perp}\beta_{\perp})^{-1}\beta'_{\perp}\alpha_{\perp}\Lambda_1^{-1'}(\int W_1 W'_1)^{-1}\Lambda_1^{-1}\alpha'_{\perp}\beta_{\perp}(\beta'_{\perp}\beta_{\perp})^{-1}\beta'_{\perp}\otimes\Sigma).$$

So,

$$Q_T(\widehat{\alpha}, \widehat{\beta})$$

$$\Rightarrow \mathrm{vec}(\Lambda_1(\int W_1 dW_1')'\Lambda_1')'(\beta_\perp(\alpha_\perp'\beta_\perp)^{-1} \otimes \alpha_\perp(\alpha_\perp'\Sigma\alpha_\perp)^{-1})'$$

$$(\beta_\perp(\beta_\perp'\beta_\perp)^{-1}\beta_\perp'\alpha_\perp\Lambda_1^{-1'}(\int W_1 W_1')^{-1}\Lambda_1^{-1}\alpha_\perp'\beta_\perp(\beta_\perp'\beta_\perp)^{-1}\beta_\perp' \otimes \Sigma)$$

$$(\beta_\perp(\alpha_\perp'\beta_\perp)^{-1} \otimes \alpha_\perp(\alpha_\perp'\Sigma\alpha_\perp)^{-1})\mathrm{vec}(\Lambda_1(\int W_1 dW_1')'\Lambda_1')$$

$$\Rightarrow \mathrm{vec}(\Lambda_1(\int W_1 dW_1')'\Lambda_1')'(\Lambda_1^{-1'}(\int W_1 W_1')^{-1}\Lambda_1^{-1} \otimes (\alpha_\perp'\Sigma\alpha_\perp)^{-1})$$

$$\mathrm{vec}(\Lambda_1(\int W_1 dW_1')'\Lambda_1')$$

$$\Rightarrow \mathrm{vec}((\int W_1 dW_1')')'((\int W_1 W_1')^{-1} \otimes I_{k-r})\mathrm{vec}((\int W_1 dW_1')')$$

$$\Rightarrow tr[(\int W_1 dW_1')'(\int W_1 W_1')^{-1}(\int W_1 dW_1')].$$

Acknowledgment

I thank Bas Werker for helpful comments and discussion. Part of this research was carried out while the author was affiliated with Tilburg University. The author would also like to thank the Netherland Organization for Scientific Research (N.W.O.) for their financial support.

References

Anderson, T.W., and H. Rubin [1949]: Estimators of the Parameters of a Single Equation in a Complete Set of Stochastic Equations, *The Annals of Mathematical Statistics*, 21, 570-582.

Engle, R.F., and C.W.J. Granger [1987]: Co-integration and Error Correction : Representation, Estimation and Testing, *Econometrica*, 55, 251-276.

Hamilton, J.D. [1994]: *Times Series Analysis*, Princeton University Press, Princeton, New Jersey.

Hansen, L.P. [1982]: Large Sample Properties of Generalised Method of Moments Estimators, *Econometrica*, 50, 1029-1054.

Hausman, J.A. [**1983**]: Specification and Estimation of Simultaneous Equation Systems, in: Z. Griliches and M.D. Intrilligator, eds., *Handbook of Econometrics* , Vol.1., North-Holland Publishing Co., Amsterdam.

Johansen, S. [**1991**]: Estimation and Hypothesis Testing of Cointegrating Vectors in Gaussian Vector Autoregressive Models, *Econometrica,* 59, 1551-1581.

Kleibergen, F., and H.K. van Dijk [**1994**]: Direct Cointegration Testing in Error Correction Models, *Journal of Econometrics,* 40, 63-86.

Kleibergen, F. and H.K. van Dijk [**1994b**]: On the Shape of the Likelihood/Posterior in Cointegration Models, *Econometric Theory,* 10, 514-551.

Newey, W.K., and K.D. West [**1987**]: A Simple Positive Semi-Definite, Heteroscedasticity and Autocorrelation Consistent Covariance Matrix, *Econometrica,* 55, 703-708.

Perron, P. [**1989**]: The Great Crash, the Oil Price Shock, and the Unit Root Hypothesis, *Econometrica,* 57, 1361-1401.

Phillips, P.C.B. [**1983**]: Exact Small Sample Theory in the Simultaneous Equations Model, in: Z. Griliches and M.D. Intrilligator, eds., *Handbook of Econometrics,* Vol. 1, North-Holland Publishing Co., Amsterdam.

Phillips, P.C.B. [**1987**]: Time Series Regression with a Unit Root, *Econometrica,* 55, 277-301.

Phillips, P.C.B. [**1991**]: Optimal Inference in Cointegrated Systems, *Econometrica,* 59, 283-307.

Phillips, P.C.B. [**1994**]: Some Exact Distribution Theory for Maximum Likelihood Estimators of Cointegrating Coefficients in Error Correction Models, *Econometrica,* 62, 73-95.

Phillips, P.C.B., and P. Perron [**1988**]: Testing for a Unit Root in Time Series Regression, *Biometrika,* 75, 335-346.

Phillips, P.C.B., and V. Solo [**1992**]: Asymptotics for Linear Processes, *Annals of Statistics,* 20, 971-1001.

Quintos, C. [**1994**]: *Analysis of Cointegrating Vectors using the GMM approach,* Unpublished Manuscript, Washington University.

White, H. [**1980**]: A Heteroscedasticity-Consistent Covariance Matrix Estimator and a Direct Test for Heteroscedasticity, *Econometrica,* 48, 817-838.

Chapter 8

ESTIMATION OF LINEAR PANEL

DATA MODELS USING GMM

Seung C. Ahn and Peter Schmidt

Use of panel data regression methods has become increasingly popular as the availability of longitudinal data sets has grown. Panel data contain repeated time series observations (T) for a large number (N) of cross sectional units (*e.g.*, individuals, households, or firms). An important advantage of using such data is that they allow researchers to control for unobservable heterogeneity, that is, systematic differences across cross sectional units. Regressions using aggregated time series and pure cross section data are likely to be contaminated by these effects, and statistical inferences obtained by ignoring these effects could be seriously biased. When panel data are available, error components models can be used to control for these individual differences. Such a model typically assumes that the stochastic error term has two components: a time invariant individual effect which captures the unobservable individual heterogeneity and the usual random noise term. Some explanatory variables (*e.g.*, years of schooling in the earnings equation) are likely to be correlated with the individual effects (*e.g.*, unobservable talent or IQ). A simple treatment to this problem is the within estimator which is equivalent to least squares after transformation of the data to deviations from means.

Unfortunately, the within method has two serious defects. First, the within transformation of a model wipes out time invariant regressors as well as the individual effect, so that it is not possible to estimate the effects of time invariant regressors on the dependent variable. Second, consistency of the within estimator requires that all the regressors in a given model be strictly exogenous with respect to the random noise. The within estimator could be inconsistent for models in which regressors are only weakly exogenous, such as dynamic models including lagged dependent variables as regressors. In response to these problems, a number of studies have developed alternative GMM estimation methods.

In this chapter we provide a systematic account of GMM estimation of linear panel data models. Several different types of models are considered, including the linear regression model with strictly or weakly exogenous regressors, the simultaneous regression model, and a dynamic linear model containing a lagged dependent variable as a regressor. In each case, different assumptions about the exogeneity of the explanatory variables generate different sets of moment conditions that can be used in estimation. This chapter lists the relevant sets of moment conditions and gives some results on simple ways in which they can be imposed. In particular, attention is paid to the question of under what circumstances the efficient GMM estimator takes the form of an instrumental variables estimator.[1]

8.1 Preliminaries

In this section we introduce the general model of interest, some basic assumptions, and some notation. Given linear moment conditions, we consider the efficient GMM estimator and other related instrumental variables estimators. We also examine general conditions under which the efficient GMM estimator is of an instrumental variables form.

---

[1] Here and throughout this chapter, "efficient" means "asymptotically efficient".

8.1.1 General Model

The models we examine in this chapter are of the following common form:

$$y_{it} = x_{it}\beta + u_{it}; \ u_{it} = \alpha_i + \varepsilon_{it}. \tag{8–1}$$

Here $i = 1, ..., N$ indexes the cross sectional unit (individual) and $t = 1, ..., T$ indexes time. The dependent variable is y_{it}, while x_{it} is a $1 \times p$ vector of explanatory variables. The $p \times 1$ parameter vector β is unknown. The composite error u_{it} contains a time invariant individual effect α_i and random noise ε_{it}. We assume that $E(\alpha_i) = 0$ and $E(\varepsilon_{it}) = 0$ for any i and t; thus, $E(u_{it}) = 0$. The time dimension T is held fixed, so that usual asymptotics apply as N gets large. We also assume that the data $\{(y_{i1}, \ldots, y_{iT}, x_{i1}, \ldots, x_{iT})' \mid i = 1, \ldots, N\}$ are independently and identically distributed (i.i.d.) over different i and have finite population moments up to fourth order. Under this assumption, any sample moment (up to fourth order) of the data converges to its counterpart population moment in probability, e.g., $plim_{N \to \infty} N^{-1} \sum_{i=1}^{N} x'_{it} y_{it} = E(x'_{it} y_{it})$.

Some matrix notation is useful throughout this chapter. For any single variable c_{it} or row vector d_{it}, we denote $c_i \equiv (c_{i1}, \ldots, c_{iT})'$ and $D_{it} \equiv (d'_{i1}, \ldots, d'_{iT})'$. Accordingly, y_i and X_i denote the data matrices of T rows. In addition, for any $T \times 1$ vector c_i or $T \times k$ matrix D_i, we denote $c \equiv (c'_1, \ldots, c'_N)'$ and $D \equiv (D'_1, \ldots, D'_N)'$. Accordingly, y and X denote the data matrices of NT rows. With this notation, we can rewrite equation (8–1) for individual i as

$$y_i = X_i\beta + u_i; \ u_i = e_T \otimes \alpha_i + \varepsilon_i, \tag{8–2}$$

where e_T is a $T \times 1$ vector of ones, and all NT observations as $y = X\beta + u$.

We treat the individual effects α_i as random, so that we can define $\Sigma \equiv cov(u_i) = E(u_i u'_i)$. A standard and popular assumption about Σ is the so–called random effects structure

$$\Sigma = \sigma_\alpha^2 e_T e'_T + \sigma_\varepsilon^2 I_T, \tag{8–3}$$

which arises if the ε_{it} are i.i.d. over time and independent of α_i. This covariance structure often takes an important role in GMM estimation as we discuss below.

There are two well–known special cases of the model (8–2); the traditional random effects and fixed effects models. Both of these models assume that the regressors X_i are strictly exogenous with respect to the random noise ε_i (*i.e.*, $E(x'_{it}\varepsilon_{is}) = 0$ for any t and s). The random effects model (*Balestra and Nerlove* [1966]) treats the individual effects as random unobservables which are uncorrelated with all of the regressors. Under this assumption, the parameter β can be consistently and efficiently estimated by generalized least squares (GLS): $\widehat{\beta}_{GLS} = (X'\Omega^{-1}X)^{-1}X'\Omega^{-1}y$, where $\Omega = I_N \otimes \Sigma$.

In contrast, when we treat the α_i as nuisance parameters, the model (8–2) reduces to the traditional fixed effects model. A simple treatment of the fixed effects model is to remove the effects by the (within) transformation of the model (8–2) to deviations from individual means:

$$Q_T y_i = Q_T X_i\beta + Q_T u_i = Q_T X_i\beta + Q_T \varepsilon_i, \qquad (8\text{–}4)$$

where $Q_T = I_T - P_T$, $P_T = T^{-1}e_T e'_T$, and the last equality results from $Q_T e_T = 0$. Least squares on (8–4) yields the familiar within estimator: $\widehat{\beta}_W = (X'Q_V X)^{-1}X'Q_V y$, where $Q_V = I_N \otimes Q_T$.

Although the fixed effects model views the effects α_i as nuisance parameters rather than random variables, the fixed effects treatment (within estimation) is not inconsistent with the random effects assumption. *Mundlak* [1978] considers an alternative random effects model in which the effects α_i are allowed to be correlated with all of the regressors $x_{i1}, \ldots, x_{iT}$. For this model, Mundlak shows that the within estimator is an efficient GLS estimator. This finding implies that the core difference between the random and fixed effects models is not whether the effects are literally random or nuisance parameters, but whether the effects are correlated or uncorrelated with the regressors.

8.1.2 GMM and Instrumental Variables

In this subsection we examine GMM and other related instrumental variables estimators for the model (8–2). Our main focus is a general treatment of given moment conditions, so we do not make any specific exogeneity assumption regarding the regressors X_i. We simply begin by assuming that there exists a set of $T \times k$ instruments Z_i which satisfies the moment condition

$$E(Z'_i u_i) = 0 \qquad (8\text{–}5)$$

and the usual identification condition, rank$[E(Z'_i X_i)] = p$.

Under (8–5) and other usual regularity conditions, a consistent and efficient estimate of β can be obtained by minimizing the GMM criterion function $N(y - X\beta)'Z(V_N)^{-1}Z'(y - X\beta)$, where V_N is any consistent estimate of $V \equiv E(Z_i'u_iu_i'Z_i)$. A simple choice of V_N is

$$N^{-1}\sum_{i=1}^{N} Z_i'\widehat{u}_i\widehat{u}_i'Z_i,$$

where $\widehat{u}_i = y_i - X_i\widehat{\beta}$ and $\widehat{\beta}$ is an initial consistent estimator such as two stage least squares (2SLS). The solution to the minimization leads to the GMM estimator:

$$\widehat{\beta}_{GMM} \equiv [X'Z(V_N)^{-1}Z'X]^{-1}X'Z(V_N)^{-1}Z'y.$$

An instrumental variables estimator, which is closely related with this GMM estimator, is three stages least squares (3SLS):

$$\widehat{\beta}_{3SLS} \equiv [X'Z(Z'\Omega Z)^{-1}Z'X]^{-1}X'Z(Z'\Omega Z)^{-1}Z'y,$$

where $\Omega = I_N \otimes \Sigma$. For notational convenience, we assume that Σ is known, although, in practice, it should be replaced by a consistent estimate such as $\widehat{\Sigma} = N^{-1}\sum_{i=1}^{N} \widehat{u}_i\widehat{u}_i'$. In order to understand the relationship between the GMM and 3SLS estimators, consider the following condition

$$E(Z_i'u_iu_i'Z_i) = E(Z_i'\Sigma Z_i). \tag{8–6}$$

Under this condition, the 3SLS estimator is asymptotically identical to the GMM estimator, because

$$\operatorname*{plim}_{N\to\infty} N^{-1}Z'\Omega Z = \operatorname*{plim}_{N\to\infty} N^{-1}\sum_{i=1}^{N} Z_i'\widehat{u}_i\widehat{u}_i'Z_i = E(Z_i'u_iu_i'Z_i) = V.$$

We will refer to (8–6) as the condition of no conditional heteroskedasticity (NCH). This is a slight misuse of terminology, since (8–6) is weaker than the condition that $E(u_iu_i' \mid Z_i) = \Sigma$. However, (8–6) is what is necessary for the 3SLS estimator to coincide with the GMM estimator. When (8–6) is violated, $\widehat{\beta}_{GMM}$ is strictly more efficient than $\widehat{\beta}_{3SLS}$.

An alternative to the 3SLS estimator, which is popularly used in the panel data literature, is the 2SLS estimator obtained by premultiplying (8–2) by $\Sigma^{-\frac{1}{2}}$ to filter u_i, and then applying the instruments Z_i:

$$\widehat{\beta}_{FIV} \equiv [X'\Omega^{-\frac{1}{2}}Z(Z'Z)^{-1}Z'\Omega^{-\frac{1}{2}}X]^{-1}X'\Omega^{-\frac{1}{2}}Z(Z'Z)^{-1}Z'\Omega^{-\frac{1}{2}}y.$$

We refer to this estimator as the filtered instrumental variables (FIV) estimator. This estimator is slightly different from the generalized instrumental variables (GIV) estimator, which is originally proposed by *White* [1984]. The GIV estimator is also 2SLS applied to the filtered model $\Sigma^{-\frac{1}{2}}y_i = \Sigma^{-\frac{1}{2}}X_i\beta + \Sigma^{-\frac{1}{2}}u_i$, but it uses the filtered instruments $\Sigma^{-\frac{1}{2}}Z_i$. Thus

$$\widehat{\beta}_{GIV} \equiv [X'\Omega^{-1}Z(Z'\Omega^{-1}Z)^{-1}Z'\Omega^{-1}X]^{-1}X'\Omega^{-1}Z$$
$$(Z'\Omega^{-1}Z)^{-1}Z'\Omega^{-1}y.$$

Despite this difference, the FIV and GIV estimators are often equivalent in the context of panel data models, especially when Σ is of the random effects structure (8–3). We may also note that the FIV and GIV estimators would be of little interest without the NCH assumption.

A motivation for the FIV (or GIV) estimator is that filtering the error u_i may improve the asymptotic efficiency of instrumental variables, as GLS improves upon ordinary least squares (OLS).[2] However, neither of the 3SLS nor FIV estimators can be shown to generally dominate the other. This is so because the FIV estimator is a GMM estimator based on the different moment condition $E(Z_i'\Sigma^{-\frac{1}{2}}u_i) = 0$ and the different NCH assumption $E(Z_i'\Sigma^{-\frac{1}{2}}u_iu_i'\Sigma^{-\frac{1}{2}}Z_i) = E(Z_i'Z_i)$.

We now turn to conditions under which the 3SLS and FIV estimators are numerically equivalent, whenever the same estimate of Σ is used.

THEOREM 8.1

> Suppose that there exists a nonsingular, nonstochastic matrix B such that $\Sigma^{-\frac{1}{2}}Z_i = Z_iB$ for all i (that is, $\Omega^{-\frac{1}{2}}Z = ZB$). Then, $\widehat{\beta}_{FIV} = \widehat{\beta}_{3SLS}$.

∎

The proof is omitted because it is straightforward. We note that the numerical equivalence result of theorem 8.1 holds only if the same estimate of Σ is used for both $\widehat{\beta}_{FIV}$ and $\widehat{\beta}_{3SLS}$. However, when two different but consistent estimates of Σ are used, the two estimators remain asymptotically identical.

---

[2] *White* [1984] offers some strong conditions under which the GIV estimator dominates the 3SLS estimator in terms of asymptotic efficiency.

The main point of Theorem 8.1 is that under certain assumption, filtering does not change the efficiency of instrumental variables or GMM. When Theorem 8.1 holds but the instruments Z_i violate the NCH condition (8–6), both the FIV and 3SLS estimators are strictly dominated by the GMM estimator applied without filtering. Clearly, Theorem 8.1 imposes strong restrictions on the instruments Z_i and the covariance matrix Σ, which do not generally hold. Nonetheless, in the context of some panel data models, the theorem can be used to show that filtering is irrelevant for GMM or 3SLS exploiting all of the moment conditions. We consider a few examples below.

8.1.2.1 Strictly Exogenous Instruments and Random effects

Consider a model in which there exists a $1 \times k$ vector of instruments h_{it} which are strictly exogenous with respect to the ε_{it} *and* uncorrelated with α_i. For this model, we have the moment conditions

$$E(h'_{is} u_{it}) = 0, \quad s, \quad t = 1, \ldots, T. \tag{8–7}$$

This is a set of kT^2 moment conditions. Denote $h^0_{it} \equiv (h_{i1}, \ldots, h_{it})$ for any $t = 1, \ldots, T$, and set $Z_{SE,i} \equiv I_T \otimes h^0_{iT}$, so that all of the moment conditions (8–7) can be expressed compactly as $E(Z'_{SE,i} u_i) = 0$.

We now show that filtering the error u_i does not matter in GMM. Observe that for any $T \times T$ nonsingular matrix A,

$$A Z_{SE,i} = A(I_N \otimes h^0_{iT}) = A \otimes h^0_{iT} = (I_N \otimes h^0_{iT})(A \otimes I_{kT}) = Z_{SE,i} B,$$

where $B = A \otimes I_{kT}$. If we replace A by $\Sigma^{-\frac{1}{2}}$, Theorem 8.1 holds.

8.1.2.2 Strictly Exogenous Instruments and Fixed Effects

We now allow the instruments h_{it} to be correlated with α_i (fixed effects), while they are still assumed to be strictly exogenous with respect to the ε_{it}. For this case, we may first–difference the model (8–2) to remove α_i:

$$L'_T y_i = L'_T X_i \beta + L'_T u_i = L'_T X_i \beta + L'_T \varepsilon_i, \tag{8–8}$$

where L_T is the $T \times (T-1)$ differencing matrix

$$
L_T = \begin{bmatrix}
1 & 0 & 0 & \cdots & 0 & 0 \\
-1 & 1 & 0 & \cdots & 0 & 0 \\
\vdots & \vdots & \vdots & & \vdots & \vdots \\
0 & 0 & 0 & \cdots & -1 & 1 \\
0 & 0 & 0 & \cdots & 0 & -1
\end{bmatrix}.
$$

We note that L_T has the same column space as the deviations from means matrix Q_T (in fact, $Q_T = L_T(L_T'L_T)^{-1}L_T'$). This reflects the fact that first differences and deviations from means preserve the same information in the data.

Note that strict exogeneity of the instruments h_{it} with respect to the ε_{it} implies $E(Z'_{SEFE,i}L_T'u_i) = E(Z'_{SEFE,i}L_T'\varepsilon_i) = 0$, where $Z_{SEFE,i} = I_{T-1} \otimes h_{iT}^0$. Thus, the model (8–8) can be estimated by GMM using the instruments $Z_{SEFE,i}$. Once again, given the NCH condition, filtering does not matter for GMM. To see why, define $M = [\mathrm{cov}(L_T'u_i)]^{-\frac{1}{2}} = (L_T'\Sigma L_T)^{-\frac{1}{2}}$. Then, by essentially the same algebra as in the previous section, we can show the FIV estimator applying the instruments $Z_{SEFE,i}$ and the filter M to (8–8) is asymptotically equivalent to the 3SLS estimator applying the same instruments to (8–8).

8.2 Models with Weakly Exogenous Instruments

In this section we consider the GMM estimation of the model (8–2) with weakly exogenous instruments. Suppose that there exists a vector of $1 \times k$ instruments h_{it} such that

$$
E(h_{it}'u_{is}) = 0, \quad t = 1,\ldots,T, \quad t \le s. \tag{8–9}
$$

There are $T(T+1)k/2$ such moment conditions. These arise if the instruments h_{it} are weakly exogenous with respect to the ε_{it} and uncorrelated with the effect α_i. If the instruments are weakly exogenous with respect to the ε_{it} but are correlated with the effects, we have a smaller number of moment conditions:

$$
E(h_{it}'\Delta u_{is}) = E(h_{it}'\Delta\varepsilon_{is}) = 0, \quad t = 1,\ldots,T-1, \quad t \le s, \tag{8–10}
$$

where $\Delta u_{is} = u_{is} - u_{i,s-1}$, and similarly for $\Delta\varepsilon_{is}$. In this section, our discussion will be focused on GMM based on (8–9) only. We do this because essentially the same procedures can be used for GMM based on (8–10). The only difference between (8–9) and (8–10) lies in whether GMM applies to the original model (8–2) or the differenced model (8–8).

8.2.1 The Forward Filter Estimator

For the model with weakly exogenous instruments, *Keane and Runkle* [1992] propose a forward filter (FF) estimator. To be specific, define a $T \times T$ upper–triangular matrix $F = [F_{ij}](F_{ij} = 0$ for $i > j)$ that satisfies $F\Sigma F' = I_T$, so that $\text{cov}(Fu_i) = I_T$. With this notation, Keane and Runkle propose a FIV–type estimator, which applies the instruments $H_i \equiv (h'_{i1}, , , ., h'_{iT})'$ after filtering the error u_i by F

$$\widehat{\beta}_{FF} = [X'F^{*\prime}H(H'H)^{-1}H'F^*X]^{-1}X'F^{*\prime}H('HH)^{-1}H'F^*y,$$

where $F^* = I_N \otimes F$.

The motivation of this FF estimator is that the FIV estimator using the instruments H_i and the usual filter $\Sigma^{-\frac{1}{2}}$ is inconsistent unless the instruments H_i are strictly exogenous with respect to the ε_i. In contrast, the forward-filtering transformation F preserves the weak exogeneity of the instruments h_{it}. *Hayashi and Sims* [1983] provide some efficiency results for this forward filtering in the context of time series data. However, in the context of panel data (with large N and fixed T), the FF estimator does not necessarily dominate (in terms of efficiency) the GMM or 3SLS estimators using the same instruments H_i.

One technical point is worth noting for the FF estimator. Forward filtering requires that the serial correlations in the error u_i do not depend on the values of current and lagged values of the instruments h_{it}. (See *Hayashi and Sims* [1983, pp. 788-789.]) This is a slightly weakened version of the usual condition of no conditional heteroskedasticity; it is weakened because conditioning is only on current and lagged values of the instruments. If this condition does not hold, in general,

$$\text{plim}_{N\to\infty} N^{-1} \sum_{i=1}^{N} H_i' F u_i u_i' F' H_i \neq \text{plim}_{N\to\infty} N^{-1} \sum_{i=1}^{N} H_i' F \Sigma F' H_i$$

$$= \text{plim}_{N\to\infty} N^{-1} \sum_{i=1}^{N} H_i' H_i,$$

and the rationale for forward filtering is lost. Sufficient conditions under which the autocorrelations in u_i do not depend on the history of h_{it} are given by *Wooldridge* [1996, p. 401].

8.2.2 Irrelevance of Forward Filtering

The FF and 3SLS estimators using the instruments H_i are inefficient in that they fail to fully exploit all of the moment conditions implied by (8–9). As *Schmidt, Ahn and Wyhowski* [1992] suggest, a more efficient estimator can be obtained by GMM using the $T \times T(T+1)k/2$ instruments

$$Z_{WE,i} \equiv \text{diag}(h_{i1}^0, \ldots, h_{iT}^0),$$

where, as before, $h_{it}^0 = (h_{i1}, \ldots, h_{it})$. When these instruments are used in GMM, filtering u_i by F becomes irrelevant. This result can be seen using Theorem 8.1. Schmidt, Ahn and Wyhowski show that there exists a $T(T+1)/2 \times T(T+1)/2$ nonsingular, upper-triangular matrix E such that $F Z_{WE,i} = Z_{WE,i}(E \otimes I_q)$ (Equation (10), p. 11). Thus, the FF and 3SLS estimators using the instruments $Z_{WE,i}$ are numerically identical (or asymptotically identical if different estimates of Σ are used); filtering does not matter. Of course, both of these estimators are dominated by the GMM estimator using the same instruments but an unrestricted weighting matrix, unless the instruments satisfy the NCH condition (8–6).

This irrelevance result does not mean that filtering is meaningless, even practically. In some cases, the (full) GMM estimator utilizing all of the instruments $Z_{WE,i}$ may be practically infeasible. For example, in a model with 10 weakly exogenous instruments and 10 time periods, the total number of instruments is 550. This can cause computational problems for GMM, especially when the cross section dimension is small. Furthermore, GMM with a very large number of moment conditions may have poor finite sample properties. For example, see *Tauchen* [1986], *Altongi and Segal*

[1996] and *Andersen and Sørensen* [1996] for a discussion of the finite sample bias of GMM in very overidentified problems. As a general statement, when the number of moment conditions is much larger than the number of parameters, the GMM estimates tend to have a substantial finite sample bias, which is usually attributed to correlation between the sample moments and the sample weighting matrix. Furthermore, in these circumstances the asymptotic standard errors tend to understate the true sampling variability of the estimates, so that the precision of the estimates is overstated. The trade-off between increased informational content (lower variance) and larger bias as more moment conditions are used could be resolved in terms of mean square error, but this does not yield operational advice to the practitioner. In the present context, *Ziliak* [1997] reports that the FF estimator dominates the GMM estimator in terms of both bias and mean square error, so that the FF estimator may be recommended, if the NCH condition holds. If the NCH condition does not hold, it is not clear which estimator to recommend. Clearly further research is needed to find modified versions of GMM, or reduced sets of moment conditions, that lead to estimators with reasonable finite sample properties. Some basic principles seem obvious; for example, instruments that are distant in time from the errors with which they are asserted to be uncorrelated are likely to not be very useful or important. However, the link between these basic principles and constructing reasonable operational rules for choosing moment conditions still needs to be made.

8.2.3 Semiparametric Efficiency Bound

In GMM, imposing more moment conditions never decreases asymptotic efficiency. An interesting question is whether there is an efficiency bound which GMM estimators cannot improve upon. Once this bound is identified, we may be able to construct an efficient GMM estimator whose asymptotic covariance matrix coincides with the bound. *Chamberlain* [1992] considers the semi–parametric bound for the model in which the assumption (8–9) is replaced by the stronger assumption

$$E[u_{it} \mid h_{it}^0 = (h_{i1}, \ldots, h_{it})] = 0, \quad \text{for} \quad t = 1, \ldots, T. \quad (8\text{–}11)$$

For this case, let $g_{k,it}$ be a $1 \times k$ vector of instruments which are some (polynomial) functions of h_{it}^0. Define $G_{k,i}^* = \text{diag}(g_{k,i1}, \ldots, g_{k,iT})$; so that under (8–11), $E(G_{k,i}^{*\prime} u_i) = 0$. Under some suitable regularity conditions, Chamberlain shows that the semi–parametric efficiency bound for GMM based on (8–11) is B_0^{-1}, where

$$B_0 = \lim_{k \to \infty} E(X_i' G_{k,i}^*)[E(G_{k,i}^{*\prime} u_i u_i' G_{k,i}^*)]^{-1} E(G_{k,i}^{*\prime} X_i).$$

This bound naturally suggests the GMM estimator based on the moment condition $E(G_{k,i}^{*\prime} u_i) = 0$ with large k. However, when k grows with N without any restriction, the usual asymptotic GMM inferences obtained by treating k as fixed would be misleading. In response to this problem, *Hahn* [1997] rigorously examines conditions under which the usual GMM inferences are valid for large k and the GMM estimator based on the moment condition $E(G_{k,i}^{*\prime} u_i) = 0$ is efficient. Under the assumption that

$$\lim_{N \to \infty} \frac{k^4}{N} = 0, \tag{8–12}$$

Hahn establishes the asymptotic efficiency of the GMM estimator. A similar result is obtained by *Koenker and Machado* [1996] for a linear model with heteroskedasticity of general form. They show that the usual GMM inferences, treating the number of moment conditions as fixed, are asymptotically valid if the number of moment conditions grows more slowly than $N^{\frac{1}{3}}$. These results do not directly indicate how to choose the number of moment conditions to use, for a given finite value of N, but they do provide grounds for suspicion about the desirability of GMM using numbers of moment conditions that are very large.

8.3 Models with Strictly Exogenous Regressors

This section considers efficient GMM estimation of linear panel data models with strictly exogenous regressors. The model of interest in this section is the standard panel data regression model

$$y_i = R_i \xi + (e_T \otimes w_i)\gamma + u_i \equiv X_i \beta + u_i; \quad u_i = (e_T \otimes \alpha_i) + \varepsilon_i, \tag{8–13}$$

where $R_i = [r_{i1}', \ldots, r_{iT}']'$ is a $T \times k$ matrix of time varying regressors, $e_T \otimes w_i = [w_i', \ldots, w_i']'$ is a $T \times g$ matrix of time invariant regressors, and ξ and γ are $k \times 1$ and $g \times 1$ vectors of unknown parameters, respectively. We assume that the regressors r_{it} and w_i are strictly exogenous to the ε_{it}; that is,

$$E(d_i \otimes \varepsilon_i) = 0, \qquad (8\text{--}14)$$

where $d_i = (r_{i1}, \ldots, r_{iT}, w_i)$. We also assume the random effects covariance structure $\Sigma = \sigma_\alpha^2 e_T e_T' + \sigma_\varepsilon^2 I_T$ as given in equation (8–3). For notational convenience, we treat σ_α^2 and σ_ε^2 as known. See *Hausman and Taylor* [1981] for consistent estimation of these variances.

Efficient estimation of the model (8–13) depends crucially on the assumptions about correlations between the regressors d_i and the effects α_i. When the regressors are uncorrelated with α_i, the traditional GLS estimator is consistent and efficient. If the regressors are suspected to be correlated with the effect, the within estimator can be used. However, a serious drawback of the within estimator is that it cannot identify γ because the within transformation wipes out the time invariant regressors w_i as well as the individual effects α_i.

In response to this problem, *Hausman and Taylor* [1981] considered the alternative assumption that some but possibly not all of the explanatory variables are uncorrelated with the effect α_i. This offers a middle ground between the traditional random effects and fixed effects approaches. Extending their study, *Amemiya and MaCurdy* [1986] and *Breusch, Mizon and Schmidt* [1989] considered stronger assumptions and derived alternative instrumental variables estimators that are more efficient than the Hausman and Taylor estimator. A systematic treatment of these estimators can be found in *Mátyás and Sevestre* [1995, Ch.6]. In what follows, we will study these estimators and the conditions under which they are efficient GMM estimators.

8.3.1 The Hausman and Taylor, Amemiya and MaCurdy and Breusch, Mizon and Schmidt Estimators

Following Hausman and Taylor, we decompose r_{it} and w_i into $r_{it} = (r_{1it}, r_{2it})$ and $w_i = (w_{1i}, w_{2i})$, where r_{1it} and r_{2it} are $1 \times k_1$ and

$1 \times k_2$, respectively, and w_{1i} and w_{2i} are $1 \times g_1$ and $1 \times g_2$. With this notation, define:

$$s_{HT,i} = (\bar{r}_{1i}, w_{1i}); \quad s_{AM,i} = (r_{1il}, \ldots, r_{1iT}, w_{1i}); \quad s_{BMS,i} = (s_{AM,i}, \bar{\bar{r}}_{2i}), \tag{8–15}$$

where $\bar{\bar{r}} = (r_{2i1} - \bar{r}_{2i}, \ldots, r_{2i,T-1} - \bar{r}_{2i})$. Hausman and Taylor, Amemiya and MaCurdy and Breusch, Mizon and Schmidt impose the following assumptions, respectively, on the model (8–13):

$$E(s'_{HT,i}\alpha_i) = 0; \quad E(s'_{AM,i}\alpha_i) = 0; \quad E(s'_{BMS,i}\alpha_i) = 0. \tag{8–16}$$

These assumptions are sequentially stronger. The Hausman and Taylor Assumption $E(s'_{HT,i}\alpha_i) = 0$ is weaker than the Amemiya and MaCurdy assumption $E(s'_{AM,i}\alpha_i) = 0$, since it only requires the individual means of r_{1it} to be uncorrelated with the effect, rather than requiring r_{1it} to be uncorrelated with α_i for each t. (However, as Amemiya and MaCurdy argue, it is hard to think of cases in which each of the variables r_{1it} is correlated with α_i while their individual means are not.) Imposing the Amemiya and MaCurdy assumption instead of the Hausman and Taylor assumption in GMM would generally lead to a more efficient estimator. The Breusch, Mizon and Schmidt assumption $E(s'_{BMS,i}\alpha_i) = 0$ is based on the stationarity condition,

$$E(r'_{2it}\alpha_i) \quad \text{is the same for} \quad t = 1, \ldots, T. \tag{8–17}$$

This means that, even though the unobserved effect α_i is allowed to be correlated with r_{2it}, the covariance does not change with time. *Cornwell and Rupert* [1988] provide some evidence for the empirical legitimacy of the Breusch, Mizon and Schmidt assumption. They also report that GMM imposing the Breusch, Mizon and Schmidt assumption rather than the Hausman and Taylor or Amemiya and MaCurdy assumptions would result in significant efficiency gains.

Hausman and Taylor, Amemiya and MaCurdy and Breusch, Mizon and Schmidt consider FIV estimation of the model (8–13) under the random effects assumption (8–3). The instruments used by Hausman and Taylor, Amemiya and MaCurdy and Breusch, Mizon and Schmidt are of the common form

$$Z_{A,i} \equiv (Q_T R_i, e_T \otimes s_i), \tag{8–18}$$

where the form of s_i varies across authors; that is, $s_i = s_{HT,i}, s_{AM,i}$ or $s_{BMS,i}$.

Consistency of the FIV estimator using the instruments $Z_{A,i}$ requires $E(Z'_{A,i}\Sigma^{-\frac{1}{2}}u_i) = 0$. This condition can be easily justified under (8–3), (8–14) and (8–16). Without loss of generality, we set $\sigma_\varepsilon^2 = 1$. Then, it can be easily shown that $\Sigma^{-1} = \theta^2 P_T + Q_T$ and $\Sigma^{-\frac{1}{2}} = \theta P_T + Q_T$, where $\theta^2 = \sigma_\varepsilon^2/(\sigma_\varepsilon^2 + T\sigma_\alpha^2)$. With this result, strict exogeneity of the regressors r_{it} and w_i (8–14) implies

$$E(R'_i Q_T \Sigma^{-\frac{1}{2}} u_i) = E[R'_i Q_T(\theta P_T + Q_T)u_i] = E(R'_i Q_T \varepsilon_i) = 0.$$

In addition, both (8–14) and (8–16) imply

$$E[(e_T \otimes s_i)'\Sigma^{-\frac{1}{2}} u_i] = E[\theta(e_T \otimes s_i)'(e_T \otimes \alpha_i)] = T\theta \times E(s'_i \alpha_i) = 0.$$

Several properties of the FIV estimator are worth noting. First, the usual GMM identification condition requires that the number of columns in $Z_{A,i}$ should not be smaller than the number of parameters in $\beta = (\xi', \gamma')'$. This condition is satisfied if the number of variables in s_i is not less than the number of time invariant regressors (*e.g.*, $k_1 \geq g_2$ for the Hausman and Taylor case). Second, the FIV estimator is an intermediate case between the traditional GLS and within estimators. It can be shown that the FIV estimator of ξ equals the within estimator if the model is exactly identified (*e.g.*, $k_1 = g_2$ for Hausman and Taylor), while it is strictly more efficient if the model is overidentified (*e.g.*, $k_1 > g_2$ for Hausman and Taylor). The FIV estimator of β is equivalent to the GLS estimator if $k_2 = g_2 = 0$ (that is, no regressor is correlated with α_i). For more details, see Hausman and Taylor.

Finally, the FIV estimator is numerically equivalent to the 3SLS estimator applying the instruments $Z_{A,i}$ (if the same estimate of Σ is used); thus, filtering does not matter. To see this, observe that

$$\begin{aligned}
\Sigma^{-\frac{1}{2}} Z_{A,i} &= (\theta P_T + Q_T)(Q_T R_i, e_T \otimes s_i) \\
&= (Q_T R_i, \theta e_T \otimes s_i) = (Q_T R_i, e_T \otimes s_i) \operatorname{diag}(I_{(1)}, \theta I_{(2)}) \\
&= Z_{A,i} \operatorname{diag}(I_{(1)}, \theta I_{(2)}),
\end{aligned}$$

where $I_{(1)}$ and $I_{(2)}$ are conformable identity matrices. Since the matrix $\operatorname{diag}(I_{(1)}, \theta I_{(2)})$ is nonsingular, Theorem 8.1 applies: $\widehat{\beta}_{FIV} = \widehat{\beta}_{3SLS}$. This result also implies that the FIV estimator is equally efficient as the GMM estimator using the instruments $Z_{A,i}$, if the instruments satisfy the NCH condition (8–6). When this NCH condition is violated, the GMM estimator using the instruments

$Z_{A,i}$ and an unrestricted weighting matrix is strictly more efficient than the FIV estimator.

8.3.2 Efficient GMM Estimation

We now consider alternative GMM estimators which are potentially more efficient than the Hausman and Taylor, Amemiya and MaCurdy or Breusch, Mizon and Schmidt estimators. To begin with, observe that strict exogeneity of the regressors r_{it} and w_i (8–14) implies many more moment conditions than the Hausman and Taylor, Amemiya and MaCurdy or Breusch, Mizon and Schmidt estimators utilize. The strict exogeneity condition (8–14) implies

$$E[(L_T \otimes d_i)'u_i] = E(L_T'u_i \otimes d_i) = E[L_T'(e_T\alpha_i + \varepsilon_i) \otimes d_i)]$$
$$= E(L_T'\varepsilon_i \otimes d_i) = 0,$$

where $L_T \otimes d_i$ is $T \times \{(T-1)(kT+g)\}$. Based on this observation, *Arellano and Bover* [1995] (and *Ahn and Schmidt* [1995]) propose the GMM estimator using the instruments

$$Z_{B,i} \equiv (L_T \otimes d_i, e_T \otimes s_i), \tag{8–19}$$

which include $(T-1)(Tk+g) - k$ more instruments than $Z_{A,i}$. The covariance matrix Σ need not be restricted. Clearly, the instruments $Z_{B,i}$ subsume $Z_{A,i} \equiv (Q_T R_i, e_T \otimes s_i)$ which are essentially the Hausman and Taylor, Amemiya and MaCurdy or Breusch, Mizon and Schmidt instruments. Thus, the GMM estimator utilizing all of the instruments $Z_{B,i}$ cannot be less efficient than the GMM estimator using the smaller set of instruments $Z_{A,i}$. In terms of achieving asymptotic efficiency, there is no reason to prefer to use the fewer instruments $Z_{B,i}$.

However, using all of the instruments $Z_{A,i}$ may not be practically feasible, even when T is only moderately large. For example, consider the case in which $k = g = 5$ and $T = 10$. For this case, the number of the instruments in $Z_{B,i}$ exceed the number of moment conditions in $Z_{A,i}$ by $490(= 495 - 5)$. For such cases, the GMM estimator using the Hausman and Taylor, Amemiya and MaCurdy or Breusch, Mizon and Schmidt instruments would be of more practical use.

In addition, the GMM (or FIV) estimator using the instruments $Z_{A,i}$ can be shown to be asymptotically as efficient as the GMM estimator using all of the instruments $Z_{B,i}$, under specific assumptions that are consistent with the motivation for the Hausman and Taylor, Amemiya and MaCurdy or Breusch, Mizon and Schmidt estimators. *Arellano and Bover* [1995] provide the foundation for this result.

THEOREM 8.2

Suppose that Σ has the random effect structure (8–3). Then, the 3SLS estimator using the instruments $Z_{B,i}$ is numerically identical to the 3SLS estimator using the smaller set of instruments $Z_{A,i}$, if the same estimate of Σ is used.[3]

∎

Although *Arellano and Bover* [1995] provide a detailed proof of the theorem, we provide a shorter alternative proof. In what follows, we use the usual projection notation: For any matrix B of full column rank, we define the projection matrix $P(B) = B(B'B)^{-1}B'$. The following lemma is useful for the proof of Theorem 8.2.

LEMMA 8.1

Let $L_* = I_N \otimes L_T$ and $D = [(I_{T-1} \otimes d_1)', \ldots, (I_{T-1} \otimes d_N)']'$. Define $V = I_N \otimes e_T$ and $W = (w_1', \ldots, w_N')'$, so that $X = (R, VW)$. Then, $P(L_*D)X = P(Q_V R)X$.

∎

PROOF OF THE LEMMA

Since
$$Q_V = P(L_*) = L_*(L_*'L_*)^{-1}L_*',$$
$$Q_V R = L_*[(L_*'L_*)^{-1}L_*'R].$$

In addition, since D spans all of the columns in $(L_*'L_*)^{-1}L_*'R$, L_*D must span
$$Q_V R = L_*[(L_*'L_*)^{-1}L_*'R].$$

---

[3] Even if different estimates of Σ are used, these 3SLS estimators are still asymptotically identical.

Finally, since $Q_V L_* = L_*$ and $Q_V V = 0$,

$$P(L_* D)X = P(L_* D)Q_V X = (P(L_* D)Q_V R, 0)$$
$$= (Q_V R, 0) = P(Q_V R)X.$$

■

We are now ready to prove Theorem 8.2.

PROOF OF THE THEOREM

Note that $Z_A = [Q_V R, VS]$ and $Z_B = [L_* D, VS]$, where $S = (s_1', \ldots, s_N')'$. Since L_* and Q_V are in the same space and orthogonal to both V and $P_V = P(V)$, we have $P(Z_A) = P(Q_V R) + P(VS)$ and $P(Z_B) = P(L_* D) + P(VS)$. Using these results and the fact that $\Omega^{-\frac{1}{2}} = \theta P_V + Q_V$, we can also show that the 3SLS estimators using the instruments $Z_{A,i}$ and $Z_{B,i}$, respectively, equal

$$\hat{\beta}_A = [X'\{\theta P(Q_V R) + P(VS)\}X]^{-1}X'\{\theta P(Q_V R) + P(VS)\}y;$$
$$\hat{\beta}_B = [X'\{P(L_* D) + P(VS)\}X]^{-1}X'\{\theta P(L_* D) + P(VS)\}y.$$

However, Lemma 8.1 implies $\{\theta P(L_* D) + P(VS)\}X = \{\theta P(Q_V R) + P(VS)\}X$. Thus, $\hat{\beta}_B = \hat{\beta}_A$.

■

Theorem 8.2 effectively offers conditions under which the 3SLS (or FIV) estimator using the instruments $Z_{A,i}$ is an efficient GMM estimator. Under the random effects structure (8–3), the 3SLS estimator using all of the instruments $Z_{A,i}$ equals the 3SLS estimator using the full set of instruments $Z_{B,i}$. Thus if, in addition to (8–3), the instruments $Z_{B,i}$ satisfy the NCH assumption (8–6), the 3SLS (or FIV) estimator using the instruments $Z_{A,i}$ should be asymptotically equivalent to the efficient GMM estimator exploiting all of the moment conditions $E(Z_{B,i}' u_i) = 0$. Note that both assumptions (8–3) and (8–6) are crucial for this efficiency result. If one of these assumptions is violated, the GMM estimator exploiting all of the instruments $Z_{B,i}$ is strictly more efficient than the GMM estimator using the instruments $Z_{A,i}$.

8.3.3 GMM with Unrestricted Σ

Im, Ahn, Schmidt and Wooldridge [1996] examine efficient GMM estimation for the case in which the instruments $Z_{B,i}$ satisfy the NCH condition (8–6), but Σ is unrestricted. For this case, Im, Ahn, Schmidt and Wooldridge consider the 3SLS estimator using the instruments $\Sigma^{-1}Z_{A,i} = \Sigma^{-1}(Q_T R_i, e_T \otimes s_i)$, which is essentially the GIV estimator of *White* [1984]. They show that when $s_i = s_{BMS,i}$, the 3SLS estimator using the instruments $\Sigma^{-1}Z_{A,i}$ is numerically equivalent to the 3SLS estimator using all of the instruments $Z_{B,i} = (L_T \otimes d_i, e_T \otimes s_i)$. However, they also find that this equality does not hold when $s_i = s_{HT,i}$ or $s_{AM,i}$. In fact, without the BMS assumption, the set of instruments $\Sigma^{-1}Z_{A,i}$ is not legitimate in 3SLS. This is true even if $s_i = s_{HT,i}$ or $s_{AM,i}$. To see this, observe that

$$E(R_i'Q_T\Sigma^{-1}u_i) = E(R_i'Q_T\Sigma^{-1}e_T\alpha_i) + E(R_i'Q_T\Sigma^{-1}\varepsilon_i)$$
$$= E(R_i'Q_T\Sigma^{-1}e_T\alpha_i),$$

where the last equality results from given strict exogeneity of R_i with respect to ε_i. However, with unrestricted Σ and without the BMS assumption, $E(R_i'Q_T\Sigma^{-1}e_T\alpha_i) \neq 0$, and $\Sigma^{-\frac{1}{2}}Q_T R_i$ is not legitimate.

Im, Ahn, Schmidt and Wooldridge provide a simple solution to this problem, which is to replace Q_T by a different matrix that removes the effects, $Q_\Sigma = \Sigma^{-1} - \Sigma^{-1}e_T(e_T'\Sigma^{-1}e_T)^{-1}e_T'\Sigma^{-1}$. Clearly $Q_\Sigma e_T = 0$. Thus $R_i'Q_\Sigma e_T\alpha_i = 0$, and $E(R_i'Q_\Sigma u_i) = E(R_i'Q_\Sigma\varepsilon_i) = 0$ given strict exogeneity of R_i with respect to ε_i. Thus, $Q_\Sigma R_i$ are legitimate instruments for 3SLS.

This discussion motivates modified instruments of the form $(Q_\Sigma R_i, \Sigma^{-1}e_T \otimes s_i)$. Im, Ahn, Schmidt and Wooldridge show that the 3SLS estimator using these modified instruments is numerically equivalent to the 3SLS estimator using all of the instruments $(L_T \otimes d_i, e_T \otimes s_i)$, if the same estimate of Σ is used. That is, the modified 3SLS estimator is an efficient GMM estimator, if the instruments $(L_T \otimes d_i, e_T \otimes s_i)$ satisfy the NCH condition (8–6).

8.4 Simultaneous Equations

In this section we consider GMM estimation of a simultaneous equations model, with panel data and unobservable individual effects in each structural equation. The foundation of this section is the model considered by *Cornwell, Schmidt and Wyhowski* [1992] and *Mátyás and Sevestre* [1995, Ch. 9]:

$$y_{j,i} = Y_{j,i}\lambda_j + R_{j,i}\xi_j + (e_T \otimes w_{j,i})\gamma_j + u_{j,i} \equiv X_{j,i}\beta_j + u_{j,i};$$

$$u_{j,i} = e_T \otimes \alpha_{j,i} + \varepsilon_{j,i}.$$

$$(8\text{--}20)$$

Here $j = 1, \ldots, J$ indexes the individual structural equation, so that equation (8–20) reflects T observations for individual i and equation j. $Y_{j,i}$ denotes the data matrix of included endogenous variables. Other variables are defined similarly to those in (8–13). We denote $\Sigma_{jh} \equiv E(u_{j,i}u'_{h,i})$ for $j, h = 1, \ldots, J$.

In order to use the same notation for instrumental variables as in Section 8.3, we let $R_i = (r'_{i1}, \ldots, r'_{iT})'$ and w_i be the $T \times k$ and $1 \times g$ data matrices of all time varying and time invariant exogenous regressors in the system, respectively. With this notation, we can define $d_i, s_i, Z_{A,i}$ and $Z_{B,i}$ as in Section 8.3. Consistent with Cornwell, Schmidt and Wyhowski, we assume that the variables $d_i = (r_{i1}, \ldots, r_{iT}, w_i)$ are strictly exogenous to the $\varepsilon_{j,it}$; that is, $E(d_i \otimes \varepsilon_{j,i}) = 0$ for all $j = 1, \ldots, J$. We also assume that a subset s_i of the exogenous variables d_i is uncorrelated with the individual effects $\alpha_{j,i}(j = 1, \ldots, J)$. As in Section 8.3, an appropriate choice of s_i can be made by imposing the *Hausman and Taylor* [1981], *Amemiya and MaCurdy* [1986], or *Breusch and Mizon and Schmidt* [1989] assumptions on d_i.

Under these assumptions, Cornwell, Schmidt and Wyhowski consider GMM estimators based on the moment conditions

$$E(Z'_{A,i}u_{j,i}) = 0, \quad \text{for} \quad j = 1, \ldots, J, \qquad (8\text{--}21)$$

where the instruments $Z_{A,i} = (Q_T R_i, e_T \otimes s_i)$ are of the *Hausman and Taylor* [1981], *Amemiya and MaCurdy* [1986], or *Breusch, Mizon and Schmidt* [1989] forms as in (8–18). Clearly, the model (8–20) implies more moment conditions than those in (8–21). In the same way as in Section 8.3.2, we can show that the full set of moment conditions implied by the model (8–20) is

$$E(Z'_{B,i}u_{j,i}) = 0, \quad \text{for} \quad j = 1, \ldots, J,$$

where $Z_{B,i} = (L_T \otimes d_i, e_T \otimes s_i) = 0$. We will derive conditions under which the GMM (3SLS) estimator based on (8–21) is asymptotically as efficient as the GMM estimator exploiting the full set of moment conditions.

In (8–21), we implicitly assume that the same instruments $Z_{A,i}$ are available for each structural equation. This assumption is purely for notational convenience. We can easily allow the instruments $Z_{A,i}$ to vary over different equations, at the cost of more complex matrix notation (see *Cornwell, Schmidt and Wyhowski* [1992], Section 3.4).

8.4.1 Estimation of a Single Equation

We now consider GMM estimation of a particular structural equation in the system (8–20), say the first equation, which we write as

$$y_{1,i} = X_{1,i}\beta_1 + u_{1,i}, \tag{8-22}$$

adopting the notation of (8–20). Using our convention of matrix notation, we can also write this model for all NT observations as $y_1 = X_1\beta_1 + u_1$, where $X_1 = (Y_1, R_1, VW_1)$.

GMM estimation of the model (8–22) is straightforward. The parameter β_1 can be consistently estimated by essentially the same GMM or instrumental variables as in Section 8.3. Given the assumption (8–21), the GMM estimator using the instruments $Z_{A,i}$ is consistent.

We now consider conditions under which the GMM estimator based on (8–21) is fully efficient (as efficient as GMM based on the full set of moment conditions). The following Lemma provides a clue.

LEMMA 8.2

$$(L_T \otimes d_i)[E(L_T'L_T \otimes d_i'd_i)]^{-1}E[(L_T \otimes d_i)'Y_{1,i}] = Q_T R_i[E(R_i'Q_T R_i)]^{-1}E(R_i'Q_T Y_{1,i}).$$

■

PROOF OF THE LEMMA

Consider the reduced form equations for the endogenous regressors $Y_{1,i}$:

$$Y_{1,i} = R_i \Pi_{11} + (e_T \otimes w_i) \Pi_{12} + (e_T \otimes \alpha_i) \Pi_{13} + v_{1,i},$$

where $\alpha_i = (\alpha_{1,i}, \ldots, \alpha_{J,i})$, and the error $v_{1,i}$ is a linear function of the structural random errors $\varepsilon_{j,i}(j = 1, \ldots, J)$. Since the variables $d_i = (r_{i1}, \ldots, r_{iT}, w_i)$ are strictly exogenous with respect to the $\varepsilon_{j,i}$, so are they with respect to $v_{1,i}$; that is, $E(d_i \otimes v_{1,i}) = 0$. Note also that since $L_* D$ spans the columns of $Q_V R$ (see the proof of Lemma 8.1), there exists a conformable matrix A such that $Q_T R_i = (L_T \otimes d_i) A$ for all i. These results imply

$$(L_T \otimes d_i)[E(L'_T L_T \otimes d'_i d_i)]^{-1} E[(L_T \otimes d_i)' Y_{1,i}]$$
$$= (L_T \otimes d_i)[E(L'_T L_T \otimes d'_i d_i)]^{-1} E[(L_T \otimes d_i)' Q_T Y_{1,i}]$$
$$= (L_T \otimes d_i)[E(L'_T L_T \otimes d'_i d_i)]^{-1} E[(L_T \otimes d_i)' Q_T R_i \Pi_{11}]$$
$$= (L_T \otimes d_i)[E(L'_T L_T \otimes d'_i d_i)]^{-1} E[(L_T \otimes d_i)' (L_T \otimes d_i) A \Pi_{11}]$$
$$= (L_T \otimes d_i) A \Pi_{11} = Q_T R_i \Pi_{11}.$$

However, we also have

$$Q_T R_i [E(X'_i Q_T R_i)]^{-1} E(R'_i Q_T Y_{1,i}) =$$
$$Q_T R_i [E(R'_i Q_T R_i)]^{-1} E(R'_i Q_T R_i \Pi_{11}) = Q_T R_i \Pi_{11}.$$

∎

What Lemma 8.2 means is that

$$\mathrm{Proj}(Y_{1,i} \mid L_T \otimes d_i) = \mathrm{Proj}(Y_{1,i} | Q_T R_i),$$

where $\mathrm{Proj}(B_i \mid C_i)$ is the population least squares projection of B_i on C_i. Thus, Lemma 8.2 can be viewed as a population (asymptotic) analog of Lemma 8.1. Clearly, $P(L_* D) R_1 = P(Q_V R) R_1$ and $P(L_* D) V W_1 = 0 = P(Q_V R) V W_1$. These equalities and Lemma 8.2 imply that for any conformable data matrix B_i of T rows (and B of NT rows),

$$\mathrm{plim}_{N \to \infty} N^{-1} B' P(L_* D) X_1 = E[B'_i (L_T \otimes d_i)][E(L'_T L_T \otimes d'_i d_i)]^{-1} \times$$
$$E[(L_T \otimes d_i)' X_{1,i}]$$
$$= E(B'_i Q_T R_i)[E(R'_i Q_T R_i)]^{-1} E(R'_i Q_T X_{1,i})$$
$$= \mathrm{plim}_{N \to \infty} N^{-1} B' P(Q_V R) X_1;$$

$$\operatorname*{plim}_{N\to\infty} N^{-\frac{1}{2}} B'P(L_*D)X_1 = \operatorname*{plim}_{N\to\infty} N^{-\frac{1}{2}} \sum_{i=1}^{N} B_i'(L_T \otimes d_i)$$

$$[E(L_T'L_T \otimes d_i'd_i)]^{-1} E[(L_T \otimes d_i)'X_{1,i}]$$

$$= \operatorname*{plim}_{N\to\infty} N^{-\frac{1}{2}} \sum_{i=1}^{N} B_i'Q_T R_i [E(R_i'Q_T R_i)]^{-1} \times$$

$$E(R_i'Q_T X_{1,i})$$

$$= \operatorname*{plim}_{N\to\infty} N^{-\frac{1}{2}} B'P(Q_V R)X_1.$$

Lemma 8.2 leads to an asymptotic analog of Theorem 8.2.

Theorem 8.3

Suppose that $\operatorname{cov}(u_{1,i}) = \Sigma_{11}$ is of the random effects form (8–3). Then, the 3SLS estimator $(\widehat{\beta}_{1,A})$ using the instruments $Z_{A,i}$ is asymptotically identical to the 3SLS estimator $(\widehat{\beta}_{1,B})$ using all of the instruments $Z_{B,i}$. If, in addition, the instruments $Z_{B,i}$ satisfy the NCH condition (8–6), $\widehat{\beta}_{1,A}$ is efficient among the class of GMM estimators based on the moment condition $E(Z_{B,i}'u_{1,i}) = 0$.

∎

Proof of the Theorem

Let $\Sigma_{11} = \sigma_{\alpha,1}^2 e_T e_T' + \sigma_{\varepsilon,1}^2 I_T$. Without loss of generality, we set $\sigma_{\varepsilon,1}^2 = 1$. Then, similarly to the proof of Theorem 8.2, we can show

$$\widehat{\beta}_{1,A} = [X_1'\{\theta_{11}P(L_*D) + P(VS)\}X_1]^{-1}$$
$$X_1'\{\theta_{11}P(L_*D) + P(VS)\}y_1;$$
$$\widehat{\beta}_{1,B} = [X_1'\{\theta_{11}P(Q_V R) + P(VS)\}X_1]^{-1}$$
$$X_1'\{\theta_{11}P(Q_V R) + P(VS)\}y_1,$$

where $\theta_{11}^2 = \sigma_{\varepsilon,1}^2/(\sigma_{\varepsilon,1}^2 + T\sigma_{\alpha,1}^2)$. But, Lemma 8.2 implies that $\operatorname{plim}_{N\to\infty} N^{\frac{1}{2}}(\widehat{\beta}_{1,A} - \widehat{\beta}_{1,B}) = 0$.

∎

8.4.2 System of Equations Estimation

We now consider the joint estimation of all the equations in the system (8–20). Following our convention for matrix notation, structural equation j can be written for all NT observations as $y_j = X_j \beta_j + u_j$. If we stack these equations into the seemingly unrelated regressions (SUR) form, we have

$$y_* = X_* \beta + u_*, \tag{8–23}$$

where $y_* = (y_1', \ldots, y_J')'$, $X_* = \text{diag}(X_1, \ldots, X_J)$, $u_* = (u_1', \ldots, u_J')'$ and $\beta = (\beta_1', \ldots, \beta_J')'$. We denote $\Omega_* \equiv \text{cov}(u_*)$. Straightforward algebra shows that $\Omega_* = [I_N \otimes \Sigma_{jh}]_{NTJ \times NTJ}$; that is, if we partition Ω_* evenly into $J \times J$ blocks, the $(j, h)'$-th block is $I_N \otimes \Sigma_{jh}$.

Following *Cornwell, Schmidt and Wyhowski* [1992], we consider the system GMM estimator based on the moment conditions (8–21). Define $Z_i^S = I_J \otimes Z_{A,i}$ and $u_i^S = (u_{1,i}', \ldots, u_{J,i}')'$, so that we can write all of the moment conditions (8–21) compactly as $E(Z_i^{S\prime} u_i^S) = 0$. Use of these moment conditions leads to the system GMM estimator

$$\widehat{\beta}_{SGMM} = [X_*' Z_*^S (V_N^S)^{-1} Z_*^{S\prime} X_*]^{-1} X_*' Z_*^S (V_N^S)^{-1} Z_*^{S\prime} y_*,$$

where $Z_*^S = I_J \otimes Z_A$ and

$$V_N^S = N^{-1} \sum_{i=1}^N Z_i^{S\prime} \widehat{u}_i^S \widehat{u}_i^{S\prime} Z_i^S = N^{-1} \sum_{i=1}^N [Z_{A,i}' \widehat{u}_{j,i} \widehat{u}_{h,i}' Z_{A,i}].$$

The 3SLS version of this system estimator can be obtained if we replace V_N^S by

$$N^{-1} Z_*^{S\prime} \Omega_* Z_*^S = N^{-1} \sum_{i=1}^N [Z_{A,i}' \Sigma_{jh} Z_{A,i}];$$

that is,

$$\widehat{\beta}_{S3SLS} = [X_*' Z_*^S (Z_*^{S\prime} \Omega_* Z_*^S)^{-1} Z_*^{S\prime} X_*]^{-1} X_*' Z_*^S (Z_*^{S\prime} \Omega_* Z_*^S)^{-1} Z_*^{S\prime} y_*.$$

In fact, this system 3SLS estimator is a generalization of the 3SLS estimator proposed by *Cornwell, Schmidt and Wyhowski* [1992]. To see this, we make the following assumptions, as in *Cornwell, Schmidt and Wyhowski* [1992, Assumption 1, p. 157]:

ASSUMPTION 8.1

(i) The individual effects for person i, $\alpha_i = (\alpha_{1,i}, \ldots, \alpha_{J,i})'$ are $i.i.d.(0, \Sigma_\alpha)$. (ii) The random errors for person i at time t, $(\varepsilon_{1,it}, \ldots, \varepsilon_{J,it})'$, are $i.i.d.(0, \Sigma_\varepsilon)$. (iii) All elements of α are uncorrelated with all of elements of ε. (iv) Σ_α and Σ_ε are nonsingular.

■

Under Assumption 8.1, we can show

$$\Omega_* = \Sigma_\varepsilon \otimes I_{NT} + \Sigma_\alpha \otimes (TP_V) = \Sigma_1 \otimes Q_V + \Sigma_2 \otimes P_V,$$

where $\Sigma_1 \equiv \Sigma_\varepsilon$ and $\Sigma_2 \equiv \Sigma_\varepsilon + T\Sigma_\alpha$. Using this result and the facts that $Z_*^S = I_J \otimes Z_A = (I_J \otimes Q_V R, I_J \otimes VS)$ and $R'Q_V VS = 0$, we can easily show that

$$Z_*^S (Z_*^{S'} \Omega_* Z_*^S)^{-1} Z_*^{S'} = \Sigma_1^{-1} \otimes Q_V R + \Sigma_2^{-1} \otimes VS.$$

Substituting this result into the system 3SLS estimator $\widehat{\beta}_{S3SLS}$ yields the 3SLS estimator of *Cornwell, Schmidt and Wyhowski* [1992, p. 164, equation (34)]. Thus $\widehat{\beta}_{S3SLS}$ simplifies to the Cornwell, Schmidt and Wyhowski 3SLS estimator when the errors have the random effects covariance structure implied by Assumption 8.1; otherwise, it is the appropriate generalization of the Cornwell, Schmidt and Wyhowski estimator.

8.5 Dynamic Panel Data Models

In this section we consider a regression model for dynamic panel data. The model of interest is given by:

$$y_i = y_{i,-1}\delta + R_i\xi + (e_T \otimes w_i)\gamma + u_i \equiv X_i\beta + u_i; \quad u_i = e_T \otimes \alpha_i + \varepsilon_i, \tag{8-24}$$

where $y_{i,-1} = (y_{i0}, \ldots, y_{i,T-1})'$, y_{i0} is the initial observed value of y (for individual i), and other variables are defined exactly as in (8–13).

The basic problem faced in the estimation of this model is that the traditional within estimator is inconsistent, because the within transformation induces a correlation of order $\frac{1}{T}$ between the lagged dependent variable and the random error (see *Hsiao* [1986]). A popular solution to this problem is to first difference the equation to remove the effects, and then estimate by GMM, using as instruments values of the dependent variable lagged two or more periods as well as other exogenous regressors. Legitimacy of the lagged dependent variables as instruments requires some covariance restrictions on ε_i, α_i and y_{i0}. However, these covariance restrictions imply more moment conditions than are imposed by the GMM estimator based on first differences. In this section, we study the moment conditions implied by a standard set of covariance restrictions and other alternative assumptions. We also examine how these moment conditions can be efficiently imposed in GMM.

A good survey, which emphasizes somewhat different aspects of the estimation problems, is given in *Mátyás and Sevestre* [1995, Ch. 7].

8.5.1 Moment Conditions Under Standard Assumptions

In this subsection we count and express the moment conditions implied by a standard set of assumptions about α_i, ε_{it} and y_{i0}. For simplicity, and without loss of generality, we do so in the context of the simple dynamic model whose only explanatory variable is the lagged dependent variable:

$$y_i = \delta y_{i,-1} + u_i; \quad u_i = e_T \otimes \alpha_i + \varepsilon_i. \tag{8–25}$$

Consistently with the previous sections, we assume that α_i and ε_{it} have mean zero for all i and t. (Nonzero mean of α can be handled with an intercept which can be regarded as an exogenous regressor.) We also assume that $E(y_{i0}) = 0$. We make this assumption in order to focus our discussion on the (second-order) moment conditions implied by covariance restrictions on ε_i, α_i and y_{i0}. If $E(y_{i0}) \neq 0$, the first–order moment conditions $E(u_{it}) = 0$ $(t = 1, \ldots, T)$ are relevant in GMM. Imposing these first–order moment conditions could improve efficiency of GMM estimators, as *Crépon, Karamarz and Trognon* [1995] suggest. In contrast, if $E(y_{i0}) = 0$ (and $E(\alpha_i) = 0$), the first–order moment conditions become uninformative for the unknown parameter δ because they cannot identify a unique δ. This is so because for any value of δ,

$$E(u_{it}) = E(y_{it} - \delta y_{i,t-1}) = E(y_{it}) - \delta E(y_{i,t-1}) = 0.$$

The following assumptions are most commonly adopted in the dynamic panel data literature.

ASSUMPTION 8.2

(i) For all i, ε_{it} is uncorrelated with y_{i0} for all t. (ii) For all i, ε_{it} is uncorrelated with α_i for all t. (iii) For all i, the ε_{it} are mutually uncorrelated.

∎

Under Assumption 8.2, it is obvious that the following moment conditions hold:

$$E(y_{is}\Delta u_{it}) = 0, \quad t = 2, \ldots, T, \quad s = 0, \ldots, t-2, \qquad (8\text{--}26)$$

where $\Delta u_{it} = u_{it} - u_{i,t-1} = \varepsilon_{it} - \varepsilon_{i,t-1}$. There are $T(T-1)/2$ such conditions. These are the moment conditions that are widely used in the panel data literature (*e.g.*, *Anderson and Hsiao* [1981], *Holtz-Eakin* [1988], *Holtz-Eakin, Newey and Rosen* [1988], *Arellano and Bond* [1991]). However, as *Ahn and Schmidt* [1995] find, Assumption 8.2 implies additional moment conditions beyond those in (8–26). In particular, the following $T-2$ moment conditions also hold:

$$E(u_{iT}\Delta u_{it}) = 0, \quad t = 2, \ldots, T-1, \qquad (8\text{--}27)$$

which are nonlinear in terms of δ.

The conditions (8–26) and (8–27) are a set of $T(T-1)/2+(T-2)$ moment conditions that follow directly from the assumptions that the ε_{it} are mutually uncorrelated and uncorrelated with α_i and y_{i0}. Furthermore, they represent all of the moment conditions implied by these assumptions. A formal proof of the number of restrictions implied by Assumption 8.2 can be given as follows. Define $\sigma_{tt} = \text{var}(\varepsilon_{it}), \sigma_{\alpha\alpha} = \text{var}(\alpha_i)$ and $\sigma_{00} = \text{var}(y_{i0})$. Then, Assumption 8.2 imposes the following covariance restrictions on the initial value y_{i0} and the composite errors $u_{i1}, \dots, u_{iT}$:

$$\Lambda \equiv \text{cov} \begin{pmatrix} u_{i1} \\ u_{i2} \\ \vdots \\ u_{iT} \\ u_{i0} \end{pmatrix} \equiv \begin{bmatrix} \lambda_{11} & \lambda_{12} & \cdots & \lambda_{1T} & \lambda_{10} \\ \lambda_{21} & \lambda_{22} & \cdots & \lambda_{2T} & \lambda_{20} \\ \vdots & \vdots & & \vdots & \vdots \\ \lambda_{T1} & \lambda_{T2} & \cdots & \lambda_{TT} & \lambda_{T0} \\ \lambda_{01} & \lambda_{02} & \cdots & \lambda_{0T} & \lambda_{00} \end{bmatrix},$$

$$= \begin{bmatrix} (\sigma_{\alpha\alpha} + \sigma_{11}) & \sigma_{\alpha\alpha} & \cdots & \sigma_{\alpha\alpha} & \sigma_{0\alpha} \\ \sigma_{\alpha\alpha} & (\sigma_{\alpha\alpha} + \sigma_{22}) & \cdots & \sigma_{\alpha\alpha} & \sigma_{0\alpha} \\ \vdots & \vdots & & \vdots & \vdots \\ \sigma_{\alpha\alpha} & \sigma_{\alpha\alpha} & \cdots & (\sigma_{\alpha\alpha} + \sigma_{TT}) & \sigma_{0\alpha} \\ \sigma_{0\alpha} & \sigma_{0\alpha} & \cdots & \sigma_{0\alpha} & \sigma_{0\alpha} \end{bmatrix},$$

There are $T - 1$ restrictions, that λ_{0t} is the same for $t = 1, \dots, T$; and $T(T - 1)/2 - 1$ restrictions, that λ_{ts} is the same for $t, s = 1, \dots, T$, $t \neq s$. Adding the number of restrictions, we get $T(T - 1)/2 + (T - 2)$.

Since the moment conditions (8–27) are nonlinear, GMM imposing these conditions requires an iterative procedure. Thus, an important practical question is whether this computational burden is worthwhile. *Ahn and Schmidt* [1995] provide a partial answer. They compare the asymptotic variances of the GMM estimator based on (8–26) only and the GMM estimator based on both of (8–26) and (8–27). Their computation results show that use of the extra moment condition (8–27) can result in a large efficiency gain, especially when δ is close to one or the variance $\sigma_{\alpha\alpha}$ is large.

8.5.2 Some Alternative Assumptions

We now briefly consider some alternative sets of assumptions. The first case we consider is the one in which Assumption 8.2 is augmented by the additional assumption that the ε_{it} are homoskedastic. That is, suppose that we add the assumption:

Assumption 8.3

> For all i, $\text{var}(\varepsilon_{it})$ is the same for all t.

∎

This assumption, when added to Assumption 8.2, generates the additional $(T-1)$ moment conditions that

$$E(u_{it}^2) \quad \text{is the same for} \quad t = 1, \ldots, T. \tag{8–28}$$

(In terms of Λ above, λ_{tt} is the same for $t = 1, \ldots, T$.) Therefore the total number of moment conditions becomes $T(T-1)/2+(2T-3)$. These moment conditions can be expressed as (8–26)-(8–28). Alternatively, if we wish to maximize the number of linear moment conditions, these moment conditions can be expressed as (8–26) plus the additional conditions

$$E(y_{it}\Delta u_{i,t+1} - y_{i,t+1}\Delta u_{i,t+2}) = 0, \quad t = 1, \ldots, T-2, \tag{8–29}$$

$$E(\bar{u}_i \Delta u_{i,t+1}) = 0, \quad t = 1, \ldots, T-1, \tag{8–30}$$

where $\bar{u}_i = T^{-1}\sum_{t=1}^{T} u_{it}$. Comparing this to the set of moment conditions without homoskedasticity (8–26)–(8–27), we see that homoskedasticity adds $T-1$ moment conditions and it allows $T-2$ previously nonlinear moment conditions to be expressed linearly.

Ahn and Schmidt [1995] quantify the asymptotic efficiency gain from imposing the extra moment conditions (8–27) and (8–28) (or equivalently, (8–29) and (8–30)) in addition to (8–26). Their results show that most of efficiency gains come from the moment condition (8–27). That is, we do not gain much efficiency from the assumption of homoskedasticity (Assumption 8.3).

Another possible assumption we may impose on the model (8–25) is the stationarity assumption of *Arellano and Bover* [1995]:

Assumption 8.4

> $cov(\alpha_i, y_{it})$ is the same for all t.

∎

This is an assumption of the type made by BMS (see (8–17)); it requires equal covariance between the effects and the variables with which they are correlated. *Ahn and Schmidt* [1995] show that, given Assumption 8.2, Assumption 8.4 corresponds to the restriction that

$$\sigma_{0\alpha} = \sigma_{\alpha\alpha}/(1-\delta) \tag{8–31}$$

and implies one additional moment restriction. Furthermore, they show that it also allows the entire set of available moment conditions to be written linearly; that is, (8–26) plus

$$E(u_{iT}\Delta y_{it}) = 0, \quad t = 1, \ldots, T-1;$$

$$E(u_{it}y_{it} - u_{i,t-1}y_{i,t-1}) = 0, \quad t = 2, \ldots, T.$$

This is a set of $T(T-1)/2 + (2T-2)$ moment conditions, all of which are linear in δ. *Blundell and Bond* [1997] show that the GMM estimator exploiting all of these linear moment conditions has much better asymptotic and finite sample properties than the GMM estimator based on (8–26) only. Thus the stationarity Assumption 8.4 may be quite useful.

Finally, we consider an alternative stationarity assumption, which is examined by *Ahn and Schmidt* [1997]:

ASSUMPTION 8.5

In addition to Assumptions 8.2 and 8.3, the series $y_{i0}, \ldots, y_{iT}$ is covariance stationary.

∎

To see the connection between the two stationarity assumptions, Assumptions 8.4 and 8.5, we use the solution

$$y_{it} = \delta^t y_{i0} + \alpha_i(1 - \delta^t)/(1 - \delta) + \sum_{j=0}^{t-1} \delta^j \varepsilon_{i,t-j}$$

to calculate

$$\text{var}(y_{it}) = \sigma_{00}\delta^{2t} + \sigma_{0\alpha}2\delta^t(1 - \delta^t)/(1 - \delta)$$
$$+ \sigma_{\alpha\alpha}[(1 - \delta^t)/(1 - \delta)]^2 + \sigma_{\varepsilon\varepsilon}(1 - \delta^{2t})/(1 - \delta^2),$$

where the calculation assumes Assumptions 8.2 and 8.3. Assumption 8.5 implies that $\text{var}(y_{it}) = \sigma_{00}$ for all t, which occurs if and only if $\sigma_{\alpha\alpha} = (1 - \delta)\sigma_{0\alpha}$ and also

$$\sigma_{00} = \sigma_{\alpha\alpha}/(1 - \delta)^2 + \sigma_{\varepsilon\varepsilon}/(1 - \delta^2). \quad (8\text{–}32)$$

Thus Assumption 8.5 implies $\sigma_{\alpha\alpha} = (1-\delta)\sigma_{0\alpha}$, which in turn implies Assumption 8.4. However, it also implies the restriction (8–32) on the variance of the initial observation y_{i0}. Imposing (8–32) as well as Assumptions 8.2–8.4 yields one additional, nonlinear moment condition:

$$E[y_{i0}^2 + y_{i1}\Delta u_{i2}/(1 - \delta^2) - u_{i2}u_{i1}/(1 - \delta)^2] = 0.$$

An interesting question that we do not address here is how many moment conditions we would have if the assumptions discussed above are relaxed. *Ahn and Schmidt* [1997] give a partial answer by counting the moment conditions implied by many possible combinations of the above assumptions. See that paper for more detail.

8.5.3 Estimation

In this subsection we discuss some theoretical details concerning GMM estimation of the dynamic model. We also discuss the relationship between GMM based on the linear moment conditions and 3SLS estimation. Our discussion will proceed under Assumptions 8.2–8.3, but can easily be modified to accommodate the other cases.

8.5.3.1 Notation and General Results

We now return to the model (8–24) which includes exogenous regressors r_{it} and w_i. Exogeneity assumptions on r_{it} and w_i generate linear moment conditions of the form

$$E(C_i' u_i) = 0,$$

where $C_i = Z_{A,i}$ or $Z_{B,i}$ as defined in Section 8.3. In addition, the moment conditions given by (8–26), (8–29) and (8–30) above are valid. The moment conditions in (8–26) above are linear in β and can be written as $E(A_i' u_i) = 0$, where A_i is the $T \times T(T-1)/2$ matrix

$$A_i = \begin{bmatrix} -y_{i0} & 0 & \cdots & 0 \\ y_{i0} & -(y_{i0}, y_{i1}) & \cdots & 0 \\ 0 & (y_{i0}, y_{i1}) & \cdots & 0 \\ \vdots & \vdots & & \vdots \\ 0 & 0 & \cdots & -(y_{i0}, y_{i1}, \dots, y_{i,T-2}) \\ 0 & 0 & \cdots & (y_{i0}, y_{i1}, \dots, y_{i,T-2}) \end{bmatrix}.$$

Similarly, the moment conditions in (8–29) above are also linear in β and can be written as $E(B_i' u_i) = 0$, where B_i is the $T \times (T-2)$

matrix defined by

$$B_i = \begin{bmatrix} -y_{i1} & 0 & \cdots & 0 \\ (y_{i1} + y_{i2}) & -y_{i2} & \cdots & 0 \\ -y_{i2} & (y_{i2} + y_{i3}) & \cdots & 0 \\ 0 & -y_{i3} & \cdots & 0 \\ \vdots & \vdots & & \vdots \\ 0 & 0 & \cdots & -y_{i,T-2} \\ 0 & 0 & \cdots & (y_{i,T-2} + y_{i,T-1}) \\ 0 & 0 & \cdots & -y_{i,T-1} \end{bmatrix}.$$

However, the moment conditions in (8–30) above are quadratic in β.

We will discuss GMM estimation based on all of the available moment conditions and GMM based on a subset (possibly all) of the linear moment conditions. Let $H_i = (C_i, A_i, B_i)$, which represents all of the available linear instruments. The corresponding linear moment conditions are $E[m_i(\beta)] = 0$, with

$$m_i(\beta) = H_i' u_i = m_{1i} + m_{2i}\beta, \quad m_{1i} = H_i' y_i, \quad m_{2i} = -H_i' X_i.$$

The remaining nonlinear moment conditions will be written as $E[g_i(\beta)] = 0$. Since they are at most quadratic, we can write

$$g_i(\beta) \equiv g_{1i} + g_{2i} + (I_q \otimes \beta') g_{3i}\beta,$$

where g_{1i}, g_{2i} and g_{3i} are conformable matrices of functions of data and q is the number of moment conditions in g_i. An efficient estimator of β can be obtained by GMM based on all of the moment conditions

$$E[f_i(\beta)] \equiv E[m_i(\beta)', \ g_i(\beta)']' = 0.$$

Define $f_N = N^{-1}\Sigma_i f_i(\beta)$, with m_N, m_{1N}, m_{2N}, g_N, g_{1N}, g_{2N} and g_{3N} defined similarly; and define

$$F_N = \partial f_N/\partial\beta' = [\partial m_N'/\partial\beta, \partial g_N'/\partial\beta]' = [M_N', \ G_N']',$$

where $G_N(\beta) = g_{2N} + 2(I \otimes \beta') g_{3N}$ and $M_N = m_{2N}$. Let $F = \text{plim } F_N$, with M and G defined similarly. Define the optimal weighting matrix

$$V = \begin{bmatrix} V_{mm} & V_{mg} \\ V_{gm} & V_{gg} \end{bmatrix} = E(f_i f_i').$$

Let V_N be a consistent estimate of V of the form

$$V_N = N^{-1} \sum_{i=1}^{N} f_i(\widehat{\beta}) f_i(\widehat{\beta})',$$

where $\hat{\beta}$ is an initial consistent estimate of β (perhaps based on the linear moment conditions m_i, as discussed below); partition it similarly to V.

In this notation, the efficient GMM estimator $\hat{\beta}_{EGMM}$ minimizes

$$N f_N(\beta)' V_N^{-1} f_N(\beta).$$

Using standard results, the asymptotic covariance matrix of

$$N^{\frac{1}{2}}(\hat{\beta}_{EGMM} - \beta) = [F'\Omega^{-1}F]^{-1}.$$

8.5.3.2 Linear Moment Conditions and Instrumental Variables

Some interesting questions arise when we consider GMM based on the linear moment conditions $m_i(\beta)$ only. The optimal GMM estimator based on these conditions is

$$\hat{\beta}_m = -[m'_{2N}(V_{N,mm})^{-1}m_{2N}]^{-1}m'_{2N}(V_{N,mm})^{-1}m_{1N}$$
$$= [X'H(V_{N,mm})^{-1}H'X]^{-1}X'H(V_{N,mm})^{-1}X'y.$$

This GMM estimator can be compared to the 3SLS estimator which is obtained by replacing $V_{N,mm}$ by $N^{-1}H'\Omega H = N^{-1}\sum_{i=1}^{N} H_i'\Sigma H_i$.[4] As discussed in Section 8.1, they are asymptotically equivalent in the case that $V_{mm} \equiv E(H_i'u_iu_i'H_i) = E(H_i'\Sigma H_i)$. For the case that H_i consists only of columns of C_i, so that only the moment conditions $E(C_i'u_i) = 0$ based on exogeneity of R_i and w_i are imposed, this equivalence may hold. *Arellano and Bond* [1991] considered the moment conditions (8–26), so that H_i also contains A_i, and noted that asymptotic equivalence between the 3SLS and GMM estimates fails if we relax the homoskedasticity assumption, Assumption 8.3, even though the moment conditions (8–26) are still valid under only Assumption 8.2. In fact, even the full set of Assumptions 8.2–8.3 is not sufficient to imply the asymptotic equivalence of the 3SLS and GMM estimates when the moment conditions (8–27) are used. Assumptions 8.2–8.3 deal only with second moments, whereas asymptotic equivalence of 3SLS and GMM involves restrictions on fourth moments (*e.g.*, $\text{cov}(y_{i0}^2, \varepsilon_{it}^2) = 0$). *Ahn* [1990] proved the asymptotic equivalence of the 3SLS and GMM estimators based on the moment conditions (8–26) for the case that Assumption

---

[4] Note that Assumptions 8.2 and 8.3 implies the random effects structure (8–3).

8.3 is maintained and Assumption 8.2 is strengthened by replacing uncorrelatedness with independence. *Wooldridge* [1996] provides a more general treatment of cases in which 3SLS and GMM are asymptotically equivalent. In the present case, his results indicate that asymptotic equivalence would hold if we rewrite Assumptions 8.2–8.3 in terms of conditional expectations instead of uncorrelatedness; that is, if we assume

$$E(\varepsilon_{it} \mid y_{i0}, \alpha_i, \varepsilon_{i1}, \ldots, \varepsilon_{i,t-1}) = 0,$$
$$E(\varepsilon_{it}^2 \mid y_{i0}, \alpha_i, \varepsilon_{i1}, \ldots, \varepsilon_{i,t-1}) = \sigma_{\varepsilon\varepsilon}.$$

A more novel observation is that the asymptotic equivalence of 3SLS and GMM fails whenever we use the additional linear moment conditions (8–29). This is so even if Assumptions 8.2–8.3 are strengthened by replacing uncorrelatedness with independence. When uncorrelatedness in Assumptions 8.2–8.3 is replaced by independence, *Ahn* [1990, Chapter 3, Appendix 3] shows that, while

$$E(A_i' u_i u_i' A_i) = \sigma_{\varepsilon\varepsilon} E(A_i' A_i) = E(A_i' \Sigma A_i)$$
$$E(A_i' u_i u_i' B_i) = \sigma_{\varepsilon\varepsilon} E(A_i' B_i) = E(A_i' \Sigma B_i),$$
$$E(B_i' u_i u_i' B_i) = \sigma_{\varepsilon\varepsilon} E(B_i' B_i) + (\kappa + \sigma_{\varepsilon\varepsilon}) L_{T-1}' L_{T-1}$$
$$= E(B_i' \Sigma B_i) + (\kappa + \sigma_{\varepsilon\varepsilon}) L_{T-1}' L_{T-1},$$

where $\kappa = E(\varepsilon^4) - 3\sigma_{\varepsilon\varepsilon}^2$ and L_{T-1} is the $(T-1) \times (T-2)$ differencing matrix defined similarly to L_T in Section 8.1. Under normality $\kappa = 0$ but the term $\sigma_{\varepsilon\varepsilon} L_{T-1}' L_{T-1}$ remains.

8.5.3.3 Linearized GMM

We now consider a linearized GMM estimator. Suppose that $\tilde{\beta}$ is any consistent estimator of β; for example, $\widehat{\beta}_m$. Following *Newey* [1985, p. 238], the linearized GMM estimator is of the form

$$\widehat{\beta}_{LGMM} = \widehat{\beta} - [F_N(\widehat{\beta})'(V_N)^{-1} F_N(\widehat{\beta})]^{-1} F_N(\widehat{\beta})'(V_N)^{-1} f_N(\widehat{\beta}).$$

This estimator is consistent and has the same asymptotic distribution as $\widehat{\beta}_{EGMM}$.

When the LGMM estimator is based on the initial estimator $\widehat{\beta}_m$, some further simplification is possible. Applying the usual matrix inversion rule to V_N and using the fact that $m_{2N}' V_{N,mm}^{-1} m_N(\widehat{\beta}_m) = 0$, we can write the LGMM estimator as follows:

$$\widehat{\beta}_{LGMM} = \widehat{\beta}_m - [\Gamma_N + B_N'(V_{N,bb})^{-1} B_N]^{-1} B_N'(V_{N,bb})^{-1} b_N,$$

where

$$\Gamma_N = m'_{2N}(V_{N,mm})^{-1}m_{2N}, \ V_{N,bb} = V_{N,gg} - V_{N,gm}(V_{N,mm})^{-1}V_{N,mg},$$
$$b_N = g_N(\widehat{\beta}_m) - V_{N,gm}(V_{N,mm})^{-1}m_N(\widehat{\beta}_m), \quad \text{and}$$
$$B_N = G_N(\widehat{\beta}_m) - V_{N,gm}(V_{N,mm})^{-1}m_{2N}.$$

For more detail, see *Ahn and Schmidt* [1997].

8.6 Conclusion

In this chapter we have considered the GMM estimation of linear panel data models. We have discussed standard models, including the fixed and random effects linear model, a dynamic model, and the simultaneous equation model. For these models the typical treatment in the literature is some sort of instrumental variables procedure; least squares and generalized least squares are included in the class of such instrumental variables procedures.

It is well known that for linear models the GMM estimator often takes the form of an IV estimator if a no conditional heteroskedasticity condition holds. Therefore we have focused on three related points. First, for each model we seek to identify the complete set of moment conditions (instruments) implied by the assumptions underlying the model. Next, one can observe that the usual exogenety assumptions lead to many more moment conditions than standard estimators use, and ask whether some or all of the moment conditions are redundant, in the sense that they are unnecessary to obtain an efficient estimator. Under the no conditional heteroskedasticity assumption, the efficiency of standard estimators can often be established. This implies that the moment conditions which are not utilized by standard estimators are redundant. Finally, we ask whether anything intrinsic to the model makes the assumption of no conditional heteroskedasticity untenable. In some models, such as the dynamic model, this assumption necessarily fails if the full set of moment conditions is used, and correspondingly the efficient GMM estimator is not an instrumental variables estimator.

The set of non–redundant moment conditions can sometimes be very large. For example, this is true in the dynamic model, and also in simpler static models if the assumption of no conditional heteroskedasticity fails. In such cases the finite sample properties of the GMM estimator using the full set of moment conditions may be poor. An important avenue of research is to find estimators which are efficient, or nearly so, and yet have better finite sample properties than the full GMM esitmator.

References

Ahn, S.C., [1990]: *Three essays on share contracts, labor supply, and the estimation of models for dynamic panel data,* Unpublished Ph.D. dissertation, Michigan State University.

Ahn, S. C. and P. Schmidt, [1995]: Efficient estimation of models for dynamic panel data, *Journal of Econometrics* 68, 5-27.

Ahn, S. C. and P. Schmidt, [1997]: Efficient estimation of dynamic panel data models: alternative assumptions and simplified assumptions, *Journal of Econometrics* 76, 309-321.

Altonji, J. G. and L. M. Segal, [1996]: Small-sample bias in GMM estimation of covariance structure, *Journal of Business & Economic Statistics* 14, 353-366.

Amemiya, T. and T. E. MaCurdy, [1986]: Instrumental-variables estimation of an error- components model, *Econometrica* 54, 869-880.

Andersen, T. G. and R. E. Sørensen, [1996]: GMM estimation of a stochastic volatility model: A Monte Carlo Study, *Journal of Business & Economic Statistics* 14, 328-352.

Anderson, T.W. and C. Hsiao, [1981]: Estimation of dynamic models with error components, *Journal of the American Statistical Association,* 76, 598-606.

Arellano, M. and S. Bond, [1991]: Tests of specification for panel data: Monte Carlo evidence and an application to employment equations, *Review of Economic Studies* 58, 277-297.

Arellano, M. and O. Bover, [1995]: Another look at the instrumental variables estimation of error-component models, *Journal of Econometrics* 68, 29-51.

Balestra, P. and M. Nerlove, [1966]: Pooling cross-section and time-series data in the estimation of a dynamic model: The demand for natural gas, *Econometrica* 34, 585- 612.

Blundell, R. and S. Bond, [1997]: *Initial conditions and moment restrictions in dynamic panel data models,* Unpublished manuscript, University College London

Breusch, T. S., G. E. Mizon and P. Schmidt, [1989]: Efficient estimation using panel data, *Econometrica* 57, 695-700.

Chamberlain, G., [1992]: Comment: sequential moment restrictions in panel data, *Journal of Business & Economic Statistics* 10, 20-26.

Cornwell, C., P. Schmidt and D. Wyhowski, [1992]: Simultaneous equations and panel data, *Journal of Econometrics* 51, 151-182.

Crépon, B., F. Kramarz and A. Trognon, [1995]: *Parameter of interest, nuisance parameter and orthogonality conditions,* unpublished manuscript, INSEE.

Hahn, J, [1997]: Efficient estimation of panel data models with sequential moment restrictions, *Journal of Econometrics* 79, 1-21

Hausman, J. A. and W. E. Taylor, [1981]: Panel data and unobservable individual effects, *Econometrica* 49, 1377-1398.

Hayashi, F. and C. Sims, [1983]: Nearly efficient estimation of time series models with predetermined but not exogenous instruments, *Econometrica* 51, 783-792.

Holtz-Eakin, D., [1988]: Testing for individual effects in autoregressive models, *Journal of Econometrics* 39, 297-308.

Holtz-Eakin, D., W. Newey and H.S. Rosen, [1988]: Estimating vector autoregressions with panel data, *Econometrica* 56, 1371-1396.

Hsiao, C., [1986]: *Analysis of Panel Data,* New York: Cambridge University Press.

Im, K. S., S. C. Ahn, P. Schmidt and J. M. Wooldridge, [1996]: *Efficient estimation of panel data models with strictly exogenous explanatory variables,* Econometrics and Economic Theory Working Paper 9600, Michigan State University.

Keane, M. P. and D. E. Runkle, [1992]: On the estimation of panel data models with serial correlation when instruments are not strictly exogenous, *Journal of Business & Economic Statistics* 10, 1-10.

Koenker, R. and A. F. Machado, [1997]: *GMM inferences when the number of moment conditions is large,* Unpublished manuscript, University of Illinois at Champaign.

Mundlak, Y., [1978]: On the pooling of time series and cross section data, *Econometrica* 46, 69- 85.

Mátyás, L. and Sevestre, P. [1995]: *The Econometrics of Panel Data,* Kluwer Academic Publishers, Dordrecht.

Schmidt, P., S. C. Ahn and D. Wyhowski, [1992]: Comment, *Journal of Business & Economic Statistics* 10, 10-14.

Tauchen, G., [1986]: Statistical properties of generalized method-of-moments estimators of structural parameters obtained from financial market data, *Journal of Business & Economic Statistics* 4, 397-416.

White, H., [1984]: *Asymptotic theory for econometricians (Academic Press,* San Diego, CA).

Wooldridge, J. M., [1996]: Estimating system of equations with different instruments for different equations, *Journal of Econometrics* 74, 387-405.

Ziliak, J. P., [1997]: Efficient estimation with panel data when instruments are predetermined: an empirical comparison of moment-condition estimators, *Journal of Business & Economic Statistics,* 15, 419–431.

Chapter 9

ALTERNATIVE GMM METHODS FOR

NONLINEAR PANEL DATA MODELS

Jörg Breitung and Michael Lechner

In recent years the GMM approach became increasingly popular for the analysis of panel data (*e.g., Avery, Hansen and Hotz* [1983], *Arrelano and Bond* [1991], *Keane* [1989], *Lechner and Breitung* [1996]). Combining popular nonlinear models used in microeconometric applications with typical panel data features like an error component structure yields complex models which are too complicated or even intractable to be estimated by maximum likelihood. In such cases the GMM approach is an attractive alternative.

A well known example is the probit model, which is one of the work horses whenever models with binary dependent variables are analyzed. Although the nonrobustness of the probit estimates to the model's tight statistical assumptions is widely acknowledged, the ease of computation of the maximum likelihood estimator (MLE)—combined with the availability of specification tests—make it an attractive choice for many empirical studies based on cross sectional data. The panel data version of the probit model allows for serial correlation of the errors in the latent equations. The problem with these types of specifications is, however, that the MLE becomes much more complicated as in the case of uncorrelated errors.

Two ways to deal with that sort of general problems have emerged in the literature. One is the simulated maximum likelihood estimation (SMLE). The idea of this technique is to find an estimator that only approximates the MLE but retains the asymptotic efficiency property of the exact MLE. SMLE uses stochastic simulation procedures to obtain approximate choice probabilities (see *e.g., Börsch-Supan and Hajivassiliou* [1993], or *Hajivassiliou, McFadden and Ruud* [1996]). The problem with these methods is that they can be very computer intensive, and it may still be difficult to estimate all parameters of the covariance matrix jointly with the regression coefficients.

An alternative approach sacrifices some of the asymptotic efficiency in order to obtain a simple GMM estimator. Since GMM estimators are consistent in the case of serially correlated errors, it is then not necessary to obtain joint estimates of the covariance parameters and the regression coefficients. These estimators are based on the fact that a panel probit model implies a simple probit model when taking each period separately. Therefore, simple moment conditions can be derived from the individual cross sections and asymptotic theory can be used to minimize the efficiency loss implied by such a procedure. Examples of this kind of estimators can be found in *Avery et al.* [1983] and *Chamberlain* [1980], [1984].

In a number of recent papers various other GMM estimators based on these ideas are suggested and compared asymptotically and by means of Monte Carlo simulations (*Breitung and Lechner* [1996], *Bertschek and Lechner* [1998], and *Lechner and Breitung* [1996]). The results of these studies are quite promising. The appropriate GMM estimator provides an estimation procedure that is robust, flexible, easy and fast to compute, and results in a small (in some case negligible) efficiency loss compared to full information maximum likelihood.

In this chapter we review some earlier work on the GMM estimation of nonlinear panel data models and suggest some new estimators as well. In particular we consider the joint estimation of mean and covariance parameters. Most of the previous studies focused on first order moment conditions, *i.e.,* restrictions on the conditional mean, while here we will consider restrictions on higher moments as well.

The chapter is organized as follows. Section 9.1 defines the nonlinear panel data model and gives some examples. Section 9.2 sketches the earlier work concerning the GMM estimation of parameters for the conditional mean. Section 9.3 considers higher order moments for estimating the complete parameter vector and Section 9.4 applies the new approach of *Gallant and Tauchen* [1996] to select appropriate moment conditions. A minimum distance version of the resulting estimator is suggested in Section 9.5. Section 9.6 presents the results of a small Monte Carlo experiment and in Section 9.7 the estimation procedures are applied to an empirical example. Section 9.8 concludes.

9.1 A Class of Nonlinear Panel Data Models

Let y_{it} be an $m \times 1$ vector of jointly dependent variables and x_{it} is a $k \times 1$ vector of independent variables. The indices $i = 1, \ldots, N$ and $t = 1, \ldots, T$ indicate the cross section unit and the time period of the observation. It is convenient to stack the observations into matrices such that $Y_i = [y_{i1}, \ldots, y_{iT}]'$ and $X_i = [x_{i1}, \ldots, x_{iT}]'$. Next we consider the asymptotic properties for T fixed and $N \to \infty$.

For the time period t, the nonlinear model is characterized by its conditional density function $h(y_{it}|x_{it}; \theta_0)$ (cf. *Gouriéroux* [1996]). Defining the conditional mean function as $E(y_{it}|x_{it}) = \mu_1(x_{it}; \theta_0)$, the model may be rewritten as

$$y_{it} = \mu_1(x_{it}; \theta_0) + v_{it} , \tag{9-1}$$

where $E(v_{it}|x_{it}) = 0$ and $E(v_{it}v_{jt}|x_{it}, x_{jt}) = 0$ for $i \neq j$.

EXAMPLE 9.1 **Binary Choice Model**

Let $y_{it}^* = x_{it}'\beta_0 + \varepsilon_{it}$, where $\varepsilon_i = [\varepsilon_{i1}, \ldots, \varepsilon_{iT}]'$ is i.i.d. and ε_{it} has a constant marginal distribution function $F_\varepsilon(z)$. If $y_{it}^* > 0$, we observe $y_{it} = 1$. Otherwise we have $y_{it} = 0$. The conditional mean function for this model is given by

$$E(y_{it}|x_{it}) = \mu_1(x_{it}; \theta_0) = F_\varepsilon(x_{it}'\beta_0).$$

∎

EXAMPLE 9.2 **Multinomial Logit Model**

Let $P_{j,it}$ denote the probability of choosing alternative $j = 0, 1, \ldots, J$ given by

$$P_{j,it} = \frac{\exp(x'_{it}\beta_0^j)}{1 + \sum\limits_{j=1}^{J} \exp(x'_{it}\beta_0^j)},$$

where $\beta_0^0 = 0$. We define J indicator variables[1] $y_{j,it}$ ($j = 1, \ldots, J$) which takes a value of one if alternative j is chosen by individual i at time period t and zero otherwise. The conditional mean function for $y_{it} = [y_{1,it}, \ldots, y_{J,it}]'$ is

$$E(y_{it}|x_{it}) = \mu_1(x_{it}; \theta_0) = \begin{bmatrix} P_{1,it} \\ \vdots \\ P_{J,it} \end{bmatrix}$$

∎

EXAMPLE 9.3 **Poisson Model**

Let y_{it} be a integer valued random variable drawn from a Poisson distribution with conditional mean function

$$\mu_1(x_{it}; \theta_0) = \exp(x'_{it}\beta_0).$$

∎

In the examples we give the conditional mean functions for an individual i at time t. Stacking the means of different time periods into a $T \times m$ matrix gives

$$\mu_1(X_i; \theta_0) = \begin{bmatrix} \mu_1(x_{i1}; \theta_0)' \\ \vdots \\ \mu_1(x_{iT}; \theta_0)' \end{bmatrix}.$$

We may include lagged or lead values of the exogenous variables in x_{it}, so that the conditional mean may depend on the exogenous variables from other time periods. Moreover, we may include weakly exogenous variables in the sense that x_{it} is uncorrelated with v_{it}

---

[1] Note, that the moment condition for $y_{0,it}$ is redundant because the probabilities of the choices sum up to one.

but may be correlated with v_{is} for $s \neq t$. Accordingly, the model may include weakly or strongly exogenous variables. However, it is important to notice that the mean function is the same for all cross section units. This excludes many models with heterogeneity in the mean such as fixed effects models.[2]

Unobserved heterogeneity may be represented by including an individual specific random effect α_i. For example, a random component version of the binary choice model may be constructed as in the following example.

EXAMPLE 9.4 **Error Components Probit Model**

Let y_{it}^* be a latent variable given by

$$y_{it}^* = x_{it}'\beta_0 + \alpha_i + \varepsilon_{it},$$

where x_{it} is a vector of strongly exogenous variables, α_i and ε_{it} are mutually and serially uncorrelated random variables distributed as $\alpha_i \sim \mathcal{N}(0, \sigma_\alpha^2)$ and $\varepsilon_{it} \sim \mathcal{N}(0, \sigma_\varepsilon^2)$, where we normalize the variances as $\sigma_\varepsilon^2 + \sigma_\alpha^2 = 1$. The observed dependent variable y_{it} is one if $y_{it}^* > 0$ and zero otherwise. The parameter vector of the model is $\theta = [\beta_0', \rho_0]'$, where $\rho_0 = \sigma_\alpha^2/(\sigma_\varepsilon^2 + \sigma_\alpha^2)$ denotes the serial correlation and the mean function is identical to the one of Example 9.1, where $F_\varepsilon(z)$ is the standard normal c.d.f.

■

This error component probit model is a special case of Example 9.1 and will serve as the leading example in what follows.

---

[2]   The reason is that in nonlinear models it is not easy to deal with heterogeneity in the mean. For discrete choice models there are some special cases allowing for fixed effects estimation such as count data models and conditional binary logit models. If the latent dependent variable is partly observable, as in censored or truncated regression models, semiparametric methods may be an attractive alternative (cf. *Honoré* [1992], [1993]).

9.2 GMM Estimators for the Conditional Mean

Assume that we are interested in the conditional mean function given by $\mu_1(X_i; \theta)$. In many applications, the mean function does not depend on the complete parameter vector. In this case we may write $\mu_1(X_i; \theta) = \mu_1(X_i; \theta^{(1)})$, where $\theta^{(1)}$ is a $p_1 \times 1$ subvector of θ. The remaining parameters are treated as nuisance parameters. For example, in the error components probit model given in Example 9.4 we may be interested in β_0 but not in the correlation coefficient ρ_0. Accordingly, it is convenient to focus on the conditional mean when constructing a GMM estimator. We define first order moments as

$$f_1(y_i, X_i; \theta^{(1)}) = y_i - \mu_1(X_i; \theta^{(1)}) \tag{9-2}$$

with the moment condition

$$E[f_1(X_i; \theta_0^{(1)})|X_i] = 0. \tag{9-3}$$

Using the law of iterated expectations the conditional moment restrictions can be expressed as a set of unconditional moment restrictions

$$E[B(X_i)f_1(y_i, X_i; \theta_0^{(1)})] = 0, \tag{9-4}$$

where $B(X_i)$ is a $p_1 \times T$ matrix of functions on X_i. The optimal choice of $B(X_i)$ is (cf. Newey [1993])

$$B^*(X_i) = C \cdot D(X_i; \theta_0^{(1)})'\Omega(X_i; \theta_0)^{-1}, \tag{9-5}$$

where

$$D(X_i; \theta^{(1)}) = E[\partial f_1(y_i, X_i; \theta^{(1)})/\partial\theta^{(1)'}|X_i]$$
$$\Omega(X_i; \theta) = E[(f_1(y_i, X_i; \theta^{(1)})f_1(y_i, X_i; \theta^{(1)})'|X_i]$$

and C is some nonsingular squared matrix.

For the panel probit model (Example 9.4) we obtain:

$$D(X_i; \beta) = \begin{bmatrix} -\phi(x_{i1}'\beta_0)x_{i1}' \\ \vdots \\ -\phi(x_{iT}'\beta_0)x_{iT}' \end{bmatrix}$$

$$\Omega(X_i; \beta, \rho) = (\omega_{ts,i}) \tag{9-6}$$

$$\omega_{ts,i}(x_{it}, x_{is}; \beta, \rho) = \begin{cases} \Phi(x_{it}'\beta)[1 - \Phi(x_{it}'\beta)] & \text{for } t = s \\ \Phi^{(2)}(x_{it}'\beta, x_{is}'\beta, \rho) - \Phi(x_{it}'\beta)\Phi(x_{is}'\beta) & \text{otherwise} \end{cases}$$

where $\phi(x'_{it}\beta)$ denotes the p.d.f. of the univariate standard normal distribution and $\Phi^{(2)}(x'_{it}\beta, x'_{is}\beta, \rho)$ indicates a bivariate normal c.d.f. with correlation ρ.

It is important to note that $D(X_i; \beta)$ does not depend on the covariance parameter ρ, whereas the computation of $\omega_{ts,i}$ requires the value of ρ. Accordingly, for the asymptotically optimal instruments we need estimates of the mean and the covariance parameters. There are several strategies to deal with this problem. First, ρ may be fixed at some arbitrary level, say $\rho = 0$. This gives a computationally simple estimator that is consistent but inefficient. The second possibility is to apply some rough approximation such as the "small sigma approximation" (cf. *Breitung and Lechner* [1996]). Again, an efficiency loss may result from this approximation.

The third possibility is to estimate $T(T-1)/2$ bivariate probit models to obtain direct estimates. This approach is asymptotically efficient, but quite time consuming. In particular, convergence problems may occur, as it often happens in fairly small sample sizes. Finally, *Bertschek and Lechner* [1998] suggest the use of nonparametric methods, (*e.g.*, the k–nearest neighbor method) to avoid the estimation of the correlation coefficient. Based on an empirical application and an extensive Monte Carlo study they find that the nonparametric GMM estimator approaches the efficiency of the MLE.

Another possibility is to use a high dimensional simple function such as

$$B(X_i) = I_T \otimes \text{vec}(X_i)'$$

or

$$B(X_i) = \begin{bmatrix} x_{i1}/s_{i1} & 0 & \cdots & 0 \\ 0 & x_{i2}/s_{i2} & & 0 \\ \vdots & & & \vdots \\ 0 & 0 & \cdots & x_{iT}/s_{iT} \end{bmatrix},$$

where $s_{it} = \Phi(x'_{it}\beta)[1 - \Phi(x'_{it}\beta)]$ (see *Avery et al.* [1983], *Breitung and Lechner* [1996]). The main problem with this approach is that a large number of moment conditions is needed to approach the efficient GMM estimator. In finite samples, however, GMM estimators perform poorly if the number of moment conditions gets large relative to the sample size (*e.g.*, *Breitung and Lechner* [1996]).

9.3 Higher Order Moment Conditions

So far we confine ourselves to the moment restrictions for the conditional mean. Accordingly, this approach does not provide estimates for other parameters like the conditional variance. Moreover, the efficiency of the GMM procedure may be improved by considering higher order moment conditions. If y_i is univariate (as for the cross section probit model, for example) we may define moments of degree k as

$$f_k(y_i, x_i; \theta) = [y_i - \mu_1(x_i; \theta)]^k - \mu_k(x_i; \theta)$$

where $\mu_k = E\{[y_i - \mu_1(X_i; \theta)]^k | x_i\}$. The corresponding moment condition is

$$E[f_k(y_i, x_i; \theta_0) | x_i] = 0 . \tag{9–7}$$

If y_i is a vector, all relevant moments are stacked into an appropriate vector. For the panel probit model the typical element for a vector with $k = 2$ is given by

$$f_2^{(ts)}(y_i, X_i; \beta, \rho) = [y_{it} - \Phi(x'_{it}\beta)][y_{is} - \Phi(x'_{is}\beta)] - \omega_{ts,i}(x_{it}, x_{is}; \beta, \rho), \tag{9–8}$$

where $\omega_{ts,i}$ is defined as in (9–6). For $t \neq s$, the moment condition requires the evaluation of the bivariate normal c.d.f. and is, therefore, more complicated than imposing just the conditional mean restrictions.

Intuitively, as we include an increasing number of moment conditions, the moment conditions will give an accurate characterization of the conditional distribution. Therefore, the GMM estimator will tend to the MLE. There are, however, serious problems with such an approach. First, higher order moment conditions easily become quite complicated so that the GMM procedure may even be more burdensome than the corresponding MLE. Second, the number of moment conditions increase rapidly with k. It is therefore desirable to have an alternative method for generating moment conditions rather than considering higher order conditional moments.

9.4 Selecting Moment Conditions: The Gallant–Tauchen Approach

Gallant and Tauchen [1996] suggest to use an auxiliary (possibly misspecified) model to generate moment conditions from the scores of the pseudo MLE. The idea behind this approach is that the scores of an accurate representation of the main features of the model (the score generator) may provide efficient moment conditions. In fact, if the auxiliary model "smoothly embed" the structural model, then the GMM estimator derived from the score generator is asymptotically efficient (*Gallant and Tauchen* [1996]).

Consider the panel probit model given in Example 9.4. Using a linear error component model $y_{it} = x_{it}'\gamma + \alpha_i^* + \varepsilon_{it}^*$ as auxiliary model gives rise to the following moments[3]

$$s_{N,1}(\lambda) = \frac{1}{\sigma_{\varepsilon^*}^2 NT} \sum_{t=1}^{T} \sum_{i=1}^{N} (u_{it} - \psi \bar{u}_i) x_{it} \qquad (9\text{--}9)$$

$$s_{N,2}(\lambda) = \frac{1}{N} \sum_{i=1}^{N} \bar{u}_i^2 - \sigma_{\alpha^*}^2 - \frac{1}{T}\sigma_{\varepsilon^*}^2 \qquad (9\text{--}10)$$

$$s_{N,3}(\lambda) = \frac{1}{N(T-1)} \sum_{t=1}^{T} \sum_{i=1}^{N} (u_{it} - \bar{u}_i)^2 - \sigma_{\alpha^*}^2 , \qquad (9\text{--}11)$$

where $\lambda = [\gamma', \sigma_{\alpha^*}^2, \sigma_{\varepsilon^*}^2]'$, $u_{it} = y_{it} - x_{it}'\gamma$, $\bar{u}_i = T^{-1} \sum_t u_{it}$, and $\psi = T\sigma_{\alpha^*}^2 / (T\sigma_{\alpha^*}^2 + \sigma_{\varepsilon^*}^2)$. It is important to note that the variance of the errors in a probit model is not identified and is therefore set to one. As a consequence the moment $s_{N,3}(\lambda)$ is dropped to obtain a nonsingular covariance matrix of the conditional moments.

Although the linear model is misspecified, it may approximate the crucial features of the underlying nonlinear model. Whenever it is possible to derive the relationship between the parameters of the structural and auxiliary model, we are able to compute estimates for the structural model from the estimated auxiliary model.

Let θ denote the vector of structural parameters, (*i.e.*, $\theta = [\beta', \rho]'$ in our example) and

$$f_N(\theta, \lambda) = E_\theta[s_N(\lambda)], \qquad (9\text{--}12)$$

---

[3] These expressions are derived from the scores given in *Hsiao* [1986, p. 39].

denotes the expected scores, where

$$s_N(\lambda) = [s_{N,1}(\lambda), s_{N,2}(\lambda), s_{N,3}(\lambda)]'$$

and E_θ indicates the expectation with respect to the structural model given the parameter vector θ. Then, *Gallant and Tauchen* [1996] suggest to estimate θ by minimizing the objective function

$$\widehat{\theta}_{GT} = \operatorname{argmin}_\theta \{ f_N(\theta, \widetilde{\lambda})' A_N f_N(\theta, \widetilde{\lambda}) \}, \qquad (9\text{--}13)$$

where $\widetilde{\lambda}$ is the pseudo MLE given by $s_N(\widetilde{\lambda}) = 0$ and A_N tends to the optimal weight matrix as $N \to \infty$. If the dimension of $f_N(\theta, \widetilde{\lambda})$ is the same as the number of structural parameters, we can compute $\widehat{\theta}_{GT}$ from solving $f_N(\widehat{\theta}_{GT}, \widetilde{\lambda}) = 0$.

In our example, the moments $f_N(\theta, \widetilde{\lambda})$ can be computed by using the bivariate normal c.d.f. (see Section 9.2). Another possibility, which is particularly useful for more complicated models, is to approximate (9–12) using Monte Carlo techniques (see, *e.g.*, *Gouriéroux and Monfort* [1993] and *Gallant and Tauchen* [1996]).

To compute the GMM estimator we need (estimates for) the derivatives

$$F_N(\theta) = \frac{\partial E_\theta \{ f_N[\theta, \widetilde{\lambda}] \}}{\partial \theta'}, \qquad (9\text{--}14)$$

which is a quite complicated function in general. It is important to notice that in (9–12) the expectation is computed by treating λ as given while in (9–14) $\widetilde{\lambda}$ is a random variable depending on θ. In practice, this expression is estimated using simulation methods.

Usually, the variance of the GMM estimator with optimal weight matrix is estimated as

$$\widehat{V}_N = [F_N(\widehat{\theta})' A_N F_N(\widehat{\theta})]^{-1}.$$

However, for the consistency of this estimator it is required that the auxiliary model is correctly specified so that there exists a value λ^* such that the "score contributions" satisfy

$$E_\theta[s(y_i, X_i; \lambda^*)] = 0 \quad \text{for all } i = 1, \dots, N,$$

where $s_N(\lambda) = \sum_i s(y_i, X_i; \lambda)$. For misspecified auxiliary models we therefore need to apply a different estimator for the covariance matrix of $\widehat{\theta}$ given by

$$\overline{V}_N =$$
$$[F_N(\widehat{\theta})' A_N F_N(\widehat{\theta})]^{-1} F_N(\widehat{\theta})' A_N \overline{\Sigma}_f A_N F_N(\widehat{\theta}) [F_N(\widehat{\theta})' A_N F_N(\widehat{\theta})]^{-1}$$

where

$$\overline{\Sigma}_f = \frac{1}{N} \sum_{i=1}^{N} [s(y_i, X_i; \widetilde{\lambda}) - m_i(\widetilde{\lambda})][s(y_i, X_i; \widetilde{\lambda}) - m_i(\widetilde{\lambda})]' \qquad (9\text{--}15)$$

and

$$m_i(\lambda) = E_\theta[s(y_i, X_i; \lambda)].$$

Obviously, this modification, suggested by *Gallant and Tauchen* [1996] implies a considerable increase in computational burden compared with the conventional estimator.

In sum, although the approach suggested by *Gallant and Tauchen* [1996] is attractive for selecting suitable moment conditions, it implies a great deal of computational effort. Hence, this approach is not recommended for rather simple models considered here for the ease of exposition. If the model becomes much more complex and no convenient expressions for the first moments are available, the Gallant–Tauchen approach seems to be an attractive devise to select useful moments for the GMM procedure.

9.5 A Minimum Distance Approach

It is possible to construct a computationally more convenient minimum distance procedure with the same asymptotic properties as the Gallant–Tauchen estimator. This approach was suggested by *Gouriéroux, Monfort and Renault* [1993].

Applying a Taylor series expansion to the moments derived from the auxiliary model gives

$$
\begin{aligned}
f_N(\theta, \widetilde{\lambda}) &= E_\theta[s_N(\widetilde{\lambda})] \\
&= E_\theta[s_N(\lambda^*)] + H_N(\lambda^*)(\widetilde{\lambda} - \lambda^*) + o_p(T^{-1/2}) \\
&= H_N(\lambda^*)(\widetilde{\lambda} - \lambda^*) + o_p(T^{-1/2})
\end{aligned}
$$

where $H_N(\lambda) = \partial E_\theta[s_N(\lambda)]/\partial \lambda'$ and λ^* is the value of λ such that $E_\theta[s_N(\lambda^*)] = 0$. As the sample size tends to infinity, θ^* converges to the "pseudo-true value" defined in *White* [1982]. If $H_N(\lambda^*)$ is a regular matrix, then minimizing $f_N(\theta, \widetilde{\lambda})' A_N f_N(\theta, \widetilde{\lambda})$ is asymptotically equivalent to

$$\widehat{\theta}_{MD} = \underset{\lambda}{\mathrm{argmin}}\{(\widetilde{\lambda} - \lambda^*)' V_{\widetilde{\lambda}}^{-1} (\widetilde{\lambda} - \lambda^*)\},$$

where $V_{\widetilde{\lambda}} = H_N(\lambda^*)'A_N H_N(\lambda^*)$ tends to the covariance matrix of $\widetilde{\lambda} - \lambda^*$. For convenience the notation does not make explicit the dependence of λ^* on θ.

For computing $\widehat{\theta}_{MD}$ the derivative

$$D_\lambda^*(\theta) = \frac{\partial \lambda^*}{\partial \theta'}$$

needs to be evaluated. Usually, this derivative is much easier to compute than the derivative $F_N(\theta)$ needed to compute the Gallant–Tauchen estimator. Since $E_\theta(\widetilde{\lambda})$ tends to λ^* as $N \to \infty$, this derivative is asymptotically equivalent to

$$\widetilde{D}_\lambda(\theta) = \frac{\partial E_\theta(\widetilde{\lambda})}{\partial \theta'},$$

which can easily be estimated by simulation techniques.

A second important advantage of this variant of the Gallant–Tauchen approach is that the covariance matrix $\Sigma_{MD} = E[(\widehat{\theta}_{MD} - \theta)(\widehat{\theta}_{MD} - \theta)']$ can be estimated as

$$\widetilde{\Sigma}_{MD} = \widetilde{D}_\lambda(\theta)'\widetilde{\Sigma}_\lambda \widetilde{D}_\lambda(\theta)$$

where $\widetilde{\Sigma}_\lambda = E_\theta[(\widetilde{\lambda} - \lambda^*)(\widetilde{\lambda} - \lambda^*)']$, which is much easier to estimate than the expression (9–15).

9.6 Finite Sample Properties

9.6.1 Data Generating Process

To compare the small sample properties of different GMM estimators, we simulate data according to the following model:

$$
\begin{aligned}
y_{it} &= \mathbf{1}(\beta^C + \beta^D x_{it}^D + \beta^N x_{it}^N + u_{it} > 0) \\
x_{it}^D &= \mathbf{1}(\widetilde{x}_{it}^D > 0), & P(\widetilde{x}_{it}^D > 0) &= 0.5 \\
x_{it}^N &= 0.5 x_{i,t-1}^N + 0.05t + \eta_{it}, & \eta_{it} &\sim U[-1,1], \\
u_{it} &= \delta c_i + \varepsilon_{it}, & c_i &\sim N(0,1), \\
\varepsilon_{it} &= \alpha \varepsilon_{i,t-1} + \sigma \widetilde{\varepsilon}_{it}, & \widetilde{\varepsilon}_{it} &\sim N(0,1), \\
i &= 1,\ldots,N, \quad t = 1,\ldots,T.
\end{aligned}
$$

which is also used in *Breitung and Lechner* [1996] and *Bertschek and Lechner* [1998]. The parameters $(\beta^C, \beta^D, \beta^N, \delta, \alpha, \sigma)$ are fixed coefficients and $\mathbf{I}(\cdot)$ is an indicator function, which is one if its argument is true and zero otherwise. The parameter σ is chosen such that the variance of u_{it} is unity. All random numbers are drawn independently over time and individuals. The first regressor is a serially uncorrelated indicator variable, whereas the second regressor is a smooth variable with bounded support. The dependence on lagged values and on a time trend induces a correlation over time. This type of regressor has been suggested by *Nerlove* [1971] and was also used, for example, by *Heckman* [1981].

We set $\beta^C = -0.75$, $\beta^D = \beta^N = 1$ in all simulations and $T^{-1} \sum_{t=1}^{T} \text{var}(u_{it}) = 1$. To represent typical sample sizes encountered in empirical applications we let $N = 100, 400$ and $T = 5, 10$. Depending on the DGP, 500 or 1000 replications (R) were generated. In order to diminish the impact of initial conditions, the dynamic processes have been started at $t = -10$ with $x_{i,t-11}^N = \varepsilon_{i,t-11} = 0$.

In the simulations two different specifications are considered. First, a pure error component model with serially and mutually uncorrelated error components is obtained by setting $\alpha = 0$ and $\delta = \sqrt{0.5}$. Furthermore $\sigma = \sqrt{0.5}$ so that $E(u_{it}) = 1$. The correlation coefficient is $\rho = 0.5$.

The second specification removes the equi-correlation pattern by setting $\alpha = 0.8$, $\delta = 0.2$ and $\sigma = 0.5$. In such a specification, the serial correlation is persistent but declines with an increasing lag length. The maximum correlation coefficient is 0.8 for a single lag and the correlation decrease to 0.4 for a lag length of four (the maximum lag length when letting $T = 5$).

9.6.2 Estimators

The first estimator is the MLE computed as in *Butler and Moffitt* [1982]. The number of evaluation points is set to 5 as a compromise between computational speed and numerical accuracy. The robust estimator according to *White* [1982] is used to estimate the standard errors. The results for this estimator are indicated by the acronym *ML–RE*. The *pooled* estimator denotes the ML estimator ignoring the panel structure of the data. The standard errors are estimated allowing for serial correlation as in *Avery et al.* [1983].

The *infeasible GMM–IV* estimator is the optimal GMM estimator using the conditional mean restrictions (see Section 9.2). To compute the optimal instrument matrix the true correlation ρ_0 is used. *Bertschek and Lechner* [1998] propose a feasible GMM estimator that estimates the unknown quantities in the expression for the optimal instruments by nonparametric methods. The version that performs best in their Monte Carlo study is labeled *GMM–WNP*.

Another approach to obtain the optimal instruments is to get a consistent estimate of the unknown correlation coefficient. The estimator *GMM–IV(param)* proposed here consists of three steps. In the first step a pooled probit model is estimated to obtain consistent estimates $\tilde{\beta}$. Then $T(T-1)/2$ second moments as in eq. (9–8) are used to compute consistent estimates of the correlations. For given values of β, each moment condition depends only on the unknown correlation coefficient, which is bounded between -1 and $+1$. Hence, grid search methods are used to determine the correlation coefficients. For a random effects model, using one such moment condition is sufficient for obtaining a consistent estimate of ρ. However, our estimation procedure allows for different values of the $T(T-1)/2$ correlation coefficients ρ_{ts} $(t, s = 1, \ldots, T)$. This estimator is still optimal even when the covariance structure is more general than the equi-correlation structure of a random effects model.

The pooled probit estimator as well as the GMM estimators with asymptotically optimal instruments are consistent no matter of the true error correlation. Furthermore, all GMM estimators have the same limiting distribution whether the true or consistently estimated optimal instruments are used. To yield a nonparametric estimate of the optimal instruments, a nearest–neighbor approach is applied (see *Bertschek and Lechner* [1998] for details). This resulting estimator is labeled as *GMM–WNP*.

Following *Gallant and Tauchen* [1996] we employ simple auxiliary models as score generators. First we use a linear error components model with scores given in (9–9) and (9–10). To compute the expectation of the scores $f_N(\theta, \tilde{\lambda})$ we generate 100 replications of the model and compute the average of the scores. Using a Taylor expansion

$$f_N(\theta + \delta, \widetilde{\lambda}) = f_N(\theta, \widetilde{\lambda}) + \frac{\partial f_N(\theta, \widetilde{\lambda})}{\partial \theta'} \delta + \widetilde{r}, \qquad (9\text{--}16)$$

where $\widetilde{r}$ is a remainder term of order $O(\delta^2)$, the derivatives are estimated by a least squares regression of $f_N(\theta + \delta, \widetilde{\lambda}) - f_N(\theta, \widetilde{\lambda})$ on δ, where δ is a vector of normally distributed random numbers with zero mean and $E(\delta^2) = 0.02$. We use 100 realizations of δ for computing the regression lines. This regression estimator has the advantage that it does not suffer from problems due to the discontinuity and non-differentiability of the simulator. At every iteration step of θ, the same sequence of random numbers are used. Using the *pooled* estimator with an estimate of ρ based on the small–sigma estimate (*Breitung and Lechner* [1996]) as initial values, the algorithm usually converges after 5-10 iterations. The resulting estimates are labeled as *GT–score*.

Our practical experiences with such an algorithm suggest that the convergence properties crucially depend on the number of replications used to estimate the conditional mean and derivatives of the moments. In particular, the least squares estimate of the derivatives requires at least 100 replications to obtain reliable estimates of the gradients. Furthermore, the step–length δ in the Taylor expansion should be small enough to avoid a substantial bias but must be large enough to achieve acceptable properties of the least squares estimator. In our simulations we found that a value of $E(\delta^2) = 0.02$ provides a reasonable trade–off for our data generating process. For other processes, however, suitable values for δ or the number of replications may be different.

Adding the scores from the (cross section) probit estimator applied to the pooled dataset we obtain three additional moments. The weight matrix are computed using the *GT–score* estimator. The computational details for the simulations are the same as for the *GT–score* procedure. The resulting estimator is labeled as *GT–score$^+$*. Since the estimator employs the instruments of the pooled probit estimator, it is asymptotically more efficient than the *pooled* estimator.

For both estimators using the Gallant–Tauchen approach the respective minimum distance estimators are computed. Accordingly, we denote these estimators as *GT–MD* and *GT–MD$^+$*. We use 300 Monte Carlo realizations of the model for computing the moments. The matrix of derivatives $\tilde{D}_\lambda(\theta)$ were computed by least squares using a Taylor expansion of $\tilde{\lambda}$.

To compare the performance of the estimators we compute the root mean square error (RMSE) and the median absolute error (MAE). For the estimated standard errors of the coefficient we compute the relative bias. The precise definitions of these measures are given in Table 9.1.

9.7 Results

Table 9.2 presents the results for the specification with pure random effects. It turns out that with respect to RMSE and MAE the MLE performs best among all estimators. The second best estimator is the GMM estimator based on the optimal instruments derived from the conditional mean restrictions (*Infeasible GMM*). However, this estimator is based on a known correlation parameter ρ_0 so that such an estimator is of limited use in practice.

With respect to the other GMM estimators, the ranking is not as clear. Generally, the GMM procedures using information about the error correlation like the feasible versions of *GMM–IV* or the estimators using a linear error component model as a score generator perform better than the *pooled* estimator ignoring the error correlation altogether.

Comparing the small sample properties of the two asymptotically equivalent GMM estimators *GMM–IV(param)* and *GMM–WNP*, the latter estimator appears to be superior for all DGP's, with the exception of the random effects DGP with $N = 400$ and $T = 5$. The potential small sample problems of these estimators is related to the estimation of the inverse of the conditional covariance matrix of the residuals for each individual. *GMM–WNP* uses nonparametric methods that perform very well even in fairly small samples (see *Bertschek and Lechner* [1998] for details). The problem with *GMM–IV(param)* is that some of the estimated ρ_{ts} coefficients may end up at the boundary of the parameter space [-1,+1] when N is 'not large enough'. This is a particular problem when the number of coefficients to be estimated gets large (45 in the case of $T = 10$). A potential remedy is to enforce equality of the ρ_{ts} in the second step of the estimation. There are however two drawbacks of such a procedure. First, the estimator is no longer asymptotically efficient when the true DGP is different from the random effect model. Second, the simplicity of the estimator is lost. Therefore, we conclude that in applications *GMM–IV(param)* may be a preferable option only if an estimate of the correlation structure of latent residuals is of interest and if the dimension N is sufficiently large relative to the dimension T.

The Gallant–Tauchen estimators derived from a linear error component model seem to work well. This is perhaps surprising since the linear model is quite a crude approximation to the panel probit model. In fact, there is much room for improving the fit of the auxiliary model. For example, the nonlinear mean function and heteroskedasticity of the errors are important features which are neglected by the linear approximation. Nevertheless, the scores of the linear model obviously provide useful moment conditions to be exploited by a GMM procedure.

In small samples, the original version and the minimum distance variant perform somewhat differently. For the smaller set of moment conditions the Gallant–Tauchen GMM estimator (*GT–Score*) outperforms the respective minimum distance estimator (*GT–MD*), while for the enhanced set of moment conditions the (*GT–MD+*) estimator performs better than the (*GT–Score+*) estimator. In all, however, the differences are small relative to the simulation error.

The estimation of the standard errors for the coefficients are extremely biased for Gallant–Tauchen estimators. The reason is that the standard errors are estimated assuming a correctly specified auxiliary model. Of course, this is not true in our application and it turns out that the resulting bias can be immense. Unfortunately, the computational effort for correcting the estimates along the lines suggested by *Gallant and Tauchen* [1996] was beyond the time schedule for the present work.

The problems with the estimation of the standard errors can be side-stepped by using the minimum distance approach. In fact, the estimation of the standard errors for the (*GT–MD+*) procedure seems to perform acceptable. However, the standard errors for the (*GT–MD*) estimator still possess a substantial bias.

To study the performance of the estimators under more general conditions, we introduce a persistent autocorrelation in addition to the random effects. Obviously, such a data generating process is difficult to distinguish empirically in a sample with a small number of time periods. All GMM estimators designed for the error component model remain consistent in the presence of a more general form of serial correlation. Thus, it is interesting to know whether the efficiency ranking is robust to differences in the autocorrelation pattern. Table 9.3 presents the results for such a process.

The conclusions from simulations with other sample sizes are qualitatively similar. It turns out that the relative performance of the estimators is roughly similar to the case of a pure random effects model. However, it appears that the *ML–RE* estimator looses most of its relative advantages. Furthermore, the Gallant–Tauchen type of estimators perform worse than the competitors based on the conditional mean function. On the other hand, the *GMM–WNP* estimator turns out to have the most attractive properties. It is simple to compute and has favorable small sample properties for the DGP considered here.

9.8 An Application

An empirical example for our discussion of panel probit models is the analysis of firms' innovative activity as a response to imports and foreign direct investment (FDI) as considered in *Bertschek* [1995]. The main hypothesis put forward in that paper is that imports and inward FDI have positive effects on the innovative activity of domestic firms. The intuition for this effect is that imports and FDI represent a competitive threat to domestic firms. Competition on the domestic market is enhanced and the profitability of the domestic firms might be reduced.

As a consequence, these firms have to produce more efficiently. Increasing the innovative activity is one possibility to react to this competitive threat and to maintain the market position. The dependent variable available in the data takes the value one if a product innovation has been realized within the last year and the value zero otherwise. The binary character of this variable leads us to formulate the model in terms of a latent variable that represents for instance the firms' unobservable expenditures for innovation that is linearly related to the explanatory variables.

The firm–level data have been collected by the Ifo-Institute, Munich ('Ifo-Konjunkturtest') and have been merged with official statistics from the German Statistical Yearbooks. The binary dependent variable indicates whether a firm reports having realized a product innovation within the last year or not. The independent variables refer to the market structure, in particular the market size of the industry *ln(sales)*, the shares of imports and FDI in the supply on the domestic market *import share* and *FDI–share*, the *productivity* as a measure of the competitiveness of the industry as well as two variables indicating whether a firm belongs to the *raw materials* or to the *investment goods* industry. Moreover, including the *relative firm size* allows us to take account of the innovation — firm size relation often discussed in the literature. Hence, all variables with the exception of the firm size are measured at the industry-level (for descriptive statistics see Table 9.4).

The estimators applied to the example include the simplest one (*pooled* with GMM standard errors), both feasible GMM estimators based on second order moments and the minimum distance versions of the Gallant–Tauchen estimator. For the latter estimator, we use 1000 Monte Carlo replications for the simulated moments as well as its derivatives. Results for other estimators for that example can be found in *Bertschek and Lechner* [1998].

The results of the different GMM procedures are presented in Table 9.5. In all they are quite similar and yield the same conclusions. Both *import share* and *FDI–share* have positive and significant effects on product innovative activity. As expected by the Schumperian hypothesis that large firms are more innovative than small firms the *firm size* variable has a positive and significant impact. The coefficient of *productivity* is significantly negative for *pooled*, *GMM–IV(param)* and *GMM–WNP* but insignificant when using the *GT–MD*.

An interesting finding is that the estimated standard errors of *GT–MD* tend to be substantially greater than the corresponding estimates of the alternative estimators. We have tried different numbers of replications or values of δ. The problem is that if δ is a small number, then the simulation error is large in relative terms, while for large values of δ, the estimates of the derivative are biased. The standard errors presented in Table 9.5 are based on 10.000 replications and $\delta = 0.05 \cdot \tilde{\beta}_P$, where $\tilde{\beta}_P$ denotes the *pooled* estimator. We decided to choose a relative step size, because the parameter values appears to be quite different in magnitude. Repeating the computation of the standard errors using a different sequence of random numbers shows that these estimates reveal a considerable variability. Hence, these estimates do not seem very reliable and must be interpreted with caution.

It is interesting to consider the serial correlation of the errors between different time periods (see Table 9.6) They are obtained as a by-product in the computation of the second step of *GMM–IV(param)* (see Section 9.6.2). It turns out that the autocorrelation function decays with increasing lag length. This result suggests that an autoregressive pattern is more suitable than the equi-correlation implied by an error component model. In any case, the GMM estimators remain consistent regardless of the form of the autocorrelation function.

9.9 Concluding Remarks

GMM is an attractive approach for estimating complex models like nonlinear error component models popular in current econometric research. Simple estimators can be constructed by using restrictions implied by the conditional mean function. Asymptotically optimal GMM estimators based on the conditional mean function are obtained by using a parametric or nonparametric approach. Our Monte Carlo results clearly indicate that the nonparametric approach is superior in small samples.

In addition we consider further moment conditions derived from higher order moments or the "score generator" as proposed by *Gallant and Tauchen* [1996]. From a practical perspective the latter approach is appealing, because it provides simple moment conditions and may yield highly efficient estimators. However, the computational effort is considerable for such estimators. Following *Gouriéroux et al.* [1993], we adopt a minimum distance analog of the Gallant–Tauchen estimator, which is much simpler to compute and generally renders valid estimates of the standard errors.

Our Monte Carlo results demonstrate that the GMM procedures considered in this paper perform well relative to the MLE. Although the Gallant–Tauchen estimator is based on a very simple "score generator", the efficiency comes close to the MLE. However, the computational burden of the Gallant–Tauchen approach is immense and there are serious problems when estimating the standard errors for the parameters. Therefore, we do not recommend this estimator for models like the error component probit models, where much simpler GMM procedures with better small sample properties are available. However, if the model is more complicated and simple GMM estimators do not exist, the Gallant–Tauchen approach may be a useful devise for providing efficient moment conditions.

Table 9.1: Measures of Accuracy Used in the Monte Carlo Study

RMSE:	root MSE	$\sqrt{\frac{100}{R}\sum_{r=1}^{R}(\widehat{\theta}_r - \theta_0)^2}$
MAE:	median abs. error	$\text{median}_r |\widehat{\theta}_r - \theta_0|$
BIAS(SE):	bias of est. stand. error in %	$\frac{100}{R}\sum_{r=1}^{R}[\widehat{\sigma}_r(\widehat{\theta}_r) - \sigma(\widehat{\theta})]/\sigma(\widehat{\theta})$

Note: $\widehat{\theta}_r$ denotes the rth realization of the simulated estimator for θ. $\widehat{\sigma}_r(\widehat{\theta}_r)$ indicates the rth estimate of the standard errors of $\widehat{\theta}$ based on the asymptotic standard errors. $\sigma(\widehat{\theta})$ indicates the standard errors computed from the Monte Carlo replications.

Table 9.2: Simulation Results for Pure Random Effects
$(\alpha = 0, \delta = \sqrt{0.5})$

	RMSE × 10		MAE × 10		bias (SE) in %	
	β_D	β_N	β_D	β_N	β_D	β_N
N=100			$T = 5$, 1000 replications			
ML-RE	1.09	1.22	0.69	0.78	−5.4	0.4
Infeasible GMM	1.09	1.29	0.73	0.84	0.2	−3.9
Pooled	1.21	1.34	0.75	0.85	−1.4	−0.3
GMM–IV(param)	1.35	1.62	0.83	0.93	−10.4	−14.3
GMM–WNP	1.14	1.29	0.76	0.86	−0.7	−0.3
GT-Score	1.24	1.24	0.84	0.97	82*	27*
GT-Score$^+$	1.22	1.30	0.73	0.97	−85*	−84*
GT-MD	1.37	1.37	1.01	0.91	−12.2	−9.1
GT-MD$^+$	1.21	1.31	0.75	1.00	−3.6	−4.3
N=400			$T = 5$, 1000 replications			
ML-RE	0.52	0.61	0.35	0.42	0.8	−2.2
Infeasible GMM	0.55	0.60	0.37	0.39	-0.5	2.4
Pooled	0.58	0.67	0.39	0.45	2.0	−1.0
GMM–IV(param)	0.55	0.62	0.38	0.42	−1.9	1.4
GMM–WNP	0.54	0.63	0.36	0.43	1.9	−0.6
GT-Score	0.58	0.67	0.36	0.47	215*	108*
GT-Score$^+$	0.62	0.67	0.41	0.46	−87*	−86*
GT-MD	0.66	0.75	0.41	0.50	9.2	8.5
GT-MD$^+$	0.58	0.65	0.37	0.43	−5.7	−6.1
N=100			$T = 10$, 500 replications			
ML-RE	0.74	0.85	0.52	0.53	1.2	5.7
Infeasible GMM	0.80	0.89	0.55	0.61	−4.8	1.1
Pooled	0.86	0.94	0.58	0.61	−0.5	5.0
GMM–IV(param)	2.72	3.71	1.38	1.54	4458	739
GMM–WNP	0.84	0.96	0.58	0.60	−2.4	1.2
GT-Score	0.82	0.99	0.56	0.70	14.9*	−12.0*
GT-Score$^+$	0.80	1.00	0.53	0.64	−85.0*	−86.1*
GT-MD	0.93	1.13	0.66	0.71	8.9	−5.4
GT-MD$^+$	0.78	0.98	0.53	0.62	−0.7	−8.2

Table 9.2: (continued)

	RMSE $\times$ 10		MAE $\times$ 10		bias (SE) in %	
	β_D	β_N	β_D	β_N	β_D	β_N
N=400			$T = 10$, 500 replications			
ML-RE	0.37	0.45	0.24	0.30	1.4	-0.3
Infeasible GMM	0.37	0.45	0.24	0.30	1.4	-0.3
Pooled	0.41	0.49	0.28	0.34	3.9	0.2
GMM–IV(param)	0.58	0.77	0.34	0.40	-19	-27
GMM–WNP	0.40	0.47	0.26	0.32	-1.4	-1.7
GT-Score	0.41	0.46	0.27	0.29	159*	129*
GT-Score$^+$	0.43	0.47	0.27	0.31	-86*	-85*
GT-MD	0.46	0.48	0.30	0.32	-12	-8.9
GT-MD$^+$	0.45	0.42	0.26	0.28	-5.8	4.6

Note: * The estimates of the standard errors are based on the assumption of a correctly specified model.

Table 9.3: Simulation Results for AR(1) and Random Effects
$$(\alpha = 0.8, \delta = 0.2)$$

	RMSE × 10		MAE × 10		bias (SE) in %	
N=100			$T = 5$, 1000 replications			
ML-RE	0.61	0.64	0.40	0.44	4.0	2.2
Infeasible GMM	0.61	0.56	0.41	0.45	−0.2	−1.3
Pooled	0.70	0.73	0.47	0.51	−1.3	0.9
GMM–IV(param)	0.63	0.68	0.42	0.47	−0.2	−1.7
GMM–WNP	0.61	0.68	0.41	0.46	2.2	−0.3
GT-Score	0.68	0.71	0.47	0.47	472*	388*
GT-Score+	0.68	0.70	0.45	0.47	−85*	−85*
GT-MD	0.68	0.71	0.45	0.47	−22	-19
GT-MD+	0.60	0.64	0.41	0.40	−8.3	−4.6

Note: * The estimates of the standard errors are based on the assumption of a correctly specified model.

Table 9.4: Descriptive Statistics

		mean	std.dev.
ln(sales)	ln of ind. sales in DM	10.540	1.00
Rel. firm size	ratio of empl. in business unit to empl. in industry	0.074	0.290
Imp. share	ratio of industry imps. to (sales + imps.)	0.250	0.120
FDI-share	ratio of industry FDI (sales + imports)	0.046	0.047
Productivity	ratio of industry V.A. to industry empl.	0.090	0.033
Raw mat.	= 1 if firm is in 'raw mat.'	0.087	0.280
Invest.	= 1 if firm is in 'invest. goods'	0.500	0.500
Dept. var.	= 1 if prod. in. is realized	0.600	0.490

Table 9.5: Estimation Results for the Innovation Probit

	pooled	GMM-WNP	GMM-IV (param)	GT-MD	GT-MD+
ln(sales)	0.18	0.15	0.17	0.15	0.17
	(0.04)	(0.04)	(0.04)	(0.06)	(0.03)
R. size	1.07	0.95	1.20	0.90	0.95
	(0.31)	(0.20)	(0.31)	(0.21)	(0.20)
Imp. sh.	1.13	1.14	1.12	0.99	1.05
	(0.24)	(0.24)	(0.24)	(0.29)	(0.21)
FDI sh.	2.85	2.59	2.78	2.87	2.88
	(0.68)	(0.59)	(0.68)	(0.79)	(0.53)
Prod.	-2.34	−1.91	−2.54	−2.49	−2.50
	(1.32)	(0.82)	(1.24)	(1.67)	(0.70)
R. mat.	−0.28	−0.28	−0.24	−0.20	−0.24
	(0.13)	(0.12)	(0.13)	(0.11)	(0.07)
Invest.	0.19	0.21	0.19	0.20	0.20
	(0.06)	(0.06)	(0.06)	(0.08)	(0.05)
Const.	−1.96	−1.74	−1.86	−1.68	−1.90
	(0.38)	(0.37)	(0.37)	(0.54)	(0.31)

Table 9.6 Estimated Correlation Matrix

	1985	1986	1987	1988
1984	0.60	0.65	0.58	0.48
1985		0.64	0.56	0.37
1986			0.68	0.58
1987				0.64

References

Arellano, M. and Bond, S. [1991]: Some Tests of Specification for Panel Data: Monte Carlo Evidence and an Application to Employment Equations, *Review of Economic Studies,* 58, 277–297.

Avery, R., Hansen, L. and Hotz, V. [1983]: Multiperiod Probit Models and Orthogonality Condition Estimation, *International Economic Review,* 24, 21-35.

Bertschek, I. [1995]: Product and Process Innovation as a Response to Increasing Imports and Foreign Direct Investment, *Journal of Industrial Economics,* 43[4]; 341–357.

Bertschek, I. and Lechner, M. [1998]: Convenient Estimators for the Panel Probit Model, *Journal of Econometrics,* (forthcoming).

Boersch-Supan, A. and Hajivassiliou, V.A. [1993]: Smooth Unbiased Multivariate Probabilities Simulators for Maximum Likelihood Estimation of Limited Dependent Variable Models, *Journal of Econometrics,* 58, 347-368.

Breitung, J. and Lechner, M. [1996]: Estimation de modèles non linéaires sur données de panel par la méthode des moments généralisés, *Economie et Prevision,* 126, 191–204. (The English version is available as SFB discussion paper No. 67 / 1995 , Humboldt-University, Berlin).

Butler, J.S. and Moffitt, R. [1982]: A Computationally Efficient Quadrature Procedure for the One-Factor Multinomial Probit Model, *Econometrica,* 50, 761-764.

Chamberlain, G. [1980]: Analysis of Covariance with Qualitative Data, *Review of Economic Studies,* 47, 225-238.

Chamberlain, G. [1984]: Panel Data, in Griliches, Z. and Intriligator, M.D. [eds.], *Handbook of Econometrics,* Vol. II, Ch. 22, Amsterdam: North-Holland.

Gallant, A.R. and Tauchen, G. [1996]: Which Moments to Match, *Econometric Theory,* 12, 657–681.

Gouriéroux, C. [1996]: Introduction to Nonlinear Models, in: L. Mátyás and P. Sevestre [eds], *The Econometrics of Panel Data,* 2. vol., Chap. 15, 399–409, Dordrecht: Kluwer.

Gouriéroux, C. and Monfort, A. [1993]: Simulation-based Inference: a survey with special reference to panel data models, *Journal of Econometrics,* 59, 5–33.

Gouriéroux, C. Monfort, A. and Renault, E. [1993]: Indirect Inference, *Journal of Applied Econometrics,* 8, S85–S118.

Guilkey, D.K. and Murphy, J.L. [1993]: Estimation and Testing in the Random Effects Probit Model, *Journal of Econometrics,* 59, 301-317.

Hajivassiliou, V.A. [1993]: Simulation Estimation Methods for Limited Dependent Variable Models, in: Maddala, G.S., Rao, C.R. and Vinod, H.D. [eds.], *Handbook of Statistics,* Vol. 11: Econometrics, Ch. 19, Amsterdam: North-Holland.

Hansen, L.P. **[1982]:** Large Sample Properties of Generalized Methods of Moments Estimators, *Econometrica,* 50, 1029–1055.

Heckman, J.J. **[1981]:** The Incidental Parameters Problem and the Problem of Initial Conditions in Estimating a Discrete Time - Discrete Data Stochastic Process and Some Monte Carlo Evidence, in: Manski, C. and McFadden, D. [eds]: *Structural Analysis of Discrete Data,* Cambridge: MIT-Press.

Honoré, B. **[1992]:** Trimmed LAD and Least Squares Estimation of Truncated and Censored Regression Models with Fixed Effects, *Econometrica,* 60, 533–565.

Honoré, B. **[1993]:** Orthogonality Conditions for Tobit Models with Fixed Effects and Lagged Dependent Variables, *Journal of Econometrics,* 59, 35–61.

Hsiao, C. **[1992]:** Logit and Probit Models, in: Matyas, L. and Sevestre, P. [eds.], *The Econometrics of Panel Data,* Ch. 11, Dordrecht: Kluwer.

Keane, M.P. **[1993]:** Simulation Estimation for Panel Data Models with Limited Dependent Variables, in Maddala, G.S., Rao, C.R. and Vinod, H.D. (eds.), *Handbook of Statistics,* Vol. 11: Econometrics, Ch. 20, Amsterdam: North-Holland.

Keane, M.P. **[1994]:** A Computationally Practical Simulation Estimator for Panel Data, *Econometrica,* 62, 95-116.

Lechner, M. and Breitung, J. **[1996]:** Some GMM Estimation Methods and Specification Tests for Nonlinear Models, in: L. Mátyás and P. Sevestre [eds], *The Econometrics of Panel Data,* 2. vol., Chap. 15, 399–409, Dordrecht: Kluwer.

McFadden **[1989]:** A Method of Simulated Moments for Estimation of Discrete Response Models Without Numerical Integration, *Econometrica,* 57, 995–1026.

McFadden, D. and Ruud, P.A. **[1995]:** Estimation by Simulation, *The Review of Economics and Statistics,* 76, 591-608.

Nerlove, M. **[1971]:** Further Evidence on the Estimation of Dynamic Economic Relations From a Time Series of Cross Sections, *Econometrica,* 39, 359-383.

Newey, W.K. **[1993]:** Efficient Estimation of Models with Conditional Moment Restrictions, in Maddala, G.S., Rao, C.R. and Vinod, H.D. [eds.], *Handbook of Statistics,* Vol. 11: Econometrics, Ch. 16, Amsterdam: North-Holland.

Newey, W.K. and McFadden, D.L. **[1994]:** Large Sample Estimation and Hypothesis Testing, in: Engle, R.F and McFadden, D.L. [eds], *Handbook of Econometrics,* Vol. IV, Elsevier: North Holland.

White, H. **[1982]:** Maximum Likelihood Estimation of Misspecified Models, *Econometrica,* 50, 1–26.

Chapter   10

SIMULATION BASED METHOD OF

MOMENTS

Roman Liesenfeld and Jörg Breitung

The estimation of unknown parameters generally involves optimizing a criterion function based on the likelihood function or a set of moment restrictions. Unfortunately, for many econometric models the likelihood function and/or the relevant moment restrictions do not have a tractable analytical form in terms of the unknown parameters rendering thereby the estimation by maximum likelihood (ML) or the generalized method of moments (GMM) infeasible. This estimation problem typically arises when unobservable variables enter the model nonlinearly, leading to multiple integrals in the criterion function, which cannot be evaluated by standard numerical procedures. Prominent examples of such models in financial econometrics are continous–time models of stock prices or interest rates and discrete–time stochastic volatility models.

Until recently, estimation problems due to the lack of some kind tractable criterion function were often circumvented by using approximations of the model producing criterion functions simple enough to be evaluated. However, using such approximations may lead to inconsistent estimates of the parameters of interest. An alternative solution in such cases which has received increased attention over the last few years, is the use of Monte Carlo simulation methods to compute an otherwise intractable criterion function.[1]

---

[1]   It is worth noting that Monte Carlo simulation methods have already been used for a long time in Bayesian econometrics to evaluate posterior distributions, see *e.g., Kloek and van Dijk* [1978].

Seminal for the development of this type of estimation procedures were the contributions of *McFadden* [1989] and *Pakes and Pollard* [1989] who introduced the Method of Simulated Moments (MSM) in a cross sectional context. This approach, which was extended to time series applications by *Lee and Ingram* [1991] and *Duffie and Singleton* [1993], modifies the traditional GMM estimator by using moments computed from simulated data rather than the analytical ones. Like the GMM estimator, the MSM estimator is consistent and asymptotically normal when the number of observations approaches infinity, and is asymptotically equivalent to the "usual" GMM estimator if the number of simulations goes to infinity. However, in a fully parametric model the MSM, just as the GMM, is inefficient relative to procedures based on the full likelihood due to the arbitrary choice of moment restrictions. This issue is addressed by the indirect inference estimators proposed by *Gouriéroux, Monfort and Renault* [1993], *Bansal, Gallant, Hussey and Tauchen* [1993], [1995] and *Gallant and Tauchen* [1996a]. These approaches which represent extensions of the MSM introduce an auxiliary model in order to estimate the parameters of the model of interest. The first version of the indirect inference as proposed by *Gouriéroux, Monfort and Renault* [1993] uses the parameters of the auxiliary model to define the GMM criterion function, whereas in the second version as suggested by *Bansal, Gallant, Hussey and Tauchen* [1993], [1995] and *Gallant and Tauchen* [1996a] the scores of the auxiliary model generate the moment restrictions used in the GMM criterion function. Since in both procedures the GMM criterion is an intractable function in terms of the parameters of interest, simulations are used to evaluate it. Both indirect inference estimators are consistent and asymptotically normal as the number of observations goes to infinity and approach the fully efficient estimator if the auxiliary model is appropriately chosen. When the auxiliary model is based on the semi–nonparametric model of *Gallant and Nychka* [1987], as proposed by *Gallant and Tauchen* [1996a], one may hope that the loss of efficiency of the indirect inference estimator is small.

The purpose of this chapter is to give a selective review of the MSM techniques, and to illustrate their applications to financial models.

Besides these moment based simulation approaches, a variety of other simulation estimators are proposed in the literature including simulated maximum likelihood (*Danielsson and Richard* [1993] and *Richard and Zhang* [1997]), and Markov Chain Monte Carlo procedures (*Jacquier, Polson and Rossi* [1994] and *Kim, Shephard and Chip* [1996]). Surveys on these likelihood based simulation methods are given by *Ghysels, Harvey and Renault* [1996] and *Shephard* [1996]. An extensive overview of simulation based estimation methods including MSM and likelihood based procedures can be found in *Gouriéroux and Monfort* [1996].

This chapter is organized as follows. In Section 10.1 we outline the estimation context and give some examples. The MSM and the indirect inference estimator are discussed in Sections 10.2 and 10.3, respectively. Section 10.4 reviews the semi–nonparametric auxiliary model and in Section 10.5 we address selected practical issues concerning the application of these estimators. We conclude in Section 10.6.

10.1 General Setup and Applications

Let y_t, $t = 1, \ldots, T$ denote an n-dimensional vector of observable dependent variables and x_t a k-dimensional vector of observable strongly exogenous variables. For expositional convenience it is assumed that y_t and x_t are stationary. The nonlinear dynamic model is characterized by the conditional density $h_0(y_t|z_t)$, where $z_t = [y'_{t-1}, \ldots, y'_1, y'_0, x'_t, \ldots, x'_1]'$ is the vector of conditioning variables and the initial conditions are represented by y_0. We want to estimate the p-dimensional parameter vector θ from the model $\mathcal{M} := \{h(y_t|z_t; \theta), \theta \in \Theta\}$, where Θ denotes the parameter space. The true value θ_0 is a unique value of θ such that $h_0(y_t|z_t) = h(y_t|z_t; \theta_0)$. In the following, we use $h(\cdot)$ as a generic notation for all density functions.

The estimation of θ_0 is generally based on the likelihood function $L_T(\theta) = \prod_{t=1}^{T} h(y_t|z_t; \theta)$ or on moment restrictions based on a set of moments such as $E[y_t|z_t]$ or $E[y_t y'_t|z_t]$. Here we are interested in the cases where the likelihood function or the relevant moments have an intractable form, making the ML or GMM procudures infeasible. Nevertheless, we assume that the model allows us to simulate values of the process $\{y_t\}$ for a given value of the parameter vector θ and the initial conditions y_0.

For dynamic models with lagged endogenous variables two different simulation schemes exist (see, *Gouriéroux and Monfort* [1996, p. 17]). If the model admits a *reduced form* $y_t = \varrho(z_t, \varepsilon_t; \theta)$, where ε_t is an error term stochastically independent of z_t and with a known distribution independent of θ, simulated random variables $y_t^{(r)}(\theta)$, $(r = 1, \ldots, R)$ from the distribution $h(y_t|z_t; \theta)$ can be generated as follows. Artificial random variables $\varepsilon_t^{(r)}$ from the distribution of ε_t are generated and used to calculate

$$y_t^{(r)}(\theta) = \varrho(z_t, \varepsilon_t^{(r)}; \theta)$$

for the observed values of $z_t = [y'_{t-1}, \ldots, y'_1, y'_0, x'_t, \ldots, x'_1]'$ and a value of the parameter vector θ. For a large number of replications R, the empirical distribution of the simulated values $y_t^{(r)}(\theta)$, $(r = 1, \ldots, R)$ approximates the conditional distribution $h(y_t|z_t; \theta)$ for every t. Since the simulations are performed conditionally on the observed lagged endogenous variables, this simulation scheme is called *conditional simulations*. The second approach, termed *path simulations*, is to generate simulated values of y_t conditionally on simulated lagged endogenous variables, *i.e.*, conditionally on $z_t^{(r)}(\theta) = [y_{t-1}^{(r)}(\theta)', \ldots, y_1^{(r)}(\theta)', y'_0, x'_t, \ldots, x'_1]'$, using some kind of recursion. For large R, the empirical joint distribution of $y_1^{(r)}(\theta), \ldots, y_T^{(r)}(\theta)$, $(r = 1, \ldots, R)$ approximates the distribution $h(y_1, \ldots, y_T|x_1, \ldots, x_T; \theta)$.

We illustrate next these procedures using some financial applications.[2]

EXAMPLE 10.1 **Discrete–time Stochastic Volatility Model**

The standard discrete–time stochastic volatility (SV) model proposed by *Taylor* [1986], [1994] and others is given by

$$y_t = \exp\{w_t^*/2\}u_t \tag{10–1}$$

$$w_t^* = \gamma + \delta w_{t-1}^* + \nu\eta_t, \qquad t = 1, \ldots, T, \tag{10–2}$$

---

[2] As in most financial econometrics applications, a time series framework is used here. Examples for cross sectional applications are given by *Gouriéroux and Monfort* [1993], [1996] and *Stern* [1997].

where y_t is the observable return of a financial asset and w_t^* is the unobservable log volatility. The error processes u_t and η_t are mutually and serially independent with known distributions. In accounting for the observed autocorrelation in the variance of financial time series, this SV model represents an alternative to the ARCH and GARCH specifications proposed by *Engle* [1982] and *Bollerslev* [1986]. Since the latent log volatility w_t^* enters the model in a nonlinear form, the conditional density $h(y_t|z_t; \theta)$ with $\theta = [\gamma, \delta, \nu]'$ and $z_t = [y_{t-1}, \ldots, y_1, y_0]'$ does not have an explicit analytical form. To obtain the (marginal) likelihood function associated with the observable variables, the latent variables are "integrated out" from the joint distribution of $y_1, \ldots, y_T, w_1^*, \ldots, w_T^*$ denoted by $h(y_1, \ldots, y_T, w_1^*, \ldots, w_T^*|\theta)$. This distribution can be factorized as $h(y_1, \ldots, y_T, w_1^*, \ldots, w_T^*|\theta) = \prod_{t=1}^{T} h(y_t|w_t^*; \theta)h(w_t^*|w_{t-1}^*; \theta)$, where $h(y_t|w_t^*; \theta)$ is the conditional density of the returns given the log volatility and $h(w_t^*|w_{t-1}^*; \theta)$ denotes the conditional density of the log volatility given its past value. Hence, for a given initial value of the log volatility w_0^* the marginal likelihood has the following form

$$L_T(\theta) = \int \cdots \int \prod_{t=1}^{T} h(y_t|w_t^*; \theta)h(w_t^*|w_{t-1}^*; \theta) \, dw_1^* \ldots dw_T^* \, .$$

For this T-dimensional integral no closed form solution exists, nor can standard numerical methods be applied to evaluate it making the ML estimation infeasible. Furthermore, even if the standard SV model could be estimated by GMM using unconditional moments such as $E[|y_t|]$, $E[y_t^2]$ or $E[y_t^2 y_{t-1}^2]$, GMM is relatively inefficient, especially, if the persistence parameter δ is close to one (see, *e.g.*, *Jacquier, Polson and Rossi* [1994] and *Andersen and Sørensen* [1996]). However, the SV model given by (10–1) and (10–2) defines a simple data generating process which allows to generate values from the joint distribution $h(y_1, \ldots, y_T|\theta)$ implied by the model using path simulations. Note though, that conditional simulations from $h(y_t|y_{t-1}, \ldots, y_0; \theta)$ appear to be infeasible since the SV model does not admit an explicit expression of

the reduced form in terms of lagged endogenous variables
$y_t = \varrho(y_{t-1}, \ldots, y_0, \varepsilon_t; \theta)$.

∎

EXAMPLE 10.2 **Stochastic Differential Equations**

Consider the following scalar stochastic differential equation:

$$dv_t = a(v_t, \theta)dt + b(v_t, \theta)dW_t , \qquad 0 \leq t \leq N , \qquad (10\text{--}3)$$

where $a(v_t, \theta)$ and $b(v_t, \theta)$ are the drift and the diffusion function, respectively, and W_t is a Brownian motion. Such continuous–time processes are often used to model stock prices and interest rates. In practice, however, the variables are observable only at some discrete (possibly equispaced) points. Hence, the observable variables y_t, $(t = 1, \ldots, T)$ are given by $y_t = v_{t\cdot\Delta}$ for some $\Delta > 0$, where the time interval between two observations is $[t, t+\Delta)$. For arbitrary drift and diffusion functions, the distribution of the observable variables generally does not have a closed form expression. A closed form can be obtained only for some special drift and diffusion functions. As an example, consider the square root process proposed by *Cox, Ingersoll and Ross* [1985] to model the evolution of interest rates

$$dv_t = (\alpha_0 + \alpha_1 v_t)dt + \beta_0 \sqrt{v_t}dW_t .$$

This stochastic differential equation implies a joint distribution of the observable variables $y_1, \ldots, y_T$ given by

$$\prod_{t=1}^{T} h(y_t|y_{t-1}; \theta) ,$$

where $h(y_t|y_{t-1}; \theta)$ is a non–central χ^2 distribution. However, for more complicated specifications the conditional density $h(y_t|y_{t-1}\theta)$ and, in general its moments, do not have a tractable form since $h(y_t|y_{t-1}\theta)$ appears as a multiple integral (see, *e.g.*, *Gouriéroux and Monfort* [1996, p. 10f]). This motivates the use of alternative procedures to the standard ML and GMM estimators. An example for a specification with an intractable density $h(y_t|y_{t-1}; \theta)$

is the following generalisation of the Cox–Ingersoll–Ross model:

$$dv_t = (\alpha_0 + \alpha_1 v_t)dt + \beta_0 v_t^{\beta_1} dW_t \,,$$

which is proposed by *Chan, Karolyi, Longstaff and Sanders* [1992]. To simulate values of the observable discrete–time variables according to a continous–time model, one can use a discrete–time approximation, for example, the Euler approximation. If the time interval between two observations $[t, t + \Delta)$ is divided into subintervals of length τ, the corresponding Euler approximation of (10–3) becomes

$$v_{t+k\tau} = v_{t+(k-1)\tau} + \tau\, a(v_{t+(k-1)\tau}, \theta) + \sqrt{\tau}\, b(v_{t+(k-1)\tau}, \theta)\eta_{t,k},$$
$$k = 1, 2, \dots \,,$$

where $\eta_{t,k}$ is an *i.i.d.* $N(0,1)$ random variable. If the time interval τ is sufficiently small, this approximation can be used to simulate values from $h(y_1, \dots, y_T | \theta)$ according to $y_t = \varrho(y_{t-1}, \varepsilon_t; \theta)$, where $\varepsilon_t = [\eta_{t,1}, \dots, \eta_{t,1/\tau}]'$ is the vector of error terms.   ∎

The common feature of Examples 10.1 and 10.2 is that (partially) unobservable processes enter the model nonlinearly, making criterion functions commonly used for estimation intractable. Further examples for this in financial econometrics are the continous–time stochastic volatility models of *Hull and White* [1987] and *Chesney and Scott* [1989], the market microstructure model proposed by *Forster and Viswanathan* [1995], the dynamic equilibrium model for asset prices estimated by *Bansal, Gallant, Hussey and Tauchen* [1995] and the multifactor latent ARCH models of *Diebold and Nerlove* [1989] and *Engle, Ng and Rothschild* [1990].

10.2 The Method of Simulated Moments (MSM)

Consider a dynamic model with a well defined reduced form $y_t = \varrho(z_t, \varepsilon_t; \theta)$ which can be used to simulate values of y_t from $h(y_t | z_t, \theta)$ for observed values of the conditioning variables

$$z_t = [y'_{t-1}, \dots, y'_1, y'_0, x'_t, x'_{t-1}, \dots, x'_1]'.$$

We will focus on the m-dimensional moment function of the form

$$\varphi(y_t, z_t; \theta) = s(y_t, z_t) - \sigma(z_t; \theta) , \qquad (10\text{--}4)$$

with $m \geq p$ and where $s(y_t, z_t)$ is a function on the data and $\sigma(z_t; \theta)$ is the theoretical counterpart defined as

$$\sigma(z_t; \theta) = E_\theta[s(y_t, z_t)|z_t].$$

Here $E_\theta(\cdot|z_t)$ indicates that the expectation is computed with respect to the density $h(y_t|z_t; \theta)$ and $\sigma(z_t; \theta)$ represents conditional moments as, for example, $E_\theta(y_t|z_t)$ or $E_\theta(y_t y_t'|z_t)$. The index is dropped if the expectation is taken with respect to the true process, *i.e.*, , $E \equiv E_{\theta_0}$. We assume that for θ_0 the empirical moment condition

$$E[\varphi(y_t, z_t; \theta_0)|z_t] = 0 \quad \text{for all } t$$

is satisfied. Let $f(y_t, z_t; \theta_0) = B(z_t)'\varphi(y_t, z_t; \theta_0)$, where $B(z_t)$ is some nonlinear matrix function on z_t, then the corresponding set of unconditional moment restrictions is given by (see, *e.g.*, Newey [1993])

$$E[f(y_t, z_t; \theta_0)] = 0 \quad \text{for all } t .$$

If the expression $\sigma(z_t; \theta)$ cannot be computed analytically, it may be approximated using simulation methods. Since $\sigma(z_t; \theta)$ is the expectation value of $s(y_t, z_t)$ evaluated with respect to $h(y_t|z_t; \theta)$, a natural unbiased estimator for $\sigma(z_t; \theta)$ is given by

$$\widehat{\sigma}_R(z_t; \theta) = \frac{1}{R} \sum_{r=1}^{R} s[y_t^{(r)}(\theta), z_t] , \qquad (10\text{--}5)$$

where $y_t^{(r)}(\theta)$, $(r = 1, \ldots, R)$ are simulated random variables drawn from the distribution $h(y_t|z_t; \theta)$ for the observed values of z_t. The natural estimator of $\sigma(z_t; \theta)$ given in equation (10–5) results from sampling data using $h(y_t|z_t, \theta)$. However, this estimator may have undesirable properties. For example, it may not be differentiable with respect to θ or it may have a large variance. Therefore, alternative methods of estimating $\sigma(z_t, \theta)$ such as importance sampling procedures were proposed to obtain an estimator with improved properties (see, *Gouriéroux and Monfort* [1993] and *Stern* [1997]).

If the natural Monte Carlo estimator (10–5) is used to estimate the moment restrictions the method of simulated moments (MSM) estimator for θ_0 is obtained by minimizing the criterion function

$$\widehat{\theta}^R_{MSM} = \overset{\text{argmin}}{\theta}$$

$$\left[\sum_{t=1}^{T} f_R(y_t, z_t; \theta)\right]' A \left[\sum_{t=1}^{T} f_R(y_t, z_t; \theta)\right] \tag{10–6}$$

where

$$f_R(y_t, z_t; \theta) = B(z_t)'[s(y_t, z_t) - \widehat{\sigma}_R(z_t; \theta)]$$

and A denotes an appropriately chosen positive definite weighting matrix. If the simulation sample size R tends to infinity, $\widehat{\sigma}_R(z_t; \theta)$ converges almost surely to $E_\theta[s(y_t, z_t)|z_t]$ and the MSM estimator equals the corresponding GMM estimator. However, as the sample size T tends to infinity, the MSM estimator is consistent for any fixed $R \geq 1$ as long as different random draws are used across t (cf. *McFadden* [1989]). The reason for this is that for the estimator $\widehat{\theta}^R_{MSM}$ the simulation error is "averaged out" by using the *mean* of $\widehat{\sigma}_R(z_t; \theta)$, $(t = 1, \ldots, T)$.

The fact that the MSM estimator is consistent for any $R \geq 1$ should not be taken as an indication that R is irrelevant for the asymptotic properties of $\widehat{\theta}^R_{MSM}$ as $T \to \infty$. This becomes clear from considering the asymptotic distribution of the MSM estimator, which results as $T^{1/2}(\widehat{\theta}^R_{MSM} - \theta_0) \overset{d}{\longrightarrow} N(0, \text{avar}(\widehat{\theta}^R_{MSM}))$. The asymptotic covariance matrix of $\widehat{\theta}^R_{MSM}$, as it results from the fact that $\{f(y_t, z_t; \theta_0)\}$ is by construction serially uncorrelated with identical distributions, has the form (see, *Gouriéroux and Monfort* [1996, p. 29])

$$\text{avar}(\widehat{\theta}^R_{MSM}) =$$

$$\Sigma_1^{-1} \Sigma_2 \Sigma_1^{-1} + \frac{1}{R} \Sigma_1^{-1} D' A \text{ var}[f(y_t^{(r)}(\theta_0), z_t; \theta_0)] A D \Sigma_1^{-1}, \tag{10–7}$$

where

$$D = E\left[B(z_t)' \frac{\partial \sigma(z_t; \theta_0)}{\partial \theta'}\right]$$

$$\Sigma_1 = D' A D$$

$$\Sigma_2 = D' A \text{ var}[f(y_t, z_t; \theta_0)] A D .$$

The lower bound of the asymptotic covariance matrix obtained for $R \to \infty$ is given by the asymptotic covariance of the corresponding

GMM estimator $\Sigma_1^{-1}\Sigma_2\Sigma_1^{-1}$. However, the asymptotic covariance matrix of the MSM estimator contains, compared to that of the GMM estimator, an additional component which is due to the variation in the Monte Carlo estimates of the moment restrictions. This additional Monte Carlo sampling variance vanishes as the simulation sample size increases and the MSM estimator attains the efficiency of the corresponding GMM estimator.

The asymptotic optimal weighting matrix which minimizes the asymptotic covariance of $\widehat{\theta}_{MSM}^R$ for a given set of moment restrictions is:

$$A_0 = \left(\operatorname{var}[f(y_t, z_t; \theta_0)] + \frac{1}{R} \operatorname{var}[f(y_t^{(r)}(\theta_0), z_t; \theta_0)] \right)^{-1}.$$

For this optimal choice of the weight matrix the asymptotic covariance matrix of the MSM estimator is $\operatorname{avar}(\widehat{\theta}_{MSM}^R) = [D'A_0D]^{-1}$.

The MSM estimator given above is based on conditional moments of the function $s(y_t, z_t)$ given

$$z_t = [y_{t-1}', \ldots, y_1', y_0', x_t', x_{t-1}', \ldots, x_1']'.$$

A necessary requirement for using such conditional moments for MSM estimation, is that the model admits a well defined reduced form $y_t = \varrho(z_t, \varepsilon_t; \theta)$ in terms of exogenous and lagged endogenous variables in order to perform conditional simulations from $h(y_t|z_t; \theta)$. These conditional simulations are necessary to obtain unbiased estimates for $\sigma(z_t, \theta)$ based on estimators such as the one given in equation (10–5). However, for models which include unobservable variables nonlinearly as, for instance, the SV model in Example 10.1, a reduced form in terms of lagged endogenous variables is generally not available. Hence, in such cases the MSM estimation based on conditional moments given lagged endogeneous variables is infeasible. Then one may use restrictions based on moments conditional only on the exogenous variables or for pure time series models restrictions derived from unconditional moments. Such MSM approach for pure time series applications has been proposed by *Duffie and Singleton* [1993], and has been applied by *Forster and Viswanathan* [1995] and *Gennotte and Marsh* [1993] for estimating a market microstructure model and a dynamic asset pricing model, respectively.

This unconditional version of the MSM estimator is based on a m-dimensional moment function of the form

$$f(y_t, \ldots, y_{t-l}; \theta) = s(y_t, \ldots, y_{t-l}) - \sigma(\theta) , \qquad t = 1, \ldots, T ,$$
$$(10\text{–}8)$$

where $\sigma(\theta)$ represents the unconditional expectation

$$E_\theta[s(y_t, \ldots, y_{t-l})].$$

The corresponding set of moment restrictions is given by

$$E[f(y_t, \ldots, y_{t-l}; \theta_0)] = 0 .$$

These restrictions include moments such as

$$E_\theta(y_t) \quad \text{and} \quad E_\theta(y_t y_t')$$

as well as cross order moments of the form $E_\theta(y_t y_{t-i}')$. If $y_t(\theta)$, $(t = 1, \ldots, R)$ denotes a simulated path from the distribution $h(y_1, \ldots, y_R|\theta)$ implied by the model, the MSM estimator based on these unconditional moments is obtained by

$$\widehat{\theta}^R_{MSM} = \overset{\text{argmin}}{\theta}$$

$$\left[\frac{1}{T} \sum_{t=1}^T s(y_t, \ldots, y_{t-l}) - \widehat{\sigma}_R(\theta) \right]' A \left[\frac{1}{T} \sum_{t=1}^T s(y_t, \ldots, y_{t-l}) - \widehat{\sigma}_R(\theta) \right]$$

where

$$\widehat{\sigma}_R(\theta) = \frac{1}{R} \sum_{t=1}^R s[y_t(\theta), \ldots, y_{t-l}(\theta)] .$$

The matrix A denotes the weight matrix and $\widehat{\sigma}_R(\theta)$ is an unbiased Monte Carlo estimator for $\sigma(\theta)$. As the moment function (10–8) derived from the dynamic model $h(y_t|z_t; \theta)$ is expected to be serially correlated, the asymptotic optimal weight matrix is given by

$$A_0 = \left(\lim_{T \to \infty} \left[\operatorname{var} \left\{ \frac{1}{\sqrt{T}} \sum_{t=1}^T s(y_t, \ldots, y_{t-l}) \right\} \right] \right)^{-1} .$$

Since $s(y_t, \ldots, y_{t-l})$ is independent of the parameter θ and independent of the simulated values $y_t(\theta)$, the matrix A_0 can be estimated by procedures discussed in Chapter 3. Like the MSM estimator based on conditional moments, the MSM estimator using unconditional moments is consistent and asymptotically normally distributed as T goes to infinity. The asymptotic distribution for the optimal weight matrix A_0 results as $T^{1/2}(\widehat{\theta}^R_{MSM} - \theta_0) \overset{d}{\longrightarrow} N(0, \operatorname{avar}(\widehat{\theta}^R_{MSM}))$, with $\operatorname{avar}(\widehat{\theta}^R_{MSM}) = [1 + (1/R)][D' A_0 D]^{-1}$

and $D = E[\partial\sigma(\theta_0)/\partial\theta']$ (see, *Duffie and Singleton* [1993]). The factor $[1 + (1/R)]$ in the asymptotic variance accounts for the additional variation of the estimator due to the Monte Carlo sampling variance which vanishes as R goes to infinity.

10.3 Indirect Inference Estimator

The MSM approach is used to optimize a GMM criterion function, which is too complicated to be computed analytically. Another approach proposed by *Gouriéroux, Monfort and Renault* [1993], is to use a criterion function derived from an *auxiliary*, possibly misspecified model and to recover the *structural* parameters of the original model from the parameter estimates of the misspecified model. Unfortunately, the relationship between the auxiliary and the structural model is too complicated to admit an explicit solution. Therefore, simulation techniques are used to derive the final estimates. Another view about the indirect inference estimator followed by *Gallant and Tauchen* [1996a] is that the derivatives of the criterion function for the auxiliary model (usually the log–likelihood function) can be used as a moment function for a GMM procedure. Thus, the scores of the Quasi–ML procedure of the possibly misspecified auxiliary model are the moments to be matched by a GMM approach. Hence, in this context the auxiliary model is also termed the *score generator*. However, if the indirect inference estimator is combined with some flexible data dependent choice of the auxiliary model, the resulting estimator can be expected to be more efficient than a GMM procedure based on an ad hoc selection of the moments. For this reason, an indirect inference estimator based on such a flexible auxiliary model is called *Efficient Method of Moments* (EMM).

Consider a dynamic model characterized by $h(y_t|z_t; \theta)$ which allows us to simulate values of y_t using path simulations but with intractable criterion functions commonly used for estimation. Furthermore, let $\mathcal{M}^* = \{h^*(y_t|z_t; \lambda), \lambda \in \Lambda\}$ denote the auxiliary model with the q-dimensional vector of auxiliary parameters λ, where $q \geq p$, that is, the auxiliary model has at least as many parameters as θ. The model is misspecified, if there exists no parameter vector λ^* such that $h_0(y_t|z_t) = h^*(y_t|z_t; \lambda^*)$. However, it is assumed that the auxiliary model has some tractable criterion function (here the log–likelihood) allowing us to estimate λ. For example, if we are interested in estimating the SV model in Example 10.1, a possible auxiliary model may be a GARCH model which is relatively easy to estimate by ML compared to the SV model.

The Quasi–ML estimates of λ are computed by maximizing the criterion function $Q(Y, X; \lambda) = T^{-1} \sum_{t=1}^{T} \log h^*(y_t|z_t; \lambda)$ with $Y = [y_1, \ldots, y_T]$ and $X = [x_1, \ldots, x_T]$, that is

$$\tilde{\lambda}_T = \overset{\text{argmax}}{\lambda} \ Q(Y, X; \lambda) .$$

The first order condition is that the score vector

$$g(Y, X; \lambda) = \frac{\partial Q(Y, X; \lambda)}{\partial \lambda} = \frac{1}{T} \sum_{t=1}^{T} \frac{\partial \log h^*(y_t|z_t; \lambda)}{\partial \lambda} \qquad (10\text{–}9)$$

equals zero. An important concept linking the structural parameters θ with the auxiliary parameters λ, is the so-called *binding function* $\lambda = b(\theta)$ (see, *Gouriéroux and Monfort* [1996, p. 67]). The binding function is obtained from the solution of the equation $E_\theta g[Y, X; b(\theta)] = 0$, where the expected value is evaluated with respect to the joint distribution $h(Y, X|\theta)$ implied by the structural model.

From *White* [1994] it is known that the estimates $\tilde{\lambda}_T$ converge in probability to the *pseudo–true* value given by $\lambda_0 = b(\theta_0)$. Hence, if λ and θ are of the same dimension and if it is assumed that there exists an inverse function $b^{-1}(\cdot)$, it is possible to obtain an indirect inference estimator for θ_0 as $\hat{\theta}_T = b^{-1}(\tilde{\lambda}_T)$. The practical problem is, however, that usually the function $b(\theta)$ is unknown and must be evaluated using Monte Carlo simulations. Therefore, we generate R simulated paths $y_1^{(r)}(\theta), \ldots, y_T^{(r)}(\theta)$, $(r = 1, \ldots, R)$ from the distribution $h(y_1, \ldots, y_T|x_1, \ldots, x_T; \theta)$ for observed values of the exogenous variables. For each simulated path we obtain an estimate of the vector of auxiliary parameters denoted by $\tilde{\lambda}_T^{(r)}(\theta)$. Then the unknown binding function $b(\theta)$ can be approximated by

$$\hat{b}_R(\theta) = \frac{1}{R} \sum_{r=1}^{R} \tilde{\lambda}_T^{(r)}(\theta).$$

If $b(\theta)$ is replaced by $\hat{b}_R(\theta)$ we can construct a simulated minimum distance estimator as

$$\hat{\theta}_{MD}^R = \overset{\text{argmin}}{\theta} \ [\tilde{\lambda}_T - \hat{b}_R(\theta)]' A [\tilde{\lambda}_T - \hat{b}_R(\theta)], \qquad (10\text{–}10)$$

where A is a positive definite weight matrix. This indirect inference estimator suggested by *Gouriéroux, Monfort and Renault* [1993] searches for a value of θ, for which simulated data from the structural model approximate the properties of the observed data summarized by the estimate $\tilde{\lambda}_T$ as close as possible.

As the sample size T goes to infinity, the indirect inference estimator is consistent and asymptotically normal for any fixed $R \geq 1$. The asymptotic optimal weight matrix is given by

$$A_0 = J_0 I_0^{-1} J_0 \,,$$

where

$$J_0 = \lim_{T \to \infty} E \left\{ \frac{\partial^2 Q(Y, X; \lambda_0)}{\partial \lambda \partial \lambda'} \right\}$$
$$I_0 = \lim_{T \to \infty} \text{var} \left\{ \sqrt{T} g(Y, X; \lambda_0) - E[\sqrt{T} g(Y, X; \lambda_0)|X] \right\} \,.$$

For this optimal choice of the weight matrix the asymptotic distribution of the minimum distance estimator (10–10) is obtained as $T^{1/2}(\hat{\theta}_{MD}^R - \theta_0) \overset{d}{\longrightarrow} N(0, \text{avar}(\hat{\theta}_{MD}^R))$, where the asymptotic variance of $\hat{\theta}_{MD}^R$ is given by $\text{avar}(\hat{\theta}_{MD}^R) = [1 + (1/R)][B'A_0 B]^{-1}$ with $B = \partial b(\theta_0)/\partial \theta'$ (see, *Gouriéroux, Monfort and Renault* [1993]).

The second approach for deriving an indirect estimate from the auxiliary model suggested by *Gallant and Tauchen* [1996a] is to use the moment conditions implied by the scores of the auxiliary model

$$E\, g[Y, X; b(\theta_0)] = 0 \,. \tag{10–11}$$

Using path simulations from the structural model to approximate $E_\theta\, g[Y_T, X_T;\, b\,(\theta)]$, the GMM estimation procedure based on the scores of the auxiliary model results as

$$\hat{\theta}_{GT}^R = \overset{\text{argmin}}{\theta} \; \hat{g}_R(\theta, \tilde{\lambda}_T)' A\, \hat{g}_R(\theta, \tilde{\lambda}_T) \,, \tag{10–12}$$

where

$$\hat{g}_R(\theta, \tilde{\lambda}_T) = \frac{1}{R}\sum_{r=1}^{R} \frac{1}{T}\sum_{t=1}^{T} \frac{\partial \log h^*[y_t^{(r)}(\theta)\,|\,z_t^{(r)}(\theta); \tilde{\lambda}_T]}{\partial \lambda} \tag{10–13}$$

is the simulated score function which approximates the moment conditions (10–11) and A is a positive definite weight matrix. For this estimator the asymptotic optimal weight matrix is given by $A_0 = I_0^{-1}$. Notice, that the score vector (10–9) for the observed data and the estimate $\tilde{\lambda}_T$ is equal to zero as implied by the first order condition. Hence, the estimator $\hat{\theta}_{GT}^R$ searches for a value of θ, for which the simulated data from the structural model mimic this first order condition.

Both estimators $\widehat{\theta}^R_{MD}$ and $\widehat{\theta}^R_{GT}$ are derived from similar principles although the criterion function is different. Indeed *Gouriérioux, Monfort and Renault* [1993] show that both approaches yield asymptotically equivalent estimators as T goes to infinity. Thus, the choice between these estimators is a matter of computational convenience. As far as this is concerned the following should be considered. As usual for nonlinear optimization problems, estimations based on $\widehat{\theta}^R_{MD}$ and $\widehat{\theta}^R_{GT}$ are performed with iterative optimization algorithms. However, at every iteration step of the optimization with respect to θ, the parameter based estimator $\widehat{\theta}^R_{MD}$ requires "secondary" optimizations to estimate the auxiliary parameters λ, whereas the score based estimator $\widehat{\theta}^R_{GT}$ requires only one optimization concerning λ. Furthermore, the estimator $\widehat{\theta}^R_{MD}$, using the optimal weight matrix A_0, requires an estimate of J_0 based on the Hessian matrix which is not necessary for the estimator $\widehat{\theta}^R_{GT}$. On the other hand, for the computational efficiency of the score based estimator $\widehat{\theta}^R_{GT}$, it is necessary that the score vector of the auxiliary model (10–9) is available in a closed form which is not essential for the parameter based estimator.

The asymptotic efficiency of the indirect inference estimators depends on the potential of the auxiliary model to approximate the true process. In fact, if $h(y_t|z_t; \theta_0) = h^*(y_t|z_t; b(\theta_0))$ in some neighborhood of θ_0, the structural model is "smoothly embedded within the score generator" (see, *Gallant and Tauchen* [1996a]), and it follows that the indirect inference estimator is asymptotically efficient. However, in principle two different approaches to select an appropriate auxiliary model (or score generator) exists. The first approach is to search for an auxiliary model that is able to mimic the salient features of the structural model, and is as close to it as possible. For the SV model (see Example 10.1), for instance, a potential candidate may be a GARCH specification as the predictions concerning the stochastic behavior of the returns resulting from a GARCH model and the SV model are very similar. The second approach as advocated by *Gallant and Tauchen* [1996a] is a data dependent choice of the auxiliary model. Specifically, they propose to adopt a flexible, possibly nonparametric, score generator which can be expected to capture any dynamic and distributional features of the observed data. Such a data dependent procedure associated with the term EMM is considered in the next section in greater detail.

10.4 The SNP Approach

To achieve a high level of efficiency for the indirect inference estimator, *Gallant and Tauchen* [1996a] consider the class of semi-nonparametric (SNP) models of *Gallant and Nychka* [1987] for constructing the score generator. As shown by *Gallant and Long* [1997], these SNP models can be expected to capture the probabilistic structure of any stationary and Markovian time series.

The SNP model as applied by *Gallant and Tauchen* [1996b], *Andersen and Lund* [1997], and *Gallant, Hsieh and Tauchen* [1997] to various financial time series can be represented by the following conditional density:

$$h_q^*(y_t|z_t; \lambda_q) = \frac{[\mathcal{P}(u_t, z_t)]^2 \, \phi(u_t)/|\det(S_t)|}{\int [\mathcal{P}(v, z_t)]^2 \, \phi(v)dv} . \qquad (10\text{--}14)$$

Here $z_t = [y'_{t-1}, \ldots, y'_{t-l}]'$ and λ_q is a q-dimensional parameter vector. The n-dimensional vector u_t is obtained from a standardization of y_t, i.e., , $u_t = S_t^{-1}(y_t - \mu_t)$, where μ_t and S_t are a location and a scale functions, respectively. The density function of a multivariate normal distribution with mean zero and unit covariance matrix is denoted by $\phi(\cdot)$, and $\mathcal{P}(u_t, z_t)$ is a polynomial in u_t with coefficients depending on z_t. The integration constant $\int [\mathcal{P}(v, z_t)]^2 \, \phi(v)dv$ ensures that $h_q^*(y_t|z_t; \lambda_q)$ integrates to unity.

The parametrizations of the location function, the scale function, and the polynomial are as follows. To accommodate the dynamic structure in the mean, the location function is the conditional mean corresponding to a vector autoregression given by

$$\mu_t = b_0 + \sum_{i=1}^{l_\mu} B_i y_{t-i} . \qquad (10\text{--}15)$$

To capture the dynamics in the variance, the following ARCH–type scale function is applied

$$\text{vech}\,(S_t) = c_0 + \sum_{i=1}^{l_S} C_i |y_{t-i} - \mu_{t-i}| , \qquad (10\text{--}16)$$

where $\text{vech}(S_t)$ is the vector containing the $[n(n + 1)/2]$ distinct elements of S_t and $|y_{t-i} - \mu_{t-i}|$ indicates the elementwise absolute value. Alternative scale functions applied by *Andersen and Lund* [1997] and *Andersen, Chung and Sørensen* [1998] are based on corresponding GARCH–type specifications. In order to account for non–Gaussianity and dynamic dependencies of the standardized process u_t the normal density $\phi(\cdot)$ is expanded using the square of the polynomial

$$P(u_t, z_t) = \sum_{|\alpha|=0}^{k_u} a_\alpha(z_t)u_t^\alpha , \qquad (10\text{--}17)$$

where $u^\alpha = \prod_{i=1}^{n} u_i^{\alpha_i}$ and $|\alpha| = \sum_{i=1}^{n} |\alpha_i|$. The parameter k_u denotes the degree of the polynomial and controls the extent to which $h_q^*(y_t|z_t; \lambda_q)$ deviates from the normal density. For $k_u = 0$ the density function $h_q^*(y_t|z_t; \lambda_q)$ reduces to that of a normal distribution. To achieve identification, the constant term of the polynomial is set to 1. To allow for deviations from normality to depend on past values of y_t, the coefficients $a_\alpha(z_t)$ are polynomials in z_t given by

$$a_\alpha(z_t) = \sum_{|\beta|=0}^{k_z} a_{\alpha\beta}z_t^\beta ,$$

where $z^\beta = \prod_{i=1}^{(n \cdot l)} z_i^{\beta_i}$ and $|\beta| = \sum_{i=1}^{(n \cdot l)} |\beta_i|$. For $k_z = 0$ the deviations from the shape of a normal distribution are independent from z_t.

Summing up, the leading term of the SNP model, obtained for $k_u = k_z = 0$, is a Gaussian VAR–ARCH specification depending on the lag lengths l_μ and l_S. This leading term captures the heterogeneity in the first two moments. The remaining features of the data such as any remaining non–normality and possible heterogeneity in the higher–order moments are accommodated by an expansion of the squared Hermite polynomial $P(u_t, z_t)^2 \phi(u_t)$ controlled by k_u and k_z. To estimate the parameter vector λ_q, whose dimension is determined by l_μ, l_S, k_u, and k_z, the ML method can be used. For this purpose, the integration constant of the SNP model (10–14) can be computed analytically by applying the recursive formulas for the moments of a standard normal distribution (see, *e.g., Patel and Read* [1982]).

If the dimension of the SNP model q increases with the sample size T, the Quasi–ML estimate of the SNP model $h_q^*(y_t|z_t; \lambda_q)$ is, under weak conditions, an efficient nonparametric estimate of the true density $h_0(y_t|z_t)$ (see, *Fenton and Gallant* [1996a,b]). Furthermore, *Gallant and Long* [1997] show that the indirect inference estimator with the SNP model as the score generator (or EMM estimator) attains the asymptotic efficiency of the ML estimator by increasing the dimension q. However, how to determine the adequate specification of the SNP model, *i.e.*, to select l_μ, l_S, k_u and k_z, remains a difficult problem. In most practical applications (see *e.g.*, *Gallant, Rossi and Tauchen* [1992], *Gallant and Tauchen* [1996b] and *Tauchen* [1997]) the dimension q of the SNP model is successively expanded and the AIC or BIC model selection criteria are used to determine a preferred specification. Then, in order to prove the adequacy of the chosen specification, diagnostic tests based on the standardized residuals are conducted. An alternative approach to prove the adequacy of the chosen SNP specification is followed by *Liu and Zhang* [1998], who propose an overall goodness of fit test for the auxiliary model based on the partial sum process of the score series of this auxiliary model.

10.5   Some Practical Issues

In many cases the application of simulation techniques require an immense amount of computer power and thus some care is necessary when implementing the simulation procedures. In this section we therefore address some practical problems and report implications of recent Monte Carlo studies concerning the properties of simulation based estimators.

10.5.1 Drawing Random Numbers and
Variance Reduction

In most applications the simulation based estimator is obtained by optimizing the criterion function using an iterative algorithm. At each iteration step the criterion function must be estimated through simulations for the current parameter values. For such an algorithm to converge, it is important to use *common random numbers* at every iteration step. With regard to the reduced form $y_t = \varrho(z_t, \varepsilon_t; \theta)$ of the model, the use of common random numbers means that for every value of θ during the iterative optimization procedure, the same set of simulated random variables $\{\varepsilon_t^{(r)}\}$ is used to generate simulated values of y_t. If at each iteration step new values of ε_t were drawn, some additional randomness would be introduced and the algorithm would fail to converge (see, *e.g.*, *Hendry* [1984]).

As shown above, the overall variance of simulation based estimators consists of two components. The first one represents the variance of the estimator as if it was based on the exact criterion function and the second one is the Monte Carlo sampling variance due to the use of simulations to evaluate the criterion function. The first component is irreducible whereas the second component can be made arbitrarily small by increasing the simulation sample size. Unfortunately, this often leads to an enormous increase in computing costs. However, there exists a number of techniques developed for reducing the Monte Carlo sampling variance without increasing the computing costs, for instance, the *antithetic variates* and *control variates* procedures.

The idea of the antithetic variates procedure as applied, for example, by *Andersen and Lund* [1997] for an indirect inference estimator is as follows. If we want to estimate a quantity ω by simulations, here for example, the moment conditions (10–11), we construct two estimates for these moment conditions according to estimator (10–13), say $\widehat{\omega}_1$ and $\widehat{\omega}_2$, that are negatively correlated. Then the average $\frac{1}{2}(\widehat{\omega}_1 + \widehat{\omega}_2)$ has a lower variance than either of the two individual estimates. Assuming that the error term ε_t in the reduced form of the model has a symmetric distribution around zero, negatively correlated estimates of moment conditions ω can be produced by using a set of simulated values $\{\varepsilon_t^{(r)}\}$ for $\widehat{\omega}_1$ and the same set of simulated values but with the opposite sign, *i.e.*, $\{-\varepsilon_t^{(r)}\}$, for $\widehat{\omega}_2$. The additional computing costs of these procedure are negligible and the reduction of the Monte Carlo sampling variance may be considerable as reported by *Andersen and Lund* [1997].

The control variates technique, as applied by *Calzolari, Di Iorio and Fiorentini* [1998] for indirect inference, uses two components for the final Monte Carlo estimate of the quantity of interest ω. The first component is the natural Monte Carlo estimate of ω denoted by $\widehat{\omega}^\star$, and the second one is an estimate $\widetilde{\omega}$ created from the same set of simulated random numbers as $\widehat{\omega}^\star$ with known expectation and a positive correlation with $\widehat{\omega}^{\star}$. Then the final estimate of ω based on the control variate $\tilde{\omega}$ is given by $\widehat{\omega} = (\widehat{\omega}^{\star} - \tilde{\omega}) + E(\tilde{\omega})$. Under suitable conditions, the variance of $\widehat{\omega}$ is considerably smaller than that of the natural estimator $\widehat{\omega}^{\star}$. *Calzolari, Di Iorio and Fiorentini* [1998] adjust the parameter based indirect inference estimator by control variates created from the difference $(\widehat{\lambda} - \tilde{\lambda}_T)$, where $\tilde{\lambda}_T$ is the estimate of the auxiliary parameter λ based on the observed data and $\widehat{\lambda}$ is an estimate of λ using simulated data from the auxiliary model. These simulated data are generated using $\tilde{\lambda}_T$ as the parameter vector and the same set of simulated random numbers as for the indirect inference procedure itself. Based on Monte Carlo experiments, they show that the indirect inference estimator combined with control variates and applied to continuous–time models (see Example 10.2) reduces the Monte Carlo sampling variance substantially relative to the simple indirect inference estimator.

10.5.2 The Selection of the Auxiliary Model

Indirect inference has been applied to a variety of financial time series models. Next, we discuss strategies used to select an auxiliary model (or score generator).

A data dependent choice of the auxiliary model based on an expansion of the SNP model (10–14) has been followed by *Gallant and Tauchen* [1996b], *Tauchen* [1997] and *Andersen and Lund* [1997] to estimate continuous–time models for interest rates, as the Cox-Ingersoll-Ross and Chan-Karolyi-Longstaff-Sanders specification (see Example 10.2). The same approach is used by *Gallant, Hsieh and Tauchen* [1997] for the estimation of discrete–time SV models (see Example 10.1) for interest rates, stock returns and exchange rates. In these applications the dimension q of the SNP auxiliary model determined by model selection criteria, is typically quite large, resulting in a multitude of auxiliary parameters and hence in a large number of moments. It turns out, that an expansion of the scale function as that in equation (10–16) is necessary to accomodate for the typically observed conditional heteroskedasticity of financial time series. The expansion of the polynomial (10–17) is important to capture, for instance, the leptokurtic distribution of financial time series not accomodated by a time varying scale function and possible asymmetries of this distribution.

Simpler auxiliary models, which are close to the structural model, resulting in a similar number of auxiliary and structural parameters, are chosen by *Broze, Scaillet and Zakoian* [1995] and *Engle and Lee* [1996]. To estimate the Cox-Ingersoll-Ross and Chan-Karolyi-Longstaff-Sanders specification for interest rates *Broze, Scaillet and Zakoian* [1995] use auxiliary models based on simple discrete–time Euler approximations of the corresponding continuous–time model. *Engle and Lee* [1996] apply GARCH specifications as auxiliary models to estimate continuous–time SV models for exchange rates, interest rates and stock returns.

However, the data dependent SNP approach to select an auxiliary model is motivated by asymptotic arguments indicating that this approach ensures a high level of efficiency of the indirect inference estimator when the maintained structural model is true. Clearly, if the structural model is true, a simple auxiliary model very close to it in the sense that it reflects all salient features of the structural model can also be expected to ensure a high level of efficiency. Nevertheless, the data dependent SNP approach seems to be more adequate if we are interested in detecting possible misspecifications of the structural model based on corresponding specification tests (not discussed here).[3]

10.5.3 Small Sample Properties of the Indirect Inference

As we saw, the theory of the indirect inference estimator, as developed by *Gouriéroux, Monfort and Renault* [1993], *Gallant and Tauchen* [1996a] and *Gallant and Long* [1997], is based on asymptotic arguments. This raises the question of its finite sample properties. A comprehensive Monte Carlo study of the performance of EMM in finite samples is conducted by *Andersen, Chung and Sørensen* [1998]. They use the stochastic volatility model (see Example 10.1) to compare EMM with GMM and likelihood based estimators and to address the adequate parametrization of the auxiliary model. Their key findings are that EMM provides, regardless of the

---

[3] For specification tests based on indirect inference, see *e.g.*, *Gouriéroux, Monfort and Renault* [1993], *Tauchen* [1997] and *Gallant, Hsieh and Tauchen* [1997].

sample size, a substantial efficiency gain relative to the standard GMM procedure. Furthermore, the likelihood based estimators are generally more efficient than the EMM procedure, but EMM approaches the efficiency of the likelihood based estimators with increasing sample size, in harmony with the asymptotic theory of the EMM estimator. Finally, they find evidence that score generators based on an over–parametrized SNP model lead, especially in smaller samples, to a substantial loss of efficiency. Specifically, they show that the substitution of an ARCH type scale function in the SNP model as given in equation (10–16) by a GARCH type specification, improve the efficiency of the EMM estimator. In fact, this substitution reduces the number of parameters necessary to capture the autocorrelation in the variance.

10.6 Conclusion

Recently, simulation based inference procedures have become popular in particular in empirical finance. This is due to the complexity of the standard models implied by latent factors or continuous–time processes, for example. This chapter reviewed different approaches for the estimation of the parameters of interest based on a GMM criterion function. The MSM approach is the simulated counterpart of the traditional GMM procedure and is applicable when the theoretical moments cannot be computed analytically. However, in many applications it is not clear how to choose the moment conditions. In nonlinear models the structure implies restrictions on a wide range of moments and, therefore, it is difficult to represent the main features of the model using a few moment conditions. In such cases it seems attractive to use a simple auxiliary model which approximates the main features of the structural model. In most cases, however, the relationship between the parameters of the auxiliary model and the parameters of interest is too complicated to admit an explicit solution. Hence, simulation techniques are applied to evaluate the binding function linking the parameters of interest with the parameters of the auxiliary model. Two asymptotically equivalent approaches for such indirect infererence are available. *Gouriéroux, Monfort and Renault* [1993] use a minimum distance procedure whereas *Gallant and Tauchen* [1996a] use the scores of the auxiliary model as the moment condition to be matched by a (simulation based) GMM procedure.

Since the efficiency of an indirect inference procedure crucially depends on the potential of the auxiliary model to approximate the model of interest, it seems attractive to use flexible nonparametric models as score generators. Such estimation procedures are known as EMM estimators in the literature and seem to be a fruitful and a promising field of future research.

References

Andersen T.G., Chung, H.J. and B.E. Sørensen [1998]: Efficient Method of Moments Estimation of a Stochastic Volatility Model: A Monte Carlo Study , Working Paper No. 97–12, Brown University.

Andersen T.G. and J. Lund [1997]: Estimating Continuous-Time Stochastic Volatility Models of the Short-Term Interest Rate, *Journal of Econometrics*, 77, 343–377.

Andersen, T.G., and B.E. Sørensen [1996]: GMM Estimation of a Stochastic Volatility Model: A Monte Carlo Study , Journal of Business & Economic Statistics, 14, 328–352.

Bansal, R., Gallant, A.R., Hussey, R. and G. Tauchen [1993]: Computational Aspects of Nonparametric Simulation Estimation, in: D.A. Belsley, ed., *Computational Techniques for Econometrics and Economic Analysis* , Kluwer Academic Publishers, Boston, Massachusetts.

Bansal, R., Gallant, A.R., Hussey, R. and G. Tauchen [1995]: Nonparametric Estimation of Structural Models for High-Frequency Currency Market Data, *Journal of Econometrics*, 66, 251–287.

Bollerslev, T. [1986]: Generalized Autoregressive Conditional Heteroskedasticity, *Journal of Econometrics*, 31, 307–327.

Broze, L., Scaillet, O. and J. Zakoian [1995]: Testing for Continuous-time Models of the Short-term Interest Rate, *Journal of Empirical Finance*, 2, 199–223.

Calzolari, G., Di Iorio, F. and G. Fiorentini [1998]: Control Variates for Variance Reduction in Indirect Inference: Interest Rate Models in Continuous Time, *The Econometrics Journal*, forthcoming.

Chesney, M. and L. Scott [1989]: Pricing European Currency Options: A Comparison of the Modified Black-Scholes Model and a Random Variance Model, *Journal of Financial and Quantitative Analysis*, 24, 267–284.

Chan, K.C., Karolyi, G.A., Longstaff, F.A. and A.B. Sanders [1992]: An Empirical Comparison of Alternative Models of the Short-Term Interest Rate, *Journal of Finance*, 47, 1209–1227.

Cox, J.C., Ingersoll, J.E. and S.A. Ross [1985]: A Theory of the Term Structure of Interest Rates, *Econometrica*, 53, 385–407.

Danielsson, J. and J.F. Richard [1993]: Accelerated Gaussian Importance Sampler with Application to Dynamic Latent Variable Models, *Journal of Applied Econometrics*, 8, S153–S173.

Duffie, D. and K.J. Singleton [1993]: Simulated Moments Estimation of Markov Models of Asset Prices, *Econometrica*, 61, 929–952.

Diebold, F.X. and M. Nerlove [1989]: The Dynamics of Exchange Rate Volatility: A Multivariate Latent Factor ARCH Model, *Journal of Applied Econometrics*, 4, 1–21.

Engle, R.F. [1982]: Autoregressive Conditional Heteroscedasticity with Estimates of the Variance of United Kingdom Inflation, *Econometrica*, 50, 987–1007.

Engle, R.F., and G.G.J. Lee [1996]: Estimating Diffusion Models of Stochastic Volatility, in: Rossi, P.E., ed., *Modelling Stock Market Volatility: Bridging the Gap to Continuous Time*, Academic Press, San Diego.

Engle, R.F., Ng, V.K. and M. Rothschild [1990]: Asset Pricing with a Factor-ARCH Covariance Structure: Empirical Estimates for Treasury Bills, *Journal of Econometrics*, 45, 213–237.

Fenton, V.M., and A.R. Gallant [1996a]: Convergence Rates of SNP Density Estimators, *Econometrica*, 64, 719–727.

Fenton, V.M., and A.R. Gallant [1996b]: Qualitative and Asymptotic Performance of SNP Density Estimators, *Journal of Econometrics*, 74, 77–118.

Forster, F.D., and S. Viswanathan [1995]: Can Speculative Trading Explain Volume-Volatility Relation?, *Journal of Business & Economic Statistics*, 13, 379–396.

Gallant, A.R., Hsieh, D.A. and G.E. Tauchen [1997]: Estimation of Stochastic Volatility Models with Diagnostics, *Journal of Econometrics*, 81, 159–192.

Gallant, A.R., and J.R. Long [1997]: Estimating Stochastic Differential Equations Efficiently by Minimum Chi-Squared, *Biometrica*, 84, 125–141.

Gallant, A.R., and D.W. Nychka [1987]: Semi-Nonparametric Maximum Likelihood Estimation, *Econometrica*, 55, 363–390.

Gallant, A.R., Rossi, P.E., and G.E. Tauchen [1992]: Stock Prices and Volume, *The Review of Financial Studies*, 5, 199–242.

Gallant, A.R., and G.E. Tauchen [1996a]: Which Moments to Match?, *Econometric Theory*, 12, 657–681.

Gallant, A.R., and G.E. Tauchen [1996b]: Specification Analysis of Continuous Time Models in Finance, in: Rossi, P.E., ed., *Modelling Stock Market Volatility: Bridging the Gap to Continuous Time*, Academic Press, San Diego.

Gennotte, G., and T.A. Marsh [1993]: Variations in Economic Uncertainty and Risk Premiums on Capital Assets, *European Economic Review,* 37, 1021–1041.

Ghysels, E., Harvey, A.C., and E. Renault [1996]: Stochastic Volatility, in: Maddala, G.S. and C.R. Rao, ed., *Handbook of Statistics, Vol.14,* Elsevier Science B.V., Amsterdam.

Gouriéroux, C., and A. Monfort [1993]: Simulation Based Inference: A survey with special reference to panel data models, *Journal of Econometrics,* 59, 5–33.

Gouriéroux, C., and A. Monfort [1996]: *Simulation Based Econometric Methods,* CORE Lectures, Oxford University Press, New York.

Gouriéroux, C., Monfort. A. and E. Renault [1993]: Indirect Inference, *Journal of Applied Econometrics,* 8, S85–S118.

Hendry, D.F. [1984]: Monte Carlo Experimentation in Econometrics, in: Griliches, Z. and M.D. Intriligator, ed., *Handbook of Econometrics, Vol 2,* Elsevier Science B.V., Amsterdam.

Hull, J., and A. White [1987]: The Pricing of Options on Assets with Stochastic Volatilities, *Journal of Finance,* 42, 281–300.

Jacquier, E., Polson, N.G. and P.E. Rossi [1994]: Bayesian Analysis of Stochastic Volatility Models, *Journal of Business & Economic Statistics,* 12, 371–389.

Kim, S., Shephard, N. and S. Chib. [1996]: *Stochastic Volatility: Likelihood Inference and Comparison with ARCH Models,* working paper, Nuffield College, Oxford University.

Kloek, T., and H.K. van Dijk [1978]: Bayesian Estimates of Equation System Parameters: An Application of Integration by Monte Carlo, *Econometrica,* 46, 1–19.

Lee, B. and B.F. Ingram [1991]: Simulation Estimation of Time-Series Models, *Journal of Econometrics,* 47, 197–205.

Liu, M. and H. Zhang [1998]: *Specification Tests in the Efficient Method of Moments Framework with Application to the Stochastic Volatility Models,* Working paper, Carnegie Mellon Ubiversity, Pittsburgh.

McFadden, D. [1989]: A Method of Simulated Moments for Estimation of Discrete Response Models Without Numerical Integration, *Econometrica,* 57, 995–1026.

Newey, W.K. [1993]: Efficient Estimation of Models with Conditional Moment Restrictions, in: Maddala, G.S., Rao, C.R. and H.D. Vinod, ed., *Handbook of Statistics, Vol. 11,* North-Holland, Amsterdam.

Pakes, A. and D. Pollard [1989]: Simulation and the Asymptotics of Optimization Estimators, *Econometrica,* 57, 1027–1057.

Patel, J.K. and C.B. Read [1982]: *Handbook of the Normal Distribution,* Marcel Dekker, New York.

Richard, J.F. and W. Zhang [1997]: *Accelerated Importance Sampling,* working paper, University of Pittsburgh.

Shephard, N. [1996]: Statistical Aspects of ARCH and Stochastic Volatility, in: Cox, D.R., Hinkley, D.V. and O.E. Barndorff-Nielsen, ed., *Time Series Models In Econometrics, Finance and Other Fields,* Chapman & Hall, London.

Stern, S. [1997]: Simulation-Based Estimation, *Journal of Economic Literature,* 35, 2006–2039.

Tauchen, G.E. [1997]: New Minimum Chi-Square Methods in Empirical Finance, in: Kreps, D. and K. Wallis, ed., *Advances in Econometrics: Theory and Applications, Seventh World Congress, Vol.3,* Cambridge University Press, Cambridge.

Taylor, S.J. [1986]: *Modelling Financial Time Series,* John Wiley & Sons, Chichester.

Taylor, S.J. [1994]: Modeling Stochastic Volatility: A Review and Comparative Study, *Mathematical Finance,* 4, 183–204.

White, H. [1994]: *Estimation, Inference and Specification Analysis,* Cambridge University Press, Cambridge.

Chapter 11

LOGICALLY INCONSISTENT LIMITED

DEPENDENT VARIABLES MODELS

J. S. Butler and Gabriel Picone

Simultaneous equations models involving limited dependent variables can have nonunique reduced forms, a problem called logical inconsistency in the econometrics literature. In response to that problem, such models can be compelled to be recursive (*Maddala* [1983], *Amemiya* [1985]) or recast in terms of the latent variables (*Mallar* [1977]). In labor economics and elsewhere, this approach is often contrary to structural modelling; theory involving education, childbearing, and work, for example, naturally leads to models with simultaneously related limited dependent variables. Restricting these models to be recursive is inconsistent with the theory.

It is widely believed among economists that logically inconsistent models cannot be data generating processes (see *Amemiya* [1974] and *Maddala* [1983]). However, *Jovanovic* [1989] showed that the structural form of a model with nonunique reduced forms can be identified. That raises the possibility that these models can produce outcomes which are random variables even if the process is logically inconsistent.

An alternative interpretation of these models is that they can generate more than one equilibrium for the endogenous variables for some values of the exogenous variables and disturbances. Viewed this way, the problem can be solved by using a selection rule (*Dagsvik and Jovanovic* [1991], *Goldfeld and Quandt* [1968]], *Hamilton and Whiteman* [1985]) or collapsing the possibly nonunique equilibria into one outcome for purposes of estimation (*Bresnahan and Reiss* [1991]).

This chapter combines the use of a selection rule to choose among alternative equilibria with the insights of *Jovanovic* [1989] and standard GMM estimation theory to suggest an alternative to the method of Bresnahan and *Reiss* [1991] to identify and estimate simultaneous equations models of limited dependent variables. Section 11.1 shows a logically inconsistent model that describes a data generating process. Section 11.2 shows that the model is uniquely identified. Section 11.3 argues that by standard GMM estimation theory the model can be estimated independent of the selection rule. Section 11.4 concludes the chapter and discusses extensions of the results.

11.1 Logical Inconsistency

Consider the following model of two simultaneous equations in endogenous dummy variables:

$$
\begin{aligned}
y_1^* &= \gamma_{21} y_2 + \underline{x}_1' \underline{\beta}_1 + u_1 = \gamma_{21} y_2 + z_1 + u_1 \\
y_2^* &= \gamma_{12} y_1 + \underline{x}_2' \underline{\beta}_2 + u_2 = \gamma_{12} y_1 + z_2 + u_2 \\
y_1 &= 1, \quad \text{if} \quad y_1^* > 0; \quad 0, \quad \text{otherwise;} \\
y_2 &= 1, \quad \text{if} \quad y_2^* > 0; \quad 0, \quad \text{otherwise}.
\end{aligned}
\tag{11-1}
$$

Only $y_1, y_2, \underline{x}_1$, and $\underline{x}_2$ are observed. This model could be widely used in labor economics and elsewhere. *Bresnahan and Reiss* [1991] showed that this model can be derived as the result of a simultaneous move game, where the researcher observes only the players' actions, but the players observe each other's payoffs, providing one possible economic interpretation of the above model when y_1 and y_2 represent the actions of two different players. However, y_1 and y_2 may represent also the actions of only one individual.

Let γ_{21} and γ_{12} be positive. The reduced form correspondence $\Psi_\phi(u)$, where ϕ indexes structural relationships between observed and latent endogenous variables, associated with model (11–1) is

$$y^1 = (1,1) \quad \text{if} \quad u \in A = \{u : (u_1, u_2) \in (-z_1, \infty) \times (-z_2, \infty)\}$$
$$\cup \{u : (u_1, u_2) \in (-z_1, \infty) \times (-z_2 - \gamma_{12}, -z_2)\}$$
$$\cup \{u : (u_1, u_2) \in (-z_1 - \gamma_{21}, -z_1) \times (-z_2, \infty)\};$$

$$y^2 = (1,0) \quad \text{if}$$
$$u \in B = \{u : (u_1, u_2) \in (-z_1, \infty) \times (-\infty, -z_2 - \gamma_{12})\};$$

$$y^3 = (0,1) \quad \text{if}$$
$$u \in C = \{u : (u_1, u_2) \in (-\infty, -z_1 - \gamma_{21}) \times (-z_2, \infty)\};$$

$$y^4 = (0,0) \quad \text{if}$$
$$u \in D = \{u : (u_1, u_2) \in (-\infty, -z_1 - \gamma_{21})(-\infty, -z_2 - \gamma_{12})\};$$
$$\cup \{u : (u_1, u_2) \in (-\infty, -z_1 - \gamma_{21}) \times (-z_2 - \gamma_{12}, -z_2)\}$$
$$\cup \{u : (u_1, u_2) \in (-z_1, -\gamma_{21}, -z_1) \times (-\infty, -z_2 - \gamma_{12})\}; \text{ and}$$

$$y^1 \text{ or } y^4 \text{ if}$$
$$u \in E = \{u : (u_1, u_2) \in (-z_1 - \gamma_{21}, -z_1) \times (-z_2 - \gamma_{12}, -z_2)\}.$$

Note that $A \cup B \cup C \cup D \cup E = \{u : (u_1, u_2) \in \mathbb{R}^2\}$.

The reduced form is a correspondence, and it would be a function if the equilibrium were unique. Note that the multiple equilibria arise in only one region, and in any other region there is a unique equilibrium. Let $\Psi_1(u)$, $\Psi_2(u) \in \Psi_\phi(u)$, where $\Psi_1(u)$ is the function such that if $u \in E$ then $\Psi_1(u) = y^1$, while $\Psi_2(u)$ is the function such that if $u \in E$ then $\Psi_2(u) = y^2$. Then $\Psi_1(u)$ and $\Psi_2(u)$ are identical unless $u \in E$.

In model (11–1), $\gamma_{12} > 0$ and $\gamma_{21} > 0$, but if both are negative, there is also a range of values of u_1 and u_2 which produces multiple equilibria. If $\gamma_{12}\gamma_{21} < 0$, there is a set of values of u_1 and u_2 which produces no equilibrium. If $\gamma_{12}\gamma_{21} = 0$, the model produces unique equilibria.

To solve the problem of nonuniqueness two solutions have been proposed. One is to treat the events where the multiple equilibria arise as one event. See *Bresnahan and Reiss* [1991]. In model (11–1), y^1 and y^4 are the same event. The other alternative is to allow for a selection rule that assigns the nonunique region to y^1 if $u \in F \subseteq E$ or to y^4 if $u \in (E - F)$. Then the selected alternative can be written as:

$$\Psi_F(u) = I_F(u)\Psi_1(u) + (1 - I_F(u))\Psi_2(u), \qquad (11\text{–}2)$$

where $I_F(u)$ is an indicator function that takes the value 1 if $u \in F$ and 0 otherwise. With the help of this selection rule we can select any $\Psi_i \in \Psi_\phi$. If $u \in E^c$ then $\Psi_i(u) = \Psi_1(u) = \Psi_2(u)$ and if $u \in E$ then we can construct a set F such that if $\Psi_i(u) = y^1$ then $u \in F$ and if $\Psi_i(u) = y^4$ then $u \in (E - F)$. It follows that for each $\Psi_i(u) \in \Psi_\phi(u)$ there exists a unique set F such that $\Psi_i(u) = \Psi_F(u)$. The use of a selection rule to deal with econometric models with multiple equilibria was first proposed by *Goldfeld and Quandt* [1968]. For more recent applications, see *Hamilton and White* [1985] and *Dagsvik and Jovanovic* [1991].

The problem with models with multiple equilibria is that they cannot define a random variable for the dependent variable. For example, in model (11–1) the sum of the probabilities of the four distinct outcomes do not add to one and model (11–1) cannot completely define the random vector $y = (y_1, y_2)$ unless we impose certain restrictions to preclude multiple solutions. See *Maddala* [1983, p. 119]. A necessary and sufficient condition for this model to have a unique solution is that the model be recursive. See *Amemiya* [1974]. This econometric assumption is often contrary to many theoretical structural models. Therefore, the above model has rarely been used.

Thus, it is important to find the conditions under which any function $\Psi_i(u) \in \Psi_\phi(u)$ generates a random variable. By definition, a random variable is a real–valued measurable function. The following proposition states that if there is a measurable selection rule to select between the two equilibria, model (11–1) generates a random variable.

PROPOSITION 11.1

$\Psi_i(u) \in \Psi_\phi(u)$ is a random variable if F is a measurable set where F is the set such that $\Psi_i(u) = \Psi_F(u)$.

■

PROOF OF THE PROPOSITION

Note $\Psi_i(u) : \mathbb{R}^2 \to \mathbb{R}^2$ so $\Psi_i(u)$ is measurable if and only if each component of Ψ_i is measurable (see *Billingsley* [1986,

p. 184]). $\Psi_i(u) = (\Psi_i^1(u), \Psi_i^2(u))$ where

$$\Psi_i^1(u) = \begin{cases} 1 & \text{if } u \in H_1 = (A \cup B) \cup (E \cap F) \\ 0 & \text{if } u \in H_1^c = (C \cup D) \cup (E \cap F^c) \end{cases}$$

and

$$\Psi_i^2(u) = \begin{cases} 1 & \text{if } u \in H_2 = (A \cup C) \cup (E \cap F) \\ 0 & \text{if } u \in H_2^c = (B \cup D) \cup (E \cap F^c) \end{cases}$$

$\Psi_i^1(u)$ and $\Psi_i^2(u)$ are characteristic functions which are measurable if and only if H_1 and H_2 are measurable sets (see *Royden* [1988]), but A, B, C, D, and E are by definition measurable sets. It follows that H_1 and H_2 are measurable sets if and only if F is a measurable set, since the union and intersection of measurable sets are measurable.

■

11.2 Identification

The identification problem in econometrics is the one of drawing inferences from the probability distribution of the observed variables to an underlying theoretical structure. In this section we show that model (11–1) is identified in the sense of equation (11–2) of *Jovanovic* [1989].

Jovanovic defines structure to be a pair $s = (G, \phi)$, where $G(u)$ is a particular distribution function of the latent variable u, and $\phi(u, y) = 0$ is a particular structural relationship between observed and latent endogenous variables. He shows that if a model has multiple equilibria then there is a set of distribution functions for the endogenous variable consistent with a given structure s. Let $\Gamma(s)$ be this set. Then a necessary and sufficient condition for a model to be identified is:

$$\Gamma(s) \cap \Gamma(s') = \emptyset \qquad \forall s \neq s'.$$

In model (11–1) $\phi(u, y)$ can be characterized by the parameters $\beta_1, \beta_2, \gamma_{21}$, and γ_{12}. The distribution function for the latent variable u can be any bivariate distribution function $G(u)$ with support $\mathbb{R}^2$. Without loss of generality assume that it is any continuous distribution that can be characterized by vector σ of parameters. Then the structure of the model is $s = (\underline{\beta}, \gamma, \sigma)$.

The observed endogenous variable is a discrete bivariate random vector that takes four different outcomes: y^1, y^2, y^3, and y^4. Then its distribution function is described by a vector μ_T, such that

$$\mu^T = [Pr_s(y^1), Pr_s(y^2), Pr_s(y^3), Pr_s(y^4)]$$

and

$$Pr_s(y^1) + Pr_s(y^2) + Pr_s(y^3) + Pr_s(y^4) = 1.$$

$Pr_s(y^i), i = 1, 2, 3, 4$, is a function of s, the structure.

By Proposition 11.1 every measurable selection from the correspondence generates a particular distribution for the endogenous variable. For example, let $\Psi_F(u)$ be the selected alternative; then the associated distribution function for the endogenous variable is

$$\mu_F = \begin{bmatrix} P_r(A) + P_r(F) \\ P_r(B) \\ P_r(C) \\ P_r(D) + P_r(E) - P_r(F) \end{bmatrix}.$$

Assuming that $P_r(E) \neq 0$, then μ_F can be written as:

$$\mu_F = \frac{Pr(F)}{P_r(E)} \begin{bmatrix} P_r(A) + P_r(E) \\ P_r(B) \\ P_r(C) \\ P_r(D) \end{bmatrix} + \frac{1 - P_r(F)}{P_r(E)} \begin{bmatrix} P_r(A) \\ P_r(B) \\ P_r(C) \\ P_r(D) + P_r(E) \end{bmatrix}$$

$$\mu_F = (P_r(F)/P_r(E))\mu_1 + (1 - P_r(F)/P_r(E))\mu_2, \qquad (11\text{--}3)$$

where μ_1 and μ_2 are the distribution function associated with $\Psi_1(u)$ and $\Psi_2(u)$ respectively. Thus, the set of distribution functions consistent with the model, $\Gamma(s)$, is given by all the μ_F defined as in equation (11–3) such that (a) F is measurable and (b) $F \subseteq E$. The following proposition proves that if u is an absolutely continuous random variable and $P_r(E) > 0$ then $\Gamma(s)$ is given by all of the possible convex combinations of μ_1 and μ_2.

PROPOSITION 11.2

If u is an absolutely continuous random variable and $P_r(E) > 0$, then for the endogenous variable consistent with the structure given by model (11–1), the set of distributions is given by

$$\Gamma(s) = \{\mu_\alpha : \mu_\alpha = \alpha\mu_1 + (1 - \alpha)\mu_2, \quad \alpha \in [0, 1]\}.$$

■

PROOF OF THE PROPOSITION

Assume that $P_r(E) = c > 0$. We need to show that

a) If $\Psi_F(u) \in \Psi_\phi(u)$ then $\mu_F = \alpha\mu_1 + (1 - \alpha)\mu_2$ where $\alpha \in [0, 1]$.

b) If $\mu_\alpha = \alpha\mu_1 + (1 - \alpha)\mu_2$ for $\alpha \in [0, 1]$ then $\mu_\alpha \in \Gamma(s)$. Part a) follows from equation (11–3), since the probability distribution associated with any $\Psi_F \in \Psi_\phi$ can be written as $\mu_F = (Pr(F)/c)\mu_1 + (1 - Pr(F)/c)\mu_2$, where $c = Pr(E)$. Because $F \subseteq E, Pr(F) \leq Pr(E) = c$. Thus $0 \leq Pr(F)/c = \alpha \leq 1$. Part b) follows from *Jovanovic* [1986], Theorem 3.1, which says that if u is an absolutely continuous random variable and μ_1 and μ_2 belong to $\Gamma(s)$ then all of the convex combinations of μ_1 and μ_2 also belong to $\Gamma(s)$.

∎

If u is an absolutely continuous random vector with pdf f then

$$\int_{a_1}^{b_1} \int_{a_2}^{b_2} f(u_1, u_2)du_1 du_2 =$$

$$G(b_1, b_2) - G(b_1, a_2) - G(a_1, b_2) + G(a_1, a_2)$$

and the probabilities of the different regions can be written as

$$Pr(A) = \int_{-z_2}^{\infty} \int_{-z_1}^{\infty} f(u_1, u_2)du_1 du_2 + \int_{-z_2}^{\infty} \int_{-z_1-\gamma_{21}}^{-z_1} f(u_1, u_2)du_1 du_2$$

$$+ \int_{-z_2-\gamma_{12}}^{-z_2} \int_{-z_1}^{\infty} f(u_1, u_2)du_1 du_2$$

$$Pr(A) = 1 - G(\infty, -z_2 - \gamma_{12}) + G(-z_1, -z_2 - \gamma_{12}) - G(-z_1, -z_2)$$

$$+ G(-z_1 - \gamma_{21}, -z_2) - G(-z_1 - \gamma_{21}, \infty)$$

$$Pr(B) = \int_{-\infty}^{-z_2-\gamma_{12}} \int_{-z_1}^{\infty} f(u_1, u_2)du_1 du_2$$

$$= G(\infty, -z_2 - \gamma_{12}) - G(-z_1, -z_2 - \gamma_{12})$$

$$Pr(C) = \int_{-z_2}^{\infty} \int_{\infty}^{-z_1-\gamma_{21}} f(u_1, u_2)du_1 du_2 = G(-z_1 - \gamma_{21}, \infty)$$

$$- G(-z_1 - \gamma_{21}, -z_2)$$

$$Pr(D) = \int_{-z_2-\gamma_{12}}^{-z_2} \int_{-\infty}^{-z_1-\gamma_{21}} f(u_1, u_2)du_1 du_2 + \int_{-\infty}^{-z_2-\gamma_{12}} \int_{-z_1-\gamma_{21}}^{-z_1}$$

$$f(u_1, u_2)du_1 du_2 + \int_{-\infty}^{-z_2-\gamma_{12}} \int_{-\infty}^{-z_1-\gamma_{21}} f(u_1, u_2)du_1 du_2$$

$$Pr(D) = G(-z_1, -z_2 - \gamma_{12}) -$$
$$G(-z_1 - \gamma_{21}, -z_2 - \gamma_{12})$$
$$- G(-z_1 - \gamma_{21}, -z_2)$$

$$Pr(E) = \int_{-z_2-\gamma_{12}}^{-z_2} \int_{-z_1-\gamma_{21}}^{-z_1} f(u_1, u_2) du_1 du_2$$
$$= G(-z_1, -z_2) - G(-z_1, -z_2 - \gamma_{12}) - G(-z_1 - \gamma_{21}, -z_2)$$
$$+ G(-z_1 - \gamma_{21}, -z_2 - \gamma_{12}).$$

Thus, the set of distribution functions associated with structure $s = (Y, \sigma)$ is given by

$$\Gamma(s) = \{\mu_\alpha : \mu_\alpha = [(1 - G(\infty, z_2 - \gamma_{12}) - G(-z_1 - \gamma_{21}, \infty)$$
$$+ \alpha G(-z_1 - \gamma_{21}, -z_2 - \gamma_{12})$$
$$+ (1 - \alpha)(G(-z_1, -z_2 - \gamma_{12}) + G(-z_1 - \gamma_{21}, -z_2)$$
$$- G(-z_1, -z_2)),$$
$$(G(\infty, -z_2 - \gamma_{12}) - G(-z_1, -z_2 - \gamma_{12})),$$
$$(G(-z_1 - \gamma_{21}, \infty) - G(-z_1 - \gamma_{21}, z_2)),$$
$$\alpha(G(-z_1, -z_2 - \gamma_{12}) - G(-z_1 - \gamma_{21}, -z_2 - \gamma_{12})$$
$$+ G(-z_1 - \gamma_{21}, -z_2)) + (1 - \alpha)(G(-z_1, z_2))], \alpha \in [0, 1]\}.$$

Now, consider a different structure $s' = (Y', \sigma)$ such that $\gamma_{12} \neq \gamma'_{12}, \gamma_{21} \neq \gamma'_{21}, \underline{\beta}_1 \neq \underline{\beta}'_1$ or $\underline{\beta}_2 \neq \underline{\beta}'_2$ but with the same distribution function for u that can be characterized by the same vector of parameters σ. Then the model is uniquely identified since

$$Pr_s(B) = G(\infty, -z_2 - \gamma_{12}) - G(-z_1, -z_2 - \gamma_{12}) \neq$$
$$G(\infty, -z'_2 - \gamma'_{12}) - G(-z'_1, -z'_2 - \gamma'_{12}) = Pr_{s'}(B)$$

or

$$Pr_s(C) = G(-z_1 - \gamma_{21}, \infty) - G(-z_1 - \gamma_{21}, -z_2) \neq$$
$$G(-z_1 - \gamma'_{21}, \infty) - G(-z_1 - \gamma_{21}, -z_2) = Pr_{s'}(C)$$

or both, except for exactly offsetting combinations of z_1 and γ_{21} or z_2 and γ_{12}, which have measure zero for continuously distributed $\underline{x}$ or require exact matches between discrete values of $\underline{x}$ and coefficients.

If a different structure $(s") = (Y', \sigma')$ implies also a different vector of parameters σ' then the model is not identified and we need to impose further restrictions, such as normalizing the variances or covariances, but this is a problem also shared with logically consistent models.

The proofs presented here and the GMM estimation strategy which follows from it apply directly to bivariate, binomial probit and logit but could be adapted readily to tobit models, ordered probit or logit models, and to combinations of those models with regression, for example, a selection bias model with selection affected by the outcome of the selected equation.

11.3 Estimation

Model (11–1) can be estimated using the joint probability distribution or the conditional probabilities of each outcome given the other.

Model (11–1) can be estimated using the structural probabilities of the various outcomes if and only if the selection method is fully specified. Whether the likelihood function is used in MLE or the expectations of the proportions found in each outcome are used in GMM estimation, the result is inconsistent unless the selection method is correctly specified.

Bresnahan and Reiss [1991] combine the equilibria which may overlap, but we suggest an alternative method which does not abandon the direct estimation using the above equations which are so convenient given the familiarity of equation–by–equation methods in econometrics and the usefulness of estimates of marginal impacts in applied research. The alternative approach does not require additional assumptions to be embodied in the estimation, using only the conditional expectations of y_1 given y_2 and the exogenous variables and of y_2 given y_1 and the exogenous variables. For example, if $y_1 = 1$, then y_2 is determined by $\gamma_{12} + x_2'\beta_1 + u_2$ regardless of whether $y_1 = 0$ is also possible, or what selection rule is used to choose y_1. In the case of linear probability models, which result from uniform marginal distributions of the disturbances, the result is two–stage least squares applied to the two (or more) equations. Other distributions result in nonlinear equations which may be identified either with exclusions or nonlinear functions of the instruments and estimated with GMM. *Butler and Mitchell* [1990] apply these ideas to a bivariate normal model.

To illustrate the estimation, assume model (11–1) with a probit model specification, *i.e.*, standard bivariate normally distributed disturbances. Let $\{\underline{z}\} = \{\underline{x}_1\} \cup \{\underline{x}_2\} \cup \{\underline{x}_3\}$, where $\underline{x}_3$ consists of nonlinear functions of $\underline{x}_1$ and $\underline{x}_2$, be the instrumental variables. Identification by exclusions is usually less collinear and more reliable when it is feasible. The orthogonality conditions based on model (11–1) could be as follows.

$$E[\underline{z}(y_1 - \Phi(\gamma_{21}y_2 + \underline{x}_1'\underline{\beta}_1))] = \underline{0}$$
$$E[\underline{z}(y_2 - \Phi(\gamma_{12}y_1 + \underline{x}_2'\underline{\beta}_2))] = \underline{0}. \tag{11–4}$$

The estimation presents no more difficulty than the usual probit model. *Butler and Mitchell* [1990] estimate a simultaneous probit model of cardiovascular disease and having earnings, each measured as a discrete outcome. They find, other things equal, that cardiovascular disease reduces the probability of having earnings and that having earnings reduces the probability of cardiovascular disease ($\gamma_{21} < 0$ and $\gamma_{12} < 0$). Perhaps because of weak instruments, they also find that the standard errors rise considerably relative to estimates assuming all regressors are exogenous; that can be a problem in any instrumental variable, two–stage least squares, or GMM estimation.

By extending the results in this chapter, earnings could be estimated as a continuous outcome. The bivariate ordered probit model could also be adapted to this estimation.

A Hausman test of the specification of the selection method is possible, since more efficient estimation of the model is possible with the rule, and less efficient but consistent estimation of the model is possible without the rule. The Hausman test has a null of a joint hypothesis including the specification of the distribution of the disturbances.

11.4 Conclusion and Extensions

Logically inconsistent models with multiple equilibria consistent with observable distributions of data can be estimated (1) by restricting parameters; (2) by treating nonunique equilibria as observationally equivalent, collapsing the potentially overlapping equilibria in all cases, as suggested by *Bresnahan and Reiss* [1991]; or (3) by finding identified parameters with testable implications, estimating the conditional expectations of the endogenous variables.

This chapter explores the last option, suggesting a GMM estimator which does not require the selection rule to be specified.

The most efficient estimation specifies the rule used to find equilibria in the regions left ambiguous by the standard limited dependent variable models, and uses the rule to specify the likelihood function. If a proposed rule is available, it forms the basis of a Hausman test versus the GMM estimator presented in this chapter.

The model presented here is a bivariate probit or logit model, but the same arguments could be applied to multivariate models, ordered probit, logit, or ordered logit models, and simultaneous regression and probit, logit, or tobit models. A selection bias model in which selection is affected by the outcome of the regression could be estimated with the methods of this chapter.

References

Amemiya, T. [1985]: *Advanced Econometrics;* Cambridge, MA, Harvard University Press.

Amemiya, T. [1974]: Multivariate Regression and Simultaneous Equation Models When the Dependent Variables are Truncated Normal; *Econometrica*, 42, 999–1012

Billingsley, P. [1986]: *Probability and Measure;* Second Edition, New York, John Wiley & Sons.

Bresnahan, T.F., and Reiss, P.C. [1991]: Empirical Models of Discrete Games; *Journal of Econometrics*, 48, 57–81.

Butler, J.S., and Mitchell, J.M. [1990]: A Simultaneous Equations Model of Cardiovascular Disease and Earnings; *Metron*, 48, 283–295.

Dagsvik, J., and Jovanovic, B. [June 1991.]: Was the Great Depression a Low–Level Equilibrium? *National Bureau of Economic Research Working Paper* No. 3726.

Goldfeld, S., and Quandt, R. [1968]: Nonlinear Simultaneous Equations: Estimation and Prediction; *International Economic Review*, 9, 113–136.

Hamilton, J.D., and Whiteman, C.H. [1985]: The Observable Implications of Self–Fulfilling Expectations; *Journal of Monetary Economics*, 16, 353–373.

Jovanovic, B. [September 1986]: Inference in Models with Multiple Equilibria. *C. V. Starr Center for Applied Economics, R. R.* 86-17.

Jovanovic, B. [1989]: Observable Implications of Models with Multiple Equilibria; *Econometrica*, 57, 1731–1732

Maddala, G.S. [1983]: *Limited Dependent and Other Qualitative Variables in Econometrics;* Cambridge, UK, Cambridge University Press.

Mallar, C.P. [1977]: The Estimation of Simultaneous Probability Models; *Econometrica,* 45, 1717–1722.

Royden, H.L. [1988]: Real Analysis; *Third Edition,* New York, Macmillan Publishing Company.

INDEX